MORAL THEOLOGY:
Challenges for the Future

RICHARD A. McCORMICK, S.J.

MORAL THEOLOGY:
Challenges for the Future

edited by
Charles E. Curran

ESSAYS IN HONOR OF RICHARD A. MCCORMICK

PAULIST PRESS
New York/Mahwah

Library of Congress Cataloging-in-Publication Data

Moral theology: challenges for the future: essays in honor of
  Richard A. McCormick/edited by Charles E. Curran.
      p.   cm.
    Includes bibliographical references.
    ISBN 0-8091-3168-4
    1. Christian ethics.   2. Social ethics.   3. McCormick, Richard A.,
  1922–   . I. McCormick, Richard A., 1922–   . II. Curran, Charles E.
  BJ1249.M666   1990
  241′.042—dc20   90-33545
                                                             CIP

Published by Paulist Press
997 Macarthur Boulevard
Mahwah, New Jersey 07430

Printed and bound in the
United States of America

Contents

v

SEXUAL AND MEDICAL ETHICS

SOCIAL AND POLITICAL ETHICS

The Contributors

Walter J. Burghardt, S.J., Theologian-in-residence at Georgetown University, Washington, D.C., editor-in-chief of *Theological Studies,* co-editor of *Ancient Christian Writers,* and associate fellow of the Woodstock Theological Center, is author of *The Image of God in Man according to Cyril of Alexandria* and *Preaching: The Art and the Craft.*

Lisa Sowle Cahill is Professor of Christian Ethics at Boston College and is the author of *Between the Sexes: Toward a Christian Ethics of Sexuality.*

James F. Childress is Kyle Professor of Religious Studies and Professor of Medical Education, University of Virginia, and is the co-author of *Principles of Bioethics* and co-editor of *The Westminster Dictionary of Christian Ethics.*

Charles E. Curran is Visiting Firestone Professor in the School of Religion, University of Southern California, and author of *Tensions in Moral Theology* and *Catholic Higher Education, Theology, and Academic Freedom.*

Margaret A. Farley is Gilbert L. Stark Professor of Christian Ethics at Yale University Divinity School and is the author of *Personal Commitments: Beginning, Keeping, Changing.*

Josef Fuchs, S.J., was Professor of Moral Theology at the Pontifical Gregorian University in Rome from 1954, emeritus from 1982; in recent years Georgetown University Press has published three volumes of his work in English.

Leslie Griffin formerly taught moral theology at the University of Notre Dame, edited *Religion and Politics in the American Milieu,* and is currently pursuing legal studies.

James M. Gustafson is Henry R. Luce Professor of Humanities and Comparative Studies at Emory University, whose recent publications include John R. Meyer and James M. Gustafson, eds., *The U.S. Business Corporation: An Institution in Transition* and *Varieties of Moral Discourse: Prophetic, Narrative, Ethical, and Policy,* Stob lectures given at Calvin College and Seminary.

Bernard Häring, C.SS.R., is Professor Emeritus of Moral Theology at the

Alphonsian Academy in Rome and the author of two three-volume works in moral theology, *The Law of Christ* and *Free and Faithful in Christ.*

J. Bryan Hehir is Joseph Kennedy Professor of Ethics at Georgetown University, Counselor for Social Policy for the United States Catholic Conference, and author of numerous articles in social ethics.

Kenneth R. Himes, O.F.M., is Associate Professor of Moral Theology at the Washington Theological Union, co-editor of *Introduction to Christian Ethics: A Reader,* and associate editor of *New Theology Review.*

Louis Janssens is Professor Emeritus of the Faculty of Theology at Katholieke Universiteit te Leuven, Belgium, and author of over one hundred studies in moral theology, including some recent English articles in *Louvain Studies.*

Jack Mahoney, S.J., is F.D. Maurice Professor of Moral and Social Theology at King's College, University of London, and author of *Bioethics and Belief* and *The Making of Moral Theology.*

James J. McCartney, O.S.A., is Associate Professor in the Department of Philosophy at Villanova University and the author of *Unborn Persons: Pope John Paul II and the Abortion Debate,* which was originally a dissertation directed by Richard A. McCormick.

Joseph F. Rautenberg did his doctoral dissertation under Richard McCormick at Georgetown University and is currently ethicist at St. Vincent's Hospital and Health Care Center and associate pastor at Holy Name Parish in Indianapolis.

Norbert J. Rigali, S.J., is Professor of Moral Theology at the University of San Diego and has contributed articles on moral theology to many theological journals.

James J. Walter is Professor of Christian Ethics at Loyola University of Chicago, a contributor to many theological journals, and co-author of *Conversion and Discipleship: A Christian Foundation for Ethics and Doctrine.*

Introduction: Why This Book?

Charles E. Curran

The purpose of this book is twofold—to honor and celebrate the contribution of Richard A. McCormick and to assess the present state and possible future developments in the discipline of moral theology. This volume can readily accomplish this dual purpose because Richard McCormick has been a central figure in the development of Catholic moral theology in the post-Vatican II period. The contributors to this festschrift in honor of Father McCormick are well qualified to carry out the purpose of this volume. The authors assembled here include internationally respected scholars in the discipline of moral theology as well as some younger scholars who have been associated with Professor McCormick and his work.

An understanding of the past is necessary to assess properly the present and the future of moral theology. Most of the studies in this book deal with particular areas or issues in moral theology, so this introduction will focus on the broader methodological aspects of the discipline. Like so many other realities in the Catholic Church, moral theology has undergone significant and widespread changes in the period since the close of the Second Vatican Council in 1965. Before the council, the manuals of moral theology were the textbooks of the discipline, having their origin in the *Institutiones Theologiae Moralis,* which came into existence in response to the reforms proposed by the Council of Trent. Moral theology today differs from the manuals of moral theology with regard to scope, method, and context.

SCOPE

The primary purpose of the manuals of moral theology was to train confessors to perform their function as "judges" in the sacrament of penance. Confessors had to know what acts were sinful and whether the sin was mortal or venial. Because of this narrow scope, the manuals of moral theology were individualistic, act-centered, and minimalistic.

The scope of contemporary moral theology is life-centered, with emphasis not just on the acts or the "doing" of the person, but on the "being" of the person. Christian anthropology includes the basic orientations, attitudes, values, and virtues which should characterize a follower of Jesus. The Christian is called to the fullness of discipleship and not just to the minimum of avoiding sin. The roles of groups, associations, and nations also must receive greater attention in discussing the contemporary moral realities.

METHOD

The manuals employed a legal or juridical model of the Christian life. The objective norm of morality was viewed almost exclusively in terms of *law,* both in the church and in civil society. Law included the eternal law, divine positive law, natural law, and human law. Conscience was the subjective norm of morality and conscience had to conform itself to the various laws comprising the objective norm of morality. An extrinsic and voluntaristic mindset supported such a legal model. For the voluntarist the source of obligation comes not from the moral reality itself, but from the will of the legislator: something is good because it is commanded.

Ironically, such an approach, while evident in the manuals, deviated dramatically from the position of Thomas Aquinas, who had insisted on an intrinsic and rational approach to morality. For Aquinas, something is commanded because it is good. The legal, juridical, and voluntaristic approach of the manuals naturally interpreted official Catholic teaching of the hierarchical magisterium in the same way. The teaching authority of the church required submission and obedience on the part of Catholics.

The manuals of moral theology did not give much importance to the theological aspects of the discipline. For all practical purposes a natural law approach, understood as human reason reflecting on human nature, was the method employed. Appeal was made to scripture, but only as a proof text, often taken out of context, to support a conclusion which had been reached on the basis of a natural law approach. Aspects of Christology, grace, eschatology, and other theological disciplines did not enter into the arena of moral theology.

From a philosophical perspective, the manuals of moral theology were wedded to a neoscholasticism which frequently had wandered away from the best of Thomas Aquinas. This neoscholasticism was looked upon as if it were the perennial philosophy. Behind such an understanding lay a classicist mentality, with its emphasis on eternal truths and immutable essences. A deductive methodology cohered with such philosophical underpinnings. Such a philosophy had not made the "turn to the subject," so the emphasis was almost exclusively focused on the object or end of the act itself.

Contemporary moral theology has been moving away from the approach used in the manuals of moral theology in all of these areas. The inadequacies of a legal model are apparent to all. There always will be a place for law in the moral life, but law ought not be the primary model used to understand the God-human relationship. Teleological, deontological (but not juridically deontological), and responsibility models have been proposed in place of the older legal model of the manuals. Official church teaching by the hierarchical magisterium is viewed primarily under the category of doctrine or "teaching," not as juridical authority imposing answers by decree.

Attempts have been made in recent years to understand moral theology as a distinct *theological* discipline in dialogue with systematic theology, spiritual theology, and sacramental theology. Christology, pneumatology, anthropology, and eschatology all have important bearing on moral theology. However, significant questions arise in this attempt to make moral theology more theological. How can one integrate all these aspects? How does Christian morality relate to human morality? Two essays in this volume deal with these important questions.

From a philosophical perspective, Catholic moral theology is no longer wedded to neoscholasticism. Moral theology has a variety of philosophical dialogue partners today. One must recognize a legitimate pluralism of philosophical approaches. The demise of the perennial philosophy is a direct result of the rejection of classicism and the acceptance of historical consciousness. Greater emphasis is now given to the particular, the contingent, and the developing. Such an approach does not rely on eternal essences because it embraces a more inductive methodology.

The "turn to the subject," a greater emphasis on the person acting, has characterized much of contemporary Catholic theology, as is evident in the works of Karl Rahner and Bernard Lonergan. The person is both subject and agent, who expresses and molds himself or herself as a person in the act of doing something. Moral theology's focus on the role of fundamental option and of conversion reflects this emphasis on the subject in contemporary thought.

CONTEXT

Three changing contexts have greatly affected the discipline of moral theology—the church, the world, and the academy. The moral theology of the manuals existed in a church which largely accentuated the institutional, the hierarchical, and the juridical approach to its own life and existence. The church was often withdrawn from the world, existing in its own parochial and cultural ghetto. Fear of contamination by contemporary developments in the world led to the erection of barricades, to keep the church pure from outside defilements. Truth was sought and found solely within the Catholic tradition, which claimed to have a timeless philosophy and theology capable of withstanding the changing tides of modern philosophies. Theology in general, and moral theology in particular, found their natural home in seminaries and theologates which, with their high walls and rustic settings, embodied this separation from the world.

By contrast, the Second Vatican Council emphasized the church as the "people of God" on pilgrimage. Many biblical metaphors were employed to emphasize communal unity in Christ and to move away from a single institutional model of church. The office of the hierarchy exists as a service within the church and for the church, but the episcopacy is not identical with the church. The role and gifts of *all* the people of God have become more important, both for the moral life of the church and for systematic reflection on that life. With its Decree on Ecumenism, Vatican II opened up a dialogue with other Christians and even with non-Christians. In an earlier era, "non-Catholic" Christians appeared in the manuals of theology only as adversaries. Now, true dialogue began to take place. As this volume well illustrates, moral theology must be done today in and with an ecumenical perspective.

The whole approach of Vatican II stressed the need for dialogue with the modern world. Catholic Christians could learn from the world and from other religious seekers in the world. The ghetto walls were being torn down. While dialogue does not mean acceptance of everything in the world, it does require a critical openness to the input and ideas of others. For example, in order to deal with the complex social and political issues facing humankind, the moral theologian has to be in contact with the appropriate human sciences.

The church has gone through decisive changes in the last twenty-five years, but so has the world. Advances in technology have brought ethical questions to the fore. A greater recognition of the responsibility of all for a more just, peaceable, participative, and sustainable society has changed the political and social map of the world. In the United States issues of peace, poverty, and human equality have forced us to recognize that we all belong to the one human family on planet earth.

Likewise, the context or "place" in which moral theology is done has changed within Roman Catholicism. The seminary, with its isolation, was the primary place where theology was done before Vatican II. Moral theology is no longer done only in the seminary for those studying for the ministry; it is also an academic discipline housed in the university. Richard McCormick's personal history well illustrates this change. McCormick studied theology at the Jesuit theologate in West Baden, Indiana. Later he taught there and at its subsequent relocations to more urban centers in attempts to make the theologate less isolated. In 1974 he became the Rose F. Kennedy Professor of Christian Ethics at the Kennedy Institute of Ethics, which had been established at Georgetown University. In 1986 he became the John A. O'Brien Professor of Christian Ethics at the University of Notre Dame. Just as the discipline of moral theology moved into the wider academic arena, so too its scholars have become increasingly more diverse. As this volume illustrates, moral theologians are no longer exclusively priests, but include all the people of God who share this academic vocation.

However, despite the monumental change experienced in recent decades, there is also significant continuity of post-Vatican II moral theology with the earlier Catholic tradition. *Mediation* has always characterized the Catholic theological approach. In the area of morality the divine is seen as working in and through the human. In the Catholic tradition grace does not destroy or do away with the human, but infuses, enhances, and builds on it. The core Christian emphasis on the divine gift of faith does not do away with the need for the human response of works.

While many moral theologians today question some aspects of the neoscholastic understanding of the natural law methodology, they agree with its basic theological insight that human reason can arrive at true ethical wisdom and knowledge. The emphasis on the role of human reason in the epistemological sphere illustrates the Catholic emphasis on mediation. Detailed rational analysis of human action is necessary for the moral theologian in order to arrive at moral truth.

In the light of this emphasis on mediation, the Catholic tradition has given great importance to the life and actions of Christians in this world. The Christian and the church are not called to withdraw from the world but to help transform it. Active participation in the life of this world has been emphasized in the Catholic tradition at its best. The church works with all people of good will to bring about greater justice and peace in the world. Modern Catholic social teaching has been associated largely with the papal social encyclicals, beginning with Leo XIII in 1891. Lately, this social mission is seen as a constitutive dimension of the preaching of the gospel and of the church's mission for the redemption of the human race.

The Catholic tradition in morality, with its recognition of the importance of human actions and the role of reason, has employed casuistry as a means of arriving at the ethical evaluation of particular actions. Casuistry has been abused in the past, but the discussion and comparison of cases does contribute to the forming of apt moral judgments about particular human actions.

Moral theology, even if done in a broader, more historically conscious context, continues to be a discipline in the service of the church. The church community and its individual members seek counsel from moral theology in the proper formation of conscience. For better or worse, the development of moral theology has been greatly affected by the penitential discipline in the church. Such a narrow understanding of the role of moral theology has contributed to the need for its renewal at the present time. Still, moral theology always will serve an important role in the total life of the church.

RICHARD MCCORMICK AND THE CONTENT OF THIS VOLUME

The vision of moral theology briefly outlined above is shared by many in the Catholic Church today. Richard McCormick has made a lasting contribution to this vision. The authors who have written for this volume intend both to celebrate and to examine the thought of McCormick, and, in the process, to assess the present and the future of moral theology.

Richard A. McCormick, born in 1922, entered the Society of Jesus at the age of eighteen. He received his B.A. in 1945 from Loyola University in Chicago, and an M.A. in 1950 from the same institution. He completed his theological studies at the Jesuit theologate in West Baden, Indiana, and was ordained a priest in 1953. He received his S.T.D. (doctorate in sacred theology) from the Pontifical Gregorian University in Rome in 1957, with a thesis on the removal of a probably dead fetus to save the mother's life. McCormick began his career as a moral theologian that same year, at the theologate of the Jesuits, which was then still in West Baden, Indiana. After seventeen years in seminary education, he moved on, accepting the Rose F. Kennedy professorship at the Kennedy Institute, Georgetown University. In 1986 he accepted appointment to his current position as the John A. O'Brien Professor of Christian Ethics at the University of Notre Dame.

Our author's greatest contribution to moral theology is the "Notes on Moral Theology," which he published for twenty consecutive years, from 1965 to 1984, in *Theological Studies*. The custom for *Theological Studies* was to have two different authors review the literature in moral theology, alternating every six months. Such a policy was followed until the first issue of 1977, when McCormick began reviewing all the literature from the previous year, publishing his "Notes" in the March issue. Father McCormick was such a master at his work that no others could be found to match his amazing gifts and abilities. Since 1985 a team of different authors, including McCormick, have contributed to the yearly "Notes." McCormick's "Notes" subsequently have been collected and published in two volumes: *Notes on Moral Theology 1965 through 1980* and *Notes on Moral Theology 1981 through 1984*.

A word must be said about the literary genre of the "Notes." The purpose was to review, analyze, and critique the current periodical literature dealing with moral theology. The task is daunting. Selectivity is necessary amid such a large annual output. Objectivity calls for a brief but accurate description of the author's thesis. Analysis and criticism require perceptive and penetrating comments and responses. Space limitations demand that this all be done in a comparatively short form. The range of material covers the whole field of moral theology, requiring a breadth and depth that few people have. Richard McCormick became the acknowledged master of this genre, which is so much more than just a bibliographical survey. Since he resigned in 1984 the editor of *Theological Studies* has had to divide up the work among a number of different authors.

As author of the "Notes" from 1965 to 1984 McCormick chronicled, discerned trends, and gave some direction to the tremendous changes that were taking place in Catholic moral theology. By carefully selecting, summarizing, and responding to the most important aspects of the current literature, he helped set the agenda for Catholic moral theology in one of the most tumultuous periods of its development. At times authors of outstanding books can make very original and pace-setting contributions to a particular field, but such works, by definition, cannot touch the *whole* field. Richard McCormick, through this genre, helped to shape and direct the entire field of moral theology.

Thus, the acclaimed author of the "Notes on Moral Theology" exemplifies well how one can and should work theologically in and with a living ecclesial tradition. To do this well, knowledge of the rich tradition of Catholic theology is essential. But also one must recognize that such a tradition continually needs development, change, and reappropriation in the light of ongoing historical, social, and cultural evolution. One must avoid both the rigidity of an inflexible traditionalism and also the itch for novelty that refuses to recognize the importance of tradition. The moral theologian truly conserves and serves the tradition by making it a living tradition, responding to the contemporary developments which, in this particular period in time, have been momentous, within both the church and the world.

The twenty years of McCormick's "Notes" well illustrate the characteristics necessary for one who deals with a living tradition. One must be respectful, dialogical, open, critical, objective, serene, while never losing a sense of humor. As the studies in this volume show, our author has been willing to change his mind in the course of this ongoing dialogue. He has remained open to better arguments and clarifying reasons. At times he even has embraced some positions about which he earlier raised critical problems.

McCormick's mastery of this genre owes much to his own character traits as well as to his writing skills. A moral theologian should be a judicious, objective, calm, well balanced observer of the scene. He or she needs to be convinced, but not unduly hesitant to decide, and must have the courage of his or her own convictions. McCormick abounds in all these virtues. He does not have an enlarged ego or a need to dominate or control. Humility, honesty, and forthrightness characterize his person and his professional life. The author of "Notes" obviously has a penchant for the practical, rather than the speculative, and combines a rigorous ability for rational analysis with a pastor's concern for the dilemmas faced by many in the church.

His literary style fits the genre of "Notes" perfectly. His writing is clear, crisp, succinct, respectful, and always to the point. His lucid and accurate summaries and his penetrating analysis show the work of a marvelous crafter of sentences and paragraphs. The approach and style of the "Notes" has become so much a part of this Jesuit moralist that he approaches almost all his writing as a dialogue with other authors. Thus, in his "Notes on Moral Theology," McCormick has made a significant and singular contribution to moral theology.

However, there are limits to the literary genre which consumed so much of our author's time and energy. Such a genre, by definition, does not provide opportunity for a systematic development of the field of moral theology in general or of any one topic. The material dealt with, of necessity, will be somewhat limited. In this book some authors point out the areas that are not covered by McCormick. For example, theological methodological issues, such as Christology and eschatology, are missing; questions dealing with orientation, character, and the virtues receive relatively little attention. Broader social issues, such as ecology and the very concept of social responsibility, are not fully developed. Quandary ethics and particular problems receive the most discussion.

However, the fault, or perhaps better the limitation, is not only McCormick's. Yes, he selected the materials to be discussed each year in his "Notes." But the genre itself, the traditional acts-oriented role of the Catholic moral theologian, and the concrete issues facing society to a large extent have set the agenda for the "Notes." The genre of the "Notes" first involves review of the recent *periodical* literature. Therefore, books and monographs are not explicitly treated. Usually longer monographs or book-length volumes deal with the more theoretical and methodological issues. Periodical literature is more adapted to discuss the particular problems and moral issues that arise in any given year. A survey of current periodical literature does not give one the opportunity to stand back and analyze the deeper issues and trends.

At the same time, Catholic moral theology has consistently dealt with the particular problems facing the church community in its life in the world and in the church itself. A pastoral dimension consistently has been an important part of Catholic moral theology. This strong practical orientation is evident in the "Notes." For example, in the area of medical ethics, McCormick has responded to many of the health care dilemmas facing individuals and society today, as is evident in the essays in this book on medical ethics.

In his attempt, as a moral theologian in the Catholic Church, to make this tradition a living reality, our author has been more reactive than proactive. He has responded to the work of others in the "Notes" and thereby has pushed forward his own understanding and agenda. This is one very important way of dealing with a tradition and keeping it alive. Others will adopt more innovative and even more radical approaches in their dealing with the tradition and trying to move it forward. The genre of the "Notes" makes its most expert practitioner an incrementalist and reformer by definition.

The generalist in moral theology well might be a dying breed, and one can understand why. However, in the "Notes" McCormick has shown how one can combine the breadth of the generalist with the depth of perceptive criticism in a variety of moral subspecialties. In general, social ethics has received less attention from McCormick than any other part of the discipline of moral theology. The area of his greatest interest has been bioethics, which also was the focus of his own doctoral dissertation. Perhaps McCormick was influenced in this direction by the fact that his father was a well-known physician in Toledo, Ohio, and a president of the American Medical Association. Especially during his twelve years at the Kennedy Institute of Ethics at Georgetown, McCormick devoted much time to bioethics. His books in this area, which often follow the approach and style of the "Notes," are *How Brave a New World?* and *Health and Medicine in the Catholic Tradition.*

The American Jesuit's most significant contribution to fundamental moral theology has been his works on proportionalism or the grounding of moral norms. This question arises in the moral discussion about many traditional behavioral norms in Catholic sexual morality. The debate about the role of absolute norms in contemporary Christian ethics and moral philosophy is also important in relation to situation ethics, utilitarianism, and other methodological questions. McCormick has addressed this issue frequently in the "Notes" and in his Père Marquette Lecture at Marquette University, *Ambiguity in Moral Choice,* as well as in a subsequent volume edited with Paul Ramsey, *Doing Evil to Achieve Good.*

In 1989 Georgetown University Press published *The Critical Calling,* which contains updated and expanded versions of essays that have appeared in the last few years as well as some previously unpublished chapters. I have had the privilege of working with Dick in coediting what is now a seven-volume series of *Readings in Moral Theology,* dealing with significant topics in fundamental moral theology. A full bibliography of Richard McCormick's writings is published at the end of this book.

Father McCormick's contributions to moral theology have been widely recognized. He was the recipient of the Cardinal Spellman award of the Catholic Theological Society of America as the outstanding theologian for the year 1969 and was elected president of the Catholic Theological Society. He has served on numerous scholarly, church, and public boards and committees, such as the Ethics Advisory Board of the then Department of Health, Education, and Welfare. Eleven institutions in this country and abroad have granted him honorary doctorate degrees.

The contributors to this volume all know Richard McCormick personally. We have all profited from his dialogue with and criticism of our work. He has taught us much about moral theology and the ways of keeping this tradition living in the midst of great change and diversity. In his person, as in his writings, he combines humility with courage, dialogue with decisiveness, and support with criticism.

There is no better or more apt way for us, as colleagues and friends, to celebrate the work of Richard McCormick than by following his example of critical dialogue. The studies in this volume not only dialogue with McCormick, but also assess the present and future of Catholic moral theology. The book is structured so that the major themes as well as issues of moral theology are considered. In addition to articles on the role of the scholar and the moral theologian in the church many significant questions in contemporary fundamental moral theology are addressed, including the foundation of norms, the uniqueness of Christian morality and ethics, theological aspects of moral theology, personalism, conscience, natural law, human rights, the teaching role of the church, and a Protestant perspective. Sexuality, divorce, and remarriage receive careful attention, as do the bioethical issues related to abortion, death and dying, and artificial reproduction. The social issues of peace and war as well as the relationship between morality and public policy are the subjects of two final essays.

The contributors to these pages wish both to pay tribute in a critical fashion to the work of Richard McCormick and to appraise the present status and the future possibilities of moral theology.

FUNDAMENTAL
MORAL THEOLOGY

1

The Role of the Scholar
in the Catholic Church

Walter J. Burghardt, S.J.

The title of this article and the context that shapes it call for three distinct but related questions: (1) What is this creature called scholarship? (2) How does the Roman Catholic Church relate to scholarship so described? (3) Where does Richard McCormick fit in this picture?

SCHOLARSHIP

What is a scholar? In the restricted sense that hovers over this festschrift, a scholar is defined in Webster's Second Edition Unabridged (1958) as "one who has engaged in advanced study and acquired the minutiae of knowledge in some special field, along with accuracy and skill in investigation and powers of critical analysis in interpretation of such knowledge." Scholar and student, scholar and searcher for knowledge, are not interchangeable terms.[1] A college student who studies seriously, masters the class material, and produces a first-rate term paper is not necessarily a scholar. Genuine scholarship involves certain criteria over and above sheer intelligence and diligence.

First, scholarship implies *methodology,* a disciplined approach to a subject, a way of reaching truth, reality, knowledge either commonly accepted within the field or at least acceptable to one's colleagues and peers. There is not just one scholarly method; methods are as diverse as the fields. Historian Barbara Tuchman (no graduate degree, by the way), preparing *The Guns of August,*[2] simply had to plumb primary sources (e.g. memoirs and letters, archival material), had to expect bias in such sources (e.g. personal accounts, tendentious and possibly mendacious, from generals), had to be selective (with all the risks selectivity embodies), had to avoid imposing her own self on the sources, had to use secondary literature judiciously (lest she simply repeat others' research, even their errors), felt she must drive personally over the battle areas of August 1914.[3]

Scholars in the physical and life sciences (e.g. astronomy, biology, chemistry, geology, paleontology, physics, psychology), concerned on broad lines with the nature of the universe and with living organisms, study tiny atoms and vast galaxies, the earth and earth's events, plants and animals, the structure of organisms, fossils, the behavior of man and woman. But not with carefree abandon. In each area the scholar is bound by experiment, observation, measurement; constant repetition of experiments; experiments so designed that other scientists may repeat them; constant correction. If Alexander Fleming discovered penicillin accidentally, it was still in the laboratory that he found it, in the midst of disciplined research, not on the playing fields of Eton.

Philosophy has no single definition, and in consequence no single methodology. Nevertheless, from Greek philosophy through the scholastic systems to Descartes and Locke and Spinoza, Kant and Hegel and Comte, James and Dewey and Whitehead, Russell and Husserl, Heidegger and Sartre, Dewey and Lonergan, philosophy has not been a haphazard hobby. It has consistently been a rational quest for the real: God, the world, and the human person; being, knowledge, and function. Each philosopher or system had certain presuppositions that seemed certain or at least usable as working hypotheses; amassed data from speculation and experience; drew conclusions, principles, even at times a synthesis. It involves rational demonstration, struggle with one's peers and one's culture, correction and retraction, fresh evidence and fresh reflection, intellectual agony, near despair, and rare ecstasy.

Second, scholarship implies extraordinary *accuracy.* Not in its strict sense—utter freedom from error. Rather, consistent care, even reverence, in handling the raw material of research, in selecting the significant evidence, in interpreting the data at hand, in deriving conclusions. Humility in the face of ages that yield only scattered fragments of the past, in the face of a nature at once limitless in its richness and reluctant to surrender it, in the face of my own intellectual limitations, unacknowledged prejudices, in the face of ceaseless revisions of science and history, philosophy and theology, reason and revelation. Openness to criticism, even the harsh and hostile, the attack that threatens to undermine my life's work.[4]

Third, scholarship demands undeviating *dedication.* Normally, the scholarly life is a vocation, very much as medicine and the law are vocations, rather than part-time avocations. Vocation calls for an involvement of the whole person. Not simply time and talent, but heart and emotions. I recall a striking sentence in A.J. Cronin's novel *The Green*

Years, where young Robert Shannon, doctor in embryo, says of Dr. Galbraith: "I then perceived his interest to be purely scientific: that strange, beautiful, and wholly disinterested emotion which had already stirred me as I sat at my microscope and which in later years was to afford me some of the rarest joys of my life."[5] Disinterested does not suggest lack of interest, passionless objectivity—only freedom from selfish motive, not biased or prejudiced.

Ideally, dedication ought to spark enthusiasm. Barbara Tuchman tells glowingly of her experience at Radcliffe in C.II. McIlwain's course on the constitutional history of England:

> ... McIlwain was conducting a passionate love affair with the laws of the Angles and the articles of the Charter. . . . Like any person in love, he wanted to let everyone know how beautiful was the object of his affections. He had white hair and pink cheeks and the brightest blue eyes I ever saw, and though I cannot remember a word of Article 39, I do remember how his blue eyes blazed as he discussed it and how I sat on the edge of my seat. . . .[6]

Tuchman's own goal? "To write history so as to enthrall the reader and make the subject as captivating and exciting to him as it is to me. . . . A prerequisite . . . is to be enthralled one's self and to feel a compulsion to communicate the magic."[7]

Fourth, the scholar should be convinced, with Samuel Eliot Morison, that the cultivation of scholarship is "*a necessity for national survival*—nay, for the survival of the Hellenic-Hebraic-Christian civilization upon which our polity is based."[8] Morison has asserted that America never respected the scholar as did Europe: "In a growing, practical, go-ahead country the scholar was regarded at best as a dreamer, at worst as a subversive, bent on shattering cherished beliefs."[9]

What specific factors fashioned this negative attitude? (1) Jacksonian democracy: "in part . . . a revolt of the common man against the scholar; of those who had just enough education to think they knew everything, and really knew nothing, against the well-educated scholar who believed he knew something, and knew that nobody could know everything."[10] (2) American scholars themselves: from 1830 on, their typical attitude toward their country "was either evasion or despair."[11] (3) The promise of wealth and success offered by business and finance. (4) The burden on teachers and clergy to convey the rudiments of education and supply basic pastoral needs. (5) The challenge to fundamentalist Protestantism by evolution and the findings of geologists. (6) The challenge to politics and the marketplace from standards of ideal or permanent values.[12]

Today the situation of the scholar is vastly improved—the scientist's far more than the humanist's. For national defense and the conquest of space and AIDS, the mathematician, the physicist, and the chemist are widely recognized as indispensable. For American culture and civilization, a corresponding respect does not greet the classicist or ethicist, the historian, philosopher, or theologian. Practical Americans can see the fruits of science in the mushroom cloud over Hiroshima, in Neil Armstrong walking on the moon, in AZT and pentamidine lengthening the time between AIDS diagnosis and death. It is far more difficult to grasp how significant a Barbara Tuchman is to our self-understanding as a nation, a John Courtney Murray to our religious freedom, a Paul Tillich to our "courage to be," the *Oxford Book of American Verse* to a richer culture, the Kennedy Institute of Ethics to our commitment to life in the womb and near the tomb.

Nevertheless, all genuine scholarship, publicly recognized or not, should stem from an inner urge to employ one's talents in a rigorous, disciplined, often frustrating effort to plumb the endless mysteries hidden in time and space, in nature and person, not only for "national survival" but for our increase in life and love on all levels. The summons turns tragic whenever it turns out pedants and drones, charlatans and quacks.

Roman Catholic Scholarship

When we move to scholarship in the Roman Catholic Church, a distinction seems in order. Some men and women are scholars *and* Catholic; others are Catholic scholars. The former engage in scholarly pursuits according to recognized standards *and* remain faithful to their Catholic commitment, but for any number of reasons their profession and their confession are not closely interrelated. Not necessarily cause for self-flagellation. Perhaps the subject matter does not call for such connection: ancient arrowheads in Arizona; Alleluia tropes in the tenth to twelfth century west; legal research into torts; a life devoted to the Greek iota subscript, *Beowulf,* the fission of heavy atoms, General George Patton and the Battle of the Bulge. I venture to say that most scholars in the Roman Catholic community, particularly such as ply their art or craft in secular situations, fall into this category. Such service to scholarship I do not denigrate; it can be, often is, a contribution to human understanding, human living, human loving. In fact, it is unfortunate that, from astronomy to zoology, American Catholicism has produced far fewer scholars of prominence than our numbers promise or warrant.[13]

In the context of this festschrift, I am not interested so much in the scholar who is a Catholic as in the Catholic scholar. Authors descant in depth on what they mean by scholarship—for example, high-level publication, recognized in awards, in fellowships, in tenure at the best secular universities. But I discover precious little effort to fathom the meaning of the adjective "Catholic" in its relation to the noun "scholar." I submit that "Catholic scholar" is not interchangeable with a scholar who "keeps the faith." I submit that practicing Catholics will make their distinctive contribution to American scholarship not in the first instance because they accept what the church teaches, obey church law, and share in liturgical worship, but to the extent that their Catholicism is integral to their scholarship. How, in the concrete, might that wedding be consummated? Five suggestions.[14]

1. One of the significant reasons for the dearth of Catholic scholarship has been the failure of lay and clerical Catholics to appreciate the *vocation* of the intellectual. A profound grasp of the genuine Catholic tradition would reveal that scholarship should be as authentic a vocation as priesthood or marriage.

The tradition goes back to the first Christian "university" in third century Alexandria, to a provocative thinker and theologian named Origen, with his four remarkable insights: (1) recognition of the rights of reason, awareness of the thrilling fact that the Word wore our flesh not to destroy what is human but to perfect it; (2) acquisition of knowledge, a sweepingly broad knowledge, the sheer materials for the student's contemplation; (3) the indispensable task that is Christian criticism, the intelligent confrontation of the old with the new, the ceaseless effort to link the highest flights of naked reason with God's self-disclosure, to communicate Clement of Alexandria's conviction that "there is one river of truth, but many streams fall into it on this side and on that"; (4) love of truth wherever it is to be found, in the mind of man or woman as well as in the mind of God, and a profound yearning to include all the scattered fragments of discovered truth under what a later pupil of Origen, Gregory of Neocaesarea, called "the holy Word, the loveliest thing there is."[15] This fourth facet anticipates a striking sentence penned by the incomparable theologian-in-a-wheelchair Yves Congar in a little book about Archbishop Lefebvre: "As for me, I want to gather up every small fragment of truth, wherever it is to be found, with the same care that I would use in picking up a tiny piece of a consecrated host."[16]

That sense of vocation runs through the Benedictine tradition of education and is admirably synthesized in the title of Dom Jean Leclercq's minor classic *The Love of Learning and the Desire for God.*[17] It is implicit in the twenty-eight Jesuit colleges and universities created at stunning sacrifice in the United States. It was set irrevocably in the heavens by astronomers like Clavius and Secchi; multiplied over and over by mathematicians like Kircher and Boscovich; carried to the ends of the earth by missionaries like humanist-scientist Matteo Ricci; brought into our own era by Maritain and Dawson, John Courtney Murray and Teilhard de Chardin, Sandra Schneiders and Lisa Cahill. For these and uncounted others, Catholicism and scholarship were not isolated compartments, two parts of the human psyche. In all they accomplished, faith was the motivating force, the energy that drove them relentlessly. To be a Catholic was to prize intelligence, to respect scholarship.

Succinctly, if our scholarship is to be authentically Catholic, I see a desperate need for Catholics, educated or not, clerical and lay, to etch on their minds and hearts a profound truth. Within Catholicism, scholarship, research, the life of the mind is not a game, not a hobby for such as can afford the time or have leisure for loafing, not a dispensable occupation like skink catching or kite flying, not irrelevant to the gospel and to salvation. Scholarship is a response to God, to God's call to serve, to open up the wonders of created and redeemed reality, to pay reverence to what creation's God saw "was very good" (Gen 1:31), to an earth that the fathers of the church saw transformed in its entirety by the touch of God-in-flesh. Realize it or not, behind each intellectual discipline is a divine summons. Unless our students and budding scholars sense this, academe is just a blastoff for the three top goals Harvard's incoming freshpersons declared on its 350th anniversary: money, power, reputation.[18]

2. Given faith as motive, Catholic scholars are challenged to move beyond that, to *integrate* Catholicism and professionalism even more intimately. I am aware, as suggested above, that certain areas of research render such an integration difficult or even impossible. I am concerned about fields and issues where the integration is not only possible but imperative.

Take a concrete example. The science of eugenics is ushering us into a future where the New Human will reveal qualities significantly greater than any we experience at present. A doctrinal question confronting the church now is the relationship between the New Human of scientific/technical development and the eschatological New Human of Christian tradition. The human body, therefore the human person, is going to be "transfigured" through the power of God and/or through the power of human beings. We are on the threshold of being able to remake ourselves according to a human image of humankind. But our Christian calling summons us to share in the humanity of Jesus, and so in his bodiedness, sacramentally now, integrally in the final kingdom. The consequent question, as posed by Robert Brungs, director of the Institute for Theological Encounter with Science and Technology:

> Does the conformity of our bodied form to [Jesus'], both now and in the resurrection, militate against any significant changing of that form through the use of the technologies we are gathering to ourselves? We must seriously probe into the question of whether and how Christ's body is normative for our bodies. . . . Does [the incarnation, death, and resurrection of Christ] help us in determining the extent to which we may deliberately alter the body, and hence the person? We know that there are faith limits to living in the community of God. We know that there are moral limits to such living. Now, in the light of our growing technological capacity, we must ask if there are physical limits to that living in God's community.[19]

Now Vatican II, in its Pastoral Constitution on the Church in the Modern World, has affirmed a Christian position on the biotechnologies.[20] God does not see divinity diminished by human efforts to master the secrets of creation, as long as our mastery is neither whimsical nor tyrannical. But the council has not supplied specific direction. Understandably so; for at the moment the possibilities latent in bioengineering exceed our ability to fantasize. It will be the task not only of Rome but more immediately of the Catholic technologist to work out the answers to five crucial questions Brungs has articulated.[21] (1) Does a particular biological alteration enhance the innate, internal dignity of the human—which involves the sacramental and covenantal character of the body? (2) Does a particular enhancement foster personal freedom? (3) Does the proposed bodily alteration preserve (and increase) the bodily integrity needed for conformity with the body of Christ? (4) Does the alteration promote a closer integration into the human community and a closer entry into the sacramental living and growing of the covenantal community? (5) Does the projected enhancement tend to promote worship of God, or does it lead away from that worship?

Such is the kind of involvement I see as indispensable if the technologist is to be Catholic precisely as a technologist. It demands (1) a broad grasp of the church's tradition as a whole and (2) intimate involvement in the ceaseless struggle to link mastery of creation with submission to creation's Master—what I dare to call a contemporary version of human freedom and divine sovereignty. Good indeed is a Catholic who is also a scholar; better still are scholars whose competence is part and parcel of their Catholicism. For only such Catholic scholars are in a position to confront effectively a type of technological, rational mentality that in ever new ways and on a global level is producing a new atheism.

A new atheism. Precisely there is a second concrete example of potential and desirable integration. In a profound reflection on American atheism, Michael Buckley writes:

> The critical point to bear in mind ... is that contemporary atheism does not emerge from an argument for the freedom of physics from theological assertions nor from the development of the human above the present state of humanity. Atheism in the U.S. arises spontaneously from a climate of mind which both segregates religious thought from serious inquiry and makes the authority of experience depend upon its codification in those experiential methods that took their rise from the physical and biological sciences. Religious denial or disinterest emerges from the unquestioned and unquestionable persuasion that only some such procedure enables human beings to move with honesty and respectability toward warranted assertions, that outside of these rigorous, objective procedures there are only enthusiasms, taste, and sentiment, mindless or ungrounded mythological thinking, and the projections of wish-fulfilment. The confused situation which confronts the contemporary religious mind in the intellectual culture of the U.S. is not so much argument or even hostility. It is dismissal—a cultural indifference to the entire and increasingly discredited theological enterprise itself.[22]

In every area of science the Catholic Church needs men and women like the Anglican priest and physical biochemist Arthur Peacocke, richly knowledgeable in Christian tradition and widely respected for his research, e.g. into DNA. In a post-Darwinian world Peacocke is struggling to restructure an understanding of God, nature, and the human person. His *God and the New Biology*[23] has been described by a Jesuit physicist as "a short but magisterial approach, rich in its contacts with the past, open in its conversation with the present, and unafraid of the unforeseeable developments that must of necessity soon be rushing upon us."[24]

3. To integrate Catholicism with professionalism, it is not enough for the scholar to be proficient in a particular segment of Catholic belief and morality: that a geneticist, for example, be cognizant of the official position on surrogate motherhood. Catholic experience must be catholic;

individual experience must be contextualized by the *community experience* that spans ages and continents.

Ideally, I want Catholic scholars to feel the Hebrew experience of Sinai and the desert; the New Testament experience of God's breakthrough in the flesh of Jesus; the conciliar experience from Nicaea I to Vatican II; the experience of theologians from Origen and Augustine through Aquinas and Bonaventure to Balthasar and Rahner—yes, mystics like Tauler and Teresa. I would like them to share the experience of non-Roman Christian communities, their pens and pews and pulpits; to listen to the Spirit speaking through the Jewish community as it alternately affirms and denies that "God died in Auschwitz," through our black brothers and sisters as they protest in their poverty that they are not quite "free at last." I would have their knowledge leavened by the arts, from *Les Miserables* through Rodin's *St. John the Baptist* to Samuel Beckett's frightening "Two times anything equals zero." I want them to agonize over the experience of living men and women, as these cry to us that they cannot discover God in our abstractions, stand mute before an immutable God who does not weep when they bleed, insist that, if they are to find God at all, they must somehow find God in earth's humans.

An ideal, of course. But so is the divine command to love God with all our hearts, love our neighbor as we love ourselves.

4. Catholic scholarship dares not remain mired in the sheerly rational. The life of the mind must be fired by what William F. Lynch saw as the Christian or Christic *imagination.*[25] Not the fantastic, the grotesque, the bizarre. Rather, the capacity we have to make the material an image of the immaterial or spiritual; a breaking through the obvious, the surface, to the reality beneath and beyond; the world of intuition and wonder, of amazement and delight, of festivity and play. Concretely, it is the vision and the dream, ritual and symbol, story and the fine arts. It is the Bible with its vast array of symbols from the creation story in Genesis through the parables of Jesus to the four horsemen in the Apocalypse. It is Michelangelo's *Last Judgment* and Beethoven's *Missa solemnis;* Kazantzakis' *Report to Greco* and Hopkins' "The Blessed Virgin Compared to the Air We Breathe"; Martin Luther King's dream of freedom and God as mother, God as lover, God as friend of the earth.

I am not downgrading abstract thought, conceptual analysis, rational demonstration, historical data, scientific experiment. These are basic to scholarship. I am suggesting that, for Catholic scholarship to come alive, the clear and distinct idea, rich as it is, is often not rich enough. There are areas where we need the image, more open-ended than the concept, more susceptible of different understandings; therein lie the risk and the joy. We need more than one Teilhard de Chardin: his interest in the human person, dominating his technical research; his situating "Christianity in human history precisely as man himself is situated in nature, that is, as informing and consolidating man's axial and leading role and transforming all his human psychic energy";[26] what Cardinal Feltin called his seductive "global vision of the universe wherein matter and spirit, body and soul, nature and supernature, science and faith find their unity in Christ."[27]

I do not claim that without imagination Catholic scholars are necessarily unhappy or unsuccessful. I do claim that without it they may miss much of the thrill in human living, run a greater risk of finding existence unexciting; that x-number of the dead and despairing will not be quickened to life by them, may fail to touch in love a living God whose glory challenges not so much our logic as our imagining. For, as metaphysician Jacques Maritain insisted, the culmination of knowledge is not conceptual but experiential; I "feel" God.

5. The Catholicism of a scholar should be a faith that does *justice.* Catholics whose lives are largely consecrated to ideas, to research, are not exempt from the charge laid on the People of God by the programmatic opening of Vatican II's Pastoral Constitution on the Church in the Modern World: "The joys and the hopes, the griefs and the anxieties of the men and women of this age, especially those who are poor or in any way afflicted, these too are the joys and hopes, the griefs and anxieties of the followers of Christ."[28] The charge is laid not only on women and men of medicine, but on the philosopher and the atomic scientist, on the speculative theologian and even the editor of *Theological Studies.* Precisely how this responsibility is to be implemented by a given scholar will depend on the scholar, the situation, and God's specific call and gracious self-giving.

RICHARD MCCORMICK

Scholarship as a vocation, a Christian calling; integration of professionalism and Catholicism; a grasp of the community experience from Sinai to Vatican II and beyond; faith and reason fleshed out and inflamed by a Christic imagination; a faith that does justice—if these facets are basic to Catholic scholarship, then Richard McCormick ranks high among Catholic scholars.

1. No need to dwell on his *vocation.* One point, however, calls for clarification. McCormick's decades-long existence as ethicist/moralist is not something that has coexisted with his priesthood, side by side with it.

A defensible theology of priesthood rejects a hard-and-fast distinction between priestly and nonpriestly activities, proclaims that whatever a priest does in authentic response to the call of the church at a given moment in its mission is priestly. Jesuit Pietro Angelo Secchi, cofounder of astrophysics; Augustinian Gregor Johann Mendel, laying the foundations of modern genetics; Dominican Gilbert Hartke, establishing the Speech and Drama Department at the Catholic University of America; diocesan priest Raymond A. McGowan, expert in industrial relations— these were not clerics with side interests approved by superiors, leaving "priestly" works to the parish. Quite the contrary. A fortiori, McCormick's involvement as a practitioner of moral theology and ethics is part and parcel of his vocation to the ordained priesthood. Not indeed necessary to that vocation, but in point of fact the primary path the vocation has taken.

The Origen I described earlier anticipated McCormick's response: rich recognition of the rights of reason; comprehensive knowledge; critical confrontation of reason and revelation; love of truth wherever found, and submission of truth's countless fragments to the holy Word. And Origen's pupil, Gregory of Neocaesarea, might apply to McCormick today what he wrote of his teacher then:

> . . . from the first day . . . he used every turn of language, pulled every string . . . employed every resource of his abilities . . . insisting that they only lived the life befitting the reasonable beings who studied to live rightly, who "knew themselves," first their own nature, and secondly, the things essentially good which a human being ought to follow after, and the really evil things which he ought to avoid. . . . Like some spark falling in the midst of my soul there was kindled and there blazed forth my love . . . both for the holy Word, the loveliest thing there is, and for this man, His friend and His prophet.[29]

2. In Richard McCormick professionalism and Catholicism form a remarkably *integrated* unity. Not only does faith motivate his scholarship; the substance of his research is a moral theology that intends to commend itself to reason and revelation. An increasingly difficult task, particularly from the year (1965) when he yielded to the persuasions of John Courtney Murray, S.J., to "have a try at" the "Notes on Moral Theology" in *Theological Studies.* The "try" lasted into 1987.

The basic problem that confronted McCormick? Moral theology as a discipline was changing radically. The first sentence of McCormick's first "Notes" reads: "For quite a few years now, theologians have, without disowning casuistry, disowned an excessively casuistic approach to the moral life."[30] In the 1940s and 1950s Catholic moral theology, though "very pastoral and prudent, critically respectful, realistic, compassionate, open and charitable, well-informed," nevertheless "was all too often one-sidedly confession-oriented, magisterium-dominated, canon law-centered, and seminary-controlled."[31]

Through the past three decades McCormick has been in the forefront of what Daniel Callahan in 1964 called a theological "revolution."[32] McCormick has listed ten of "the revolutionary phases or ingredients": the influence of Vatican II's ecclesiology; Karl Rahner's theology of fundamental freedom; a quarter century of discussion about moral norms and moral method, revolving in great measure around the umbrella-term "proportionalism"; the Birth Control Commission and *Humanae vitae;* the emergence of feminism; the maturation of bioethics; the influence of liberation theology; the person as criterion of the morally right and wrong; the Charles Curran affair; and the effort to "tighten things up" in the church, especially by authoritative intervention in matters theological.[33] Where are we now? McCormick has replied by describing ten "ages." We are in the age of settling, of specialists, of justice, of experience, of cultural diversity, of technology, of holiness and witness, of theological anthropology, of ecumenism, of women.[34]

This is not the place to appraise McCormick's positions; such an appraisal demands time and perspective. If scores of scholars say amen to his so-called proportionalism, prominent opponents of this methodological move have not been silent: e.g. Joseph Boyle, John Connery, John Finnis, Germain Grisez, and William May. The point I am stressing is not that McCormick has won the anguished Catholic struggle on moral methodology or definitively solved such crucial issues as direct sterilization or heterologous technologically-assisted reproduction, but that he merits regard as a model for moral/ethical scholarship. He has given his life to scholarly research. He has been ceaselessly in search of moral method, of fundamental norms. He possesses a knowledge of the field unsurpassed in our time, commanding a rare control of the literature in French, German, Italian, and Spanish. He keeps close contact not only with Protestant ethics but with Protestant ethicians as well, aware that his discipline cannot flourish in Catholic isolation. Rigorous logic is a demand he makes on himself as well as on others. He jousts with adversaries firmly but courteously, presents their positions succinctly but accurately, is open to opposition and contradiction, reinterpretation and revaluation.[35] He has put his scholarly life on the line—in countless lectures and seminars, in a handful of significant books and hundreds of articles, in publications that take respectful but carefully crafted issue with individual facets of official Catholic doctrine. If philosophical literature on moral theory is not prominent in his published work, it may confirm what needs no demonstration: no single scholar in any field is omnicompetent.[36]

3. Richard McCormick knows the Catholic moral *tradition*—and much of our broader theological tradition—from scripture through medieval scholasticism to the twentieth century. From long experience and contemplation it is resident in his bones and blood. I trust he will be a living reproach to a generation of scholars who know Augustine only as a born-again Catholic who foisted on the western world a hellish doctrine of original sin and a pessimistic view of marriage; who cannot spell Chalcedon, even though a quarter century ago Harvey Cox argued that apart from Chalcedon technopolis is unintelligible; who can anathematize Aquinas and scuttle scholasticism without ever having read a word thereof; who sneer at the mere mention of "medieval," as if the middle ages were darker than our own; who could not care less about a papal pronouncement, much less peruse it.

Moreover, McCormick possesses a quality that keeps tradition from degenerating into traditionalism: historical consciousness. He recognizes that truth, objective though it be, is not something "already out there now," existing apart from its possession by anyone, apart from history, formulated in propositions verbally immutable. He knows that in no facet of its existence is the church of Christ a sort of Platonic idea suspended in midair, that in every phase of its pilgrim life the church is inescapably involved in the ebb and flow of history. And so he realizes that, whether in Rome or South Bend, theology must be a ceaseless struggle in each age to grasp the gospel anew. In this connection I must avow my conviction that, despite his occasional tilting with official Catholic teaching, McCormick's scholarship does not clash with *obsequium religiosum* properly understood.[37]

4. Richard McCormick's theology is enriched by *imagination*. I mean, concretely, an uncommon ability to see beneath the surface of issues, together with a fine power of association: e.g. his realization that a coercive theological atmosphere weakens the episcopal and papal magisterium, marginalizes theologians, demoralizes priests, reduces the laity to a no-account theological status, compromises future ministry, and threatens loss of the Catholic leaven in significant areas such as technology and science.[38] I mean a certain creative gift—taking the elements of past moral reasoning (e.g. object-end-circumstances as determinative of moral evaluation) and shaping them into a fresh pattern, a new synthesis.

I mean a consistent but not pollyanna openness to the future, to what tomorrow's technology and theology may bring.

5. McCormick's scholarship is not embowered in an ivory tower; his word written and spoken, his involvement with government and health care, with religious congregations and secular leaders, are built around the human person, with an almost fierce focus on *justice.* The areas are amazingly many: dignity of the human person, contraception, civil disobedience, business morality, heart transplants, political protest, genetic engineering, ecology, death and dying, divorce and remarriage, abortion, sexuality, nuclear warfare, homosexuality, and women's liberation. If ideas have consequences, uncounted unknowns are living and will live a more human existence because Richard McCormick set mind to moral and pen to paper, thundered ethical truth in high places and low, listened to the powerful and the powerless, engaged graciously in John Courtney Murray's "civilized conversation," and took praise and diatribe with Ignatian "indifference." And never forget, this scholar sat at the bedside of comatose Karen Ann Quinlan.

Perhaps a summary statement on the object, end, and intention of Catholic scholar Richard McCormick's life might be borrowed from the prayer sung in the musical *Godspell:* "see you more clearly, love you more dearly, follow you more nearly."

Notes

1. Here I clearly part company with renowned historian Samuel Eliot Morison, who wrote in one of the smallest published books (thirty-two pages) I have ever seen: "For the purpose of this essay [delivered 'in a somewhat different form' at Rockhurst College, Kansas City, Mo., in 1960], I venture to define a scholar as a person engaged in the pursuit of knowledge, whether it be classical, literary, mathematical, or in the natural sciences, including nuclear physics. I would not exclude the so-called creative artists and writers—the musicians, painters, sculptors, poets, and prose writers, many of whom also are scholars; and I would certainly include those for whom scholarship is an avocation rather than a vocation. There are many people in business or professional life who pursue some branch of learning as a hobby; and who, like as not, turn out to be better scholars than the full-time professionals" (*The Scholar in America: Past, Present, and Future* [New York: Oxford University, 1961] 6). I prefer to employ the genus intellectual, placing under it species such as scholar, artist, editor, novelist, etc. Scholarship is a specific way of living the life of the mind.

2. New York: Macmillan, 1962.

3. See Barbara W. Tuchman, *Practicing History: Selected Essays* (New York: Knopf, 1981) 17ff.

4. A vivid example: the controversy that raged throughout the scientific community in early 1989, after two scientists claimed to have produced controlled nuclear fusion in a jar at room temperature—heralding the end of the world's energy problems. Charges were aired: faulty techniques, lack of thoroughness, impetuous announcement. As this paper was being prepared, more exhaustive tests were under way. A factor apparently contributing to "impetuous" scientific announcements is the felt need to rush one's research into print before others do.

5. A.J. Cronin, *The Green Years* (Boston: Little, Brown, 1944) 128.

6. Tuchman, *Practicing History* 14.

7. Ibid. 17.

8. Morison, *The Scholar in America* 8; italics mine.

9. Ibid. 7. A strange development; for scholars were respected in our colonial period, led the American Revolution, and guided the early Republic. "The era from 1760 to 1830 was, par excellence, that of the scholar in American politics" (ibid. 11).

10. Ibid. 7.

11. Ibid. 15.

12. See ibid. 16–18.

13. See, e.g., the ground-breaking article by John Tracy Ellis, "American Catholics and the Intellectual Life," *Thought* 30 (1955) 351–88, and the interview with Ellis thirty years later in the *U.S. Catholic Historian* 4 (1985) 188–94. Factors Ellis saw contributing to this "poverty" before 1955 include (1) profound anti-Catholic prejudice, (2) immigrant character of U.S. Catholicism, (3) absence of an intellectual tradition, (4) general lack of serious reading habits, (5) captivity to the prevailing American material-goods ethos, (6) failure to appreciate the vocation of the intellectual. In 1985 Ellis saw improvement, but nothing like what it should be. More optimistic about Catholic intellectual life in general (not exclusively scholarship) is Andrew M. Greeley's "Is There an American Catholic Elite?" *America* 160, no. 17 (May 6, 1989) 426–29.

14. These suggestions were first set forth in my keynote address to a faculty conference at Georgetown University on "The State of American Catholic Intellectual Life Today," March 2, 1989, where the focus was not narrowly on scholarship but more broadly on the whole range of intellectualism. The address was published as "Intellectual and Catholic? Or Catholic Intellectual?" *America* 160, no. 17 (May 6, 1989) 420–25.

15. Gregory of Neocaesarea, *Panegyric Addressed to Origen* 6:83 (*Sources chrétiennes* 148:128).

16. Yves Congar, *Challenge to the Church: The Case of Archbishop Lefebvre* (Huntington, Ind.: *Our Sunday Visitor,* 1976) 42.

17. New York: New American Library, 1961.

18. See *Time* 128, no. 10 (Sept. 8, 1986) 57.

19. Robert A. Brungs, S.J., "Biology and the Future: A Doctrinal Agenda," *Theological Studies* 50 (1989) 707.

20. See *Gaudium et spes,* no. 34.

21. See Brungs, "Biology" 710–13.

22. Michael J. Buckley, S.J., "Experience and Culture: A Point of Departure for American Atheism," *Theological Studies* 50 (1989) 459.

23. San Francisco: Harper and Row, 1987.

24. Review by Frank R. Haig, S.J., in *Theological Studies* 49 (1988) 371.

25. See William F. Lynch, S.J., *Christ and Apollo: The Dimensions of the Literary Imagination* (New York: Sheed and Ward, 1960) esp. 187–98, 227–67; *Images of Hope: Imagination as Healer of the Hopeless* (Baltimore: Helicon, 1965); *Images of Faith: An Exploration of the Ironic Imagination* (Notre Dame: University of Notre Dame, 1973).

26. E.L. Boné, "Teilhard de Chardin, Pierre," *New Catholic Encyclopedia* 13 (1967) 977.

27. In *Documentation catholique* 58 (1961) 1523.

28. *Gaudium et spes,* no. 1.

29. Gregory of Neocaesarea, *Panegyric Addressed to Origen* 6:73–75, 83 (*Sources chrétiennes* 148:124, 128; translation in part from M. Metcalfe, *Gregory Thaumatourgos: Address to Origen* [London/New York: SPCK/Macmillan, 1920] 57–58, 60).

30. Richard A. McCormick, S.J., "Notes on Moral Theology," *Theological Studies* 26 (1965) 596.

31. Richard A. McCormick, S.J., "Moral Theology 1940–1989: An Overview," *Theological Studies* 50 (1989) 3–4.

32. Daniel Callahan, "Authority and the Theologian," *Commonweal* 80 (1964) 319–23.

33. McCormick develops these items at some length in "Moral Theology 1940–1989" (n. 31 above) 7–18.

34. See ibid. 19–23.

35. See, e.g., McCormick's "Notes on Moral Theology 1977: The Church in Dispute," *Theological Studies* 39 (1978) 108: "Through the kind criticisms of thoughtful colleagues, I have modified this teleological understanding of the wrongfulness of many direct killings, without, however, abandoning the teleology itself. . . ."

36. As far as the "Notes on Moral Theology" are concerned, McCormick's contributions have been supplemented by articles such as that of John Langan, S.J., "Recent Philosophical Work in Moral Theory," *Theological Studies* 41 (1980) 549–67, a critical survey of significant books by John L. Mackie, Gilbert Harman, Richard Brandt, Alan Gewirth, and Alan Donagan.

37. See the penetrating pages on *obsequium* in Vatican II by Ladislas Örsy, S.J., "Magisterium: Assent and Dissent," *Theological Studies* 48 (1987) 473–97, at 487–90. He calls it a "seminal locution," i.e. "a term or expression which contains the truth but without circumscribing it with precision; it needs to be developed further. It is a broad and intuitive approach to a mystery that leaves plenty of room for future insights and discoveries" (488). As with *subsistit* in *Lumen Gentium* 8, so with *obsequium* in *LG* 25, the council did not intend to

give a precise meaning to the term; it "set the parameters for research" (ibid.). When it "spoke of religious *obsequium,* it meant an attitude toward the Church which is rooted in the virtue of religion, the love of God and the love of His Church. This attitude in every concrete case will be in need of further specification, which could be 'respect' or could be 'submission,' depending on the progress the Church has made in clarifying its own beliefs" (490).

38. See Richard A. McCormick, S.J., "Dissent in Moral Theology and Its Implications," *Theological Studies* 48 (1987) 102–5.

2

The Role of the
Catholic Moral Theologian

Bernard Häring, C.SS.R.

In order to honor Richard McCormick, an outstanding moral theologian, I—having spent more than fifty years in the study and teaching of moral theology—will try to share my own understanding of the role of the Catholic moral theologian, and my hopes, based on the experience of past and present moral theologians, for the young generation of moral theologians. I shall avoid the term *moralist* except in cases where I hesitate to recognize the legitimacy of the role played by such a person within the field of moral theology.

The precise question under consideration is this: What, in our opinion, constitutes the proper mission and ethos of the Catholic moral theologian?

I. A Ministry of Mediation

Catholic moral theologians are not lawgivers or mere interpreters of law, norm-makers or inculcators of existing norms. Their mission is greater than this, and their ministry, more humble. The mission and ethos of the moral theologian (who is at the same time both learner and teacher) are those of a very alert mediator within the community of Christ's disciples—a mediator who is a member of the community of theologians, and a learner and fellow-pilgrim along with all the redeemed.

1. Mediator of the Biblical Message for the Here and Now

Moral theologians should constantly be nourished by the word of God (cf. Vatican II, *Optatam totius,* n. 16). Always learning from the work of biblical scholars, they treasure the good news in their hearts and minds, pondering it in order to discern what helps us to come to a deeper knowledge of Christ, of the Father, and of his salvific plan for humankind. Good exegesis teaches us to understand the word of God within the ongoing history of salvation by explaining what each part of the Bible meant at that time. The rules of hermeneutics enable us to mediate the biblical message for here and now—of course, only insofar as we live alertly, with vigilance and readiness in this our "time of salvation," in full solidarity with the people to whom we minister. A moral theologian should possess and exercise the capacity to bring together the biblical message and human experience, especially the experiences of contemporary people (without neglecting those of past cultures).

2. A Discerning Mediator of Tradition

One of the great themes of all theology is the right understanding of tradition and traditions. In my view, *tradition* refers to a stream of life and truth under the guidance of the Holy Spirit, who introduces each generation in its dynamic historical context into the one great truth revealed by Jesus Christ. The Spirit enriches God's people with new experiences, enabling them faithfully to discern the abiding heritage in its various historical expressions, so that they may measure human experiences in the abiding light of Christ, treasuring what is valuable, purifying what needs purification, and discarding what cannot become part of the constructive history of salvation.

A moralist who is a traditionalist, clinging to mere formulas and a set of laws, is not a theologian; such a person does not, and cannot, convey the faith in the living God who was, who is, and who is to come—the God who is a wonderful householder who brings together old and new things. Today, a moral theologian must carefully use the tools of the sociology of knowledge, the sociology of culture, and the other human sciences in order to avoid a dead and deadly traditionalism, the mere transmission of a set of time-bound norms without recognition of just how time-bound they were and are.

The proper ethos of the moral theologian is a grateful memory, a spirit of appreciation for what we have received from past generations and cultures, combined with a great eagerness to cultivate the spirit of discernment. In this way, and only in this way, can past experiences and human reflection—the whole stream of tradition and traditions—become fruitful for the here and now. One aspect of the moral theologian's vocation is the task of indicating in a lively way how the stream of divine and human tradition can and should become fruitful for the present.

The Second Vatican Council is a model of this theological spirit which combines appreciation of the past with discernment in order to make the tradition fruitful for the here and now. In contrast, traditionalist movements like that of Bishop Lefebvre can produce moralists in the worst sense of the term, but not helpful moral theologians.

3. The Moral Theologian as Learner-Teacher

Richard McCormick exemplifies the role I intend to describe in this section. I never failed to read his "Notes on Moral Theology," published for many years in *Theological Studies*. His knowledge of languages has enabled him to inform himself and others about what is going on in the worldwide community of moral theologians regarding their relationship with the magisterium and with the problems of their people. He is a learner, eager to distinguish what is valuable from what is dead and deadly, who informs his readers in such a way that they are challenged and helped to pursue discernment in a spirit of mature responsibility.

Authentic moral theologians do not imagine themselves as standing over, and above, other people. Their path of knowledge is not a one-way street. They continually realize that they cannot be teachers without always becoming better students as disciples of Christ who are docile to the Holy Spirit, and as co-disciples in the faith community which extends even beyond the boundaries of the Roman Catholic Church. Believing in the Holy Spirit, they realize that the Spirit of Christ can work in all, and through all. The catholicity of their ethos urges Catholic moral theologians to appreciate the traditions and the present efforts of the Eastern Orthodox churches as well as those of the churches which emerged from the Reformation.

Believing in the universal call to salvation and the power of the Holy Spirit, Catholic moral theologians must be willing to learn from all people: those who adhere to other religions, and even those not affiliated with any organized religion. We consider the so-called "natural law" (cf. Rom 2:15) to be a law written into the hearts of all people, and brought to life by the presence of the Holy Spirit. To give an example—how much could we Christians learn from a man like Mahatma Gandhi? We cannot be genuine Catholic moral theologians if we confine our learning and teaching efforts to one stream of the Christian tradition, to one culture, or even to what the Holy Spirit has brought forth as the fruit of love, peace, and justice within Christianity. We are "catholic" (worldwide) learner-teachers, breaking down the barriers persons have constructed and honoring God's presence everywhere. I think that I have learned more from the writings of Confucius and from some Jewish writers than from the traditional manuals of Catholic moral theology.

II. THE RELATIONSHIP WITH THE MAGISTERIUM

Concerning the sometimes unavoidable tension between the papal or episcopal magisterium on the one hand and the moral theologians on the other, we not infrequently hear the warning that there is only one magisterium in the church—that of the pope and the bishops (under and along with him)—and that there is no such thing as a second kind of magisterium in the church, i.e., that of moral theologians, or of theologians in general. The most important response to this argument is that of Jesus: "But you must not be called 'master': for you have only one 'master,' and you are all brothers and sisters. . . . Nor must you be called 'teacher'; you have one teacher, the messiah" (Mt 23:8–10). Under the one master and the one teacher, Jesus Christ, we are all learners; but to some extent, and in proportion to our humility and docility, we also have some modest share in the mission of Christ. The particular share of that mission accorded to moral theologians requires that they fully acknowledge and appreciate the share accorded to others. This is also true—although in a somewhat different way and degree—of the magisterium of the successor of Peter and all the successors of the apostles. Therefore, before explicitly discussing the relationship of the moral theologians to the official magisterium of the successors of the apostles, we must remind ourselves of the various other forms of participation in the one, unique magisterium of Christ.

1. The Magisterium of the Saints

The saints are the models for all teachers of the moral life, which may be understood as life in Christ Jesus, the life of discipleship of all the followers of Christ. One cannot be a good moral theologian without believing in one's own call to holiness and in the universal call to holiness (cf. chapter 5 of *Lumen Gentium*).

The saints do not teach us with empty words, empty cries of "Master, Master!" With heart and mind and will they follow the divine master whom the Father has sent us. They teach by their example, and also by their words of wisdom. They teach in concrete historical circumstances, and in an existential way which is always actualized anew. In their unity under Christ and in their wonderful diversity, their type of teaching is more valuable than abstract casuistry. Their magisterium is also an indispensable aid for the learner-teacher of moral theology's perception of the historical dynamism and inculturation of the moral message. When discussing the saints in this way, I am not thinking only of the canonized saints of past and recent times (although the significance of the papal magisterium's assurance of their authenticity should in no way be belittled). I think of the many great and humble saints with whom we come into contact throughout the course of our lives. They are a letter written "not with ink but with the Spirit of the living God . . . not on stone tablets but on the pages of the human heart" (2 Cor 3:3). The saints are on the wavelength of the wisdom that comes from God. The chorus of saints whom we know and meet directly or encounter through study-meditation leads us most directly to Christ, the only master.

Among the saints, those recognized by the universal church as "doctors of the church" play a special role. They complete and sometimes correct each other as our teachers of the life in Christ Jesus.

From those doctors of the church such as Augustine, Thomas Aquinas, and Alphonsus Liguori, who have made the most important contributions to moral theology, we can and must learn that moral theology requires an ongoing readiness for revision and correction. Augustine, for example, published two whole books of "retractions"; Alphonsus Liguori provided several lists of opinions which he had changed over the course of the years. There is no danger of loss of substance if we follow the example of the great doctors of the church, and thus imitate their increasing faithfulness toward the divine master.

2. The Magisterium of the Little Ones

"Jesus exulted in the Holy Spirit and said: 'I thank you, Father, Lord of heaven and earth, for hiding these things from the learned and self-important, while revealing them to the simple' " (Lk 10:21). The ethos of the moral theologian includes the attempt to belong to the "simple." One of the best ways to reach this privileged state is through readiness to learn from simple, humble people. I think that many moral theologians have, as I have, both experienced and admired the wisdom of parents, brothers, and sisters, who not infrequently manifest an astonishing wisdom in resolving their own moral problems and in giving advice to others who acknowledge their "competence," even though they have no official position whatsoever. By "competence," I refer to the competence of an alert, sensitive conscience, a competence in discerning what true love is and requires.

Moralists who, led by the conviction that ordinary people are morally immature and incapable of being brought to maturity, believe it appropriate to dictate and inculcate their own solutions are poor learners. They may well belong to the group of self-important people to whom God refuses to reveal himself and the true countenance of love. If we ignore the wisdom of our most humble fellow-pilgrims, we are—as teachers of moral theology—in great danger of missing our road.

3. The Magisterium of the Merciful and Those in Need of Mercy

The core of the New Testament's moral message is: "Be merciful as your heavenly Father is merciful" (Lk 6:36). I can fulfill the difficult mission of a moral theologian only insofar as I orient, not only my private life, but also my theological ethos and activity, according to the beatitude: "How blest are those who show mercy; mercy shall be shown to them" (Mt 5:7). We can learn from our Lord, and (in view of him) from the great doctors of the church and from all the saints, what mercy and compassion mean. We cannot marvel enough at how much God loves us poor sinners. Theologians cannot boast about their merits. We are far from attaining perfect fulfillment of the great law of love and compassion. If we but realize that we live by God's undeserved compassion and grace, we will never dare to impose unproven burdens upon people's consciences.

We have to listen not only to those who show compassion, but also to the cry of those who need mercy, understanding, and encouragement in their difficult situations. I want to mention just one example: How many divorced people have been alienated from the sacraments and from the church? How many have been refused an annulment, even though there is sufficient proof that their first marriage was not viable and had no chance to succeed? Persons who struggle heroically to save their first marriage, find themselves unjustly abandoned, and remarry because of particular needs are nonetheless treated as public sinners by those who in many respects are greater sinners—sinners against the all-embracing law of love. The ethos of Catholic moral theologians obliges them to listen to such people, and, when the need arises, to speak out in their favor.

Moral theologians who live in economically powerful societies as well as those who live among the poorest peoples of the third world cannot be true to their vocation and ethos unless they allow themselves to be deeply touched by these situations. How can a Catholic moral theologian waste time fighting about minutiae or imposing doubtful burdens— burdens very probably not willed by God—when the people "without voice" have such obvious needs?

4. Learning from Those of Outstanding Ability in the Human Sciences

The vocation to fullness of life in Christ impels all the faithful to strive continuously for deeper knowledge of Jesus Christ, of the Father (through Christ), and of the human person in his or her situation. Moral theologians have a particular professional obligation to excel in understanding humanity, men and women, within actual historical, cultural, social, socio-economic, and political situations. Inadequate understandings of the human person, deeply-rooted ideologies (e.g. about the nature and role of woman, and her proper relation to man), and/or historical conditions which no longer exist have grounded many of the traditional norms and are responsible for the emphasis traditionally accorded to certain norms.

Some churchmen in high positions think that the moral theologian's role is limited to the explanation of the existing norms and the display of their proper forms of application. This is a dangerous error which must be unmasked. Moral theologians, in full solidarity with one another, with members of other professions, and with church authorities, must test the traditional norms and the traditional emphasis upon certain norms, since norms are for people—not people for norms. To do so, they need personal pastoral experience, or at least constant contact with the best pastoral workers (men and women), as well as with lay people, who frequently excel in knowledge of the human condition—a knowledge which is both a great art and an aspect of wisdom.

5. Solidarity with the Magisterium of Pope and Bishops

It is inconceivable to think of the community of theologians (particularly moral theologians) as a kind of second magisterium other than or even against that of the pope and bishops. To the theologian belongs not a magisterium, but a ministry, a *diakonia,* undertaken for the benefit of the whole people of God, and, in a special way, for the benefit of the pastoral teaching office of the pope and the bishops.

The teaching of the pope and bishops is more directly pastoral than that of theologians, but moral theologians, in order to fulfill their *diakonia* to those in authority and to all people, must also be pastorally-minded. Moral theologians must constantly be in contact with the joys and sorrows, the anguish and hopes, of people, particularly those in distress. They must be in close contact with the priests and lay people who have pastoral experience, and can reveal their experiences and problems. Theologians should give voice to "voiceless," marginalized people. Frequently, they must think more about the sheep who have gone astray or who have been unjustly alienated than those who are described as "just" or "obedient."

Moral theologians' *diakonia* is not a "one-way" ministry, i.e. a ministry of explaining the official magisterium's teachings to people in an understandable way; they also have the duty (through solidarity with the people of God) to let the bishops and the pope know what people feel and think. To carry out this duty they should strive to bring together the shared experiences and co-reflections of various kinds of people from different cultures, socio-economic backgrounds, etc. Should theologians become mere yes-men and yes-women who say only what pleases those in high places, they would sin gravely against covenant-fidelity toward those in authority and those under authority.

Theologians, of course, must faithfully and sympathetically present the teachings of popes, bishops, councils, and synods, but they should also respond honestly and straightforwardly to the doubts and objections of various kinds of people. Particularly in this era, when culture is both critical in its assessments and rapidly-changing, theologians must educate themselves in order to acquire the virtue of constructive criticism; one of their main concerns must be assisting people to become discerning and responsible members of both church and society. It is a grave sin to tell people that "popes" and the holy office have never erred in matters of morality.

III. Speaking and Doing the Truth in Love

Moral theologians ought to be indefatigable searchers for existential truth, at the heart of which is divine and human love. They are to be spokespersons in the ongoing history of salvation, individuals rooted in the word of God and in tradition, yet open to the here and now, accepting the constantly approaching challenge of the future. They should combine a sensitivity concerning continuity in faithfulness toward the Lord of history with a readiness to scrutinize the signs of the times, the indications of the necessity of a change which requires both personal conversion and structural renewal. Deeply-rooted in faith and love, theologians must constantly be on the move with the Lord of history and with the pilgrim-church. Believing that we all are "not under law, but under grace" (Rom 6:14), they cannot regard the proposal of a code of unchanging law-norms (i.e. prohibitive, limiting norms) as their first duty; indeed, in the sphere of norms, and even in the sphere of aspirations and emphases, they must constantly strive to distinguish what is abiding from what is time-bound and culturally conditioned. Much more fundamental is their mission to communicate, in an attractive way, the true countenance of redeemed and redeeming love, and, with love, all the fruits of the Spirit. "The harvest of the Spirit is love, joy, peace, kindness, goodness, fidelity, gentleness (nonviolence), and self-control. There is no law dealing with such things as these" (Gal 5:22–23). Their proper point of departure, and of arrival, therefore, is "to know Jesus Christ" with heart and mind, to know the Father, and to know human beings both in their lofty "vocation to Christ" (*Optatam totius,* n. 16) and (through the help of the human sciences) in their historical condition. As fellow sojourners sharing in the ongoing pilgrimage of history, they should emphasize the goal commandments, with their liberating and compelling dynamics, before pointing to the forbidden side-paths and dangerous dead-ends.

Faithful to the biblical thought-patterns, theologians must care more—more, I say!—about helping to form the Christian person, Christian communities, Christian character ("virtues"), healthy and healing human relationships, and sound conditions of life, than about the mere repetition of prohibitions. Prohibitions should be described in the context of a clear picture of the ongoing struggle between the Spirit and the incarnate selfishness ("*sarx*"): in this way, bare and harsh do's-and-don'ts will not stand along the people's road.

To put it in a nutshell, Christian moral theologians should never become *moralists,* part of a system of "normers" and controllers; instead, they must present the "law of the Spirit who gives life in Christ Jesus." Their main moral discourse, therefore, is *paraclese* in view of the *Paracletos,* the Holy Spirit, the enabler, the consoler, the one who introduces us kindly and firmly into the truth revealed in Jesus Christ, with its marvelous mirror-images in the great saints and prophets.

1. *A* Satyagrahi, *Witnessing to Truth Forcefully*

Mahatma Gandhi was the great *satyagrahi,* the forceful witness to *truth* whose heart is love and whose way is *ahimsa,* the strength of love expressed by courageous nonviolence. As a *satyagrahi,* the moral theologian must never be a utilitarian consequentialist who thinks primarily in terms of immediate success; instead the theologian must aim forcefully for the liberation of humankind from every type of falsehood, violence, manipulation, sterile rigorism, and legalism. A *satyagrahi* is a challenger, a messenger of peace; but for those who are prisoners of legalistic systems and hurtful power-structures, such a person is inevitably a troublemaker. The moral theologian must be aware of this, and must take the necessary risk of being rejected as an enabler of justice and peace, of being treated instead like a mere troublemaker.

In order to avoid unnecessary conflicts and dangerous misinterpretations, theologians must keep careful watch over their motives, and look for the right time to speak and the right manner in which to witness. As a *satyagrahi,* the authentic moral theologian is also a healer who speaks with healing love and healing understanding. Such a person will sympathize with those in authority who, through their pursuit of order and search for observance of law, fall easily into a rigorism and a legalism which deprive their ministry of the force of paraclesis. Moral theologians must not be harsh judges looking for signs of malice; instead, they must exhibit healing warmth and understanding, while constantly asking: What would happen to me if I were in their position?

To put it another way, the true *satyagrahi* moral theologian constantly combines a theology of liberation with a healing approach. Such theologians never think of their prophetic role without understanding it within the context of Christ, *the prophet,* and the whole chorus of authentic prophets. Theologians must allow themselves to be challenged by these prophets, by church authorities, and, at the same time, by simple, humble people, especially those in trouble because no one dares to speak in their favor.

2. The Courage for the Provisional

One of the great insights of the Second Vatican Council is that the church as a whole, including the magisterium, does not have ready-made solutions for every new personal, interpersonal, and socio-cultural problem. In many situations sometimes—indeed, often—both the official magisterium and the moral theologians can give only a tentative response. Both groups need the courage to offer that which is provisional.

It is sickening when even moral theologians, as well as those in authority, are not aware of their limitations and of the tentativeness which frequently characterizes their utterances. Authentic moral theologians will never be intolerant or arrogant; by their whole manner of life and of theologizing they will unmask the evil of intolerance, and the unhealthiness of a claim for certainties and security where we should accept the humble and yet noble value of the provisional insofar as it is explicitly acknowledged as such. One of the remedies for clinging attachment to false sources of security and for undue claims of certainty is indicated by the Pastoral Constitution on the Church in the Modern World (*Gaudium et spes*), n. 16: "In faithfulness to their conscience, Christians will unite themselves with others in the search for truth and truthful solutions of questions which arise. . . ." This point is of enormous importance for all the faithful, but particularly for the bearers of the official magisterium and for moral theologians. We should never make claims concerning the assistance of the Holy Spirit unless we honor the Holy Spirit by this shared reflection, this shared search for enlightenment. The Holy Spirit works in all, through all, and on behalf of all—although surely with particular richness in the successors of the apostles, if, faithful to a lively conscience, they unite themselves with the rest of the faithful, and try to bring together these shared experiences and reflections in accordance with the very nature of the *catholic* (worldwide) church and the promptings of the Holy Spirit.

To make oneself the slave of just one school, one trend, one social class, one human tradition, is a tragedy, a betrayal of the Christian conscience and vocation. Moral theologians should be the very last to expose themselves and their role to such a temptation to "monopoly," such an offense against the Holy Spirit. I regard the avoidance of such an attitude as an important measure of faithful adherence to the spirit and words of Vatican II. Moral theology should play an outstanding role in the ecumenical learning process, and should assist the magisterium in this area, even though its results might not immediately be "honored."

The moral theologian should be gratefully docile to the "grace of doubt," and should constantly help others to obtain the grace of doubt. Thus, the moral theologian must often be content to raise helpful questions instead of asserting final solutions.

IV. A WHOLISTIC VISION

When I speak of a vision of wholeness, I am thoroughly aware that each one of us, and humanity in general, will not reach full wholeness, full health, full peace, etc. before the second coming of Christ. We live in a wounded world and are, at our very best, no more than "wounded healers." We cannot even attain a complete vision of wholeness. I see two particular dangers or enemies to what I call a vision of wholeness. One danger is the pursuit of a closed, perfect systematization—a ready-made "scientific system" of ethics; the other is the chaos of a thousand do's and don'ts—a chaotic collection of problems and advice.

1. A NO to Any Kind of Final "System" in Moral Theology

The holy scriptures do not offer a theological system of concepts and norms. To a great extent, the Bible is narrative theology, an unsystematized account of great events in the history of creation and salvation; it is also a call for a grateful memory. However, there is no lack of keys by which to unlock this history. There are highlights which shed their light upon the whole history of creation, salvation, and expectation.

The scriptures contain reflections and thought patterns which cannot be neglected. At this point, I just want to mention the biblical eschatological virtues which insert the believer into the dynamics of the ongoing history of salvation. Gratitude (particularly the grateful memory) opens the Christian to an inheritance of wealth from the past: everything that God has done for us, and the leaven brought into history by the lives of the saints. Christians are called to make these blessings fruitful for the here and now, and for the future. There are also special virtues which help us to confront present opportunities and risks: alertness, vigilance, readiness, and discernment. The divine promises and the promptings of the Spirit guide the believer to hope, and to creative commitment for the future. (A static systematization of the Greek cardinal virtues is unacceptable, and must be rejected if it is regarded as automatically appropriate for other cultures.) Other significant aspects characteristic of revelation include the primacy of grace, a faith which is fruitful in love and filled with hope, and the coming of God's kingdom.

A moral theology for the practice of the Christian life cannot have automatic recourse to leitmotives, but it should propose them in such a way that individuals and groups can adopt them while adapting them to their own situations.

2. Helping Believers To Find a Healing Vision of Wholeness

The great oriental tradition of the Orthodox churches presents a vision of wholeness which does not separate a moral theology of static norms from a spirituality which is reserved for a privileged group. A developed pneumatology and eucharistic faith-experience fosters that kind of vision—a vision which radiates from the eucharist into all realms of life. The churches which arose during the sixteenth century offer a vision of wholeness centered around the primacy of justification through faith and grace, generally leading to great emphasis upon the biblical model of "faith fruitful in love," or (in the same spirit) upon the "harvest of the Spirit" in the struggle against embodied selfishness. In all traditions, emphasis upon the discipleship of believers as followers of Christ and upon the Pauline–Johannine vision of "life in Christ Jesus" provide both impetus and direction for a vision of wholeness.

Under certain circumstances, liberation (viewed in light of the liberty for which Christ has set us free) can and should be a guiding thought-pattern, providing a leitmotiv for judging what represents saving justice and redeemed and redeeming love. As already mentioned, the emphasis upon liberty-liberation cannot exclude an integrating vision of healing love and nonviolence.

Any kind of one-sidedness should be avoided. An authentic vision of wholeness favors integration, and thus also promotes ecumenism. The legalistic moral theology of the last three centuries, written primarily for confessor-judges, was absolutely alien to the other Christian traditions. A renewed Catholic moral theology for this ecumenical age must strive to the utmost to address the central concerns of the Oriental and Protestant churches, which maintain the great Christian tradition of the centuries prior to the separation. This requires our own reintegration into the central, common stream of tradition. This will foster a rich vision of wholeness, providing a substantial contribution to Christian unity.

Within such a vision of wholeness, the biblical model of "bearing fruit in love" and the sacramental attitude toward the whole of Christian life are indispensable elements. Equally indispensable, in my view, is the reevaluation of the biblical virtues, understood as enabling the creative insertion of the faithful into the ongoing history of salvation.

Whatever the moral theologian's particular preference concerning a general approach to the moral life, one concern must remain at the center: to help Christians (by means of an attractive vision) to gain deep knowledge of the loftiness of their vocation in Christ, and its dynamic to bear fruit for the life of the world (Vatican II, *Optatam totius,* n. 16).

V. Alertness Toward the Signs of the Times

More than any other type of theology, moral theology requires excellent historical-consciousness. Moral theologians must constantly scrutinize the "signs of the times" concerning both their own cultures and the whole human race. One of the most evident signs of our time is the experience of a unique solidarity among all the inhabitants of our deeply wounded planet. The existence or absence of solidarity among all human beings, and particularly among Christians in service of all humanity, is now a matter of survival.

As a young student of moral theology during the era of Hitler, I became angry when I saw our moral theologians concentrating on relative trivialities while we were faced with the most horrifying events and the most cruel deeds, with diabolical lusts for power, and with slavishly "obedient" Christians. Today, questions which I would have regarded as significant in those days appear to be trivial when one sees so much energy expended upon them, while the big issues are almost totally overlooked.

1. Peace and Nonviolence in a Nuclear Age

The time has come when humanity must set itself free from the age-old slavery of war and related ideologies. Every war can escalate into a nuclear holocaust. Training for war—even if "only" for defensive war —heightens the already tremendous potential for violence in our cultures, which are themselves violent in a thousand forms. The lust for power, the lust for wealth through ruthless competition, and the ingenuous dream of liberation through counter-violence against institutionalized violence create innumerable threats to our humanity, and even to human existence on earth. Just-war theories don't work anymore; even on the basis of their own premises, they are useless in this age.

In this situation, Christian ethics must give high priority to the exploration of the healing dimensions of love of enemy and nonviolence as signs of God's coming kingdom. Some moral theologians will simply advocate the reduction of the use of violence to its very minimum, while others will try to form Christian elites in the spirit of the gospel and, looking to heralds of nonviolence like Gandhi, will espouse the radical option of a life of absolute nonviolence as a compelling ideal. A major concern will be to demonstrate that the genuine freedom for which Christ has set us free cannot be defended by war, while recognizing that true freedom and basic human rights belonging to our vocation for freedom must be defended. Therefore, the alternative of an ongoing civil defense through creative use of nonviolent strategy and spirituality must be explored and effectively presented in the moral theology of today and tomorrow. A moral theologian should be an expert and convincing witness concerning nonviolence at all levels of personal, social, socio-economic, and political life.

Only the radical option for nonviolent liberation and nonviolent defense will deliver us from the many ideologies which can survive only in an ambiance of armament, in which trade in weapons of all kinds is big business. The option for nonviolent civil liberation and defense would free enormous energies for the pursuit of justice, a healthy lifestyle, and healthy human relationships. It would radically transform both capitalism and socialism. An option for nonviolent liberation and civil defense could bring about reconciliation between the wealthy industrialized countries and those of the third world.

A moral theologian who spends great time and energy in order to prove that masturbation is always "objectively" a grave sin (with a presumption even of mortal sin), while almost completely overlooking the incredible scandal of trillions of dollars spent on arms, is a ripe candidate for a mental asylum. And what can one say about a moralist who resists the interruption of pregnancy when it is the only way to save the life of the mother (thus avoiding the loss of a second life), and yet allows governments to use nuclear holocaust as a threat, or even justifies the possibility of a morally licit first use of nuclear weapons? We can, however, reasonably argue that a mother should refuse abortion (even though this entails a very great risk for her own life), when we have decided once and for all that we would prefer to risk all kinds of suffering, and even our own lives, relying upon the option of nonviolent defense, which is marked by profound signs of a totally new way of thinking.

2. *A New Vision in the Light of the Ecological Crisis*

The mutual nuclear threat, with an arsenal which can destroy all human life seven times over and make the planet uninhabitable for years, is but one possible way in which an irresponsible humanity might eventually bring human history to an end. A danger no less real is a collapse of the ecological balance. Ruthless competition in socio-economic life and a culture characterized by waste, air and water pollution have brought the human race to the edge of an abyss. In our day, the moral theologian must constantly envision the results for the planet should the so-called third world imitate the highly "developed" nations in the waste of earthly goods, engaging in production like that of our industrialized great "powers." Before a century passed, the ozone layer protecting our planet would be completely destroyed. The human race would vanish as once, ages before, the ichthysaurs did.

The Second Vatican Council did not devote sufficient attention to this sacrilegious threat to our planet, and to the whole human family. Within the commissions there were some who raised the issue, but at the time adequate awareness and sufficient knowledge of the whole situation, and of its extremely critical status, had not yet developed. Although there was an awareness of the overpopulation problem, concern was focused upon the question of how to feed a doubling world-population. The problems of preserving clean air, clean water, and, last but not least, the ozone layer—as well as the increased danger of violence in proportion to the excessive growth of population—were not properly recognized. The council, however, was merely reflecting the general level of awareness in the church and the world at that time.

Up to now, I have spoken of these problems in the tone of one relating "alarming signs of the times." We must have the courage to face them. We can do it if we are generally able to recognize the encouraging signs of the times. Regarding even the grave problems previously mentioned there is an encouraging sign: throughout the whole Christian community, and even throughout the whole world, there is a new attention to the most vital questions for the future of humanity. There is preparation for the convocation of a conciliar process on "Peace, Worldwide Justice (solidarity) and the Conservation of God's Creation." If the whole Christian community—all Christian churches and all believers—can rally around the indefatigable search for better knowledge, and can pursue the greatest fidelity to the creator and redeemer in reference to these issues, then the gospel and particularly moral theology (Christian ethics) will become meaningful in a new, unexpected way. A commitment (in solidarity) to these burning issues will be the greatest mark of a truly Christian conscience, as described by the Second Vatican Council: "In fidelity to conscience, Christians are joined with the rest of humankind in the search for truth and for genuine solutions to the numerous problems which arise in the life of individuals and from social relationships" (*Gaudium et spes,* n. 16). Let all moral theologians unite their energies and voices to promote this great program of creative fidelity-solidarity. Then these three issues—peace, solidarity-justice, conservation of God's creation—will shed their saving light on many other questions of ethics: e.g. the role of women, sexual morality, the whole socio-economic realm, and political and international ethics

3

The Contribution of Theology to Catholic Moral Theology

Kenneth R. Himes, O.F.M.

INTRODUCTION

Several years ago James Gustafson delivered the Père Marquette lecture at that Jesuit University in Wisconsin. He entitled his address "The Contribution of Theology to Medical Ethics."[1] In that presentation Gustafson stated theology's contribution to medical ethics was not unmistakably clear to those who work in the latter field. I would take Gustafson one step further and say that theology's contribution even to moral theology is not always evident.

The previous statement may, on the face of it, seem odd. Yet, recall Richard McBrien's definition of theology as "the ordered effort to bring our experience of God to the level of intelligent expression."[2] Now one can read a good deal of the literature in moral theology without ever finding the experience of God brought to the level of intelligent expression; that is, God-language is often unused by moral theologians in any explicit way. Some moral theologians have complained that one of the difficulties with contemporary moral theology is that it is insufficiently theological.[3] Too much of moral theology reads like moral philosophy. Once this is acknowledged my reason for stating that the contribution of theology to moral theology requires attention is more easily understood.

The reform of Roman Catholic moral theology called for by Vatican II has been underway for twenty-five years.[4] One can read the review of literature found in the "Moral Notes" written by Richard McCormick to attain some indication of how impressive has been the scholarly response to the council's call. If the present state of moral theology is judged inadequate it is not to denigrate the work that has been accomplished. Rather, it is to note that the agenda for moral theology is unfinished. After these twenty-five years since Vatican II where do we stand? A reader of the essays in this volume will gain a sense of the answer to that large question. Here I wish to touch upon but one aspect of the topic, the *theology* that informs Catholic moral theology.

In what follows I will offer some introductory remarks on the place of theology in moral theology before examining Richard McCormick's writing to discern his contribution. Discern is the correct word here since much of McCormick's theology is only implicitly stated in his writing. This essay will conclude with some remarks for future directions in Catholic moral theology.

Faced with the dilemmas of modern living and the collapse of certitude regarding the answers to those dilemmas, many moral theologians have been practitioners of what is called "quandary ethics." A good deal of intelligent and thoughtful writing by a large cast of scholars has been devoted to discussing problems in the moral life. Less energy, however, has been given over to relating our moral experience with the creedal statements we espouse.

There are reasons in both the history of Catholic moral theology and more recent events that encouraged a focus on "quandary ethics." For many years moral theology was the discipline that was most directly linked to the training of future priest-confessors. The pastoral care of penitents was a central task of priestly ministry, and it was moral theology which bore the largest part of the responsibility in the seminary curriculum for that apostolate. It is not necessary to rehearse the act-centered, negative tone which the focus on penance brought to moral theology.[5]

The separation of moral theology from dogmatic theology in post-Tridentine seminary curricula also contributed to the decline of theological reflection among moralists. And the polemical context of post-reformation theology undercut the degree to which Catholic moral theologians utilized the Bible in their study. On most seminary faculties the moral theologians had more in common with their colleagues in canon law than with systematic theologians or scripture scholars. Within moral theology the paradigm of law rose to prominence, and the symbols, metaphors and images more common to dogmatic and biblical theology fell into neglect.[6]

In our own time two factors have discouraged explicit appeal to theological themes in moral theology. The first factor is the audience which moral theologians address. Many Catholic moralists no longer work in seminaries or other church-related institutions. This change in setting has caused a change in moral theologians' awareness when thinking of their audience. The academy or the public policy arena may be as much in mind as the ecclesial community when moral theologians speak and write. Individuals in the former categories are apt to be disinterested in the theological horizon that stands behind a moralist's ethical principles.

This lack of interest may be due to an ideology of secularism, but there is also the quite sensible position that theological differences can stand in the way of building consensus on an issue. Practical considerations limit the agenda of public policy makers to attainment of consensus on a specific course of action. The broader topic of examining the varying theoretical frameworks which stand behind the consensus is not readily taken up in our democratic polity. Why should policy discussions move beyond agreement on the conclusions only to risk disagreement over the reasoning process? In our pluralistic society if agreement is reached on the place of human rights in foreign policy it can be bothersome and fruitless to engage in further discussion on foundational beliefs about why we have human rights at all.

Whether the issue is the status of the pre-embryo, the proper care of the dying, or public health with regard to AIDS, it is safer for policy formulation and implementation to focus on the narrow agenda of concrete conclusions. As a result, moral theologians often narrow rather than widen their focus when seeking to influence, or at least converse with, the broad range of nonecclesial groups in society. This tendency has been especially strong in Catholic moral theology with its adherence to the natural law tradition. Sometimes the role of theology in moral reasoning was limited to providing the rationale for appeal to natural law, and once that was done theology's further contribution was unclear.

The second contemporary reason for the nontheological character of much moral theology was the situation ethics debate of the 1960s.[7] The ensuing reconceptualization of the nature of moral principles and rules led to a preoccupation with normative ethics. Due to Joseph Fletcher's provocations interest was high in "getting down to cases," but that meant theological reflection routinely was slighted as moralists attended to the resolution of pastoral problems.

The outcome of this focus on problem-solving has been mixed for moral theology. We have seen an outpouring of material on sexual ethics, bioethics, justice and peace issues that has been insightful and learned. Nonetheless, whenever the agenda of moral theology is restricted to formulating and applying normative principles, which in conjunction with empirical considerations guide our moral choices, then we skew the task of moral theology. Moral theology must be related to what we believe, including what we believe about God, creation and the divine plan.

THE PLACE OF THEOLOGY IN MORAL THEOLOGY

Those who practice the discipline of moral theology owe believers more than problem-solving, as useful and important as that can be. The "more" is the responsibility to discuss how the moral life relates to religious convictions. If the study of morality is to be theological and not just philosophical, then theologians must help believers understand the world in the light of faith. The theologian ought to place the realm of morality within the context of belief in how God creates, orders and sustains.

In 1971 John Rawls published his landmark work, *A Theory of Justice*.[8] Among the many interesting ideas espoused therein was Rawls' notion of "reflective equilibrium."[9] Reflective equilibrium is a state arrived at when a person's considered judgments about a specific issue are in harmony with that same person's consciously held moral principles.

It can happen that some moral principle a person espouses leads to an unacceptable conclusion or that a particular judgment is made which is unsupportable by an individual's set of moral principles. In such cases, human beings can revise their thinking so as to bring about a balance between specific choices and moral principles. We may rethink our practical judgments in light of our principled convictions. Alternatively, we may revise, abandon or develop moral principles that are adequate to the reality we experience. The aim is to reestablish consistency between our principles and our choices. Reflective equilibrium is the end result of such a process.

As Rawls notes, however, the equilibrium attained is not necessarily stable. It can be upset by new situations that provoke new reflection on the proper fit between principle and choice. Rarely is there total consistency by anyone on the subject of abstract principle and concrete decision. Persons of critical intellect often refine the relationship between the two as their life progresses.

When the process of moral decision-making is played out in such a schema the role of theology is not readily apparent. The difficulty, however, is not that theology has little to say to ethics, but that the outline of ethical theory is too narrowly drawn. What is needed, I believe, is a "wide reflective equilibrium" which examines the fuller range of moral reflection. If that is done, if a genuine ethical theory is developed which examines not only the fit of principle and choice but the foundation of moral beliefs and the grounding of moral principles, then theology's role is more obvious.

In schematic form Charles Curran has provided an understanding of moral theology which illustrates the framework of wide reflective equilibrium. Curran examines the theory that lay behind the moral principles which inform decision-making.[10] He suggests a tripartite theory of stance, anthropology and ethical model. This interest in the theory behind one's normative ethics reflects the influence of Curran's teacher, Bernard Häring.

Since the 1950s Häring has striven to demonstrate the import of theology for the task of the moralist. His early writing illustrates a sensitivity to the moral life as being more than problem-solving, and his later work exhibits even greater awareness of the richness of the discipline of moral theology.[11] Häring's view that the task of moral theology is relating creedal beliefs with moral experience finds expression in his student's understanding of moral theology. (See figure below.)

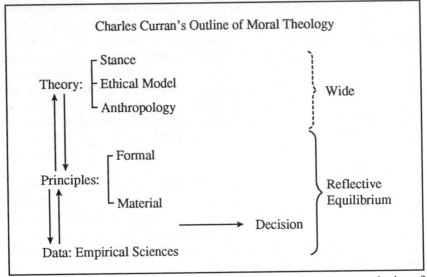

Charles Curran's Outline of Moral Theology

Theory:
- Stance
- Ethical Model
- Anthropology

} Wide

Principles:
- Formal
- Material

Data: Empirical Sciences

→ Decision

} Reflective Equilibrium

Curran's framework for moral theology illustrates the complexity of the discipline since the background theory forces the moralist to play out ethical discourse on a broader field than a narrow reflective equilibrium suggests. By the term "stance" Curran means the way we perceive reality, our worldview. How is it that we understand our existence? The answer given by Curran is unabashedly theological. Reality is interpreted through the Christian tradition. In order to provide a manageable summary of that faith Curran employs five great mysteries as cluster-concepts under which various sub-themes can be grouped. These five mysteries—creation, incarnation, sin, redemption, resurrection-destiny—are unpacked to reveal their ethical import.

Essentially, Curran's use of the category of stance is what other moralists call the element of narrative in theology. Curran's version of the Christian story, using the shorthand of five basic themes, is a rendition that will not gain acceptance in all quarters, however. For example, he reads creation in such a way that natural law theory is useful, redemption is understood as universal extending beyond the Christian church in history, and incarnation is viewed as supporting a Christian humanism.

What Curran provides is a helpful way of relating ethics to theology by examining the way foundational symbols of the Christian community shape our moral outlook. Yet it is a formal framework and grounded on a number of taken-for-granted positions of the Roman Catholic tradition. What is offered is more by way of exposition than argument. The fact that many Christians hold different interpretations than Curran about the five mysteries is not resolved by his methodological schema. That requires more comprehensive and intensive treatment of Curran's rendering of the story. The fivefold stance functions more as a heuristic tool for Curran's analysis of other authors than as a developed systematic method of constructive theology.

The second sub-element of Curran's moral theology is the ethical model he endorses. On this matter Curran sides with the position developed by H. Richard Niebuhr, what is called a relational-responsible approach to the moral life. The nature of moral existence is viewed primarily in terms of relationships with God, self, neighbor and world. The source of the ethical demand in this model is best expressed not in terms of duties or ends but in the responsibility to maintain and develop relationships. The experience of value emerges out of the matrix of social existence. It is a model with roots in the biblical notion of covenant.

Covenant is the biblical term expressing the ideal of fidelity and intimacy in the divine/human relationship. That reality is the touchstone for all other moral relationships. Moral experience and reflection throughout the scriptures testify to the necessary ongoing struggle to broaden the network of relations a person acknowledges so that tribalism, nationalism, racism, and sexism are overcome. In our time we are rediscovering the value of humanity's relationship with the nonhuman dimensions of the cosmos as well.

Implicit in the ethical model Curran chooses is an aspect of his anthropology, the social nature of personhood. This third sub-element in his moral theory, the understanding of the human person, requires of moral theologians an examination of the nature of the moral agent as well as moral acts. Reflection on the moral agent as subject directs Curran to topics such as epistemology, character, freedom, conversion, spirituality, and sin. This area constitutes what has come to be called "the ethics of being" as contrasted with an "ethics of doing" which takes up the normative questions involved in human actions. The ethics of being allows for the introduction of broader moral concerns than quandary ethics and provides the moral theologian with a larger canvas on which to sketch the interplay of theology and moral reasoning.

Throughout his writing Curran exhibits an understanding of central theological symbols that stands in the mainstream of Catholic theology. As mentioned earlier, his method is not fully elaborated, and what he offers by way of illustrating his understanding of stance in the schema requires further amplification. Still, the formal outline which he presents is helpful for understanding how theology contributes to the work of the moral theologian. In the next section the publications of Richard McCormick will be studied in order to see the theology at work in his background ethical theory.

McCormick's Moral Theory

In any author as productive and widely published as Richard McCormick it becomes possible to identify certain typical expressions or catch-phrases that frequently appear. Such language usage can be an indication not only of favorite words but favorite ideas, concepts that are central to understanding the mind of the writer. Several expressions provide this key for grasping McCormick's perspective on the theology of moral theology. For purposes of illustration I will examine four phrases which McCormick employs regularly. Each of these will be analyzed to show the theology behind Richard McCormick's moral theology.

1. The first expression is "reason informed by faith." This is not a novel turn of phrase coined by McCormick, but it is an expression which McCormick has explored in several places when he treats the topic of epistemology.[12] By investigating his understanding of it one can see both the debt McCormick owes to the Catholic theological tradition and the manner whereby he develops his own insights into the tradition. In particular we can discover something of his theological beliefs about creation.

For McCormick reason is neither replaced by faith nor functions without it. Rather it is *informed* by faith. How that informing occurs moves McCormick to shift moral theology's attention away from problem-solving and toward the development of moral persons. His comments on the informing process explore the "ethics of being," the way whereby a person's attitudes, values and perspective are shaped by faith.

In such a framework the role of narrative or story in the moral life is evident since moral reasoning takes place within a context. It is not merely the rationalist application of abstract norms to concrete problems. The moral agent is a human person who brings to the exercise of moral reasoning a fuller life than the ability to apply principles. The context of moral reasoning is the whole range of feeling, perceiving, valuing that each individual has come to experience. Stories, images, metaphors all play a part in shaping this context, for they offer the person a way of construing the world, suggestions for what is to be cherished, and aids to understanding.[13]

Thus, the role of reason cannot be easily divorced from the realm of faith, for it is within the larger faith context that reason operates. Christian faith offers a means of deepening and rooting one's moral convictions within an overarching vision or worldview. Without such a context the risk is ever present that moral reasoning will occur in an atmosphere too heavily influenced by self-interest or faddishness.[14] A Christian faith stance gives the believer a better grasp of truth by underlining fundamental elements of the true understanding of reality.

Faith brings not "originating" but "confirmatory" power to moral reasoning.[15] What is known by means of the Christian vision is truth which is, in principle, open to others who do not share in the commitment of faith. Moral truth can be grasped by others, however difficult it may be to overcome the distortions of personal and cultural bias without the wisdom that comes from faith. Faith allows a person to more readily see truth and hold onto it in the face of powerful forces that work against sound human reasoning.[16]

Faith does not provide moral truth at the level of a material content imperceptible to those outside the believing community. The Christian story does not allow the claim that at the level of specific action Christian believers know what others cannot know. On this point McCormick likes to quote Franz Böckle who distinguishes between "morally relevant insights" and concrete "moral judgments." Faith has a direct influence on the former, not the latter.[17] Faith sharpens our ability to perceive the full range and depth of moral values and it is values which are the "parents of more concrete norms and rules."[18]

The reason why McCormick holds that nonbelievers can come to the same judgments as Christians about "concrete norms" and their application to specific cases is his adherence to the natural law tradition. Through the use of "recta ratio" the person is able to determine appropriate behavior. While the discernment process is assisted by the insights of faith it is not mandated that faith alone permits one to know moral truth. Wisdom in this area is attainable by all who would conscientiously seek to know the morally right. That is so due to the nature of the moral order which is rooted in the created order of things, the order of being.

As James Gustafson notes, McCormick might be considered a moderate revisionist in his attitude toward natural law. He believes norms are grounded in being but the nature of being is more historical, communal and developmental than previously thought within the Catholic tradition.[19] By adhering to the natural law tradition McCormick belongs to the category of those who hold for the objectivity of the moral order, rooted in the nature of reality. This order can be known through the use of reason. Such knowing requires more than a simple reading of the physical order, however, since the world of *human meaning* can only be known through an epistemology of "critical realism."[20]

Briefly, this epistemology accepts the nature of the real as a basis for moral judgment but demands a process of critical questioning that takes the subject beyond the world of sense data to the world of meaning. Objectivity in the world of sense data requires functional sensory organs. Objectivity in the world of meaning asks of us to wed sense data with intelligence and reason. Thus, to obtain moral meaning it is insufficient to rely upon the immediacy of sense data alone. Meaning comes to be in the encounter of the subject with the object of the world of immediacy. The criteria for an authentic encounter are the transcendental precepts: Be attentive! Be intelligent! Be reasonable! Be responsible![21]

When McCormick argues that the moral meaning of an action cannot be known apart from the *fontes moralitatis* of object, end and circumstances, he is rejecting a crude form of realist epistemology which relies upon the object of the act alone, simple sense data, for moral meaning.[22] What is being proposed is a more critical epistemological method that requires taking into account the role of the subject in discovering the meaning of the objective order. This way of thinking about the matter echoes Lonergan's idea that "objectivity is simply the consequence of authentic subjectivity."[23] This, of course, hardly places him outside the realm of natural law theorists and the commitment to an objective moral order.

2. It is obvious that in a background theory of epistemology which gives such a large place to the role of the subject one's anthropology is central. Here we can note a second favorite phrase of McCormick's, one which is taken from the official commentary on *Gaudium et Spes* of Vatican II. The standard for judging human activity is "the human person integrally and adequately considered."[24] The phrase itself, like the statement "reason informed by faith," is a formal principle. McCormick's skill is once again seen by the persistence he shows in clarifying the expression.

The person "integrally and adequately considered" leads McCormick into the realm of anthropology. In two places where he cites the phrase McCormick expands upon it by using the ideas of Louis Jans-sens.[25] Janssens suggests that to adequately consider the person is to consider all the essential aspects. He has listed eight: the person is a subject, normally conscious and called to free and responsible action; the person is a corporeal subject; a corporeal subject united with the material world; essentially social and directed to the other for fulfillment; social persons require appropriate institutions and structures for group life; persons are religious and called to encounter God; as historical beings there is a developmental aspect to human life; finally, there is a funda-mental equality to all persons.[26]

Two points: first, it must be recalled that McCormick cites the Jans-sens article approvingly.[27] It can be fairly interpreted that it reflects McCormick's own anthropology. Second, each of these "essential aspects" of the person deserves more comment than will be given here. My remarks simply will be suggestive so as to show McCormick's aware-ness of major themes in systematic theology as he develops his anthro-pology.

The emphasis given to freedom at the outset of a descriptive anthro-pology of the person "adequately considered" is in accord with Karl Rahner's stress on the ability of the human subject to be self-determining as well as self-choosing. Behind the claim that the person is called to consciousness and freedom as well as being a participant in the historical processes of material existence is Rahner's view of the person as "spirit in world." This anthropological position highlights both the transcendence and the materiality of human existence. Thus, the unfolding of genuine personhood through the free disposition of oneself is a necessarily histori-cal and communal act since persons are embodied spirits in the world with others.

The Rahnerian view has radically altered the moralist's understand-ing of the depth of human action. The notion of core or basic freedom which may be actualized in particular acts of categorical freedom or free choice has become central to moral theology. The anthropology devel-oped by Rahner has forced a reconsideration of the relationship between human acts and the state of sin, as well as the processes of conversion in the fundamental moral theology of McCormick and others.[28] Also McCormick's writing on special topics like sexual ethics and genetics frequently relies upon the theological anthropology of Rahner.

The essential sociality of the person is evident in McCormick's treatment of two medical issues involving young children. In both his discussion of proper treatment of severely defective neonates and proxy consent for nonrisk experimentation upon children McCormick has ar-gued for norms which are rooted in the essential sociality of the human.

With the first case McCormick suggests that a guideline determining whether life-sustaining measures should be employed can be based on the "potential for human relationships associated with the infant's condition."[29]

In the second instance McCormick argues for the reasonableness (he uses the word "ought") of parents consenting to a child participating in nonrisk experimental procedures. His reason is that in doing so we are treating children as the "*social human beings*" they are.[30] If it is plausible to presume that adults ought on the basis of their relatedness to assist in the achievement of social goods for themselves or others when there is no significant cost or inconvenience in so doing, why not presume the same for children? To do so is not to treat the child as an adult but merely a social being.

What is the implicit theological anthropology behind such positions? Clearly, relationality looms large here and its grounding can be found, I believe, in McCormick's acceptance of another of Karl Rahner's ideas—the unity of love of God and love of neighbor.[31] Since love of God is the highest good in life all other goods are relative to that aim. Yet, if Rahner is correct that love of God is necessarily mediated in and through love of neighbor, then "the good our love wants to do Him and to which He enables us, can be done only for the neighbor."[32]

For McCormick, then, the Judeo-Christian position can be interpreted as holding that the "meaning, substance, and consummation of life are found in human *relationships*."[33] In the world of time and space it is by establishing loving relationships with others that we embody the love of the Other, life's highest good. A life devoid of any possibility for experiencing human love and care is a life sustained lacking life's meaning. Such a life is a burden and not a gift. Thus, the potential for human relationality becomes a key criterion for determining the proportionality of benefit/burden in decisions about foregoing treatment of neonates.

In other essays McCormick argues against Paul Ramsey that parents may consent to nonrisk experimentation on their children. He points out the divide between Ramsey and himself is precisely on the anthropological issue. Ramsey asserts that McCormick would treat children as if they were moral agents like adults. In reply McCormick claims his position rests not on that basis but due to the fact that children, too, are part of the social world of persons. "At the root of our disagreement, then, may be what I would suggest is Ramsey's narrowly individualistic notion of human nature. He treats the child as an unrelated entity, and thus refuses him or her entry not only into the adult world (rightly) but also into the human race (wrongly)."[34] To discuss the human person, even the youngest of humans, without attending to the social nature of the individual is to fail to consider the person integrally and adequately.

As *Gaudium et Spes* notes, "For by their innermost nature persons are social beings, and unless they relate themselves to others, they can neither live nor develop their potential." Later on, the council fathers suggest that meditation on the central mystery of God as Trinity will lead people to see that creation in the image of God means creation for community, not isolation.[35] This communitarian theme in Roman Catholic theological anthropology shapes McCormick's attitude when addressing specific issues.

3. Since the person is essentially social it becomes important to examine the influence of significant groups in human life. Within Catholic moral theology the role of the ecclesial community looms large. One of the key reasons for this is the existence of a hierarchical magisterium or teaching office and the further claim that such an office functions with the assistance of the Holy Spirit. It is this claim which founds the authority of various ecclesiastical pronouncements. Because that authority is so often questioned today it is important to understand the basis for the claim that the Holy Spirit guides the magisterium. With his typical skill McCormick probes the meaning of the phrase "assistance of the Holy Spirit." By doing so he reveals something of his own ecclesiology.

It has become popular today to speak of the Catholic tradition's adherence to a "principle of mediation." Richard McBrien captures the idea when he states the commitment to mediation suggests Catholic belief that the presence of God is made "effective" through "created realities" to all "those who avail themselves of these realities."[36] Sacraments, for instance, are but specific cases of a larger theological commitment to belief in God's activity in and through creaturely things. The church in its visible structures also mediates God's presence. Thus, it is not hard for Catholic theologians to accept the basic premise of a teaching office which can be empowered in its ministry by the Holy Spirit.

Since the ecclesial community is a community rooted in the truth of the gospel it is important that some perform the service of preaching, teaching and passing on Christian truth. Within the church the office of bishop has been established, in part, to perform this ministry. God's promised assistance to the church in its quest for truth is, quite understandably, linked to those ecclesiastical structures which have evolved in history. Belief in the assistance of the Holy Spirit in guiding the teaching office of the church is but one more instance of the principle of mediation at work in Catholic thought.

At the same time as he affirms this fundamental attitude of Catholic believers McCormick admits difficulties with some understandings of the term "assistance of the Holy Spirit." Two extremes must be avoided. One way of understanding the expression would lapse into fideism. The Spirit's help cannot be taken to mean that hierarchical teaching is immune from ordinary human processes of seeking knowledge. Catholic moral teaching cannot divorce faith and reason so that all questions and discussions are settled by exhortations to "take it on faith." On the far side of the other interpretations of the Spirit's assistance is the suggestion that the smartest and shrewdest are the most Spirit-led. This would be, according to McCormick, a form of neorationalism which overlooks the communal nature of moral wisdom.[37] What is needed is a middle way which does not separate human reasoning processes from the guidance of the Spirit yet does not simply identify the two realities.

In discussing the "assistance of the Holy Spirit," McCormick suggests that any explanation of the term must pay attention to four factors: the role of the hierarchy, the manner of the Spirit's help, the reality that error does occur in church teaching, and the role of the whole church in coming to truth.[38] He begins his reflection by suggesting that error comes about in one of two ways—inadequate evidence gathering or poor evidence assessment. At a minimum, therefore, efforts to attain adequate evidence gathering and assessment is necessary for human beings to avoid error.

These two dimensions are then related to the role of the Spirit. "Evidence gathering is inadequate when consulation is not broad enough to allow the full wisdom stimulated by the Spirit's activity in the whole Church to emerge. Evidence-assessing breaks down when consideration of the evidence is insufficient to allow the Spirit to aid in the emergence of its meaning."[39] These failures are tied to the broader ecclesial community by the further proposal that the inadequacies of evidence gathering and assessment are "traceable to a failure in the fullness of the collegial process at all levels."[40]

Bishops are well situated to overcome these handicaps since as pastoral leaders they can be in touch with the joys, hopes, fears, ideas of the local church. As collegial pastors they are able to "pool this wisdom and weigh it through a process of dialogue and debate."[41] Because the bishops are in a position to draw upon the moral wisdom of the entire church they are better able to engage in a teaching process that is open to the assistance of the Spirit. This is not to say that collegial processes control the Spirit. All that is being proposed is that we can identify certain human processes of coming to knowledge which allow greater room for the Spirit's activity.

Bishops by virtue of their office and not their scholarly credentials or personal qualities are afforded the best opportunity to gather the church's wisdom. If they merely perform their job well as pastors of the local church and collegial pastors of the universal church the hierarchy has a special advantage through their openness to the Holy Spirit present and active throughout the church. In short, the faithful execution of the responsibilities of episcopal office places the hierarchy in an advantageous position to make judgments assisted by the Holy Spirit.

The special role of the bishop of Rome in Catholic tradition is not undercut by this approach. As head of the college of bishops he is ideally suited to speak for the entire church since he has available to himself the fruits of the reflection process of the whole church. Papal primacy ought not be understood as the ability to decide matters unilaterally. That is a one-sided, overly juridical understanding of the papal prerogative. Juridical power is not the matter at stake. The issue is best understood not as what power does the pope as primate have but what conditions permit the pope to exercise his power wisely. It is an ecclesiological, not juridical, concern.[42] McCormick maintains that faithful implementation of the human processes of sound evidence gathering and evidence assessment are the conditions for wise papal teaching precisely because they are the most apt means of opening oneself to the assistance of the Spirit.

Traditionally, the Catholic believer has granted a presumption of truth to the teaching of the magisterium even on moral matters which are not declared to be infallible. The promise of Jesus concerning the Spirit's help to his church is the foundation for such a presumption. Thus, any weakening of the confidence that the Spirit's assistance is present weakens the presumption in favor of magisterial teaching. McCormick believes this is precisely what has happened on several occasions. Because the human processes which we can avail ourselves of and which mediate the Spirit's presence have been neglected, the assurance that the Spirit has guided the teaching has been undermined.[43]

This last point explains how error is still possible within a church that claims to be assisted by the Spirit. The ordinary magisterium of the church teaches with the authority due its privileged role as voice of the Spirit-led community of faith. Yet it may be that we come to recognize the necessity of further refinement of a teaching or even abandonment and reversal of some positions. That this happens is not a cause for doubt about God's presence in the church but only a reminder that even our best efforts at communal wisdom can fall short of perfection in evidence gathering and evidence assessment. Evidence not available at the time, polarized camps within the community, obsequious silence in the face of doubts, bias against certain views—these are but a few examples of the ways that the gathering and assessing processes may break down. Error comes not because of the Spirit's absence from the church in guiding our deliberations but due to the church's fallible structures which cannot always accommodate the rich variety of the mediations of the Spirit's presence.[44]

McCormick's writing has focused on the moral magisterium, yet as he himself has written, "our concept of the magisterium will be closely tied to our concept of the Church."[45] The emphasis in his writing on collegial process and dialogue among the various elements of the church suggests McCormick's view of the church is one that owes a great deal to the contemporary ecclesiology of Yves Congar, Karl Rahner, Avery Dulles, Joseph Komonchak and others who have developed a more sacramental and charismatic understanding of the church.

In McCormick's framework the diversity of gifts within the church must be respected; thus, the importance of baptism, not orders, for ecclesial responsibility is underlined. Each Christian believer is called to exercise the gifts of the Spirit given for the sake of the entire body of Christ. To ignore or marginalize any segment of the church is not simply to hurt those so ignored but to weaken the very life of the church.

McCormick writes of three interdependent charisms—the doctrinal/pastoral, the scientific and the prophetic. The first term denotes those who hold hierarchical office in the church, charged with protecting, preserving and transmitting the tradition. Those who have scholarly competence are designated by the scientific charism while the prophetic charism refers to the religious experience of all the faithful. This latter category would encompass the traditional theme of the *sensus fidelium* and the idea of the connaturality of knowledge that the graced believer enjoys.[46]

How the various charisms interrelate is determined largely by cultural variables.[47] At one time the nature of the interaction was largely modeled upon a hierarchical ordering of roles. In more recent years, and the experience of Vatican II was formative here, a communitarian model of church has given larger place to the mutuality of the charisms. Thus, the real change in ecclesiology is a paradigm shift which continues to accommodate the various charisms of the church but now seeks to rethink how they are related. McCormick's comments on the teaching office of the church presumes such a rethinking is necessary since his evidence-gathering and evidence-assessing processes require a more genuinely collegial church order.[48]

Behind the commitment to this more communitarian understanding of the church lies McCormick's commitment to the principle of mediation. There is an unwavering support for the institution of the church and its teaching office. At the same time there is a recognition that the organizational makeup of the church is historically adaptable. The acknowledgment of the cultural variables which shape the interplay of the various charisms in the church illustrates McCormick's sensitivity to the time-conditioned nature of church structures. That such historical structures can be true mediations of God's presence is presumed by McCormick. That such structures can be reworked in light of changed cultural conditions is also accepted by McCormick. Both the confidence in the church's ability to teach and the flexibility in the way this is to be done are reflective of the principle of mediation. God's truth is found in historically conditioned realities.

4. A fourth phrase which McCormick utilizes frequently has to do with what he calls the "formulation and substance" of our moral convictions.[49] It is an expression which he borrows from the opening address of John XXIII at Vatican II and subsequently is found in *Gaudium et Spes.*[50] McCormick uses the distinction between substance and formulation to suggest that dissent is not as common as believed in moral theology if one is discussing the substance of the Catholic tradition.

On matters of formulation there will be more frequent dispute precisely because of the nature of language. "We know that at a given time our formulations—being the product of limited persons, with limited insight, and with imperfect philosophical and linguistic tools—are only more or less adequate to the substance of our convictions."[51] It is the role of theology to press for greater insight and clarity in the formulation of teaching so that the substance of the tradition can be more readily grasped and maintained.

The distinction between substance and formulation should not be so emphasized that the linkage between the two is ignored. McCormick suggests that the two are so linked that at times "it is difficult to know just what the substance is amidst variation of formulation."[52] In fact, to alter the formulation may cause a change in our conclusions.

On a variety of occasions McCormick has demonstrated this by discussing topics such as masturbation, premarital intercourse and abortion. Moral norms governing these behaviors have been developed over the years that revolve around certain foundational insights concerning the meaning of sexual expression, the importance of truthfulness and intimacy, the value and protection of life. How various thinkers have worded the concrete norms meant to embody these insights differ. What the church teaches substantively cannot be simply identified with any specific formulation even if some proposals are more apt than others in a given setting.

Debates about transubstantiation in eucharistic theology is a case in point. While such a formulation about the meaning of real presence has been accepted for centuries it cannot be said that this formulation alone is the way to express Catholic belief, nor that it is unequivocally the best way. It is one adequate way.

The language of personhood in the Trinity is another example. Here, perhaps even more than in the first example of eucharist, we see how a given formulation can lose its disclosive power. Few Catholics today understand what the Greek-speaking theologians of Cappodocia meant by *hypostases* or even what Tertullian meant by *personae* when the formula of three-in-one was used to describe the Trinity. The hallowed formulation simply does not communicate the substance of the tradition accurately to most believers. Thus, rethinking the formulation of the doctrine of the Trinity for today may well lead to greater understanding of the substance of what the tradition is.

At the same time, as discussions of both the Trinity and eucharist demonstrate, there always will be concern over whether it is the substance of the tradition that is being changed or the formulation. McCormick's comment about the close linkage of substance and formulation is well taken. To a degree this is inevitable since the substance, by being given new expression, will be understood differently. The nature of language forces such different nuances, as every translator realizes. Yet this cannot prevent taking on the work of reformulation. Theology's ongoing quest is to further the knowledge of truth and in so doing promote the teaching function of the church. Archaic language that is misunderstood or meaningless is as detrimental as contemporary language that is sloppy and misleading.

Besides the distinction between substance and formulation is the related but distinct issue of doctrinal development. New formulations are one form of development, and controversial as they may seem there is the still more radical notion that the substance itself ought to change. What is necessary, in other words, is a recognition not just that linguistic development may occasion change but that development in the tradition's grasp of the truth can occur also.

Some truths essential for salvation must be substantively true if the church is to fulfill its mission. But a great many other teachings of the church, particularly moral teachings, do not seem to be of that type.[53] This idea is hinted at in the notion of a hierarchy of truths. Frequently moral norms, especially material norms applied to the contingencies of history, are several steps removed from the deposit of faith. It should not surprise or shock that such norms are open to revision, even of a substantial nature, as the community's understanding of truth grows.

McCormick tentatively has raised the prospect that this substantial revisioning is what may be going on in the area of procreation and new medical technologies. After surveying the writing of several colleagues McCormick wonders whether we are not near a stage of modifying or revising our views on the inseparability of the unitive and procreative dimensions of sexuality. The modern birth control debate first put the issue before the church.

More recently, it is the bioethical discussion surrounding two practices—artificial insemination of a woman by her husband (AIH) and the use of *in vitro* fertilization techniques—that has encouraged the revision. McCormick is not claiming that such a development of doctrine has taken place. He merely asks if we are seeing something of the same structure of development in this matter that we witnessed with the teaching on religious liberty.[54]

What stands behind this view about the revision of norms and development of doctrine is, I suggest, an eschatological perspective. McCormick has not addressed the eschatological issue in depth. Yet the notion of truth implicit in his position is one that can fairly be called eschatological. Summarizing in an approving way remarks made by another, McCormick writes that the church's "moral and ethical judgments are always *in via* and share the messy, unfinished, and perfectible character of the church itself."[55] For McCormick, the church's experience is eschatological and thus its grasp of the message of the gospel is never complete. McCormick further comments that the "ecclesial metaphors" we use "affect both the substance and method of moral inquiry in very profound and practical ways."[56]

The notion of metaphor is central to the way we can understand how truth must be seen in an eschatological framework. When we speak or write metaphorically we use one reality to express the meaning of another reality. An excellent example of how metaphors both limit and expand our understanding is to consider the varied metaphors used to describe our understanding of who Jesus is. Redeemer, prophet, pantocrator, liberator, messiah, teacher, man for others, king of kings, prince of peace, son of man, light to the Gentiles—the list is lengthy indeed.[57] No one of these is sufficient nor is any simply wrong. What is clear, however, is that any age is only as perceptive as the metaphors it has available to itself to explain reality. Richer cultures have a breadth of metaphorical usage which allows language to continually stretch to express understanding.

Expansion or revision of a truth claim need not be equated with past error. What is necessary is a certain understanding of how language and truth are related, or, in McCormick's preferred usage, how formulation and substance are related.[58] Fundamental insights possess a depth dimension which is not simply mined once and for all. Rather we can return to these deposits of truth for continual growth in understanding.

The fuller our repertoire of images and metaphors the greater the potential for not only expressing the truth more adequately but for understanding its substantive meaning.

A tension arises between this outlook and a more static perspective. The source of the tension is the differing understanding of language and how it functions within eschatological and a-historical mentalities. Xavier Seubert remarks that one way of viewing language is that "words should be univocal in meaning and correspond only to very precise realities." If that is so, then "metaphors will be seen as decorative flourishes or as educational aids for understanding the equations that are hidden behind the metaphor." However, if one's understanding is that "the essence of something is never completely had, but is always being sought, and if you further understand that the words defining something do not exhaust its meaning, but are struggles to provide markings for the fullness of reality," then metaphors become a matter of considerably greater import.[59]

Moral truth in this latter perspective is never simply captured by existing formulations, for there is an asymptotic understanding of moral truth. Our reflection as moral theologians results in "relatively adequate" formulations. Anne Patrick, commenting on the influence of linguistic studies upon moral theology, states that "aspirations to perfect certainty and absolute stability must be tempered."[60] This tempering is, at least in part, an outcome of a renewed sense of the eschatological dimension of the created order. Such a retrieval of eschatology has undermined the propositional understanding of revelation. The locus of revealed truth is no longer found in some unchanging nature. Within an eschatological mind-set nature itself is historically conditioned.

McCormick and many other Catholic theologians differ from the previous generation of moralists since they are more attuned to how God's revelation is perceived in the dynamic unfolding of history. While not dealing with eschatology at length McCormick's approach to the revisioning of moral norms can be said to imply a certain theological framework that is marked by an eschatological awareness.

THE FUTURE OF THE THEOLOGICAL DIMENSION
IN MORAL THEOLOGY

Before closing I wish to make three brief comments about McCormick's writing that indicate items for the future agenda of moral theology.

1. Revival of interest in an "ethics of being" has allowed moral

theologians to be more explicitly theological in their work. This is obviously true in McCormick's writing. Writing on topics related to character formation he is eloquent in his employment of religious language. When the matter at hand is moral decision-making, however, McCormick shifts his style. As was mentioned at the outset of this essay there are reasons, even theological ones, to justify this approach.

Still it is possible to ask whether moral theologians need to consider how an "ethics of doing" is related to theology. McCormick is aware of the difficulty.[61] It appears at times that when moralists wish to speak like theologians they focus on an "ethic of being." When the concern is an "ethic of doing," however, the language becomes purged and the connection between theological belief and ethical justification is hard to discern.

James Childress has touched on the concern in an essay on scripture and ethics.[62] He asks if it is true that biblical morality cannot provide us with a presumption in favor of certain norms, a presumption that is founded precisely on the biblical witness. This is not to argue that the biblical text is the sole reason for holding a moral norm but it may be the reason that the norm is given a weight it might not have otherwise. An example I might suggest here is the norm in the Catholic tradition regarding the indissolubility of marriage.

Irrespective of the rightness of the above example, the larger issue deserves fuller discussion among Catholic moral theologians. How can we bring theology into more direct conversation with normative discourse?

2. A second area of development in Catholic moral theology is the need for more attention to the psychology of grace. This is closely related to Christology and the doctrine of redemption. Charles Curran has written that a more functional Christology, one concerned with the saving work of Christ has greater implications for moral theology than a one-sidedly ontological or metaphysical Christology.[63] In a Christology from above, salvation is abstract, private and extrinsic, whereas in a Christology from below, salvation is concrete, communal and intrinsic.[64]

When McCormick addresses the experience of redemption he explores the Pauline image of being "in Christ" or "in the Lord."[65] What does this mean at the level of concrete existence? McCormick's answer is quite sweeping: the experience of being in Christ "totally transforms the human person" creating "new operative vitalities."[66] From here he proceeds to lay out an understanding of how charity, rooted in the experience of acceptance of Christ as Lord, forms the entirety of the moral life. McCormick borrows liberally from Gerard Gilleman in his account.[67] There is much in his presentation that is inspiring but it is also somewhat unusual in its abstractness. The statements read more like assertions that are not easily reconcilable with human experience. It appears that McCormick claims too much in his account of the experience of redemption.

Perhaps my reservation is that when McCormick speaks to the reality of redemption in the moral life his account is insufficiently eschatological. What is lacking is the element of the "not yet" and the consequent role for processes of conversion and growth. McCormick might reply to these comments by saying his writing is at the level of a formal description of the Christian moral life. He could say: "Of course, redemption is experienced more ambiguously in daily life in this world."

If that is the case, then, my point is simply to suggest we need more attention to the experience of grace at the level of concrete existence. I would hold that McCormick's "interpretive understanding of the Christian moral life" requires greater elaboration of a psychology of grace. Moral theology in general, not only McCormick's writing, would benefit from further examination of how the grace given in Jesus is experienced by people in their everyday lives.

It may be that moral theology must work more closely with spiritual theology to achieve this. Psychology is another important resource, whether it be in studies of religious experience or in the area of religion and the life cycle. The aim is not simply to dialogue with the social sciences but to make sure our moral theology is concrete and not abstract in its depictions of grace and the experience of redemption.

McCormick, I think, sees the problem when he suggests moral theology must be "centered on Christ." By this he does "not mean repetitious and cosmetic overlays of biblical paranesis." Instead, our theology "should be shaped by the fact—and implications thereof—that Jesus is God's incarnate self-gift."[68] The "fact" is, for Catholic moral theologians, undisputed. It is attending to the "implications" in an experiential way that requires more effort.

3. A final proposed item for the agenda of Catholic moral theology is the relationship of liturgy to ethics. The sacramental life of the Catholic community is one of its most distinctive and central dimensions. Yet, Catholic moral theology does not seem to accord liturgical experience a role appropriate to its standing in the life of the church.

Participation in the sacramental life of the church can introduce people to a symbol system that challenges many of the wider culture's values while providing an expression of communal values which need to be retained. Through its public prayer the church offers to people rituals that permit formation and ongoing reappropriation of one's identity through the ability of the rites to incorporate participants into a community of tradition. This transformative and educational role of liturgy is a neglected resource for moral theology.

McCormick has referred to spirituality as "a personal and corporate life-climate designed to foster and deepen belief in and insight into the basic structure of our lives as revealed in God's self-disclosure in Jesus."[69] If, as he suggests, one's spiritual life is a means not only of deepening belief but also gaining insight, then moral theology cannot ignore the import of liturgical spirituality for wisdom about the meaning of discipleship. Closer alliance with such an explicitly theological source of wisdom can assist our understanding of theology's contribution to moral reflection.

Although it is true that within the Catholic Church the liturgical assembly remains a crucial point of contact between people and the Christian tradition, a caveat must be mentioned. In appealing to liturgical experience we must be careful not to presume what the experience is. We must first identify the genuine locus of liturgical experience before we develop a moral theology rooted in liturgy. Giving too much weight to official texts—sacramentaries and codes of rubrics—as the repository of liturgical life can obscure an examination of what public prayer is actually like in a community. Just as in other areas when theology seeks to reflect upon experience, so too with liturgy we must be attentive to whose experience, and whose account of the experience, is being utilized. Only then will we discover just what is working and what is needed for the "personal and corporate life-climate" of people to be truly Christian.

In the remarks made above my intent was to show how Richard McCormick's normative moral theology rests upon a number of theological developments. While in much of his writing he only alludes to explicit theological language, McCormick is quite well versed in contemporary systematic theology. An essay like this does not permit elaboration upon all the ways in which McCormick's moral theory is integrated with his theology. It would be possible, for instance, to show that the thoroughgoing Catholic perspective he holds explains many of his differences with respected colleagues like James Gustafson, Paul Ramsey, and Stanley Hauerwas. All of these Protestant ethicians differ with McCormick at the level of background theory far more than normative morality. And the difference is that McCormick is very Catholic in his theology while these other men draw upon one or another strand of the Protestant tradition.

This essay, however, has been limited in its scope. It has attempted to illustrate how theology can contribute to moral theology. First, I suggested that for various reasons moralists have neglected the theory upon which their normative morality rests. In renewing our interest in that theory the interaction of theology and moral theology becomes easier to describe. Second, I have sketched *some* of the ways that one of our finest moralists, Richard McCormick, has reflected current theological thought. In a number of cases I have tried to make explicit what is implicit in his writing. In doing so, I hope that I have not done violence to any of the ideas of McCormick. By way of concluding the essay, several suggestions were made for future study on the contribution of theology to moral theology.

Notes

1. *The Contribution of Theology to Medical Ethics* (Milwaukee: Marquette University Press, 1975).
2. *Catholicism,* 2 vols. (Minneapolis: Winston Press, 1980) xlviii.
3. James Gustafson, *Ethics from a Theocentric Perspective,* 2 vols. (Chicago: University of Chicago Press, 1981, 1984). Stanley Hauerwas, *Against the Nations* (Minneapolis: Winston Press, 1985) chapter 2.
4. For the necessity of the renewal of the discipline the commonly cited text is found in the "Decree on Priestly Formation," n. 16. Of course the whole spirit and event of the council itself was more important than this or any other particular conciliar text.
5. Chapter 1 of John Mahoney, *The Making of Moral Theology* (Oxford: Clarendon Press, 1987), contains a fine description of the influence of confessional practice upon moral theology.
6. On the influence of the legal paradigm, ibid. chapter 6.
7. Joseph Fletcher, *Situation Ethics* (Philadelphia: Westminster Press, 1966).
8. *A Theory of Justice* (Cambridge: Belknap Press, 1971).
9. The expression "reflective equilibrium" is introduced early in *A Theory of Justice* and is used at several points in the book. It is first found on page 20 and further explained on pages 48–51.
10. Charles E. Curran, *Moral Theology: A Continuing Journey* (Notre Dame: University of Notre Dame Press, 1982) chapter 3. Another essay of Curran's that treats one level of the theory, his understanding of stance, is found in *New Perspectives in Moral Theology* (Notre Dame: University of Notre Dame Press, 1974) chapter 2.
11. The two major writings of Häring are both three-volume works. One helped alter the form of pre-conciliar moral theology and the other work demonstrated much of the best of post-conciliar moral theology. *The Law of Christ,* 3 vols. (Westminster, MD: Newman Press, 1961); *Free and Faithful in Christ* 3 vols. (New York: Crossroad/Seabury Press, 1978, 1979, 1981).
12. See Richard McCormick, "Does Religious Faith Add to Ethical Percep-

tion?" (hereafter *RFEP*) *Personal Values and Public Policy,* ed. John Haughey (New York: Paulist Press, 1979) 155–173 at 168–170 for a brief statement. For a more developed presentation, *Health and Medicine in the Catholic Tradition* (hereafter *HMCT*) (New York: Crossroad, 1984) 46–62. Also "Bioethics in the Public Forum" (hereafter *BPF*) *Milbank Memorial Fund Quarterly* 61 (1983): 113–126.

13. "The Christian story tells us the ultimate meaning of ourselves and the world. In doing so, it tells the kind of people we ought to be, the goods we ought to pursue, the dangers we ought to avoid, the kind of world we ought to seek." *HMCT,* 50.

14. Ibid.

15. Ibid. 59.

16. *RFEP,* 168–169. Also see *Notes on Moral Theology 1965–1980* (hereafter *NMT* 1) (Washington, D.C.: University Press of America, 1981) 80–82.

17. *HMCT,* 48; *BPF,* 120.

18. *RFEP,* 169.

19. James Gustafson, *Protestant and Roman Catholic Ethics* (Chicago: University of Chicago Press, 1978) 84.

20. The rejection of a moral order known simply through the physical order of creation is what McCormick opposes when he rejects "physicalism." For the many times McCormick remarks on this problem see the indexes to the collections of "Moral Notes," *NMT* 1 and *Notes on Moral Theology 1981–84* (hereafter *NMT* 2) (Lanham, MD: University Press of America, 1984).

21. The classic texts for describing an epistemology of critical realism are Bernard Lonergan's two major works. See *Insight* (New York: Philosophical Library, 1957) and *Method in Theology* (New York: Herder and Herder, 1972).

22. See his defense of the position of Josef Fuchs whose viewpoint was criticized by Gustave Ermecke. *NMT* 1, 529–533.

23. *Method in Theology,* 265.

24. "Schema constitutionis pastoralis de Ecclesia in mundo huius temporis: Expensio modorum partis secundae" (Rome: Vatican Press, 1965) 37–38.

25. *HMCT,* 16–18; "Past, Present and Future of Christian Ethics," *Called To Love: Toward a Contemporary Christian Ethic,* ed. Francis Eigo (Villanova: University of Villanova Press, 1985): 1–19 at 4.

26. Janssens' article is entitled "Artificial Insemination: Ethical Considerations," *Louvain Studies* 8 (1980): 3–29.

27. "Janssens' insistence on the 'person adequately considered' as a normative criterion is absolutely correct, and his elaboration of what that means is very helpful." *NMT* 2, 51.

28. Richard McCormick, *The Critical Calling: Reflections on Moral Dilemmas Since Vatican II* (Washington, D.C.: Georgetown University Press, 1989) chapter 10.

29. *How Brave a New World?* (hereafter *HBNW*) (Washington, D.C.: Georgetown University Press, 1981) 349.

30. Ibid. 90.

31. This theme is taken up in several writings of Rahner. One important essay

is "Reflections on the Unity of the Love of Neighbor and the Love of God," *Theological Investigations* vol. 6 (New York: Crossroads Publishing, 1969) 231–252.

32. *HBNW,* 346.

33. Ibid. (emphasis in original).

34. *HBNW,* 91.

35. "Pastoral Constitution on the Church in the Modern World," 12, 32.

36. *Catholicism,* 1180.

37. *NMT* 1, 261–262.

38. Ibid.

39. Ibid. 262–263.

40. Ibid. 263.

41. Ibid.

42. Ibid. 265.

43. *HMCT,* 69. Also various treatments of the issue can be found by consulting the pages listed under the index headings for dissent in *NMT* 1 and *NMT* 2.

44. *NMT* 1, 264.

45. Ibid. 204.

46. Richard McCormick, "The Teaching Role of the Magisterium and of Theologians," *Proceedings of the Catholic Theological Society of America* 24 (1969): 239–254.

47. Richard McCormick, "A Moral Magisterium in Ecumenical Perspective," *Studies in Christian Ethics* 1 (1988): 20–29 at 23–24; "Teaching Role of the Magisterium," 240–244; *HMCT,* 62–68.

48. "A Moral Magisterium"; "Bishops as Teachers and Jesuits as Listeners," *Studies in the Spirituality of Jesuits* 18 (1986): 1–22; "The Search for Truth in a Catholic Context" *America* 155 (1986): 276–281.

49. *HBNW,* 182; *NMT* 1, 525, 744; "Past, Present and Future," 6–7, 9–10.

50. "The deposit of faith or revealed truths are one thing; the manner in which they are formulated without violence to their meaning and significance is another." "Pastoral Constitution on the Church in the Modern World," 62.

51. "Past, Present and Future," 6.

52. Ibid. 6.

53. Josef Fuchs, *Christian Ethics in a Secular Arena* (Washington, D.C.: Georgetown University Press, 1984) chapter 4.

54. *NMT* 2, 173–182.

55. "Moral Theology 1940–1989: An Overview," *Theological Studies* 50 (1989): 3–24 at 8.

56. Ibid.

57. Jaroslav Pelikan, *Jesus Through the Centuries* (New Haven: Yale University Press, 1985) is a fine demonstration of the metaphors used to probe the meaning of Jesus.

58. My own appreciation for the importance of language has been heightened by my colleague Xavier J. Seubert, O.F.M. An as yet unpublished paper of his, "Metaphors: The Shapes of Life and Death," has been the basis for much of what I have said in this section.

59. Ibid. 3.

60. Anne E. Patrick, "The Linguistic Turn and Moral Theology," *Proceedings of the Catholic Theological Society of America* 42 (1987): 38–56 at 42.

61. *NMT* 2, 22–23.

62. James Childress, "Scripture and Christian Ethics," *Readings in Moral Theology,* vol. 4, ed. Charles E. Curran and Richard McCormick (New York: Paulist Press, 1984) 276–288.

63. Charles E. Curran, "The Person as Moral Agent and Subject in the Light of Contemporary Christology," *Called to Love* 21–46 at 24.

64. Ibid. 25.

65. *HMCT,* 30–39; "Theology and Bioethics: Christian Foundations," *Theology and Bioethics,* ed. Earl Shelp (Dordrecht, Netherlands: D. Reidel Publishing Company, 1985) 95–113 at 99–108; "Gustafson's God: Who? What? Where? (Etc.)," *Journal of Religious Ethics* 13 (1985): 53–70 at 61–64.

66. "Theology and Bioethics," 102.

67. *The Primacy of Charity in Moral Theology* (Westminster, MD: Newman Press, 1959).

68. "Moral Theology: An Overview," 24.

69. *HMCT,* 42.

4

The Uniqueness and the Distinctiveness of Christian Morality and Ethics

Norbert J. Rigali, S.J.

In a 1968 lecture in Zurich, "Gibt es eine spezifisch christliche Moral?"[1] Josef Fuchs introduced into Catholic moral theology an issue which was taken up in the United States two years later in Charles Curran's lecture, "Is There a Distinctively Christian Social Ethic?"[2] Now, after two decades of debate over the question of whether there is a specifically Christian morality, it has been boldly proposed that the dispute is merely a verbal one. Suggesting this possibility, Bruno Schüller suspects that other participants in the debate will probably have serious reasons to disagree with him.[3] Thus, in distancing itself from Schüller's suggestion this essay seeks to realize his suspicion.

The history of the debate shows that what lies at its heart often seems to be extraordinarily difficult to bring into or maintain in focus. But while this evasive quality can be interpreted as a sign that the debate is ultimately only a superficial one of words, it can be construed also, in contrary fashion, as indicating that the dispute affects depths of understanding of which even participants themselves may not always be completely aware. Far from being a mere *lis de verbis,* the long debate can be understood, in Karl Jaspers' term, as part of the *liebender Kampf* in which contemporary Catholic moral theology is making its passage from long established classicist thought-modes toward the pluralism of historical consciousness.[4]

The first matter requiring attention is the meaning of the terms in the essay title. As understood here, morality is a normative ordering, in terms of perceived meanings, values, purposes and goals of human existence, of the lives of human persons with regard to the ways in which they can choose to relate themselves to reality: themselves, other individuals, their community or communities, their world and the divine. Morality, therefore, involves a conception of the good human life and is constituted by a perceived system of human responsibilities, which is based in turn on a perceived network of human values within some world-view. It differs from morals in that the latter are factual relations, whether considered ordered or disordered, while the former is a normative order of human relations, whether actually maintained or transgressed. And ethics is the scientific study of such normative order.

Concerning Christian ethics two remarks are in order. First, if and insofar as there is a specifically Christian morality, it is self-evident that there will be specifically Christian ethics. Second, even theologians who deny that there is specifically Christian morality acknowledge that moral theology employs specifically Christian sources. Thus, no one denies that there is specifically Christian ethics;[5] what is at issue in the debate is whether there is specifically Christian morality.

UNIQUENESS AND DISTINCTIVENESS

The distinction between "unique" and "distinctive" is the same as that put forth between "specific" and "distinctive" by James Walter: whereas "the term 'specific' connotes exclusivity, the term 'distinctive' only connotes a characteristic quality or set of relations which are typically associated with any given reality."[6] Since there are obviously distinctive features of Christian morality, such as neighbor-love, forgiveness of enemies and care for the needy, the key term in the debate is "specific" or "unique": the controverted question is concerned with the specificity of Christian morality.

Before Walter made his distinction between them, the terms "specific" and "distinctive" had been used in the debate interchangeably, meaning "unique." Several years into the debate, accordingly, Curran was still understanding the two terms synonymously;[7] but in 1980 he publicly adopted Walter's distinction in a lecture.[8] And in the same year he and Richard McCormick reprinted Walter's 1975 article, with contributions of other theologians to the debate, in a volume oddly entitled *The Distinctiveness of Christian Ethics.*[9]

Another of the reprinted essays in the same volume is a translation of Fuchs' 1968 Zurich lecture, "Is There a Specifically Christian Morality?"[10] When this English version was reprinted three years later, however, in Fuchs' 1983 collection, *Personal Responsibility,* its title was changed to "Is There a Distinctively Christian Morality?" and some similar substitutions were made in its text.[11] Although from its opening lines the essay clearly raises the question of a uniquely Christian morality, its altered English version has it now attempting to ask this question by using "distinctively" instead of "specifically."[12]

Walter's distinction is between a genus ("distinctive") and a species ("specific"), not between two genera ("distinctive" and "nondistinctive") or two species ("specific" and "distinctive but nonspecific"): every specific difference is distinctive, but not every distinctive difference is specific. By employing the term "distinctive," therefore, *Readings* and *Personal Responsibility* have in effect substituted a generic for a specific term. And transposed in this way from the specific into the generic mode, the question about Christian morality now eclipses the very issue of the debate; for no one disputes that there are distinctive features of Christian morality.

SPECIFICITY AND SOURCES OF SPECIFICITY

One can ask about something whether it contains an element not found elsewhere. The unique-part paradigm underlying this question, however, is but one model of how specificity can be constituted. Especially with regard to human realities there are many other, relational models of the source of specificity. The specificity of a reality can be constituted also by a peculiar congeries of distinctive aspects; by a unique aggregation of nondistinctive aspects or of both distinctive and nondistinctive aspects; by a singular arrangement or ranking of some or all of its distinctive aspects, some or all of its nondistinctive aspects, or some or all of its distinctive and nondistinctive aspects; or by the peculiar relation of a single distinctive or nondistinctive aspect to the whole.

The question about the specificity of Christian morality, therefore, is not identical with a question, based on a unique-part model, about the existence of a unique moral element in Christian morality. Nevertheless, the existence of such an element would indicate a specifically Christian morality, since a unique part is one way in which the specificity of a reality is constituted.

The source of the specificity of an entity, moreover, is not the specificity itself. On the unique-part model, for example, the unique part is not the specificity of the entity but a source through which its specificity is constituted. The specificity of a reality is the specificity of the reality as a whole, not the specificity of a part. Thus, even on the unique-part model, the specificity of a reality is more complex than a unique part.

The specificity of a reality, furthermore, is not merely an inherent character or quality. It is also, and principally, a relational aspect of a reality, involving the outward relations of an entity to the rest of reality and its relational place within the totality of the world.

It is much easier, therefore, to identify the source of the specificity of a reality than to capture in reflective thought and precise formulation the specificity itself. Like all individuality, the specificity of a reality is given in experience but is never an object of clear and distinct ideas. Being the very relation of a reality to all other realities and to the universe itself, it cannot be reduced to an easily defined and expressed "something." The nature itself of specificity, therefore, is a reason why the subject of the present debate possesses an elusive quality.

AUTONOMOUS ETHICS AND *GLAUBENSETHIK*

An unusual feature, however, of the debate over specificity in Christian morality is the questionable name sometimes given it: autonomous ethics versus *Glaubensethik*. Reminiscent of Alfons Auer's title, *Autonome Moral und christlicher Glaube,* the name distorts the very question of the debate and is another source of its elusive quality. The false impression is created that the choice at issue is between an ethics of reason and an ethics of faith, between an autonomous ethics and a heteronomous ethics: either autonomous reason or heteronomous faith. Thus Schüller, showing the identity of the "autonomous ethics" introduced in 1971 by Auer and the natural law ethics that he himself has championed since 1966, says of the latter:

> It maintains that what it really means to be morally good and to act in a morally right way can be disclosed to human beings only by their understanding it on their own, and not by, say, leaning (in faith) upon an assertion from someone else. Now, in exactly the same sense, the term "autonomous ethics" has been used for a long time.[13]

While a simplistic distinction between autonomous-reason ethics and heteronomous-faith ethics might be serviceable in rejecting the similarly oversimplified approaches to ethics of biblical fundamentalism and ecclesiastical authoritarianism, it is useless in dealing with the real question of the debate. It is noteworthy that Auer develops his thesis of autonomous morality in dialogue with the magisterium's claims to special competence in matters of natural law, claims which, according to Auer, have sometimes been excessive.[14] Whatever the relation, however, between natural law and Catholic authority, it is essentially different from the relation of Christian morality to Christian faith; and to predicate autonomy of the former relation is quite different from defining the latter.

Contrary to how matters seem in the distinction between autonomous reason and heteronomous faith, neither fundamentalism nor authoritarianism is the issue; for neither of these excesses is necessarily implied in an affirmative answer to the question about a specifically Christian morality. Nor will introducing into it the notion of theonomy render the distinction less problematical. For theonomous morality must be understood either as religiously heteronomous morality (that leaning in faith upon someone else's moral assertions to which Schüller contrasts autonomous ethics) or religiously autonomous morality (e.g. Aquinas' understanding of natural law as participation in eternal law[15] or Vatican II's understanding of conscience as the sanctuary in which the human person is alone with God[16]).

What is missing in the dichotomy set up between autonomous reason and heteronomous faith is a third possibility: in scholastic terms, reason informed by faith. Certainly, mature human beings must understand good and evil, right and wrong, on their own. But, like graced nature and charity-informed will, faith-informed intellect is hardly an extrinsic, heteronomous principle.[17]

The question of the debate, therefore, is not about heteronomy versus autonomy but about different modes of autonomy. And it is not about reason versus faith but about whether reason uninformed by Christian faith and reason informed by it naturally create the same morality. More adequately stated—since Christian faith is a more comprehensive and holistic reality[18] than the supernatural intellectual virtue which neo-scholasticism regarded it as[19]—the question becomes whether a person informed by Christian faith and one uninformed by it naturally create the same morality. But even this way of stating the question retains an individualistic quality and fails to recognize the essentially social character of Christian faith and, indeed, of morality itself. Ultimately, the question about a specifically Christian morality is: Is morality created within the Christian faith-community naturally identical with what is created outside it?

Moreover, it is not only the affirmative answer to the question about specifically Christian morality that is distorted by the name "autonomous ethics versus *Glaubensethik.*" The negative answers that constitute the origin of the debate are likewise rendered unrecognizable. In denying that there is a specifically Christian morality neither Fuchs nor Curran sought to oppose an autonomous reason to a heteronomous faith. For both theologians, a Christian faith-informed human interiority is the intrinsic, autonomous principle of the Christian's morality. The point on which their answers differ from an affirmative one is that, according to them, faith-informed human interiority qua faith-informed creates differences only on the intentional or transcendental level of morality and not on the categorical level of its material content.[20]

DISTORTED VIEWS OF THE DEBATE

This, then, is the original debate question. And understanding it as opposition between reason and faith or between autonomy and heteronomy has seriously misrepresented it.

Lucien Richard presents the debate as a dispute between a group of theologians upholding "an autonomous morality within a Christian context" and others maintaining "a faith ethic" that views "reason as too weak to arrive at any certainty in the area of moral norms."[21] This generalization, as Richard acknowledges, has its source in an article of Jean-Marie Aubert.[22] What Aubert had characterized in this way, however, was the controversy among German-speaking theologians that followed upon the appearance of Auer's autonomous-morality thesis.[23] Consequently, what Aubert categorizes as *l'éthique de la foi* are the conservative reactions of some German-speaking theologians, especially Bernhard Stöckle's pessimistic view of the ability of human reason to know good and evil—a view which, as Aubert points out, hardly squares with theological tradition or the common teaching of the church.[24]

In initiating the debate, however, neither Fuchs nor Curran had any intention of arguing against a Barthian-type ethics—to which the very presuppositions of the entire perennial endeavor of Catholic moral theology are in opposition. They were arguing, rather, against those who would assert that Christian faith generates morality that is materially different from that of non-Christians. Neither their concern nor that of those who disagree with them can be correctly expressed in categories created to define the German controversy centered on Auer's thesis.

Another, similarly procrustean generalization about the debate is Vincent MacNamara's point of departure in discussing it. The debate, according to MacNamara, is between theologians who maintain that Christian morality has no content different from humanist morality and that "we should not expect to receive our moral norms from 'outside of ourselves'" (autonomous ethics) and other theologians who "bitterly" counter such ideas in a "crusade . . . to preserve the specific character of Christian ethics" (*Glaubensethik*).[25]

Besides making it seem that the debate is between autonomy and heteronomy and that to affirm the specifically Christian character of Christian morality is to oppose autonomy, this description of the debate adds yet another questionable element. The assertion that the so-called *Glaubensethik* seeks "to preserve" the specific character of Christian ethics is at least misleading. In fact, the affirmative answer to the question about a specifically Christian morality seeks to bring into view the Christian character of Christian morality that was overlooked in the moral theology of the past, while the negative answer preserves the more secular quality long associated with the natural law tradition of Catholic morality. Like Richard's, MacNamara's generalization about the debate attempts to force it into the mold of the dispute among German-speaking theologians into which Auer's autonomous-morality thesis deflected it.

In short, then, the debate is not about Christian ethics; not about the distinctiveness of Christian morality; not about biblical fundamentalism nor even about biblical morality or ethics; not about ecclesiastical authoritarianism nor even about ecclesiastical authority; not about whether morality should be autonomous rather than heteronomous; not about whether morality should be theonomous rather than autonomous; not about whether morality should be rooted in reason or in Christian faith; not about whether reason is too weak to achieve certainty with regard to moral norms; and not about preserving, in crusade-like or other fashion, a Christian character of morality. The debate is about whether Christian faith makes any difference with regard to the material content of moral life. And Fuchs and Curran originated the debate by asserting that it does not.

THE APPROACH OF JOSEF FUCHS

Fuchs' apparently negative answer, however, is far from simple. According to his 1968 Zurich lecture, the decisive and essential element of Christian morality is Christian intentionality, while in its materiality or categorical orientation Christian morality "is basically and substantially a *humanum*, that is, a morality of genuine being-human."[26] By designating the material content as "basically and substantially" human Fuchs appears to be leaving room to characterize it also as otherwise (accidentally? secondarily? partially? by way of exception?) *Christianum* or determined by Christian intentionality. Nevertheless, at other points in the paper Fuchs gives the impression that the material content of Christian morality is—rather than basically and substantially—exclusively "a *humanum*." He writes, for example: "Christian intentionality is an element which, while pervading and completing the particular-categorical conduct, does not determine its content."[27]

Yet, if the last statement seems flatly to deny that Christian intentionality determines the material content of morality, there are other statements that explicitly indicate the opposite: "[W]e must in no way lose sight of the distinctively Christian element in the concrete categorical conduct of Christians"; and the *Christianum* "not only motivates human conduct more deeply and inspires it, but it will also determine the *content* of our conduct."[28] Examples given by Fuchs to illustrate how moral content is determined by Christian intentionality are Christian virginity, "which should be distinguished from the single life," and "man's explicit religious and cultic relationship to God," which "is also *moral* conduct."[29]

Thus, a moral theologian who upholds the specifically Christian character of the content of Christian morality, Philippe Delhaye, correctly concludes that Fuchs, in contrast to theologians proposing more secular theories, "has actually saved the main point once his exposition is viewed as a whole."[30] Despite a general appearance to the contrary, there is in Fuchs' position an acknowledgment that Christian faith determines the material content of Christian morality. With regard to confusions such as the apparent contradictions illustrated above, Fuchs' presentation is flawed, as Delhaye notes, and "the initial statements are modified by so many exceptions and fine shadings that one may legitimately ask whether they were faultlessly formulated from the start."[31] Delhaye suggests that among the reasons for the flawed character of the presentation is the desire "to effect a connection with the morality of non-Christians."[32]

In light of this criticism it is worth noting the change between Fuchs' formulation of his thought shortly before the Second Vatican Council and his postconciliar formulations. In a work published two years before the council, Fuchs wrote:

> It cannot be denied that the new law contains new material commandments (*nova materialiter praecepta*) beyond the natural law. Nor is it to be thought that [these pertain] exclusively to the ceremonial part (concerning the sacraments) of the new law and to dogmas of faith to be believed. How without revelation can we know, e.g., the relation between Church and State or the *Christian mode* of loving God and neighbor (although *substantially* the love of God and neighbor pertains to natural law)?[33]

After the council, however, Fuchs asserted, in the Zurich lecture, that the "newness that Christ brings is not really a new (material) morality, but the new creature of grace"[34] and, elsewhere in the same year, that

"Christian morality is not determined by new moral precepts but by the grace of the Spirit."[35] Still, Fuchs continued to find, as already noted, that material content of morality is determined by Christian faith.

In spite, then, of the negative appearance and framework that Fuchs gives after the council to his position on whether there is specifically Christian morality, it is, in the final analysis, an answer quite similar to what he had given earlier—indeed, an affirmative answer. There is now, however, an obvious tendency to downplay the material content of morality determined by faith and, as some of his formulations show, even to ignore it altogether.

SERMON ON THE MOUNT

The concern underlying and shaping the postconciliar expression of his thesis on Christian morality is epitomized in Fuchs' assertion in the Zurich lecture that the morality of the Sermon on the Mount is opposed, not to "genuine human morality," but only to "the profoundly inhuman conduct of the creature who is mired in egoism."[36] Indeed, it would be difficult to find another theme to which Fuchs' postconciliar writing returns more frequently than this view of the Sermon on the Mount.[37]

This often repeated thesis is presented as a reaction against a movement within Catholic moral theology in the 1920s and 1930s. Whereas at that time the Sermon on the Mount was seen as being "in opposition to the *humanum*" and Christian morality in general as opposed to "human" morality, now moral theology, "under the impact of secular and even secularistic tendencies in theological and moral thought," is "challenged to take a new look at the *humanum* in Christian morality."[38] At the heart of Fuchs' position, then, is the conviction that the Sermon on the Mount "calls people to what is human and not a superhuman, 'distinctively Christian' behavior in the world."[39]

Perhaps one could argue that Fuchs does not engage in sufficient dialogue with biblical scholarship about the moral teaching of the gospel.[40] Be that as it may, even if it is readily and emphatically stipulated that the morality of the Sermon on the Mount is neither superhuman nor opposed to "genuine human morality," it does not follow that the sermon has no unique moral material content. Much less does it follow that Christian faith does not and cannot determine the material content of Christian morality.

Rooted in an abstract distinction between essences, Fuchs' question about the Sermon on the Mount becomes a metaphysical question of whether its morality is human or superhuman rather than a question of how its morality is related to and differs from other moralities. And with the focus on metaphysical essences instead of historical realities it is easy to lose sight of the distinction between gospel morality and Christian morality and to assume that an assertion about the former is a truth about both. In the context of Fuchs' approach, then, it cannot but seem that to affirm the existence of a specifically Christian morality is tantamount to holding that Christianity has a superhuman, nonhuman morality; and Fuchs' apparent reluctance to acknowledge the existence of a specifically Christian morality is readily understandable. Nevertheless, as already noted, even in his Zurich lecture he eventually acknowledges that a Christian's relation to "Christian realities" must find concrete expression in material content of morality; and at this point Fuchs recognizes that even on the categorical level of morality there is, in his terminology, a *humanum Christianum,* Christianly human acts.[41]

Although his concept of the *humanum Christianum* is left undeveloped and its implications unexplored, it constitutes an important development in Fuchs' thought. Indeed, it sows a seed of historically conscious pluralism. For to acknowledge that there is Christianly human behavior is a step toward raising the questions of whether there is authentic human conduct characterized by other modifiers, e.g. Israelite or Jain, and indeed of whether there can be authentic human acts that are not qualified by some historical determinant. The acknowledgment, in other words, is en route to the question of whether human nature (*natura humana adaequate sumpta*) is in fact, as classicism believes it to be, the objective norm of morality.

Not altogether without prior hint, then, an understanding of the *humanum* very different from that which had characterized his Zurich lecture appeared several years later in Fuchs' thought. In the lecture the *humanum* had been understood, in classicist manner, as acts in accord with human nature. Accordingly, the statement that in its material content Christian morality "is basically and substantially a *humanum,* a genuine being-human," meant that

> truthfulness, uprightness and faithfulness are not specifically Christian, but generally human values in what they materially say, and that we have reservations about lying and adultery not because we are Christians, but simply because we are human.[42]

Six years later, however, the *humanum* began to be seen, in the light of historical consciousness, as the concrete person in history. That "everything receives its norms from the *humanum*" now meant that "everything receives its norms from . . . the real person in an historically realized human nature." The basis for moral judgments and norms is accordingly identified as neither human nature alone nor historical particularities by themselves but "rather the two together, or even better, the one unique human reality with various aspects." There are, accordingly, "different realizations of the same humanity" in "different sociological, economic, cultural and individual contexts," and these differences can lead to "different practical solutions" to moral questions.[43]

By 1974, then, Fuchs had come to an historical consciousness of the norm of morality, a major departure from his classicist understanding of it in the Zurich lecture. If the lecture is reviewed from the perspective of this subsequent historical consciousness, the reason for its tensions and inconsistencies is apparent. While its overall understanding of morality is classicist, there emerges in the lecture an inchoately historical consciousness of Christian morality when some Christian behavior is seen as *humanum Christianum,* behavior in accord with human nature qualified by Christian faith.

Even in 1974, however, when he had arrived at an historical understanding of morality and had explicitly acknowledged that such historical determinants as sociological and cultural factors enter into the constitution of its norm, Fuchs did not advert explicitly to what is certainly, if not the most, at least one of the most important sociological and/or cultural determinants of morality—religion. Thus, the newly achieved historical consciousness of morality in general was not applied explicitly to Christian morality, and there did not emerge a thematic awareness that the norm of Christian morality is the Christian person in history, e.g. the late twentieth century western European Roman Catholic.

Significantly, the piece in which Fuchs' historical consciousness of the norm of morality emerged is not his usual essay but a collection of what might be called ethical *pensées.*[44] There are indications that Fuchs came to his historical understanding of the norm from reflecting upon sexual morality and marriage.[45] But the very nature of the work in which it comes to expression allows this historical consciousness of the norm to stand as a *pensée* and does not compel its thematic development or its systematic integration into a complete moral theology. Thus, although he has returned many times, even after 1974, to discussing the nature of Christian morality, a historically conscious understanding of it has not yet appeared, and he has continued to view it from the perspective of the same classicist understanding of the Sermon on the Mount that characterized his Zurich lecture.[46]

CLASSICISM AND HISTORICAL CONSCIOUSNESS

The question of whether the Sermon on the Mount presents super-human or human morality is a question derived from classicist presuppositions. Centered on human nature, classicist moral theology understands humanness and morality accordingly. The heart of morality is the human act (*actus humanus*), i.e. the act of deliberate will or of human nature qua human, as distinguished from the act that issues from the human organism as such (*actus hominis*). Supernatural grace is adventitious to human nature, and deliberate acts of the person in the state of grace proceed not only from nature but also from grace as supernature; hence derives the possibility of superhuman acts and, further, of superhuman morality. And this conceptual apparatus of human versus superhuman morality is the necessary common ground for the dispute between Fuchs and theologians of the 1920s and 1930s over whether the morality of the Sermon on the Mount is human or superhuman.

For historical consciousness, however, "superhuman morality" is an anomaly and "human morality" a tautology. Centered on human persons in history, historically conscious moral theology understands humanness and morality accordingly. The norm of morality is not human nature but the historical human person, to whom grace and virtue are not adventitious but intrinsic. The heart of morality, consequently, is the self-realization of the human person in history through virtue (vice), character, faith, world-view, community, friendship, commitment, political involvement, relationships, etc. as well as through the intellectual-volitional-affective activity and outward action that constitute the act of deliberate will. In a word, the realm of morality is concrete human persons as self-actualized in history. Christian faith, therefore, is not, as classicism conceives it, extrinsic to being-human and an addition to it; it is, rather, one of many intrinsic modes of being a human person in history.

Thus, while the Sermon on the Mount certainly presents morality of the graced person, to identify it as morality at all is to indicate that it is human. The inquiry into gospel morality for historical consciousness, consequently, is not the classicist query about abstract essences but rather a series of questions: (1) what is its content? (biblical scholarship); (2) how has its content been related to Christian morality in the past? (historical theology); (3) how is its content related to other moralities (comparative ethics); and (4) how should its content be related to contemporary Christian life? (fundamental moral theology). Similarly, the inquiry into

Christian morality is a question, not of whether it is human or nonhuman, but about one of the many modes of being-human; a question, not about whether and/or what Christian faith adds to "human morality," but about the Christian way of being a human person in history.

As is self-evident, the question about specifically Christian morality presupposes an answer to a more basic question about morality itself. Thus, consensus regarding the nature of morality is the common ground required for coherent discussion of Christian morality. But it is precisely such consensus, firmly established for centuries till Vatican II, that no longer exists in moral theology. Indeed, the internal variance of Fuchs' postconciliar moral theology is, in miniature, the same lack of a unanimous point of departure that characterizes contemporary moral theology as a whole: today some theologians understand morality from the classicist perspective, some from the perspective of historical consciousness, some from now one and now the other perspective, and some from an amalgam of both. Moreover, this disunity of theoretical presuppositions is largely overlooked even by theologians themselves, who, since the council, have been compelled by circumstances to address one pressing practical problem after another.

Catholic moral theology is in a stage of transition. Thrust by the council into an historically conscious era, it is undergoing radical transformation from a classicist discipline into contemporary science of Christian existence. And until this long, complicated process is accomplished and a new consensus of presuppositions created, the debate about specifically Christian morality will remain unresolved. In this respect moral theology in 1968 was, and today still is, unready for the question about specifically Christian morality.

CHARLES CURRAN'S THESIS

Far less complex than Fuchs' thesis is Curran's denial of specifically Christian morality. As presented in 1970, it is deduced from the universal offer of God's loving self-communication to humanity[47] and means only that non-Christians

> are able to arrive not only at the same ethical decisions about particular matters [at which Christians can arrive] but are also able to have for all practical purposes the same general dispositions and attitudes such as hope, freedom and love for others even to the point of sacrificing self.[48]

In a 1971 response to Curran, written from the perspective of the unique-part model of the constitution of specificity underlying his thesis, I pointed out the need to distinguish in Christian morality four spheres: essential, existential, Christian essential and Christian existential. By "Christian essential" was meant moral responsibilities incumbent on a person qua member of the Christian faith-community, e.g. the duty to witness to Christ, while "Christian existential" referred to moral responsibilities of a person as Christian individual, e.g. the duty of a religious educator to instruct a particular group of children in the Christian story. Outside of the realm of "essential" morality, understood as duties deriving from the human community as such, all persons of good will, I argued, cannot and do not arrive at the same moral decisions.[49]

In a recent reply Curran states that my concept of essential morality describes his position: his denial of specifically Christian morality is concerned with "the normative material content in Christian morality which is posed in Christian morality for all" or, in other words, with "the moral order whose normative content is the same for all as distinguished from the existential call of an individual and the obligations arising from membership in the Christian Church as such."[50] This answer seems to mean that, if obligations arising from Christian faith are prescinded from and only moral norms that apply to everyone are taken into consideration, then it follows that there is no specifically Christian morality. Even if one does not choose to dispute the logical validity of this inference, the adequacy of its premise can be readily questioned. And my thesis regarding the quadruple division of Christian morality does this.

The human essence on which Curran's essential morality is based is theological rather than philosophical: the human being oriented in salvation history toward the gracious God or, in Karl Rahner's terminology, the human being affected by the "supernatural existential." From this universal, grace-oriented human nature Curran deduces that all persons can realize the same material content of morality. The inference is persuasive, however, only if one assumes that grace-oriented human nature is the norm of morality. But it is precisely on this point that historically conscious moral theology disagrees with its classicist counterpart, finding the norm instead in the concrete person in history.

In his recent presentation of his thesis Curran adds an intermediate step between the premise and the conclusion. From all humanity's being the recipient of God's offer of love Curran first infers that "there is only one given historical moral order" and thence deduces that in principle all human beings "can arrive at the same moral norms governing human action and the same values, virtues, dispositions, and goals."[51] The addition of the new premise about only one given historical moral order, however, brings cogency to the thesis only if it is assumed that this one historical moral order is uniform rather than, like the one historical religious order, pluralistic. But this assumption is, again, precisely the issue: whereas classicism sees a uniform moral order based on a universal human nature, historical consciousness sees a multiform moral order based on concrete persons in history.

SPECIFICITY OF CHRISTIAN MORALITY

As noted earlier, to identify the specificity of a morality in terms of the unique-part model it is not enough to identify unique parts, since these are not the specificity itself but rather sources or principles of it. It is a morality, not only a part of it, that is unique; for a morality is not a sum of parts but a whole—indeed, a living, always changing whole.

Since classicism understands morality in terms of human nature, it presupposes that there is a single, uniform morality; and moral law is understood as natural law, a multitude of moral norms deduced from the principle of human nature, beginning with the most general—"Do good and avoid evil"—and moving toward increasing particularity. As each moral norm is individually deduced from human nature, it can be separately traced back to its root there. Consequently, morality can seem to be a sum of separate parts, and the question about Christian morality can appear to be a question of whether "the law of Christ" added any new norms to the already existing body of natural law norms.

Historical consciousness, however, understands moral law, not as a law of human nature, but as the human responsibilities of persons in history.[52] There is, therefore, no presupposition of a single morality; for the oneness of moral law is directly derived not from the singleness of human nature but from the unity of the human race in history. A true morality is indeed based on objective human values, but it is based on objective human values as perceived from some historico-cultural perspective. Since human values, moreover, are naturally interrelated and correlative, they can be discerned only collectively, in relation to one another, and not discretely, as if they were individual entities unto themselves. In other words, human values are perceived only as integral parts of a system of human values. And a perceived system of human values is itself possible only in light of some world-view.

A morality, then, is based on a perceived system of values that is embedded in a world-view. Sharing the unity of the value system and of the world-view in which the value system originates, it is a perceived whole, not a sum of parts. The moral norms derived from the perceived values express integral parts of a whole; they indicate aspects of a normative way of life, reflecting a value system and an underlying world-view. The question about Christian morality, therefore, is a question, not about whether Christ adds more norms to already existing ones, but about the normative way of life that originates in the value system of the world-view derived from the Christian story.

Thus, the specificity of Christian morality is something altogether different from a unique addition to an otherwise "human morality." Christian virginity, for instance, is not a value appended to an already existent, universally shared system of human values, among which is marriage. On the contrary, in a value system that encompasses both Christian virginity and marriage because each has its place in an underlying world-view, marriage itself is valued differently than in a system in which Christian virginity is not included. For in a value system all values are integral parts of a whole, and each qualifies all others, just as in the world-view underlying a value system every element is correlative to every other and to the whole.

That a human value is universal, therefore, does not mean that it is univocal. The value actually perceived, for instance, in marriage, which has varied considerably even within historical Christianity, is directly relative to how and/or whether many other values (besides Christian virginity—friendship, equality of the sexes, celibacy, single life, male and female roles, procreation, family, sexual intercourse, parenthood, sacrament, remarriage after divorce, homosexual love, marital annulment, marriage bond, Pauline privilege, marital contract—to mention but a few) are perceived. Thus, all human values and the moral norms based on them are perceived and understood only through a *conversio ad phantasma*, only in a value system rooted in a world view.

Guiding Christians into the depths of Christian life, St. Ignatius Loyola lays before them a "third kind of humility":

> Whenever the praise and glory of God would be equally served, in order better to imitate and actually be more like Christ our Lord, I desire and choose poverty with Christ poor, rather than riches; oppression with Christ oppressed, rather than honors; I desire to be considered worthless and a fool for Christ, who suffered such treatment before me, rather than to be thought wise or clever in this world.[53]

Connatural to a world-view based on the Christian story, the third kind of humility appears meaningless, indeed foolish, in any other context. And the genius of *The Spiritual Exercises* is in knowing that to adopt this value is not merely to add a value to a value system but to transvalue a value system.

Whether there is a specifically Christian morality is a classicist question. It presupposes that there is a single "human morality," based on human nature, and wonders what Christian faith adds to it. Historically conscious moral theology, however, has an altogether different point of departure and, hence, an altogether different question. Starting from the historical fact of moral pluralism, it finds specifically Christian morality —indeed moralities—as a given and wonders how it should be shaped in the contemporary world. For historical consciousness, therefore, the debate question is resolved by being dissolved.

Notes

1. *Stimmen der Zeit* 185 (1970) 99–112; English version in J. Fuchs, *Personal Responsibility and Christian Morality* (Washington, D.C.: Georgetown University, 1983), hereafter *Personal Responsibility,* 53–68.

2. Hereafter "Christian Social Ethic?" in Philip D. Morris, ed., *Metropolis: Christian Presence and Responsibility* (Notre Dame, Ind.: Fides, 1970) 92–120. "Distinctively" and "ethic" as used here by Curran are synonymous with "specifically" and "morality," respectively, in Fuchs' article. And although Curran's title speaks of a Christian social ethic, the focus of the article is Christian morality in general.

The origins of the debate are identified by Lucien Richard (*Is There a Christian Ethics?* [New York: Paulist Press, 1988] 8) as what are in fact subsequent contributions to it. Referring to Alfons Auer's 1971 work, *Autonome Moral und christlicher Glaube* (Düsseldorf: Patmos), he states that the debate "was opened by Auer in Germany" and adds that in the United States "the debate was joined by Charles Curran, who published in 1974 an essay entitled 'Is There a Catholic and/or Christian Ethic?' "

In the years preceding the debate there had been harbingers of it, such as Franz Böckle, "Was ist das Proprium einer christlichen Ethik?" *Zeitschrift fur evangelische Ethik* 11 (1967) 148–159; Richard A. McCormick, "Human Significance and Christian Significance," in Gene H. Outka and Paul Ramsey, eds., *Norm and Context in Christian Ethics* (New York: Charles Scribner's Sons, 1968) 233–261; Coenraad A.J. van Ouwerkerk, "Secularism and Christian Ethics: Some Types and Symptoms," *Concilium* 25 (1967) 97–139.

3. "Autonomous Ethics Revisited," in Joseph A. Selling, ed., *Personalist Morals: Essays in Honor of Professor Louis Janssens, Bibiliotheca Ephemeridum Theologicarum Lovaniensium* 83 (Leuven: Leuven University, 1988) 61.

4. Although not exclusively so, for the most part the debate has been within

Catholic theology. The question of a specifically Christian morality emerged in Catholic moral theology in the context of carrying forward its natural law tradition (N. Rigali, "Moral Pluralism and Christian Ethics," *Louvain Studies* 13 [1988] 305; idem, "The Story of Christian Morality," *Chicago Studies* 27 [1988] 173–174).

5. Even while maintaining that "moral theology is not theology at all" but "moral philosophy, pursued by persons who are believers," Timothy O'Connell acknowledges that it relies on "the resources of Scripture, dogmatic tradition and theological reflection" (*Principles for a Catholic Morality* [New York: Seabury, 1978] 40–41).

6. James J. Walter, "Christian Ethics: Distinctive and Specific," *American Ecclesiastical Review* 169 (1975) 483.

7. "Is There a Catholic and/or Christian Ethic?" *Proceedings: Catholic Theological Society of America* 29 (1974) 125–154.

8. Published in C. Curran, *Moral Theology: A Continuing Journey* (Notre Dame, Ind.: University of Notre Dame, 1982) 82. Subsequently Curran seems to have abandoned the distinction; in a later essay, "What Is Distinctive and Unique about Christian Ethics and Morality?" the three terms, "distinctive," "unique" and "specific," appear to be again interchangeable (*Toward an American Catholic Moral Theology* [Notre Dame: University of Notre Dame, 1987] 52–64).

9. *Readings in Moral Theology No. 2* (New York: Paulist, 1980), hereafter *Readings*, 90–110. The editors say of their book that it "centers on a very important issue in contemporary debate—is there a specifically Christian morality or ethic?" and go on to point out explicitly the need to advert to the exact meanings of "specific" and "distinctive" (1–2).

10. Ibid. 3–19.

11. *Personal Responsibility* 53–68.

12. In the earlier, 1980 English version three adverbs, "specifically," "distinctly" and "decisively," are used interchangeably to modify the adjective "Christian"; and "specifically" is the dominant member of the triad. In the 1983, modified translation are still found three interchangeable adverbs: "distinctively," "specifically" and "decisively," with "distinctively" now dominant. The revision entails substituting "distinctively" not only for the previously used "distinctly" but also at times for an earlier "specifically." Nevertheless, in other places in the revision an original "specifically" is allowed to stand.

Unfortunately, no reason for these odd changes in translation is given. But the most troublesome aspect of them is that, whether it is assumed that they were made in light of Walter's distinction or in ignorance or disregard of it, no overall pattern can be discerned in them and they appear arbitrary. Thus, whatever they were intended to accomplish, the changes in terminology generate the very confusion that Walter had sought eight years earlier to obviate.

13. "Autonomous Ethics Revisited" 62.

14. *Autonome Moral und christlicher Glaube* 137–197.

15. *Summa Theologica* 1–2, 91, 2c.

16. *Gaudium et Spes,* n. 16, in Austin Flannery, ed., *Vatican Council II: The*

Conciliar and Post Conciliar Documents (Collegeville, Minn.: Liturgical Press, 1975) 916.

17. Autonomy "does not decrease, but increases in the same proportion as dependence on God" (Karl Rahner, *Foundations of Christian Faith: An Introduction to the Idea of Christianity* [New York: Seabury, 1978] 79). Accordingly, in and through hypostatic union with divinity, the graced humanity of Christ is the perfection of humanity and the supreme realization of human autonomy (Herbert Vorgrimler, "Hypostatische Union," in *Lexikon für Theologie und Kirche,* 2nd ed., V, 82).

18. Juan Alfaro, "Faith," in *Sacramentum Mundi: An Encyclopedia of Theology* II, 313–314.

19. A. Tanquerey, *A Manual of Dogmatic Theology* (New York: Desclée, 1959) 191–202.

20. Fuchs, *Personal Responsibility* 54–58, esp. 57 (Fuchs' position, it will appear below, is more complex than what a reader would infer from this reference to his lecture); Curran, "Christian Social Ethic?" 114.

The autonomous-morality school, nevertheless, identifies Fuchs among their own number (Auer, *Autonome Moral und christlicher Glaube,* 175–176). In fact, on one occasion Fuchs linked himself with this school. To a meeting of German-speaking moral theologians in 1977 he delivered a paper entitled "Autonome Moral und Glaubensethik" ("Autonomous Morality and Morality of Faith," in *Personal Responsibility,* 84–111). Its theme, however, had been suggested to him by the organizers of the meeting (ibid. 109, n. 1); and despite the accommodation to autonomous-morality categories its theme remains that of Fuchs' original essay of 1968, namely, the relation, in his terminology, of the *Christianum* to the *humanum.*

21. *Is There a Christian Ethics?* 8.

22. "Débats autour de la morale fondamentale," *Studia Moralia* 20 (1982) 195–222.

23. Ibid. 198–209.

24. Ibid. 206.

25. *Faith and Ethics: Recent Roman Catholicism* (Washington, D.C.: Georgetown University, 1985) 3–4.

26. *Personal Responsibility* 57.

27. Ibid.

28. Ibid. 63, 64. Emphasis in original.

29. Ibid. 64–65. Emphasis in original.

30. "Questioning the Specificity of Christian Morality," in *Readings* 239.

31. Ibid. 237–238.

32. Ibid. 239.

33. *Theologia moralis generalis* (Rome: Gregorian University, 1960) I, 98–99; my translation.

34. *Personal Responsibility* 61.

35. Ibid. 23.

36. Ibid. 61.

37. See, e.g., ibid. 23, 34, 205; *Christian Ethics in a Secular Arena* (Washing-

ton, D.C.: Georgetown University, 1984) 6, 21; *Christian Morality: The Word Becomes Flesh* (Washington, D.C.: Georgetown University, 1987), hereafter *Christian Morality,* 6, 13, 50, 109–110.

38. *Personal Responsibility* 58.

39. *Christian Morality* 6.

40. Delhaye notes that Fuchs ignores the new commandment in John 13:34–35 ("Questioning the Specificity of Christian Morality" 254).

41. *Personal Responsibility* 63–65.

42. Ibid. 57–58.

43. Ibid. 214. Since the recognition of the person in history as the norm of morality implies moral pluralism, it is noteworthy that the notion of pluralism surfaces in Fuchs' subsequent writings with increasing frequency; see *Christian Morality* 56, 80, 113–114, 134–142, 173–188, 207.

Several years before Fuchs did so, Edward Schillebeeckx had argued that the concrete person in history is the norm of morality ("The Magisterium and the World of Politics," *Concilium* 36 [New York: Paulist, 1968] 26–27). Louis Janssens ("Artificial Insemination: Ethical Considerations," *Louvain Studies* 8 [1980] 3–4) and Bernard Häring (*Free and Faithful in Christ: Moral Theology for Clergy and Laity* [New York: Seabury, 1978] I, 319) likewise thematically treat the essential historicity of morality.

44. "A Summary: Clarifications of Some Currently Used Terms," in *Personal Responsibility* 200–215; with regard to its origins, see p. 229.

45. Ibid. 213.

46. See references in note 37 above.

47. "Christian Social Ethic?" 109, 114.

48. Ibid. 115–116.

49. N. Rigali, "On Christian Ethics," *Chicago Studies* 10 (1971) 227–247. McCormick adopted this fourfold understanding of Christian morality: *Notes on Moral Theology 1965 through 1980* (Washington, D.C.: University Press of America, 1981) 429–431; "Response to Professor Curran—II," *Proceedings: The Catholic Theological Society of America* 29 (1974) 163–164; "Does Religious Faith Add to Ethical Perception?" in *Readings* 157–158.

50. *Toward an American Catholic Moral Theology* 60–61.

51. Ibid.

52. N. Rigali, "Morality and Historical Consciousness," *Chicago Studies* 18 (1979) 162–168; idem, "The Unity of Moral and Pastoral Truth," ibid., vol. 25 (1986) 225–229.

53. *The Spiritual Exercises of St. Ignatius Loyola,* tr. Elisabeth Meier Tetlow (Lanham, MD: University Press of America, 1987) 56.

5

Personalism in Moral Theology

Louis Janssens

Dealing with the question of harmonizing conjugal love with the responsible transmission of life, Vatican II teaches that the moral character of any procedure must be determined by objective criteria "based on the nature of the person and his acts." To explain how the nature of the person's acts is morally relevant, the official commentary on the expression that was used states: "By these terms it is asserted that the acts must also be judged not according to their merely biological aspect, but insofar as they refer to the human person integrally and adequately considered." The comment also declares that this "is a question of a general principle."[1]

To consider the human person in an integral and adequate way, account must be taken of the person's fundamental aspects or dimensions. I discern eight such essential dimensions: 1. The human person is a subject, not an object as are the things of the world. Since the person is called to self-determination, he or she is a moral subject, deciding on all his or her doings in conscience and consequently in a responsible way. 2. The human person is a subject in corporeality. Our body forms part of the totality that we are: what concerns our human body affects our person. 3. Because of the materiality of our body, our being is a being-in-the-world. 4. Human persons are essentially directed toward each other. 5. Not only because of our openness to one another are we social beings, but also because we need to live in social groups with appropriate structures and institutions. 6. Human persons are fundamentally open to God, and it is the task of moral theology to explain how, according to our Christian revelation, our relationship to God affects us in all the dimensions of our person. 7. Human persons are historical beings since they are characterized by historicity. 8. All human persons are fundamentally equal, but at the same time each is an originality, a unique subject.[2]

In accord with a personalist criterion an act is a morally right one if, in truth, it is beneficial to the person adequately considered in all his or her fundamental dimensions. In other words, from a personalist standpoint we must examine what an action as a whole means for the promotion of the human person considered in himself or herself (as a subject in corporeality) and in his or her relationships. This demands an inductive method in which human experience and the sciences, as critical elaboration of that experience, play an indispensable role.

In this essay I will confine myself to the examination of four issues: (1) the controlling totality, (2) the person's openness to God, (3) historicity, and (4) originality.

The Controlling Totality

An action considered in abstraction—what classical moralists referred to as the uncircumstanced object of the act—cannot be appreciated in moral terms. To form a judgment on the moral rightness or wrongness of an action, two requirements must be fulfilled. We must consider the whole action with all its components, and examine whether or not this totality is promotive of the person and his or her relationships, namely in the totality of the person's dimensions.

Our activity, as active commerce with reality in ourselves or outside of us, is always liable to various limits and contingencies. Therefore, in order to determine its moral rightness or wrongness we must always start with the concrete action as it is experienced in the concrete situation. This can best be illustrated with examples.

There are actions which are harmful for one or another of the person's dimensions. They raise the question of what they mean for the person as a whole and for his or her relationships. For instance, a surgical intervention on an unhealthy organ affects the bodily integrity of the person, yet can be indicated to save his or her life. The moral rightness of the intervention is clear. There is due proportion between the means and the expected result, since a healthy life ranks prior to bodily integrity.

Nevertheless, suppose the person suffers from an advanced, incurable cancer. A surgical intervention, if successful, perhaps could somewhat prolong his or her life. However, because the person understands that this prolongation would only protract the burden of suffering, he or she refuses the operation. According to the declaration of the Congregation for the Doctrine of the Faith, based on the principle of proportionality,

> ... such a refusal is not the equivalent of suicide; on the contrary, it should be considered as an acceptance of the human

condition, or a wish to avoid the application of a medical procedure disproportionate to the results that can be expected or a
desire not to impose excessive expenses on the family or the
community.[3]

The congregation demands a due proportion between the type of treatment to be used, its degree of complexity or risk, its cost and the possibilities of using it, the investment in instruments and personnel, on the one
side, and, on the other side, the result that can be expected, taking into
account the state of the sick person and his or her physical and moral
resources.

This example makes it clear that in cases where disvalues are involved in an action, the use of the principle of proportionality is a proper
means to determine whether or not a concrete action contributes to the
promotion of the persons involved and of their relationships.

A second example attempts to show how the personalist standard
provides the necessarily broader context for evaluating the use of technical means to overcome natural deficiencies. There are, for instance, situations in which conception can only be accomplished through the intervention of artificial insemination between husband and wife (AIH). In
neo-scholastic theology, the procedure for accomplishing this would be
fragmented (the act of masturbation, replacement of sexual intercourse
by technical means, etc.) and judged according to its merely biological
aspects. This way of thinking found expression in an influential article of
F. Hürth, S.J.[4] His thesis was that procreation must be exclusively realized through the act foreseen by nature, because the intention of nature is
inscribed in the organs and their function.

It would be absurd that nature determines the means for man in
every respect (anatomical, physiological, psychological) to place
himself at the service of the species and that it indicated the
manner of acting to the smallest detail with an almost unbeliev-
able efficiency in order to then allow man the right to choose his
manner of acting as he pleases or to substitute for it another
means which he has found himself. Nature contains no such
inner contradiction.[5]

And he concluded:

Man only has disposal of the use of his organs to the end which
the Creator, in His formation of them, has intended. This end
for man, then, is both the biological law and the moral law,

such that the latter obliges him to live according to the biological law.[6]

The real question is: What is one to do in the cases in which the natural efficiency—so strongly emphasized by Hürth—of sexual intercourse to conceive new life breaks down and is, in fact, inefficient? Is it not obvious in such cases to appeal to reason, which is also part of human nature, and to investigate how to alleviate such factually present inefficiency?

I think that these questions can be answered when the procedure of AIH is considered as a whole and evaluated according to the personalist standard. I presuppose that the partners are married, foster their conjugal love, and are endowed with the qualities required to become good parents and educators. If these conditions are fulfilled, the morally relevant question concerning the totality of the procedure is: Which dimensions of the persons involved are concerned? First, *Gaudium et Spes* 48 and 50 affirm that marriage and conjugal love are by their nature ordained toward the begetting and educating of children and find in them their ultimate crown, that children are really an eminent gift of marriage and contribute very substantially to the welfare of their parents. Under the conditions I mentioned, AIH is suited to that purpose: if the procedure is successful, the wanted and expected child is a supreme gift for that marriage. It is out of their mutual love that the partners ask for AIH, and the coming child will substantially contribute to their welfare.

Second, the sexual relationship of husband and wife maintains its full meaning as the expression and promotion of their joyful, mutual self-giving (GS, 49). Third, the child is procreated by its real parents. Fourth, the mutual love of his or her parents will be the appropriate context of the child's education. Fifth, it is beneficial for the future of the larger society that good marriages grow into families. When we look at the matter as a whole, the procedure of AIH is morally defensible, since in the circumstances described here it is subservient to the promotion of the persons involved and of their relationships.

When conflict situations occur, the personalist criterion may go a long way in clarifying the most appropriate and therefore right way of acting. *Gaudium et Spes,* 51 asserts:

This Council realizes that certain modern conditions often keep couples from arranging their married lives harmoniously and that they find themselves in circumstances where at least temporarily the size of their families should not be increased. As a result, the faithful exercise of love and the full intimacy of their lives are hard to maintain. But when the intimacy of married life is broken off, it is not rare for its faithfulness (*bonum fidei*) to be imperiled and its quality of fruitfulness (*bonum prolis*) ruined. For then the upbringing of the children and the courage to accept new ones are both endangered.

This passage explicitly points out the danger of prolonged continence, a danger already indicated by St. Paul in 1 Corinthians 7:5.

It is no wonder that the council was concerned about the maintenance of intimacy and the risks that may be present in protracted continence. This directly follows from the values of the marital acts of sexual intercourse which, according to *Gaudium et Spes*, 49, "signify and promote the mutual self-giving by which spouses enrich each other with a joyful and thankful will."[7] "When there is a question of harmonizing conjugal love with the responsible transmission of life" (*Gaudium et Spes*, 51), forced continence, more often than not, induces a conflict between the priority due to the *bonum fidei* and the *bonum prolis*, both of which have been proclaimed by the whole tradition as being the supreme values of marriage. Therefore, these values must be safeguarded, even when this requires the use of artificial contraceptives, if these alone offer the necessary reliability for realizing responsible parenthood. If it is true that "the acts must be judged, not according to their merely biological aspect, but insofar as they refer to the human person integrally and adequately considered," it seems to me that in the case under consideration the intervention of artificial means in sexual intercourse promotes the personal relationship between husband and wife with its primordial values and obligations, namely the protection of the *bonum fidei* and the *bonum prolis;* and that, therefore, the procedure, taken as a totality, is beneficial to the persons involved and their relationships.

THE PERSON'S OPENNESS TO GOD

Our Christian faith informs us that it is God who always takes the initiative, and that all our actions ought to be a response to that initiative. My point of departure for the characterization of that response is Jesus' proclamation of the reign of God, *basileia*. My guides in this matter are certain prominent exegetes who take account of the ethical implications of Jesus' announcement of the *basileia*.[8]

According to the synoptic gospels, the announcement of the reign of God is the core of Jesus' activities. This same announcement is determinative for our moral life. If one wishes to know the ethic of Jesus, one must first inquire into the heart of his message, that core which makes the announcement and realization of God's will comprehensible and urgent. That core, which at once constitutes the motivation and horizon of all Jesus' activities, is the message of the *basileia* as the eschatological turning point of the age.

H. Schürmann points out that Jesus clarifies his perception of the *basileia* not only through his words and deeds, but especially through his prayer. According to Schürmann, the petition, "Father (Abba), your kingdom come," is, in all probability, Jesus' own. Accordingly, we would seem to be on solid methodological ground if we take as our point of departure the praying Jesus, who addresses God as Abba and longs for the arrival of his Father's *basileia*. On the basis of this prayer, it would seem that Jesus regards the definitive establishment of the *basileia* as the absolute prerogative of the Father, who alone knows the day and hour (Mt 13:32).

The future *basileia* (*Aus-stand*) is, however, already actively present (*Ein-stand*) in our history, in and through Jesus. The synoptic gospels are emphatic in the claim that the dynamic event of the *basileia* is inseparably bound up with the person of Jesus. They make it clear that Jesus is the immediate representative of the *basileia,* that he presents himself as one who dares to speak and act in God's place, and that the eschatological future has already begun with him. So it is that Schürmann can describe the *basileia* as eschatological salvation coming from the Father, which already comes to us and is present among us, in the words and deeds of Jesus, but especially in his prayer.

If the *basileia* is an event that has already begun in the words and deeds of Jesus, then we are able to discern, in all his activities, what the reign of his Father in our history consists in. Fundamental to that reign would appear to be his merciful and solicitous love.

God Reigns Through Merciful Love

God's initiative of merciful and forgiving love, despite our sinfulness, is especially illuminated in Jesus' words and deeds. Jesus says explicitly that he has come for sinners—and that includes all of us—and to seek out and find that which was lost (Mk 2:17f; Lk 19:1–10). He forgives the sins of those who come to him in faith (Mk 2:1–12; Lk 7:36–50). He consorts with sinners, and dines with them, and for this is mocked as the friend of publicans and sinners (Mt 11:19; Lk 5:30; 15:1–2). Luke reports that Jesus sought to answer this charge by telling the parable of the good shepherd who goes off in search of the lost sheep (Lk 15:4–7). The point of the story is the shepherd's initiative, and his great joy at finding what was lost. By means of the parable, Jesus wishes to make clear that his searching out and finding of sinners ought to engender joy, not protest. Jesus' whole performance incarnates the initiative of God's merciful love.

What this means for us is that we may entrust ourselves to God's mercy, as the publican in the temple did (Lk 18:9–14). It also means, however, that our actions are subject to certain demands. This is made quite apparent in the story of the merciful king and his hard-hearted steward (Mt 18:23–35). Matthew introduces the story with the observation that the *basileia* is like the king, and he continues his account by highlighting the sharp difference between the attitude of the king and that of his servant. The latter owes the king a great debt. He is unable to pay it, and begs for an extension. In his exceedingly great mercy, the king does even more than he is asked: he cancels the debt entirely. Immediately after his own experience of such great mercy, the servant encounters a fellow servant who owes him an insignificant sum. The fellow servant is likewise insolvent, and he, too, begs for an extension. The servant whose debt had been canceled is pitiless, however, and he turns his colleague over to the authorities. The king is made aware of what has transpired. He summons his hard-hearted servant and says to him: "You wicked servant! I forgave you all that debt because you besought me; and should you not have had mercy on your fellow servant, as I had mercy on you?" The heartless servant is then accorded the punishment he deserves. Matthew has Jesus conclude the story with the significant remark that: "So also my heavenly Father will do to every one of you, if you do not forgive your brother from your heart" (Mt 18:35).

The mercy we enjoy from God demands in response mercy on our part toward our fellow human beings. God's mercy makes us capable of forgiveness, and obliges us to forgive in imitation of the Father: be merciful *as* the Father is merciful. Matthew frequently returns to the necessity of our initiative of mercy and forgiving love. So, commenting on the prayer for God's forgiveness that is part of the Our Father, he comments that we may expect no forgiveness if we ourselves do not forgive those who have wronged us (Mt 6:14–15). He observes that our gifts are not acceptable to God if we are not first reconciled to the brother or sister who has something against us (Mt 5:23–24). And on two occasions, he remarks that God prefers mercy to sacrifice (Mt 9:13; 12:7).

Jesus specifies just how far our initiative of merciful and forgiving love ought to go when he describes how we are to love our enemies (Mt 5:38–48; Lk 6:27–36): "Do good to those who hate you, bless those who curse you, pray for those who abuse you" (Lk 6:27–28). Jesus confirms this attitude, in the first place, by pointing to the creative activity of God who makes his sun rise on the evil and the good, and sends rain on the just and the unjust. The divine model must be determinative for our attitude, so that we may be children of our Father in heaven (Mt 5:44–45). Jesus proposes the goodness of the creator God as the model for our love of our enemies. Ultimately, however, he fixes our attitude in accordance with the demands of the *basileia:* "Be merciful, even as your Father is merciful" (Lk 6:36).

God Reigns Through Solicitous Love

Jesus tells us of the Father's solicitous love for birds and plants. He informs us that we are worth more than the flowers of the field or the birds of the air, and that the Father's solicitous love is, accordingly, directed even more toward us. He concludes by affirming that the Father will give us what we need if we seek his *basileia* (Mt 6:24–34; Lk 12:6–7, 22–31). He teaches us to prayerfully ask that God the Father may provide for our daily bread, for all we need from day to day (Mt 6:11). That God's solicitous love is directed to our general well-being is, however, manifest in Jesus' deeds, as well as in his words. Mark testifies that Jesus feels compassion for the crowd in its momentary need (Mk 8:2), and that he performs miracles simply to help and to heal those he encounters (Mk 1:40–42; 6:30–44; 8:1–9; 9:14–27; 10:46–52). Jesus is extremely good to his fellows. His proximity is, quite literally, experienced as salvation. His superlative goodness makes such a powerful impression on the crowd that it cries out: "He has done all things well; he even makes the deaf hear and the dumb speak" (Mk 7:37). Jesus' behavior is the incarnation of the Father's love. The reign of God becomes apparent in his words and deeds. In Jesus' solicitous love, God's concern for the salvation of the whole man, in all his dimensions, is revealed.

It is striking that Jesus reveals his solicitous love in service, indeed, by himself assuming the role of servant, and thereby becoming an example to his disciples: "Whoever would be great among you must be your servant, and whoever would be first among you must be slave of all. For the Son of Man also came not to be served but to serve, and to give his life as a ransom for many" (Mk 10:44–45). Within the Christian community, true greatness consists in servitude. This is true for the most important, the most prominent, the leaders and authorities (Mt 23:1–12; Lk 9:46–48; 11:42–52; 22:24–27). It is no less true for those who *aspire* to greatness before God: these must become slaves of all (Mk 9:33–37; 10:43–45; Mt 20:20–28).

Jesus' announcement of the *basileia,* and the demand for merciful love and solicitous servitude which this announcement implies is the core of a moral theology built upon a personalist foundation.

Human persons are free and responsible subjects: Jesus directs his message to us all, but, out of respect for our freedom, he appeals to our responsibility as moral subjects. At the same time, he defines the situation of the human person vis-à-vis God. John the Baptist threatened Israel with God's imminent judgment (Lk 3:7–9, 16–17; Mt 3:7–12). He pointed to the sinful condition of all, and summoned all to conversion as the only means to escape God's impending wrath. As a preacher of penitence, he was *primarily* concerned to announce God's imminent judgment of Israel as it then existed. Jesus announces *primarily* the good news of the *basileia*, of God's reign, through inexhaustible love. He does, however, endorse the Baptist's anthropological point of departure: he, too, maintains that we are all sinners and in need of conversion (Lk 13:1–5; 11:13, 31–32; Mt 7:11; 12:39). However, while John calls for conversion as a means to avert God's wrath, Jesus maintains that God's merciful love precedes all conversion, and that conversion itself consists primarily in opening oneself, in faith and trust, to God's mercy, and in conducting oneself, as far as ethics and religion are concerned, in accordance with the gifts of the *basileia*. Like the Baptist, Jesus, too, often speaks of the judgment. However, while John proposes God's judgment as *absolute,* Jesus announces it as the obverse of his message of the *basileia,* and, therefore, as *conditional:* the judgment cannot affect us if we open ourselves to receive the *basileia* in the fashion of children, and vigilantly and effectively work with the talents entrusted to us.

Human persons are essentially open to one another. It is self-evident that the demands of forgiving and solicitous love must have a constant share in our relations with one another, and that we must promote the well-being of our fellows, above all the weak and marginal, through loving service, after the example of Jesus.

Human persons are also essentially social beings, called to live in social groups. The demands of the *basileia* have a claim on this social dimension of our existence as well. For example, Jesus' remarks about love for one's enemies, and our attitude toward violence, are clearly relevant to the mutual relations which obtain between communities. P. Hoffmann has demonstrated this at length in his study, "*Tradition und Situation.*"[9] Our solicitous love in service of the other has a distinct social dimension. This is, of course, true for the greatest, those in authority: their authority is a service, and that service can only be effective where there is a sensitivity to the needs and requirements of the communities for which they are responsible, and for the demands of the concrete situations in which those communities find themselves. Those concrete situations determine the nature and the content of the service rendered. However, the solicitous love to which Jesus calls us all, requires of each of us, and of the Christian community as a whole, active social engagement. The Christian community cannot be an introverted group, turned in on itself and interested only in itself.

It must be an open group which is there for everyone, including those who do not wish to join it. Just as the *basileia*—God's reign through merciful and solicitous love—is intended for all, so must the community of Jesus see itself as bearing an obligation to all.

HISTORICITY OF THE HUMAN PERSON

Historicity is an essential aspect of the human person. It is characteristic of persons to be able to take notice of the past, the present, and the future, and to raise the question of their integral meaning. The person feels obliged to respond in the present to the occurrences of the past, and has the capacity for anticipating the future in thinking and acting. Personal historicity is not subordinated to history. Rather, it functions as its constant and is the indispensable condition enabling human persons to be capable of assimilating the variety of events, actions, and experiences in their historical identity. On the strength of our historicity we are involved in history, specifically as historically conscious subjects.

The life of every person is a history in which developmental psychology can distinguish successive stages. Each stage is characterized by special possibilities, and it is the task of the person throughout the history of his or her existence to continually seize these possibilities in order eventually to progress toward integrity and wisdom. Therefore, it is, for instance, important to begin with the meaning and possibilities of young persons morally to judge behavior within that stage of life.

What is more, the history of our personal life is defined along with the fact that, in our social milieu, we are involved in a cultural history. Culture can be considered from two points of view. First, there is subjective culture, the development of our possibilities as the all-around unfolding of our talents and capacities: scientific formation, physical culture, artistic refinement, moral progress, religious improvement, etc. Second, there is objective culture, the totality of goods and values brought about in the world: sciences, technology, works of art, language, political structures and institutions, international organizations, etc. Between these two, objective and subjective culture, there is a continuous reciprocity and interaction. Our subjective culture can only be realized thanks to the support of the already accomplished objective culture. For instance, we can only develop our artistic sensitivity in contact with works of art. Then, in virtue of our already acquired subjective culture, we are, in turn, able to more or less contribute to the improvement of the objective culture. The existing objective culture is the food for our subjective culture, which in turn is the source of an increasing objective culture. Because of this unceasing inter-action, culture is both a social and an historical reality.

The fact that we are historically conscious subjects is of tremendous significance for a personalist ethics. A first illustration of this can be found in our increasing awareness of the dignity of the human person as a moral subject. In reaction to the great evils of totalitarianism, the preamble to the *Universal Declaration of Human Rights* affirms its "faith in fundamental human rights, in the dignity and worth of the human person and in the equal rights of men and women." Similarly, Vatican II, which was characterized by a sense of history and was disposed to comprehend historical facts as constituting certain "signs of the times," sanctioned the validity of the development of the doctrine of religious freedom. That the contemporary heightening of personal consciousness had an influence upon this concern is apparent from the first sentences of the *Declaration on Religious Freedom:*

A sense of the dignity of the human person has been impressing itself more and more deeply on the consciousness of contemporary man. And the demand is increasingly made that men should act on their own judgment, enjoying and making use of a responsible freedom, not driven by coercion but motivated by a sense of duty.

Second, historical development also affects the person as a subject in corporeality. Suffice it to mention the accelerating evolution of medical science and technology which raises ever new problems in bioethics. Third, interpersonal relationships evolve in the course of history: marriage, for instance, was for centuries considered as an institution primordially ordained to procreation. *Gaudium et Spes,* 48, however, defines marriage as "an intimate partnership of life and of conjugal love"; and sexual intercourse, formerly only permitted for the sake of procreation, is proposed in *Gaudium et Spes,* 49, as an essentially relational reality. Fourth, historical development mostly influences human persons as social beings, called upon to live in communities. To understand the full meaning of the social dimension of human persons today, we must not lose sight of the fact that many diverse and pluralistic societies have become part of a universal community in which solidarity, peaceableness, and collaboration are a question of survival.

Gaudium et Spes, 5, asserts:

The course of history itself is accelerating so rapidly that the individual can hardly follow it. The destiny of the human community is being unified and is no longer a matter of several different histories. Humanity is passing from a static to a more dynamic and evolutionary conception of the world order. Thus, a vast new complex of problems has come to birth, which call for new analyses and syntheses.[10]

Historical development does not always entail progress. It can happen that true values which were recognized in the past are overlooked or underestimated in the present. Therefore, a personalist ethics demands a critical attitude. New accomplishments should not be gratuitously accepted because they are new. Neither should we rashly reject them.

History testifies to many mistakes made by moral theologians, and even by the magisterium, that subsequently had to be admitted, or at the very least ignored. Sometimes we too quickly condemned something that was new without ever allowing for the time and the opportunity to verify —even by trial and error—whether or not new possibilities could lead to the real promotion of the human person. In this respect, *Gaudium et Spes,* 16, offers a valuable rule: "In fidelity to conscience, Christians are joined with the rest of men in the search for truth, and for the genuine solution to the numerous problems which arise in the life of individuals and from social relationships."

Because of historical development, an ethics of responsibility based on a personalist foundation must be a dynamic one. In virtue of the progress of science and technology, continuously new possibilities are opened for our activity. It is the task of ethics to inquire as to how these growing possibilities might best be put at the service of the human person, adequately considered. Throughout the course of history, new values have also been elaborated. A dynamic ethics has to examine how the developing experience of values is to enrich our activity. In a dynamic ethics, that which promotes human persons develops into a moral obligation insofar as it becomes possible.

THE PERSON'S ORIGINALITY

All human persons are fundamentally equal, but at the same time each is an originality, a unique subject.

We encounter each other on the same human level. In our dialogue with other persons we become aware of the fact that in knowing, feeling, and striving, we are interested in the same values and realities. All that is human concerns us (Terentius: *homo sum, humani nihil a me alienum puto*). It is even possible for us to understand foreign cultures and to begin to decipher the data from the most remote human past. Our fundamental equality explains why the fundamental moral demands are universalizable.

But within the framework and on the basis of this fundamental equality, each person is simultaneously a unique subject. This finds expression when our conversation becomes a discussion. In a real discussion, as equals we are interested in the same issues, but at the same time we experience that we are different in our ways of thinking, feeling, and evaluating with respect to the same object. Psychology substantiates the observation that everyone has his or her own temperament, personal capacities, individual tendencies, and, in interaction with the social and cultural environment, develops into an original personality with a singular, unique character.

If subjective culture is defined as the all-around development of the person's talents and capacities, the concrete expression of that subjective culture will bear the stamp of every person's uniqueness or originality. This implies as well that the person is irreplaceable, both in the expression of subjective culture and in the realization of the contribution this expression makes to the development of objective culture. In order to accomplish this task, each person requires an appropriate access to the patrimony of goods and values that we refer to as objective culture. To make that possible, nurture must take account of the uniqueness of children, and education should be as extensive and differentiated as possible, so that each can develop his or her personal talents and capacities.

The unfolding of each and every originality is a requirement for the richness and fruitfulness of our common social life. Our participation in social groups at all levels must seek to promote the goods and values of the objective culture and to make them available to the subjective culture of every member of society. A necessary condition for the accomplishment of that goal is the respect for the fundamental equality of each person, by virtue of which each one of us will have an interest in the totality of the same cultural values. But the fruitfulness of our loving and working together depends upon the originality of each individual person who participates in the project of social living. The personal uniqueness of each individual serves to realize the necessary diversity of professions, specialties, accomplishments, and works that contribute to the richness and fecundity of social collaboration.

Notes

1. *Gaudium et Spes,* 51. *Schema Constitutionis Pastoralis de Ecclesia in mundo huius temporis. Expensio Modorum Partis Secundae* (Vatican: Polyglot,

1965) 37, answer to *modi* 104: "*ex personae eiusdemaque actuum natura desumptis;* quibus verbis asseritur etiam actus diiudicandos esse non secundum aspectum merum biologicum, sed quatenus illi ad personam humanam integre et adaequate considerandam pertinent. Agitur de principio generali."

2. "Artificial Insemination: Ethical Considerations" (*Louvain Studies* 8 (1980) 3–29. In this article I more amply developed the dimensions of the human person and indicated where they are mentioned in the conciliar documents, especially in *Gaudium et Spes*.

3. Vatican Congregation for the Doctrine of the Faith, "Declaration on Euthanasia," May 5, 1980, *Origins* 10 (1980) 154–157, at 156.

4. F. Hürth, S.J., "La fécondation artificielle. Sa valeur morale et juridique," *Nouvelle revue théologique* 68 (1946) 402–426.

5. Ibid. 415.

6. Ibid. 416.

7. *Gaudium et Spes* is the first official document that explicitly recognizes mutually shared joy in marital intercourse as a positive value; it was the lay members of the commission who insistently requested the mention of this value. See the *Expensio modorum,* p. 26, answer to *modus* 57: "*Haec sententia expresse et instanter a laicis petita fuit.*"

8. I was drawn to this approach by the following exegetical works in particular: Paul Hoffmann, Volker Eid, *Jesus von Nazareth und eine christliche Moral* (Freiburg: Herder, 1975); Rudolf Schnackenburg, ed., *Die Bergpredigt: Utopische Vision oder Handlungsanweisung?* (Düsseldorf: Patmos, 1982); Wolfgang Schrage, *Ethik des Neuen Testaments* (Göttingen, Vandenhoeck und Ruprecht, 1982); Jan Lambrecht, *Maar ik zeg u: De programmatische rede van Jezus* (Leuven: Acco, 1983); Heinz Schürmann, *Gottes Reich—Jesu Geschick* (Freiburg: Herder, 1983); Helmut Merklein, *Jesu Botschaft von der Gottesherrschaft: Eine Skizze* (Stuttgart: Verlag Katholischer Bibelwerk, 1983); Helmut Merklein, *Die Gottesherrschaft als Handlungsprinzip: Untersuchung zur Ethik Jesu* (Würzburg: Echter Verlag, 3° Auflage, 1984); Paul Hoffmann, "Tradition und Situation: Zur 'Verbindlichkeit' des Gebots der Feindesliebe in der synoptischen überlieferung und in der gegenwärtigen Friedensdiskussion," in Karl Kertlege, ed., *Ethik im Neuen Testament* (Freiburg: Herder, 1984) 50–118.

9. Paul Hoffmann, "Tradition und Situation: Zur 'Verbindlichkeit' des Gebots der Feindesliebe in der synoptischen überlieferung und in der gegenwärtigen Friedensdiskussion," in Karl Kertlege, ed., *Ethik im Neuen Testament* (Freiburg: Herder, 1984) 50–118.

10. *Ipsa historia tam rapido cursu acceleratur ut singuli eam vix prosequi valeant. Consortionis humanae sors una efficitur et non amplius inter varias velut historias dispergitur. Ita genus humanum a notione magis statica ordinis rerum ad notionem magis dynamicam atque evolutivam transit, unde quam maxima nascitur problematum nova complexio, quae ad novas analyses et syntheses provocat* (translation is my own).

6

Conscience and Conscientious Fidelity

Josef Fuchs, S.J.

A considerable measure of discussion has taken place within the Catholic Church and within its moral theology in recent years concerning the concept of conscience. Some fear a current trend to over-evaluation of conscience as a "kind of apotheosis of subjectivity," "as subjectivity elevated to the ultimate criterion" against which there is no "appeal to authority (as one says)."[1] On the other hand, others denounce an under-evaluation of conscience on the part of certain authorities; for in reality conscience is not sheer subjectivity, but reflects on all objectively available facts and discoverable evaluations, striving responsibly to reach the conclusion of the ethical discourse which has been set in motion and thus to take a responsible decision; and this decision is the ultimate authority, justified subjectively and objectively, for the human person and Christian who acts responsibly.[2]

The present discussion of the question of the ethical significance of conscience is, however, less concerned with fundamental and general issues. Rather, there is a one-sided interest which concentrates in a very high degree on the question of the significance of conscience in the face of authentic (= official, but not infallible) decisions or declarations of the church's magisterium—which may take the form of declarations (or occasional statements) of the pope, of the Congregation for the Doctrine of the Faith (or other Vatican bodies), of the bishops (or episcopal conferences), or of some theologians who are gaining prominence for themselves. At the moment, this discussion concerns above all questions of moral theology (and thus of theological ethics).

The problem of the over-evaluation of conscience is raised above all by official representatives of the church's magisterium and by theologians who see themselves as bound in a particularly close fashion to this magisterium. The problem of the under-evaluation of conscience is seen especially by many representatives of Catholic theology and by priests and laypeople who sense that the traditional teaching on the significance of conscience (*in concreto* and in general) is being called into question to an excessive degree.

The title of this essay suggests that my interest is not in provoking a confrontation—magisterium *or* conscience—but above all in clearing up the concept of conscience and thus in laying the foundations of a solution that pays heed to objective reality and is acceptable to both sides of the discussion.

The contributions to the discussion (including those of the magisterium) which give rise to the suspicion that they are unfair to the traditional concept of conscience ought to be documented here precisely, and as far as possible quoted literally; this would certainly be easy to do. But it is not only texts of the magisterium that come into question here, but equally texts by theologians who follow a certain line, as well as texts by high authorities in the Catholic Church. It seems therefore less appropriate to quote them here precisely and individually in each case.[3]

VARIOUS CONCEPTS OF CONSCIENCE

Even within the recent discussion about conscience, it is striking that not only is the concept of conscience frequently insufficiently clarified, but various concepts of conscience are being employed simultaneously.

We frequently find the traditional concept of conscience as the "voice of God"—a concept that belongs to the religious sphere, and is even somewhat mystical. It is interesting that here no problem is felt to lie in the (mostly) conceded experience of the possibility of what is called an erroneous conscience, nor in the fact that even atheists and agnostics, despite their lack of faith in God, are admitted to have an experience of conscience. Especially since the Second Vatican Council (*Gaudium et Spes* 16), it is more common to employ the description of conscience as a *sacrarium* in which we find ourselves responsibly *solus cum solo* (alone with him alone) before God; this description is understood above all (though certainly not exclusively) in a Christian and religious sense. Here too, however, the question is not posed whether this holds true of agnostics and atheists, who are likewise held to have a conscience by the very fact of being human persons. The two statements that conscience is the voice of God in the human person (*solus cum solo*) and thus has absolute validity requiring obedience, and that experience shows that conscience can also err, are often placed alongside each other without any explanation. The dignity of an ultimate authority is attributed to conscience in the fullness of its situation, to which only it can have access as the voice of

God; nevertheless, the will of God, ethical norms and statements of the church's magisterium, as objective realities, have often an authority superior to that of conscience, an authority which has the function of a check on the objective competence and significance of the insight given by the conscience of the individual into his or her situation. In general, there is scarcely any attempt to find a satisfactory solution to this problematic.

There exists, however, also an understanding of conscience which is not specifically Christian or religious, *first* as the experience and insight into the objective and absolute ethical requirement which always exists *a priori* in the human person, an insight which cannot be rejected; and *then* conscience as only "organ" (and not "oracle"). There are various ways of understanding conscience as organ; for some, conscience is understood as the organ which has the responsibility to seek and find autonomously (for the believer: in the light of faith) the correct norms and concrete solutions for the decisions of life in all its multiplicity, and which takes these decisions (cf. Spaemann); for others, the character as organ is only the responsible readiness to "listen" to the word of conscience without any "creativity" of one's own and thus in a purely perceptive sense, i.e. to accept this word in a basically passive and humble way (cf. Laun), in order to be able to obey it—and thus, ultimately, to be able to obey God (thus Caffarra).

There is unanimity in rejecting an understanding of conscience as a pure super-ego or as a purely biological instinct (behavioral research), and equally as the exclusive result of sociological facts and developments, or as the product of education alone. In general, a one-sided response to such proposals—although without any noticeable attention to the enormous significance they have for the formation of the conscience—is recourse to the idea that the ethical order which comes from God's wisdom is written in the heart and the nature of the human person and of his or her personal being (whatever one understands by this). Almost without exception, the significance of faith in God and of the acceptance of the Judeo-Christian revelation is held to have the greatest importance for a deeper understanding of the phenomenon of conscience.

It is often unclear which of the various functions of conscience is intended in these individual affirmations: its deepest source (the "fundamental" conscience), its care for the ethical goodness of the person and for the moral rightness of what the person does and how he or she behaves, or the contents of the instruction given by conscience in the moment of decision ("situational" conscience), or conscience in the sense of ethical knowledge which precedes the situational conscience by indicating first and general ethical principles and more concrete ethical norms. Presumably this question is seldom considered precisely; but this means that it can remain an open question whether particular statements are to be understood of the entire realm of the functions of conscience, or only of determined functions—and which these are.

CONSCIENCE AS THE "VOICE OF GOD"

What we call, or can call, conscience expresses itself in various ways, in accordance with what has been said above. We shall now consider this in greater detail.

Fundamental Conscience. The basis of everything is the fundamental experience which alone makes it possible to talk at all about morality and ethics: viz. the experience that we—as human persons who have only a "share" in absolute personal freedom—are moral beings, i.e. we are a freedom which is oriented *absolutely* not to arbitrariness, but to what is *objectively* good and right. One can call this "the voice of God," as is often done, but not in the sense of an experience somehow "infused" by the creator and thus not accomplished in a personal manner. For we are speaking of a personal self-understanding that has been made possible in the created human person as truly his or her own—even if this is present often only in a stage of knowledge and acceptance that is as yet unreflected upon. Still, this can be taken up into the explicit intellectual reflection, even if it perhaps cannot forcibly demonstrate its correctness in such reflection. Thus absoluteness and objectivity (nonarbitrariness) always stand *a priori* in conscious acceptance as the criterion *before* (or, better, *in*) everything that has to do with morality and conscience. There are, of course, extremely various attempts in the various philosophies, world-views, ideologies and religions to give a theoretical *explanation* of this phenomenon of conscience. The Catholic theological explanation points fundamentally to the character of the human person as created by God in God's own image—in intellect and freedom. But it also knows that the Holy Spirit of God and the word of revelation can be, and are, already at work in this fundamental experience.

The basic experience of the "fundamental conscience" immediately allows us to understand two things. First, the personal human being who is aware of his own being in the fundamental conscience must seek in the free development of his life to act in accordance with what the fundamental conscience makes him experience. Earlier, this was called "being good"; today it is customary to term this more precisely the *ethical goodness of the person as such.* To this goodness there belongs also the inner readiness to behave rightly in the personal structuring of one's life and of the world, i.e. to take account, in doing this, of the reality that exists.[4] It is for this reason that the distinction is made today between the ethical goodness of the person—morality in the truest sense of the word —and *the ethical rightness of action/behavior.* Knowledge of the goodness of the person and of the rightness of the action/behavior ought to coincide, but on occasions they fall apart because of the possibility of error about what is ethically right. Both in the past and in the present (and also within the discussion which we are considering here), the rightness of behavior is still often characterized *de facto* terminologically as the "good." The significance of the distinction between the "good" as the ethical *goodness* of the person and as the ethical *rightness* of the action/ behavior in the judgment of conscience is already seen in the fact that the evaluation of the personal ethical goodness is *infallible,* while the evaluation of the ethically right action/behavior remains exposed to the possibility of *error.* Therefore only the former—not the latter, or at least not in the same sense—may be called the "voice of God," i.e. may be derived directly from God through the creation of the human person who is God's image.

The formulation that conscience—however one understands this— is the place where the human person is illuminated by a light which comes, not from his or her own reason (since this is created and always fallible), but from the wisdom of God himself, in whom everything is created, must accordingly be too simple. It cannot stand up to an objective analysis, nor can it prove helpful for the vocabulary of Christian believers.

Situational Conscience. In neo-Thomist theology, as well as in the moral theology of the church's magisterium, it has been generally less common to speak of the function of conscience as fundamental conscience, and rather to speak of it as the ultimate interior ethical "judgment" of the person who makes a decision for action or conduct. This judgment is *simultaneous* with the ethical decision—as its "light"; its priority over the personal decision is thus not to be understood chronologically, but logically. Conscience, understood in this way, is often called the "situational conscience" today, or commonly even simply "the conscience." In this concrete experience of a "judgment" of conscience, the fundamental conscience of the person who makes the decision is, of course, always present as the ultimate origin of the judgment. This requires the responsible formation of this judgment of conscience—taking into account all available helps and personal circumstances—and the decision in favor of what a responsible judgment of conscience *takes* to be what is objectively correct. If this is often called the "voice of God," then it is clear that this is only partly correct: the word of the fundamental conscience contained therein—the command to seek responsibly for what is objectively correct and to decide in favor of this—is infallible and in this sense "the voice of God." This is not necessarily true of the contents of the ethical judgment of the situational conscience for the concrete act/behavior, which could also allow or require something that is incorrect, and therefore could not be called the "voice of God" in the same sense.

Principles and Norms. Naturally, it is not possible to deduce the contents of the behavioral directive of the situational conscience from the experience-insight of the fundamental conscience, for between these two lies the immeasurable width of human, wordly and historical reality on which the human person (including the one who believes) reflects when he is called to shape it—and always does so in the entire context of the human and ecclesiastical society in which he lives—in order to discover how, as a human person and as a Christian, he has to give it the correct form. This means that he or she does not begin to reflect only in the moment in which the situational conscience demands that she make a concrete decision, i.e. he or she is always already engaged in the search for ethical self-understanding and in the attempt to orientate himself or herself to the near and the far future, and always under the experience-insight and the requirement made upon him or her by the fundamental conscience. This is why it is often (though not always) and correctly said that this seeking and finding takes place "in conscience"—thus, e.g., the Second Vatican Council (*Dignitatis Humanae* 3; cf. *Gaudium et Spes* 16)—while it is otherwise customary to attribute the recognition of ethical principles and norms to the practical reason. Thus the human person arrives at very concrete ethical norms which can provide him or her with an enormous and decisive help for the formation of the situational conscience. The concrete interpretation, evaluation and ethical judgment of the wide human world is thus possible for the personal human being—always in the manner that is proper to him or her—but without the guarantee of infallibility, i.e. not "simply" as the voice of God.

Thomas Aquinas understood the fundamental conscience (syntheresis) in a manner different from that set out here: as the certain and infallible insight into a small kernel of ethical first principles.[5] *De facto,* principles such as "doing what is good," "not behaving 'arbitrarily' toward one's neighbor," etc. are initial formulations of the fundamental conscience and just as much infallible (and hence the voice of God) as this. It follows that the principles that one must not behave "arbitrarily" in the realm of the construction of one's life and in interpersonal and societal relationships (justice, fairness, sexuality, etc.) are tautological and therefore infallibly true, and in this sense the "voice of God." But it is not possible to state with equal clarity, cogency and infallibility what such principles as ethical norms intend to say about *concrete behavior* in the wide human world. And it is a yet broader question what such concretizing norms can mean in the situation of the person who—externally and internally—is truly only himself or herself: in the last analysis, their solution can be sought and found only *"solus cum solo"*—but the contents of this solution are not unambiguously the "voice of God."

SUBJECTIVITY AND OBJECTIVITY

As fundamental conscience, conscience is subjectivity which is orientated absolutely and infallibly to ethical objectivity. It follows that when a discussion takes place today about too much subjectivity or too much objectivity, this cannot refer to the fundamental conscience, but rather to what is generally characterized simply as "conscience"—chiefly the "situational conscience," but also the insight-experience vis-à-vis concrete ethical norms.

Subjectivity. Romans 2:14ff states that Gentiles too—at least in part —*de facto* live the contents of the ethical law of the Old Testament, which was understood as given by God; thus they show that although they do not have the (Old Testament) law, they are an ethical law "for themselves," i.e. on the basis of an inner act of understanding, and that this ethical law is in this sense "written on their heart." In this context, Paul uses the Greek word "conscience" alongside the Hebrew word "heart." Thereby it is clear that he does not mean that the Gentiles—in the multiplicity of their ethical ideas—have received a "partial," passive "infusion" of ethical knowledge. He means that the Gentiles (i.e. all human persons) have been created with the capacity to arrive as subject at the concrete and objectively correct knowledge of morality, both prior to the situational conscience and also in the exercise of the situational conscience itself. It is quite clear that Paul intends an "interiority" of the "conscience"-"heart."

In its Declaration on Religious Freedom, the Second Vatican Council indicated that the human person is able to discover the objective ethical order by his or her own active search, and that he or she should do so, in order to arrive in this way at a true judgment of *conscience* (*Dignitatis Humanae* 3). In the *Pastoral Constitution on the Church in the Modern World,* the same council dedicated a whole paragraph to conscience (*Gaudium et Spes* 16), strongly emphasizing the interiority and the created subjectivity of conscience, which however shows itself to be the locus of the experience of an absolute and objective requirement, i.e. one that is not "given" by conscience itself. Thus the human person knows about the essential obligation which the ethical conscience lays upon him or her from within the self. The ethical requirement in question here is not only the word from the fundamental conscience: the council, taking up the statement in Romans 2:15, formulates thus: ". . . the human person has a law which has been inscribed by God on his heart. . . . In conscience, one recognizes in a marvelous way that law which is fulfilled in love for God and for one's neighbor." The fact that this is written on the heart means therefore here too the possibility that the human person can "recognise" ethical order with objective correctness in conscience. This becomes even clearer when the text goes on to speak of searching (in conscience) "for truth" and of the "solution, in keeping with truth, of all the many moral problems that arise both in the life of the individual and in living together in society." Here it is a question of seeking and finding "objective norms of morality"; but this seeking and finding, we are told, does not exclude an inculpable error, since the translation of the fundamental conscience and of the dignity of the human person which has its basis in this fundamental conscience into objectively correct norms of behavior, and the translation of the correct contents of the situational conscience, do not take place automatically or through a purely logical deduction. There is always a risk attached to norm-giving ethical objectivity, even in conscience (and even in the conscience of the believer: cf. *Gaudium et Spes* 43 and 33), for the fact of the search for the objective norm does not of itself mean that this objective norm already exists "somewhere" (but where—other than in God himself?) waiting to be found by us, and correspondingly (since it already exists) needs only to be sought and found.

The same paragraph of the conciliar constitution states: "Conscience is the hidden center and sanctuary in the human person, where he is alone with God whose voice can be heard in this, his most interior place"—words that are taken from a radio message of Pope Pius XII (March 23, 1952). Does this mean that there is a *"solus cum solo"* in conscience, especially in the situational conscience, in which one discovers the divine commandment in his holy presence and hears his commanding "voice" which itself gives the sought-for answer to the human person who seeks and is required to act—so that all one would have to do further would be to obey? But it is possible for an erroneous conscience to exist. There is therefore an obligation to lay down the path to the correct solution "creatively" in a responsible search (and attempt) that takes into consideration all the available realities, knowledge and known evaluations (including those of the ecclesial people of God and of the church's magisterium), and finally to be equally responsible in breaking off this process of seeking once it has been "sufficient," thus arriving at genuine conviction.[6] Such a conviction would not contain the direct voice of the God who was present, a voice that one need only "hear" perceptively and then obey; rather, it would be the last word of the situational conscience which reflected upon its own reality, containing not the infallible voice of God but the only attempt possible for a human person to give a concrete "body" to the absolute requirement of the fundamental conscience. This creative attempt would not be a subjectivist *"sola cum seipsa"* (alone with *itself*) on the part of the conscience (as has been said), but an active and living *"solus cum solo,"* i.e. alone with the creator who is present through and in the fundamental conscience and urges one to make one's own search for what is correct. The outcome would not be the *ipsissimum verbum* of God, but nevertheless would be what God requires as the only possible "objectivity" in the "sanctuary" of the conscience of his human image—i.e. as a created share (and hence only a share by participation) in his eternal wisdom, in his "eternal law," and, precisely for this reason, something that demands unconditional obedience. As has been said already above, with R. Spaemann: conscience is no oracle, but an organ that actively sketches out projects and thus seeks what is right.

Objectivity. Because of his constant awareness of the fundamental conscience, the personal human being seeks to discover in conscience, as an active organ, how he or she must deal with a given human reality if he or she is to be ethically "good." In order to reach an objectively justified judgment, one must have sufficient knowledge both of the nature of the human person and of the nature of the given reality which is to be lived in a personal manner. Today's humanity knows much more about the latter, however, than did its ancestors; one must naturally pay the proper attention to this knowledge in the search for the ultimate word of the situational conscience.

The realities of the human person and of one's human world are not meaningless, purely "material" realities which one seeks to develop further somehow or other in a "material" manner; on the contrary, this reality, as the creation maintained in being by God, is the expression of spirit and of meaning, and bears spirit and meaning in itself also in the form in which it lies before us today thanks to a long development and to the interventions through which the human person has given it form. To live this and make use of it is always an activity oriented to a near or a far future, but this is always on the basis of what the reality is now—at the point of departure, and hence in the very act of decision—*as* reality, and thus as spirit and meaning, in the presence of the creator God who always maintains it in being. This does not only involve the question of what the given reality means purely "in itself" and materially considered—for what can reality genuinely say about itself without any relationship to the human person? It involves the question of the spirit and meaning contained in this reality in the world of human persons, in human society, for particular human relationships and also for the individual in his or her own particularity.

To undertake this act of understanding through interpretation, taking into due account ethical principles, evaluations and norms that have already been discovered or that lie at hand, in order to arrive at a justifiable ethical judgment about a decision concerning behavior and activity that must be taken now, oriented toward the near or the far future: this is the work of the personal subject in conscience with the aim of finding a creative and objectively justified word in the situational conscience. This is anything but a pure "subjectivity" that would be improper for an organ; but it is also anything but a pure listening to an "objective" oracle in conscience.

FIDELITY TO CONSCIENCE

If one seeks, in keeping with the available possibilities, to discover in conscience the objectively correct directive for ethical behavior, one will be evaluated by one's fundamental conscience as "good" in the sense of personal morality. Such a person does not entrust himself to any arbitrary subjectivism. This is also the case with the inculpably erroneous conscience: the one who errs inculpably holds an objective error to be what is objectively correct, so that he is not ethically bad despite his incorrect judgment and his fidelity in conduct to this judgment (cf. Second Vatican Council, *Gaudium et Spes* 16). If one avoids this suggested distinction between "good" and "correct," but still wishes to avoid saying that one who does what is incorrect out of error is simultaneously good and not good, then one would have to follow Thomas Aquinas in the formulation that his error "excuses" him with regard to his "not good" behavior, but—because of the terminological equation of "good" and "correct"—one cannot simply call him "good."

The Contemporary Discussion. Matters are seen somewhat differently in the contemporary discussion, where the complaint is made that in today's society (including the society of the church) and even in moral theology there is often an appeal on one's own behalf and on behalf of others to conscience—against "the commandment of God," against "objective" moral norms, against the ethical natural law. This complaint is, however, justified only if the appeal to conscience is made against an ethical order that is named objective, either in an arbitrary manner or in irresponsible frivolity (cf. Vatican II, *Gaudium et Spes* 16).

This complaint raises a certain difficulty when it presupposes that God's commandment, the ethical norms and the solutions of the ethical natural law are somehow and somewhere objectively "present." But since God himself has not given them to us directly (we shall speak later about moral norms in the church), such ethical normative statements in human society exist only thanks to human ethical knowledge "in conscience." They are neither "invented" nor "created," but experienced and recognized "creatively"—although in the (merely) created human participation in God's own wisdom. To hold *absolutely* that one must adopt them simply because they express what it is customary to say in our society would be to fall victim to the logical error of deducing an ethical "ought" from an "is." Nevertheless, ethical prudence demands that one should not reject an ethical ordinance that is widely accepted or prescribed by a high authority, but that one should have great openness and should attempt to understand it or indeed to accept it, since it can contain great experience and lofty wisdom—even if it is not infallible.

On the other hand, the adoption of ethical norms which are widely accepted in society or prescribed by an authority is something that always takes place within personal responsibility.[7] In the same way, the rejection of an ethical norm or ordinance comes under personal responsibility. It follows that the adoption or rejection of ethical claims or prohibitions always takes place via the responsible, decision-making function of the personal conscience. To close one's mind against ethical reasonings proposed by others, and also by authorities, can just as well be a sign of frivolous or idiosyncratic arbitrariness, as of an honest and great sense of responsibility on the part of conscience;[8] thus it is not necessarily the sign of disobedience to the God who is represented as the authority behind the moral ordinance that is in question, but can also be the sign of a conscience with a high awareness of its responsibility.

The formulation that ultimately only the individual—in his or her conscience—can know and decide what he or she is to do is thus not simply false. Although many things and many persons may advise him or her and seek to persuade him or her away from his or her conviction, their advice must pass through the responsible judgment made by the conscience of the individual, in order to be capable of adoption or rejection by him or her in prudent responsibility. The individual can err, but so can those who advise him or her. Has he or she no *criterion,* in order to be able to distinguish unambiguously between truth and error in conscience? If this were so, it would not be possible for an erroneous conscience to exist (nor, parallel to this, erroneous advice)—unless infallible authorities exist. R. Spaemann goes beyond the problem of such a criterion to ask whether there is any *indication of the genuineness* of the decision of conscience, and answers: yes, "the willingness of the one concerned to pay the price of an unpleasant alternative."[9] Is such an indication anything more than the great exception?

Conscience and Fidelity to the Church's Magisterium. For the believing Catholic, a moral utterance of the church's magisterium is an extremely significant element that must be taken into consideration in the responsible formation of conscience. Within today's discussion, the formulation that the church's magisterium was founded for the sake of the illumination of conscience is a statement that, while not simply false, is deliberately chosen *ad hoc* and is thus one-sided; for the church's magisterium functions above all in preserving and defending the word of God which has been deposited in the church (the foundation of the faith), both in questions of faith and in questions of morals. The church's magisterium can also render this service in an infallible manner to the people of God. The believing Catholic will give a corresponding utterance a decisive role in the formation of his or her conscience.

But this protected area within which infallibility operates does not include in the same way the many concrete ethical questions of natural law dealing with our activity in the world, questions that can have significance in the formation of conscience. Because of this significance, the magisterium can certainly seek to teach the believing people of God in an official manner about such concrete ethical truths (even if they are not revealed at the same time), lest the people of God too easily fall into the danger of giving an erroneous expression to the Christian faith in the shaping of earthly realities. But the magisterium does not deduce these truths from the *faith:* it knows them from the *practical reason* which is enlightened by faith about the human person and about his or her God. Such truths must therefore lie outside the realm of infallibility. But since such ethical teaching directives have come into being in the people of God which is filled by the Holy Spirit, and have been proposed by the office-bearers who are called to lead this people and therefore have the special assistance of the Spirit, they have a great significance in the church's fellowship, and the spirit of fidelity which is required in the church obliges one to be receptive to them in the internal discourse that is the formation of conscience, and to attempt to give them a certain preference over against other considerations—even one's own—that arise; this is required by the responsible conscience itself. An aspect of the full fidelity of those who belong to the people of God in the church is that they bear witness to such concrete ethical statements.

This, at least, is how matters stand usually; this restriction is necessary because conscience also bears the responsibility—coming from the fundamental conscience—not to accept anything into itself, if the necessary discourse, carried out with sufficient competence (and thus not a disobedient discourse) within the context of the church's fellowship, shows that there are very serious arguments against it which cannot be overcome even with the greatest measure of personal openness. The dilemma "conscience *or* magisterium," which one hears frequently, does not exist. There exists only living fidelity in the church as the hierarchically ordered people of God, but this in turn cannot exist without the responsible conscience of those who bear the fidelity, for it is only via the responsibly formed conscience that the magisterium can achieve significance in the life of the person. This is Catholic tradition; in normal circumstances, it ought not to create any problem. It would be necessary to repeat here much of what was said above about fidelity to conscience. However, Thomas Aquinas indicates (in opposition to his revered Master Peter Lombard) a hard extreme situation, which should not be passed over in silence here: an ecclesiastical decision which is evaluated in conscience as certainly unacceptable, but is proclaimed under the threat of excommunication, may not under any circumstances be followed, even if this means that one must die excommunicated[10]—this would be the indication of a genuine decision of conscience, of which R. Spaemann spoke.

But even such decisions of conscience must be seen as lying within the sphere of responsible fidelity to the church's magisterium, for one is glad to take hold of the helping hand that is offered, and one seeks even in a grave case of doubt to discover responsibly how far this offer can be a genuine help for the correct shaping of the concrete world of the human person by a Christian in a particular question or in a particular case. The individual holds himself or herself under certain circumstances to be justified or even obliged in conscience to make the contribution to the church fellowship, which wishes to help those in difficulties, of a further attempt at help which he or she considers to be correct, since it is this church fellowship that one wishes to follow.

The question whether such an attempt at help in the people of God may or should also be made in public raises problems which go beyond the limits of the question posed in this essay. But we may say that here too the indication given above by R. Spaemann is appropriate if we wish to know whether such an attempt is derived from genuine concern in conscience: Is the person in question willing "to pay the price of an unpleasant alternative"? It would also be necessary to ask a further question, after the question of taking up a public stance: What freedom do the moral theologians have in scholarly discussion? Here it would perhaps be necessary to distinguish between the moral theologians who work without the commission of the church, and those who teach and research in the name of the church's magisterium;[11] research, however, entails also evidence of reflection and discussion—which in turn is open to fidelity.

Fidelity always signifies the encounter and cooperation of two partners: i.e. of the individual, and of the people of God together with its official representatives. Normally speaking, fidelity in the church's fellowship, which is filled with the Spirit, ought to be a spiritual necessity which is carried out in thankfulness. The magisterium in the church must make such a view of things possible by offering a service that is official help, rather than by behaving in an authoritarian way—although this does not mean that its utterances would be the product of complete arbitrariness—and this would be a service of the loving fellowship of the church, working through invitation (an invitation that is constantly repeated) rather than as an official ecclesiastical imposition that demands obedience; and certainly not in the form of a commandment apparently proceeding directly from God (and not only a commandment understood as such in the church because of considerations of natural law), such that even in the case of grave difficulties a responsible discourse in conscience would necessarily *ipso facto* be disobedience. And since the concrete norms of conduct are derived from practical reason illuminated by faith, rather than from the Christian faith itself (and hence can be universalized for all human persons, in principle), the magisterium in its invitation to fidelity will attempt cautiously and persuasively to make it clear to those who are basically willing to follow that such norms are based, not only on a theologically unjustifiable use of scripture, nor on a particular distorting ideology, nor on a naturalistic fallacy, nor on an excessively juridical understanding of the magisterium (which would say, for example, that one must always follow the teaching of one's own bishop, and not the teaching of another bishop, which may in particular circumstances be different),[12] but on reasons that are as a whole generally plausible and capable of being communicated to others.

It is clear that certain pre-conditions in both partners must be met if fidelity in conscience to the magisterium is to be possible. Some years ago, the American moral theologian Val J. Peter pointed in this context to Thomas' teaching about *pietas*.[13] *Pietas* is the virtue that undergirds justice, and is owed to the church as (one's own) "mother," and thereby to the church's magisterium. But the "mother" church and her magisterium likewise owe *pietas* to those who follow them. According to Yves Congar, *pietas* implies a *ius communionis*—and thereby not only a common seeking (which may not always agree at each point in time), but occasionally also a serious struggle. But this will be always a matter of *pietas* and *communio*.

RICHARD A. McCORMICK

For many years, Richard A. McCormick has lived the problematic of conscience and magisterium and discussed this privately and in public, both within the society of moral theologians and in his relationships with the official church, and he has been passionately involved in this. Those who have followed his writings, above all his "Notes on Moral Theology" which have been published for many years, have noted how this has come in a slow crescendo to be a central issue.

This began with McCormick's first reflections on the justification of concrete ethical norms of conduct. P. Knauer's 1965 study on the principle of an action with double effect as the basis of practical morality had initially provoked him to contradict this, but a process of changing his mind was begun by further discussions on this issue and by further essays in moral theology which pointed more or less in the direction indicated by Knauer. McCormick slowly became one of the strongest defenders of what is called today (above all in the United States) proportionalism. In this spirit he analyzed ethical norms of conduct and tested the soundness of the reasons adduced for them. For him, as for many other moral theologians, the encyclical *Humanae Vitae* (1968) had a catalytic effect.

McCormick believed that he saw more and more clearly the true purpose of negative norms of conduct: to help avoid as much as possible something evil in the human construction of the world and of the life of humanity. This meant that the evil to be avoided was recognized to be a nonmoral evil; it would be a *moral* evil to carry out such an evil without an *adequate* reason, and this would affect personal ethical goodness and thus salvation in Jesus Christ. This raises another thematic: How far do the formulations of negative ethical norms have validity? Is their validity in every case so absolute, without exceptions, as their habitual formulation seems to indicate? The analysis which was offered above must deny this claim.

However, when the church's magisterium condemns particular concrete norms of conduct, it customarily makes its formulations precisely in this way: this posed for McCormick the question of his attitude to such formulations of the magisterium. In the case of individual problems which seemed to him to permit no other intellectually defensible solution than a norm different from the norm upheld by the church's authority, he took up his position on the side of theological freedom. He believed that he was permitted and obliged to do this—in theory and in praxis. He was willing to pay the price of vexations for his stance—the indication of a genuine conscience.

Behind McCormick's defense of theological freedom, therefore, there stood another problem, that of the ethical conscience. He was concerned with what was ethically permissible and obligatory. He will not have overlooked the fact that other moral theologians made the problematic of conscience the explicit and clearly-stated problem for their "divergent" solutions—even in Italian and Roman books, periodicals and newspapers (even in *L'Osservatore Romano*), without (as far as one knows) provoking unpleasant reactions. The opinion was stated that it is only in conscience that one can fully see the totality of the reality which is to be realized in an action or in a behavior, and that it is therefore only in conscience that one can evaluate the defensible (inner) spectrum of validity of ethical norms of conduct.

As was remarked at the beginning, the thematic of conscience in its relationship to the ethical statements of the church's magisterium in the sphere of the norms of behavior which must be justified in terms of natural law has become more acute in recent years; this problematic has been explicitly put into the center of the stage by certain theologians and also by the magisterium itself. According to Catholic tradition, just as there exists an obligation of fidelity to conscience, there is an obligation of fidelity to the magisterium—even in noninfallible moral utterances. McCormick's further work in moral theology will be devoted to the search for a balanced solution—*in pietate* and *in iure communionis*.

Notes

1. Thus Josef Cardinal Ratzinger, "Der Auftrag des Bischofs und des Theologen angesichts der Probleme der Moral in unserer Zeit," *Int. kath. Zeitschrift "Communio"* 13 (1984) 524–538.

2. Cf. Robert Spaemann, *Moralische Grundbegriffe,* Munich 1984, 75ff.

3. Cf. Josef Cardinal Ratzinger, *loc. cit.* (n. 1 above). In his analysis of conscience, the author refers above all to R. Spaemann, *Moralische Grundbegriffe* (n. 2 above), but also to A. Laun, *Das Gewissen. Oberste Norm sittlichen Handelns,* Innsbruck 1984. One should also compare the keynote lecture "Humanae Vitae: 20 Years Later: *Quis sicut Dominus Deus noster?*" by Msgr. Carlo Caffarra, the director of the Papal Institute for Marriage and Family "John Paul II," at the exclusive congress of moral theologians organized by this institute and by the "Centro Academico" of Opus Dei (both in Rome) in November 1988 in Rome. Pope John Paul II's address at this conference on November 12, 1988 is also significant (*L'Osservatore Romano,* 13.11.1988). Further, see the informative interview Caffarra gave to the newspaper *Stampa Sera* on November 28, 1988. Significant too is the essay (unsigned, and therefore very official) "Sull'autorità dottrinale della Istruzione 'Donum Vitae,'" in *L'Osservatore Romano,* De-

cember 24, 1988, 1–2. The long pastoral document of the Italian episcopate dated January 1, 1989, *Comunione, comunità e disciplina ecclesiale,* deals in detail with the problem of conscience vis-à-vis the magisterium (text in *L'Osservatore Romano,* supplement A, n. 8, January 11, 1989).

4. R. Spaemann, *op. cit.* (n. 2 above) 91.

5. *S.T.* I 79, 12f; *De Veritate* 16f.

6. Cf. R. Spaemann, *op. cit.* (n. 2 above) 77: "Thus the individual must decide when he departs from the endlessness of weighing things up, ends the discourse and passes over with conviction to action. We call this conviction, which permits us to end the discourse, conscience."

7. Cf. ibid. 76: it is the individual who "in the last analysis must bear the responsibility of" such "obedience."

8. Cf. ibid. 82f.

9. Ibid. 84.

10. Thomas, *In 4 sent.* 38, 2, 4 qa 3; *In 4 sent.* 27, 3, 3, expos. textus; *In 4 sent.* 27, 1, 2 qa 4 ad 3.

11. On this distinction, see Norbert J. Rigali, "Moral Theology and the Magisterium," *Horizons* 15 (1988) 116–124.

12. This question has become acute also in the contemporary discussion about the teaching competence of the bishops' conferences (and the question whether this binds the individual bishop); on this, see the discussion by G. Ghirlanda and J.F. Urrutia in *Periodica de re m.c.l.* 76 (1987), especially 602f, 637, 649.

13. Val J. Peter, "The Pastoral Approach to Magisterial Teaching," in *Moral Theology Today: Certitudes and Doubts,* The Pope John Center, Saint Louis, 1984, 82–94.

7

The Foundation and Formulation of Norms

James J. Walter

In 1965 Peter Knauer, S.J. published the first[1] of several articles in which he argued that the four conditions of the principle of double effect could properly be reduced to the requirement for a proportionate reason. In other words, Knauer believed that an evil effect would be either direct or indirect according to the presence or absence of a proportionate reason. Richard McCormick's initial review of this article in his "Notes on Moral Theology"[2] was less than enthusiastic. In fact, Knauer's first volley into what would become a revolution[3] in the way that concrete behavioral norms would be formulated in Catholic moral theology was received by McCormick with some skepticism. For McCormick perceived very early in this debate that Knauer's revision of double effect, and especially of the object of the action (*objectum actus*), could destroy the traditional understanding of intrinsic evil *ex objecto*.[4] Five years later when McCormick reviewed two additional articles by Knauer,[5] he had realized that this Jesuit's revision of the principle of double effect had not only become widely accepted but that something very important was occurring.[6] Not long after he wrote this review McCormick himself would quickly become the leading proponent of "proportionalism" in the U.S. with the publication of his Père Marquette Theology Lecture *Ambiguity in Moral Choice*.[7]

In the twenty-five years that have passed since Knauer's first essay, a tremendous body of literature and commentary has been produced, and nearly every moral theologian has more or less lined up on one side or other in the debate. The discussion has sometimes been heated, even somewhat acrimonious, and, for those not initiated into the terminology and concepts, the discussions have appeared more than a little abstruse. Proponents[8] have searched for ways to articulate the essential characteristics of proportionalism, and many times they have been helped in their quests for clarity and precision by the persistent objections of their opponents.[9]

This chapter will consist of three basic parts. In the first, I will discuss the state of the question on the foundation and formulation of concrete behavioral norms. Because the traditional understanding of double effect is at the center of the revision on behavioral norms, much of this part will be concerned with analyzing this doctrine. In the second part, I will discuss the definition of proportionate reason, the criteria that establish the presence or absence of proportionality, and the ways in which we can know that a proportionate reason has been established. I will focus primarily on the writings of McCormick and on those areas in which he has developed, and even changed, his position over the years. I will conclude this part with an analysis of McCormick's contributions to the debate over behavioral norms. In the final part, I will critically evaluate a few of the issues at stake and briefly indicate where I think the discussion might go in the future.

I. STATE OF THE QUESTION

The principle of double effect has been used in the Catholic tradition to distinguish between what is directly and indirectly willed in certain actions involving conflict. The application of the principle assumed that the action under consideration would produce at least one good effect and one evil effect. Four conditions, variously formulated by the manualists, needed to be fulfilled in order to justify the permitting of the evil effect: (1) the action from which the evil would result must be good or at least indifferent; (2) the agent must intend the good effect; (3) the evil effect cannot be the cause of the good effect, or at least the good and evil effects must be caused simultaneously; (4) there must be a proportionately grave reason for allowing the evil effect. If all four conditions were fulfilled, the evil caused by or linked to the contemplated action was judged indirect, and so the agent was permitted to perform the action.

The distinction between direct and indirect voluntary, and the principle of double effect which determined this distinction in practice, was repeatedly used in three areas: actions involving the sin of another (scandal), actions involving killing, and actions that involved the use of the sexual organs. As McCormick has noted, historically the direct/indirect distinction referred to the relation of the will to the evil that was inextricably associated with the agent's action. However, as time passed the terms "direct" and "indirect" became attached to certain physical actions that were considered as necessarily entailing voluntariety. Consequently, certain actions as such were said to be "direct killings" or "direct sterilizations," and these actions were considered to be always wrong (intrinsically morally evil).[10]

To say that much is implied in the doctrine of double effect would be an understatement. A certain understanding of God's will and how God acts in the world are implied because this doctrine accepted the view that God's creative will, embodied and revealed in human nature, can be identified with the divine moral will for humanity. The doctrine also implied a way of judging the human act in which morality could be ascribed to actions (*finis operis*) apart from the intention of the agent (*finis operantis*) and the relevant circumstances (*circumstantiae*). Thus, there was the acceptance of the structural independence of the elements of the human act, championed by Peter Lombard in the twelfth century but denied by St. Thomas,[11] in assessing morality. Though in most cases all three "fonts of morality" (object, end and circumstances) were considered necessary to appraise acts morally, certain actions (*finis operis*) in themselves were considered already to contain morality. As we shall see more fully below, two classes of actions in particular were judged to be intrinsically morally evil: those actions which were against nature (*contra naturam*) and those that violated a right (*ex defectu juris in agente*). The whole doctrine of double effect relied on this theory of intrinsic moral evil, and, in fact, the first condition of the principle explicitly required that the contemplated action could not be (morally) evil in itself.

A final issue at stake in the doctrine of double effect is the foundation and formulation of certain concrete behavioral norms. Because there are classes of intrinsically morally evil actions in themselves, the proponents of this doctrine believed these actions could be normatively prohibited universally and absolutely. As Bruno Schüller has shown,[12] traditional theologians used two different forms of argument to ground norms deontologically, and these two forms correspond to the two classes of intrinsically moral evil actions mentioned above.

In the first instance, these theologians began with a natural-law position that natural ends could be ascribed to the faculties of speech and the sexual organs. God has given us the faculty of speech so that we can live together in society through truthful speech, and God has given us the sexual faculties so that we may propagate the species. These natural ends, which correspond to their respective natural faculties, have been intended by God's creative will, and thus their destruction may not be directly willed by humans regardless of the consequences. This first form of argument, then, proscribed actions that are against nature (*contra naturam*). In the second instance, the form of appeal used to establish and justify various deontological norms was to divine prerogatives. In other words, God has not granted to humans and their agency certain rights. God is the lord over life and death, and therefore suicide and the direct killing of the innocent are absolutely and universally proscribed. This second form of argument proscribed all actions that arose from a defect of a right (*ex defectu*). Whereas Schüller has argued that most other behavioral norms in the tradition were teleologically grounded, i.e. by reference to ends or disastrous consequences, these two sets of norms were grounded deontologically, i.e. without reference to ends or consequences but rather by reference either to God's creative will or to divine prerogatives.

The "revolution" which Knauer began, and which many others have joined, was really a revision not only of the doctrine of double effect and all its implications about intrinsic evil but also of the very foundation and formulation of proscriptive behavioral norms. The present debate and the revisionist attempts at reformulating these deontological norms are primarily about "those features and characteristics that make acts morally right and wrong in the first place."[13] Though the proponents of proportionalism, or revisionists as they are called, have not always formulated the issue clearly, or maybe even correctly,[14] what is under discussion is *not* the goodness/badness of the agent. This pair of terms pertains to a moral assessment of the agent's dispositions and attitudes. Rather, the discussion is about the objective rightness/wrongness of acts. The revisionist aim, then, is to attain a greater, though certainly not a total, appreciation of moral reality and objectivity than the doctrine of double effect was able to achieve in conflict situations.

In their search for a grasp of moral objectivity, in general, all proportionalists agree that no judgment of *moral* rightness or wrongness of concrete acts can be made without considering all the circumstances. To define with precision what exactly should be included in "all the circumstances" has been no easy task. Nonetheless, some common features seem to be agreed on by most of the proportionalists. First, these theologians view the human act as a structural unity, and so they deny that aspects of an act, e.g. what the tradition called the object, can be isolated and morally appraised apart from all the other components of the one unified act. Once one denies that the object (*objectum actus*) can be abstracted from the total act and judged separately, the theory of intrinsic evil *in the way* that the tradition had established this notion deontologically is also denied. Revisionists do not deny the notion of intrinsic evil altogether, but for them it can only be determined *concretely*, not abstractly, after considering all the relevant factors in a situation.[15] One of these several factors or circumstances for Fuchs, Janssens, McCormick and many others is attention to the inner act of the will of the agent.[16]

Second, when one takes into consideration "all the circumstances," it is necessary to look to all the foreseeable consequences of the action. Consequences are not the same as the end of the act (*telos* or *ratio*) aimed at by the agent, but they refer to those further ends (wanted or unwanted) caused by the action.[17] Though critics frequently have claimed that proportionalists are really consequentialists in the sense that they judge actions to be right or wrong *only* by reference to the "total net good" produced by the action,[18] in fact this has been a misunderstanding of their position.[19] What is true of proportionalism is that its structure of moral reasoning, appraisal of human acts, and its grounding of behavioral norms is teleological, i.e. it always, but not only, looks to and includes an assessment of consequences.

Though different terminology is used to express the same reality, all proponents of proportionalism argue that premoral (nonmoral or ontic) values and disvalues must also be incorporated into the assessment of the circumstances before a final moral judgment of the act is made. Premoral evil cannot be defined by what the tradition meant by natural evil (*malum naturae*), e.g. the destruction caused by a tornado, but it is similar to, though broader than, the traditional notion of physical evil (*malum physicum*). Premoral evil or disvalue refers "to the harms, lacks, pain, deprivations, etc. that occur *in or as a result of human agency*."[20] Premoral values refer to those conditioned goods that we pursue for human and nonhuman well-being and flourishing, e.g. life, health, procreation, etc. Human finiteness (temporality and spatiality) imbues all our actions with a certain ambiguity, and this is nowhere more evident than in conflict situations where a premoral disvalue is an integral part (effect or cause) of the action that promotes a premoral value.

When they emphasize the prefix "pre" in premoral values and disvalues, proportionalists refer to the fact that these values/disvalues really do exist independently of our free will. When they emphasize the "moral" aspect in pre*moral* values and disvalues, revisionists point to the fact that these values/disvalues are always relevant to our moral activity and therefore must always be taken into account.[21] Consequently, one reason why proportionalists are not consequentialists is because they maintain that actions which realize or cause premoral values/disvalues are not entirely neutral.[22] For example, when someone breaks a promise to be on time at a wedding because he or she stopped to render aid to a person in an automobile accident, the breaking of the promise is not neutral but a premoral disvalue. Revisionists argue that we have a moral duty to avoid premoral disvalue in our acts as far as possible, but the causing of premoral evil (breaking of a promise) can be justified in conflict situations where there is a proportionate reason.

Premoral disvalues or evils can be involved in our actions either as effects of the action or as causes of the premoral value that is the end (*ratio*) of the act. For revisionists, these evils, either as effect or as cause, can be justified by a proportionate reason. Thus, when only premoral evil is involved in an act, Schüller, and later McCormick following him, have argued that the distinction between direct and indirect is not always morally decisive. The distinction can be merely descriptive in that it only indicates what the agent is doing, what he or she is aiming at, and with what means. The appropriate moral categories in those instances involving premoral evil are "approval and disapproval" because they indicate whether the agent's will approved or disapproved of the premoral evil either as effect or as cause. The distinction can have a *moral* significance only to the extent that it can be shown that the agent actually approved of the premoral evil, i.e. intended the premoral evil as end or caused unnecessary disvalue. In other words, they argue that what the tradition meant by "intend as a means" and "permit" can denote the same *moral* attitude of disapproval when referring to premoral evil, and thus the traditional understanding of directness/indirectness of the intention is not morally decisive. Furthermore, when moral evil (moral wrong) is involved, e.g. an action apt to provoke others to wrong behavior, both authors have argued that the distinction between direct and indirect definitely has a moral significance. In these cases, the agent may only permit the moral wrong involved in the act.[23]

The tradition made the direct/indirect distinction morally crucial because it had already established on independent grounds, viz. deontologically by reference either to natural ends or to divine prerogatives, that the evil effect in some classes of actions was *moral* evil, i.e. moral wrong. Consequently, an agent could only permit the evil and not intend it either as end or as means. As long as the evil effect of an action was classified as a *physical* evil, for some theologians at least the *direct* willing of the physical evil did not constitute a moral wrong.[24] As we have seen, the result of this form of normative analysis led to the formulation of behavioral norms that were considered absolutely and universally prohibited. The aim of revisionists over the past twenty-five years has been to apply their general teleological structure of (1) determining moral rightness/wrongness and of (2) grounding norms and their exceptions now to those classes of behavioral norms which have been formulated deontologically.[25] This aim has been carried out, especially by McCormick, through a complex discussion of the meaning and criteria of proportionate reason.

II. McCormick's Contributions to the Discussion

Since the publication of his *Ambiguity in Moral Choice* in 1973, McCormick has become the principal proponent of proportionalism in the U.S. The sheer volume of his writings on this topic is nearly daunting, and these contributions stand as clear testimony to his importance in the discussion.[26] Nearly every issue of his "Notes" since 1965 has contained major discussions and reviews of the work that has been done in this area. McCormick has not only been a constructive theorist in the debate, but he has also been an attentive student of others who have made significant contributions. He has gained insights from Knauer, Schüller, Janssens, Fuchs and a host of others who have been proponents of proportionalism, but he has also listened to and has been a conversation partner with those who have been his staunch opponents, such as Finnis and Connery. At times McCormick's proposals on proportionalism have been tentative and somewhat sketchy, and at other times he has modified his position, changed his mind or even reversed himself. What has remained paramount in McCormick's mind since at least the early 1970s, though, is that the basic insights of the proportionalist movement are correct, even if these insights cannot be adequately stated in clear and distinct ideas.

I will organize my analysis of McCormick's contributions to proportionalism by reference to three analytically distinct but interrelated levels of inquiry: (1) the definitions of proportionalism and proportionate reason, (2) the criteria that guide and establish the fact that a proportionate reason is present or absent, and (3) the epistemic ways in which we can know that the criteria have or have not been fulfilled.[27] At each level of inquiry I will indicate where McCormick has modified or even changed his own position. Finally, I will discuss McCormick's contributions to the discussion of the foundation and formulation of concrete behavioral norms.

The Definitions of Proportionalism and Proportionate Reason

One of the persistent objections to proportionalism has been that the precise meaning of the key term "proportionate reason" is unclear. It might be helpful at the start if a distinction were made between "proportionalism" and "proportionate reason." In several places in his writings McCormick has claimed that "proportionate reason" is the basic analytic structure of moral reasoning in conflict situations[28] and moral norming.[29] McCormick is correct here in his definition, but I think that this definition more appropriately applies to "proportionalism" than to "proportionate reason." In other words, proportionalism is the general analytic structure of determining the objective moral rightness and wrongness of acts and of grounding concrete behavioral norms. This structure of moral reasoning as such is committed to assessing all relevant circumstances, viz. all aspects of the unified human act, consequences, premoral values/disvalues, institutional obligations, etc. before arriving at a final moral determination of an act.

"Proportionate reason," on the other hand, is the moral principle used by proportionalists to determine concretely and objectively the rightness or wrongness of acts and the various exceptions to behavioral norms. Obviously, proportionate reason needs criteria, but the criteria which will be discussed in the next section are analytically distinct from, but related to, the definition of the principle. This principle contains two distinguishable elements, viz. "proportionate" and "reason." Negatively, the term "reason" does not mean some serious reason which one might offer to justify the premoral disvalue in the act. Most, if not all, the manualists of this century were quite prone to interpret "reason" in the fourth condition of double effect as the offering of a "serious or excusing reason."[30] Nor should "reason" signify the "total net good" in the act as that phrase has been interpreted in consequentialism. Positively, most proponents of proportionalism mean by "reason" a premoral, i.e. a conditioned and thus not an absolute, value which is at stake in the total act. Reason, therefore, is the *ratio* in the act; it is the premoral good that the agent seeks to promote.

The proper definition of "proportionate" has also been subject to several misunderstandings. Frequently, the term has been identified with a "mathematical measuring" or "weighing" of all the premoral values and disvalues contained in the act against one another.[31] On the contrary, the term "proportionate" refers to a proper relation (*debita proportio*) that must exist between the premoral disvalue(s) contained in or caused by the means and the end (*ratio*) or between the end and the premoral disvalue(s) contained in the further ends (consequences) of the act taken as a whole.[32] Proportionalism as an analytic structure is used by revisionists in conflict situations to discern through right reason (*recta ratio*) informed by faith whether a proper relation is present by reference to certain criteria. Furthermore, in making exceptions to negative behavioral norms, e.g. no killing, no falsehoods, etc., proportionalism is used to discern if the premoral disvalue contained in or caused by the means (killing or untruth) stands in due proportion to the premoral value in the act, e.g. self-defense or protection of secrets. If a proportionate reason can be established, then revisionists argue that the norm *as stated* does not apply to *this* act under its terms of reference.[33] Exceptions to behavioral norms that prohibit premoral evil, then, are made on the basis of the presence of a proportionate reason.

Criteria That Guide and Establish Proportionate Reason

Probably the greatest constructive contribution that McCormick has made to proportionalism has been at the level of offering criteria for establishing that a proportionate reason has or has not been reached. It is also at this level that he has not only modified or changed his mind the most, but it is where he has received the greatest amount of criticism from his opponents.

In a recent issue of his "Notes" McCormick stated that he does not believe that proportionate reason can be reduced to a "single structure."[34] By "single structure" I think he meant that the criteria that establish proportionate reason cannot be reduced to a singular criterion that can be applied to all relevant situations. His explanation for holding to this view was that proportionate reason is used in a variety of different contexts: excusation from positive laws, excusation from affirmative obligations, nonimputation of unintended evil effect, etc. In addition, he has maintained that evil effects can be of many kinds, in many contexts, and caused by people with different obligational ties to others.[35]

It should not be surprising, then, to find in McCormick's writings four distinct but related criteria that he has developed over the years to establish that a proportionate reason does or does not exist in an act. Many of these criteria he shares with others, but some are specifically his own and thus they appear to form the core of his thought. McCormick has argued that a proportionate reason is present if: (1) a noncontradiction exists between the means and the end or between the end and further consequences, or (2) the means do not cause more harm than is necessary, or (3) the means are in a necessary causal relation to the end, or (4) the means (contemplated action) do not undermine the end.

Two things are important to note about these four criteria. First, whenever McCormick has referred to the end of an act, he has assumed that the agent seeks to promote a premoral good that is of great value. Thus, what he has meant by "end" in these criteria is "premoral value." Second, it is important to recall that, for McCormick, when any of these criteria is met in a situation, and thus a proportionate reason is established, he has argued that the act is justified (morally right). It is the presence of a proportionate reason that determines moral rightness; it is not the directness/indirectness of the will as this distinction was understood in the Catholic tradition that determines rightness.

McCormick appears to have adopted the first criterion of noncontradiction from Knauer[36] and Janssens.[37] However, it is debatable whether these two authors establish noncontradiction in the same way. In Knauer's later article[38] at least, he seems to mean that the end cannot be counterproductive to the *further consequences* of an act, but for Janssens noncontradiction implies that the means cannot deny the same value affirmed in the end. At one point McCormick cited the latter's definition approvingly as a way of specifying his own position,[39] so it is probable that McCormick has adopted Janssens' understanding. Because McCormick has not used this criterion very often in terms of a *direct* contradiction between means and end, one might consider it less than central to his own thought. What is surely more central to his thought, as I shall show, is his position that the means should not *indirectly* contradict the end through an association of basic goods (criterion #4 below).

The second criterion, which requires that "the means do not cause more harm than is necessary," has been formulated in several different ways by McCormick. In fact, it may be the case that he has considered each of the following three expressions as sub-criteria that can be used in different types of conflict situations. What all these sub-criteria have in common, though, is the belief that we have a moral obligation to reduce premoral disvalue in our acts as much as possible.

One expression of this criterion is that we should choose the lesser disvalue when confronted with multiple disvalues in our acts.[40] In *Ambiguity in Moral Choice* McCormick seemed to have identified the basic structure of proportionate reason with the choosing of the lesser evil.[41] Though this identification possibly points to an early confusion in his thought between the definition of proportionate reason and its criteria, McCormick is surely correct that, when confronted with more than one premoral disvalue, one must choose what is the lesser evil. How one discovers (epistemological level) what is the lesser evil, however, is no easy matter, as McCormick himself has pointed out.[42]

The second sub-criterion he has used is concerned not with premoral disvalues but with values. He has argued that if one chooses a lesser value over a higher one, then the means cause more harm than is necessary.[43] While the sub-criterion above is concerned in a sense with an *ordo malorum,* this one is concerned with an *ordo bonorum.* However, as I shall indicate later, as necessary as it may be to establish a hierarchy of goods, such an endeavor is fraught with several difficulties.

Finally, McCormick has claimed that other things being equal we should attend to a more urgent value when two premoral values are at stake but both cannot be promoted.[44] For him, to prefer a value other than the more urgent, even if lesser, value would be to cause more harm than is necessary in some conflict situations. The example of a conflict between keeping a promise to be prompt at a wedding and attending to victims in an automobile accident on the way to the church indicates a situation in which both values cannot be realized. McCormick has argued that the latter value of helping others in need is more urgent, though surely not lesser, in this situation, and so it should be preferred over the value of promise-keeping. This sub-criterion also seems to involve some form of a hierarchy of values, because one is able to determine what may be a more urgent value or what may be a more important value only when they are placed into some hierarchical relation to one another.

The third criterion states that a proportionate reason is present when "the means are in a necessary causal relation to the end." McCormick has shown that it is possible for a means to stand in a factually efficacious relation to an end without being in a necessary relation to that end.[45] For example, the direct killing of innocent people can be efficacious in the sense that it can end a war, but that does not mean the killing was thereby necessary to achieve the end. McCormick is correct on this point because, if one makes efficacy the criterion of moral rightness, then we judge actions by a crude form of consequentialism. However, McCormick has argued that certain actions involving premoral disvalue can stand in a necessary relation to the end (premoral value) sought, and when this occurs there is a proportionate reason for causing the evil. He has used the example of a pregnant woman who is found to have an aortic aneurysm. Both mother and nonviable fetus will die if something is not done to correct the life-threatening condition. McCormick has reasoned that a proportionate reason is present to justify an abortion in these circumstances because the premoral disvalue in the abortive action is intrinsically and inescapably connected with the saving of the mother's life (the only life that can be saved).[46]

The difficulty with this criterion involves the different ways in which McCormick has used the word "necessary." Sanford Levy has discovered that McCormick has chosen both "strong" and "weak" formulations of necessity to express his position. In its strong form, McCormick has understood necessary to mean that there is "an essential or inherent link between the disvalue and the good" or "there is no alternative way imaginable to attain the good." In its weak form, Levy argues that McCormick has interpreted necessary to mean that "the action is the only way to obtain the end with the means at one's disposal" or "the only way thinkable of achieving a good."[47] There is clearly a significant difference between these two forms of necessity, and I suspect that McCormick will need to clarify his position further before this criterion is truly acceptable to many. It is even possible that McCormick has already abandoned the criterion, because, in a response to John Langan in his "Notes," McCormick indicated he was far from sure that this criterion was valid.[48]

The last criterion, which requires that "the means (contemplated action) do not undermine the end," is the most complex of McCormick's criteria, and it is the one he has modified the most. In fact, McCormick has held to two different formulations of this criterion, and he has even discarded the first formulation in his later writings. Both understandings of the criterion also contain McCormick's fundamental position on the *moral* relevance of the direct/indirect distinction.

In *Ambiguity in Moral Choice,* his first real attempt constructively to state his position on proportionate reason, McCormick argued that "Both the intending and permitting will are to judged teleologically (that is, by presence or absence of proportionate reason)."[49] Like Knauer, McCormick believed that psychological directness/indirectness was not always morally decisive when premoral disvalues were involved in an act. However, he held that the potential moral relevance of the distinction vis-à-vis premoral evil could be determined (teleologically) on the basis of the long-term effects of the action. He used the principle of discrimination in the conduct of war (noncombatant immunity) to illustrate his point.

The tradition has condemned the direct killing of the innocent as intrinsically evil on the basis of divine prerogative (*ex defectu*), and consequently such killing was judged morally evil (*in se*) regardless of circumstances and independently of consequences. Though McCormick has not accepted the tradition's line of reasoning, he did believe that we should view noncombatant immunity as a "virtually exceptionless" norm.[50] He argued that the "virtually exceptionless" character of this norm could be established not on deontological considerations but rather on a long-term consideration of the disastrous consequences of destroying innocent lives in war. Consequently, he judged that there should not be any practical exceptions to the prohibition against direct killing of the innocents because of the prudential validity of a law established on the presumption of common and universal danger (*lex lata in praesumptione periculi communis*).[51] McCormick argued that the consequences would undermine the end sought in the long run, i.e. produce more evil than good, and thus one could assert that these consequences were due precisely to the *directness* of killing the innocents.[52]

It is clear here that McCormick wanted to prove the moral relevance of directness/indirectness by an appeal to a lack of proportion between the end and the long-term consequences of an action. For him, it was the directness of the killing that caused the disastrous consequences and therefore the wrongfulness of the act; it was not the consequences themselves that made the act wrong. Though McCormick never claimed that the disastrous consequences of directly killing innocents in warfare, i.e.

unleashing destructive powers that would brutalize moral sensitivities and kill more lives in the long run,[53] actually *constituted* the moral wrongfulness of the act, many of his opponents immediately branded him a consequentialist either on the basis of how he judged acts to be morally wrong and/or on the basis of how he established the conditions for making or refusing to make exceptions to behavioral norms.[54]

It was not long after he proposed his first formulation of this criterion that McCormick began to devise a second way of rendering the same criterion. Perhaps it was his recognition of the inherent weakness in the way he had distinguished the directness and indirectness of the will, and therefore how he had established the "virtually exceptionless" character of the norm against the direct killing of the innocent, that led McCormick away from his first proposal. This may be the case,[55] but what is clear is that he began to be influenced by the school of thought represented by J. de Finance, G. de Broglie, G. Grisez and J. Finnis on the concept of basic human goods.[56] McCormick's long-standing commitment to the natural law methodology, albeit revised, led him to this school of thought, which owed some of its own roots to the Thomistic tradition.

McCormick began his reflections by arguing that the origin of our basic moral commitments (moral obligations) are grounded in our natural inclinations or tendencies. Because it is impossible to act without having an interest in an object, he maintained that there is a set of natural inclinations that must exist prior to, and be the foundation of, our interest in objects of value. Without being exhaustive, he listed seven inclinations that exist in us prior to being culturally conditioned, e.g. the tendency to preserve life, the tendency to mate and raise children, the tendency to explore and question, the tendency to seek out others and seek their approval (friendship), the tendency to use intelligence in guiding action, the tendency to establish good relations with unknown higher powers (religion), and the tendency to develop skills and exercise them in play and the fine arts.[57] Though these basic values do not determine what is morally right and wrong, he reasoned, they do lay the basis for such judgments in the sense that morality is determined by the adequacy of our openness to these values.

McCormick has not been entirely consistent about how he has viewed these basic values. In one of his earliest discussions of the basic goods, he claimed that these values are "equally *basic* and irreducibly attractive,"[58] but in a later rendition he stated that the values are "equally *underivative* and irreducibly attractive."[59] The difference between these two statements was not due to a slip of McCormick's pen; a shift, albeit not substantial, had occurred in his position on axiology.

McCormick's early claim that each of these values was equally basic sounded very close to, if not the same as, Finnis' position that these values were incommensurable because basic. McCormick had wanted from the beginning to hold to the view that there is a hierarchy of values,[60] and he continued to do so even after he moved to the second formulation of this criterion under consideration.[61] All the criteria that McCormick has adopted for the determination of proportionate reason in one way or another require some form of and knowledge about a hierarchy of values. Finnis' position has categorically rejected any possibility of a hierarchy because of the incommensurability of the basic values.[62] In reaction to Finnis' position and others, e.g. Paul Ramsey, McCormick developed his notion of the "association of basic goods" in which he believed that it is possible to adopt a hierarchy and at the same time reduce the incommensurability between the basic values by reference to a single scale.

By adopting the third criterion discussed above, McCormick argued that, when an action was in a necessary causal relation to the end, a proportionate reason exists to justify the premoral disvalue in the means. However, he recognized that, whereas some actions are efficacious, they are not necessary in either a "strong" or a "weak" sense. On the other hand, McCormick has argued in this fourth criterion that when a non-necessary relation exists between a means involving premoral disvalue and its end, the value in the end can be undermined through its association with other basic values. This last criterion is similar to the first one, but McCormick has argued on the basis of an *indirect* contradiction between the means and the end in the former and a *direct* contradiction in the latter.

McCormick has used the cluster theory of virtues, in which the virtues are viewed as a kind of seamless fabric, to show that all the basic values are interrelated.[63] Without offering any proof for this cluster theory of virtues, he postulated that to weaken any one of the virtues is to weaken all the others.[64] Now, on the basis of this analogy to the virtues he assumed that to attack any one of the basic values would be to attack all the others associated with it. McCormick's reasoning here appears very close to Finnis' position on the basic goods, but the associating of these values did give him the basis on which to show why the direct killing of noncombatants is morally wrong.

McCormick has reasoned that killing noncombatants (means) does not stand in any necessary or causal relation to the aggressing nation's ceasing of its unjust actions so that lives can be saved (end). The aggressor nation is free to withdraw on its own; the doing of harm is not necessary to the aggressor's change of heart. When one denies the enemy's liberty to withdraw on its own by doing harm, in fact one undermines not only the enemy's liberty but also the value of preserving life.[65] Since preservation of life and liberty are associated values, to undermine the one is to undermine the other. The moral relevance of the direct/indirect distinction is applicable here on the basis of a lack of a proportionate reason. The means are not apt material (*materia apta*) for the end chosen because they undermine the basic value of preservation of life through the associated value of liberty. McCormick, following Schüller's analysis of the direct/indirect distinction, now argued that the doing of harm in this instance was direct in a *moral* sense because the doing of unnecessary premoral disvalue indicated *approval* of the harm.[66] Though McCormick had abandoned the long-term teleology found in his first formulation of this criterion, it should be evident that he did not abandon the teleology itself in the second formulation.[67]

Moral Epistemology and the Criteria for Proportionate Reason

The third related but distinguishable level of inquiry in the discussion of proportionalism is concerned with the ways in which we can know that the criteria used to establish a proportionate reason have or have not been fulfilled. McCormick is one of the few revisionists who has attempted to address the epistemological implications of proportionalism as a structure of moral reasoning. Even if they remain somewhat sketchy and incomplete, his contributions at this level of inquiry are significant and important.

One of McCormick's early reviews of Knauer's proposal on proportionate reason was filled with doubt about whether we could ever confidently make a judgment about proportionality. In fact, he felt that Knauer's position seemed "to demand a clairvoyance not granted to many mortals."[68] It is clear that McCormick became less skeptical of our ability to discern a proportionate reason once he became an active proponent of the position, but it is also clear he has never believed that we could arrive at these judgments with absolute certitude. As a natural-law theorist, he has been committed to the position that reality is knowable through right reason (*recta ratio*) informed by faith, but he has also realized that what we arrive at in our processes of moral reasoning is probably better defined by negation, viz. the "reasonable" means not ultimately mysterious.[69] Because McCormick has been convinced that knowledge of the presence or absence of proportionality is a human prudential judgment in a variety of irreducibly different settings, two conclusions have followed: (1) there are multiple ways of arriving at a judgment of proportionality, and (2) the best measure of these judgments is the prudent person.[70]

McCormick has explained in many of his writings that there are two forms of moral knowing: the prediscursive and the discursive.[71] Because both forms provide us with ways of knowing that proportionality is present or absent in our acts, I will briefly analyze his position on these two fonts of moral knowledge.

He has described the prediscursive elements of moral knowing somewhat differently. In his discussion of the natural inclinations, which are the bases for our interest in specific values, he claimed that our intelligence spontaneously and without reflection grasps the possibilities to which they point. In this sense, prediscursive is close to what Aquinas meant by *naturaliter nota*.[72] In another sense, prediscursive is close to what McCormick thinks Rahner meant by the "moral instinct of faith."[73] For McCormick, this latter aspect of moral knowing cannot be adequately subjected to analytic reflection, but it is responsible for one's ultimate judgments on concrete moral issues. Even though these spontaneous judgments can be affected by cultural distortions and biases, nonetheless they remain a more reliable test of proportionality than discursive arguments.[74] In addition, he maintained that our judgments about the disproportionate relation between means and end are even arrived at prediscursively via the association or interdependence of the basic goods.[75] Perhaps McCormick has not accurately rendered Rahner's notion of the "moral instinct" here, but it is clear that what he meant is that our moral sensitivities, and even intuitions, can reveal a lack of proportionality.[76]

For McCormick, discursive moral reason is concerned with analysis and the adoption of a hierarchy of values. He has proposed that, even if the basic goods are incommensurable, we still need to develop a hierarchy of values.[77] These basic values may be discovered prediscursively, as we have seen, but such apprehensions need to be tested by critical analysis. The determination of what is a more urgent value (criterion #2) to be realized in a situation cannot be merely intuited, so rational analysis within a larger community is necessary to determine when a proportionate reason is present. Our reflective experience can also discover disproportionality because we know, for example, that those who live by the sword will die by the sword, and thus we can know by reflecting on our experience that violence is often disproportionate.[78] Though McCormick has argued that long-range consequences do not constitute the disproportion itself, nevertheless a reflection on them can *reveal* how the value sought in the end is undermined through the association of basic goods.[79]

No doubt, some of the positions McCormick has taken on how we know that the criteria for proportionality have or have not been fulfilled are sketchy and incomplete. A more developed theory of moral epistemology is certainly called for, but what is surely correct is his fundamental claim that the prudent person is the true and real measure of proportionality. Again, I will return to this later when I point to some of the issues which need further attention.

The Foundation and Formulation of Norms

McCormick's contributions to the discussion of norms have also been extensive and important. First, he has tried to keep the proper terms of the discussion clearly in view. For example, he has constantly claimed that the debate has not been over either formal norms (be just, be chaste, be truthful, etc.) or synthetic norms (do not murder, do not lie, etc.). Rather, the debate has pertained to the category called concrete behavioral norms, and, more specifically, to proscriptive behavioral norms which have been considered universal and absolute in the tradition. These norms are generally formulated in a way which abstracts the physical action from the circumstances and the intention of the agent, e.g. do not utter falsehoods, do not kill, do not engage in premarital sexual relations, etc. McCormick has shown that what is new in this debate is the application of teleology to those two categories of norms traditionally founded on deontology (*contra naturam* and *ex defectu*).[80]

Second, he has attempted to define the function and meaning of behavioral norms. For McCormick and many others, the function of material norms is to prescribe premoral values or to proscribe premoral disvalues. They give instruction about what our general moral obligation to do good and to avoid evil means concretely. These norms are directly concerned with those conditioned values (premoral) that affect our well-being and flourishing; they pertain only indirectly to our goodness as moral subjects insofar as a good person will seek to promote premoral values and avoid premoral disvalues. In other words, these norms are concerned with moral rightness/wrongness and not with moral goodness/badness.

McCormick has also insisted that any assessment of the significance of our conduct that leads to a concrete moral norm must be based on the person integrally and adequately considered.[81] Thus, norms will ultimately be valid to the extent that they find their ground in the nature of a human person. Since the norms in dispute are concerned with prescribing the values or proscribing the disvalues that apply to all persons, he has denied at this level of essential ethics that Christian revelation adds anything unique to the norms.[82] This is important because it is human reason (*recta ratio*) which comprehends the truth and validity of these norms,[83] not the fact that the authority which promulgates them is legitimate.[84]

Fourth, McCormick has consistently stated that behavioral norms in the Catholic tradition, with the exception of those two classes of norms already noted, have been formulated teleologically. By a "teleological norm" McCormick has meant a norm in which consequences always play a determining but not singular role.[85] Similar to the threefold division of moral norms which Curran had proposed,[86] McCormick concluded that there are three approaches to grounding norms: (1) absolute deontology (Kant, the Catholic tradition on certain actions, Grisez, and Anscombe); (2) absolute consequentialism (J. Fletcher and some utilitarians); and (3) moderate teleology (Fuchs, Knauer, Schüller, Böckle, Curran, McCormick, etc.).[87] By "moderate teleology" McCormick has meant that the inclusion of consequences is a necessary but not sufficient condition for the determination of rightness and wrongness. Other "circumstances," in the sense that I have described them earlier, must also be included. Simply stated, if rightness or wrongness is what a norm prescribes or prohibits, and the determination of rightness and wrongness must always involve an assessment of consequences, then all norms must include a teleological foundation (moderate teleology).

McCormick has also insisted that the Catholic tradition in the past sought to narrow the range of its behavioral norms teleologically. For example, this tradition did not prohibit all killing but only the *direct* killing of the *innocent.* Thus, the norm against killing was narrowed to the direct killing of the innocent because of the disastrous consequences that would result if all killing were prohibited. His contribution here has been to show that norms are exceptionless to the extent that they resist modification by proportionate reason.[88] For example, a prescriptive behavioral norm can be exceptionless only if it prescribes a value that cannot in principle come into conflict with other values. If the value represented in the norm does conflict with another value, then the norm must imply a preference for one of the values over the other.[89] Because proscriptive behavioral norms prohibit only premoral evil, exceptions to these norms can be established on the basis of a proportionate reason. McCormick's four criteria discussed above represent the conditions under which an exception to these norms can be made in conflict situations. Another way to state the matter on exceptions to proscriptive norms is to say that these norms are limited in their application (*valent ut in pluribus*). A proportionate reason can indicate that the terms of the norm do not apply to the situation at hand,[90] and thus the contemplated action can be morally right.

Finally, McCormick has argued that concrete behavioral norms cannot be theoretically considered absolute and universal, because they only recommend or prohibit a physical action abstracted from the circumstances. Nonetheless, some of these norms can be practically viewed as "virtually exceptionless." As we have already seen, in his early writings on this issue he argued that the prohibition against the direct killing of the innocent was "virtually exceptionless" on the basis of disastrous consequences. When he later abandoned this long-term teleology in favor of a teleology which assessed moral wrongness on the basis of the means undermining the end (criterion #4), he still believed that such killing should always be prohibited.

Once he made the transition to the second formulation of his last criterion, however, it remains unclear whether McCormick has continued to construe the norm against the direct killing of the innocent in warfare as only "virtually" exceptionless. This formulation was constructed in such a way that the relevant circumstances of the act could be taken into account. Since he judged that the means indirectly contradicted the end, and thus no proportionate reason could justify either the action or an exception to the norm, then in all similar situations of warfare the contradiction would still exist. If this is true, then it seems that McCormick would have to judge the direct killing of the innocent in these circumstances as intrinsically wrong on proportionalist grounds. Consequently, it would appear that any norm formulated to prohibit such killings would have to be considered exceptionless without qualification.

If McCormick has indeed moved to the point of considering this norm truly exceptionless, it must have been his revised understanding of "directness" (Schüller's "approval") that led him to this conclusion. For him to claim that an aggressing nation "directly" killed the innocent would be the same as saying that the enemy approved of the killing, and McCormick believed this could be demonstrated on the basis of the means undermining the end through the association of basic goods. The issue, then, is not that those killed were "innocent" but that the enemy killed them approvingly (directly). Thus, the norm against killing the innocent as such is not exceptionless because it does not include in its formulation any necessary reference to the approval of the premoral evil. On the other hand, once *direct* is added to the formulation of the norm, it now includes a necessary reference to the approval of doing harm, and so the norm can be considered exceptionless on this basis. In principle, there can be no proportionate reason to justify an exception to the prohibition against approval of doing harm. Such approval not only determines an action involving premoral evil to be always morally wrong, but it also signifies that the disposition of the one doing the action is morally bad.

If this is indeed McCormick's position, then it might be helpful for him to categorize the norm against the *direct* killing of the innocent, or of anyone else for that matter, as a synthetic norm. As synthetic, the norm not only describes a physical action involving premoral evil (killing), but it also contains a reference to the agent's bad disposition (approval) toward the premoral evil. Consequently, this norm really can no longer be categorized as a concrete behavioral norm to which there could be legitimate exceptions.[91]

III. EVALUATION AND SUGGESTIONS FOR THE FUTURE

My remarks here will necessarily be brief. To begin with, I am convinced that both the proportionalist methodology and its position on norms are essentially correct, even if there are many tough questions of a theoretical or a practical nature that remain unanswered. I agree with McCormick and Janssens that there is no way that the proportionalist position can answer all questions involved in conflict situations.[92] In fact, it may be a mistake to expect that any methodology could reach such clarity. Of course, this does not mean that those who are proponents of a method should not continue to search for clarity of thought and of expression. It is to this end, then, that I would like to propose two basic issues that are in need of future study by McCormick and others who subscribe to this method of moral analysis.[93] The two issues, both central at least to McCormick's rendition of proportionalism, can be placed into the more general categories of axiology and moral epistemology. More narrowly, the first issue is concerned with the possibility, or even the advisability, of establishing a hierarchy of values (axiology), and the second is concerned with how we discern values and arrive at moral objectivity in our concrete decisions (epistemology). Both issues, as should be obvious, are intimately linked to the foundation and formulation of concrete behavioral norms.

Because McCormick has used multiple criteria to establish the presence or absence of proportionate reason, I once thought that some kind of lexical or serial ordering of these criteria might be desirable or even necessary.[94] I am now satisfied that one is either not required or one is not possible. However, I am convinced that all his criteria do rely in one way or another on some notion of a hierarchy of values. It is particularly in his second formulation of the fourth criterion that McCormick has squarely addressed this issue through the association of basic goods. It is no secret that McCormick has been severely criticized by his opponents, especially Finnis and Grisez, for taking a position which leaves open the possibility of "weighing" basic values. But Cahill has argued that it is possible that McCormick has really modified his position on proportionalism by adopting this approach to values,[95] Vacek has concluded that McCormick's position is subject to some of the same criticisms that can be brought against Finnis' theory,[96] and McKinney[97] and Hallett[98] have argued that it is not only unnecessary but impossible analytically to develop any such hierarchy. These latter assessments of McCormick's position are important not only in themselves but also because all their authors are known proportionalists.

I think that McCormick's original intuitions, if I may call them that, were correct about the need for a hierarchy of values; however, I remain relatively unconvinced of the way in which he has demonstrated his hierarchy[99] and how he has construed the conflicts between the associated goods. Certainly, many of the central differences between McCormick and most Catholic brands of deontological theory are related either to the feasibility of comparing basic goods or to the grounds for preferring one value over another in conflict situations. When they seek to protect some values in the sense that these goods may never be directly acted against, deontologists in the Catholic tradition either believe that the basic values cannot be compared in principle, e.g. Finnis and Grisez, or they believe that the basic values always take precedence over all other values in a conflict situation by reference to the design of created nature or to divine prerogatives, e.g. the manualists.

In his formulation of proportionalism at least, McCormick has claimed that the values which he classifies as basic do in fact conflict, and thus we are forced to "compare" and choose from among them. He has made this point by showing that in fact we are willing at times to sacrifice lives to protect political freedom.[100] How one is to demonstrate why political freedom should be preferred over human life is no easy matter. But one of the possible difficulties in McCormick's position, which is exemplified in this conflict situation, relates not to his claim that the basic goods are associated, but rather is concerned with the fact that he might have included both premoral and moral values into his category of the basic goods. One might argue that life is a premoral value but that liberty (political freedom) is a moral value because the latter value describes a quality of moral persons as they confront various situations.[101] If my suggestion is correct, then the conflict is not between values as associated but between values of a *different* kind.

If he accepted this construal of what really is in conflict, then McCormick might use his second criterion and argue that to prefer the value of protection of life over the value of liberty in these circumstances (unjust aggression) would be to prefer, other things being equal, a lesser over a higher value or to cause greater harm than is necessary. The two values are clearly associated *in these circumstances,* and that fact is not in dispute. Whether they are always associated *in every instance* is possibly another question. To prefer liberty in this example, however, does not commit one to hold that *in all circumstances* political freedom must be preferred. As McCormick and others have correctly stated, in some cases a more urgent, even if sometimes a lesser, value must be preferred because it is the foundation of the possibility of another value being promoted. I am not sure how McCormick would respond to this construction, but it does utilize criteria other than his fourth while at the same time relying on some form of a hierarchy of values.

Furthermore, even if McCormick's (and Finnis') claim is correct that all the basic values are equally underived in the sense that no basic value can be derived from one of the other basic values, that does not necessarily make all the basic goods equally valuable or even equally associated. It would simply mean that no hierarchy can be established on the basis of the principle of derivation.[102] Therefore, more clarity is needed about the proper categories of values and the "weight" given to each of them. Such clarity is important in itself but also because the validity of behavioral norms and their exceptions must rely on these considerations.

Another problem in developing an adequate theory of axiology, and more specifically a hierarchy of values, arises due to the lack of a developed metaphysics and moral anthropology in the writings of many proportionalists, including McCormick's.[103] Augustine's and Aquinas' theories of the *ordo caritatis,*[104] which was the foundation of their *ordo bonorum,* were grounded in a well-developed, even if inadequate, metaphysics and anthropology. Until proportionalists can give a fuller account of which goods persons should seek in their actions based on what it means to be a human person adequately considered and indicate how premoral values are interrelated yet inevitably conflict,[105] I suspect they will find it difficult to formulate a hierarchy of values. The fundamental issue is anthropology, and thus some of the basic differences between deontologists and proportionalists, or even between proportionalists, over a hierarchy of values will be located here. To put the matter simply, any position which either accepts or rejects a hierarchy of values will be adequate to the extent that the anthropology which underlies it is adequate. I would say this same statement applies also to any position on the foundation of norms, including proscriptive behavioral ones.

The second area in need of further study relates to moral epistemology and moral objectivity. McCormick's distinction between the prediscursive and the discursive is helpful and, I think, correct insofar as it rejects all forms of rationalism. There are problems, however, in the significance which he attributes to the natural inclinations and in the apparent lack of integration between these inclinations and the role of feelings at the level of the prediscursive. McCormick has held that our natural inclinations are the basis for our interest in specific values at the prediscursive level, and they form the initial foundation for our moral judgments. It may be better not to refer to *natural inclinations* here but to speak of our *aspirations,* which Janssens defines as our "dynamic openness to realities insofar as they represent values or disvalues."[106] Thus, rather than adopting a modified Thomistic thesis that our inclinations, e.g. to mate and raise children, serve as the basis for our interest in *specific* values, e.g. procreation, Janssens seems more correct to claim that our aspirations only suggest our openness to realities *which have the possibility of being valuable or disvaluable.*

Second, McCormick has discussed the role of feelings as a distinct prediscursive source of our moral knowledge. For him, feelings help us to discover the presence or absence of a proportionate reason and the relations among the basic values. Both Janssens[107] and Lonergan[108] have described a similar source of moral knowing in our intentional feelings that determine our selective orientation to our scale of values. Their description clearly demonstrates that our feelings are intentional, similar to how our consciousness itself is intentional. This seems to me to be a better way of describing how our feelings as intentional responses reveal values and disvalues. Furthermore, Janssens' description of our aspirations and intentional feelings is able to indicate an integral relation between these two in a way that McCormick's position does not or possibly cannot.

> Strictly speaking, we are directed by our intentional feeling toward *values* and *disvalues* while the dynamism of aspirations instigates us to engage ourselves with *reality* itself that we experience as a good or an evil according to its characteristics.[109]

If Janssens, Lonergan and McCormick are correct that it is primarily through our intentional feelings that we discover objective premoral values and disvalues, and I think they are, then further discussions need to take place on the relation between affective conversion and prediscursive moral knowing. By affective conversion I mean the transformation of the images and symbols which lie behind and orient our intentional feelings.[110] Can such a conversion be connected to the discussion of a hierarchy of values? Though Lonergan's writings do not contain any developed notion of a distinct affective conversion, he did believe that our intentional feelings responded to a hierarchy of values.[111] On this point, at least, I think that he was essentially correct, but at the present I probably have no adequate way of showing how this is so.

Finally, we might ask if it is the conversion of our intentional feelings that makes them reliable in the discernment of values and disvalues. If we answer in the affirmative, then this would seem similar to how revisionists make the *prudent* person the true and real measure of proportionate reason. Parenthetically, a similar question arises when theologians and philosophers want to use experience as one of the fundamental sources for normative analysis. Whose experiences or feelings should count in our discussions about objective values and disvalues? Anybody's or primarily, though not exclusively, those persons' experiences and feelings which have embodied some form of moral and affective conversion? These questions are enormously complex, and all the answers which we give probably contain some seeds of potential bias, prejudice, sexism, racism, etc. that could become the basis for unfairly or inappropriately restricting the range of experiences used in moral analysis. Nevertheless, as tough and complicated as they are, these questions need to be asked, and attention needs to be focused on proposing some constructive and fair-minded answers.

Notes

1. Peter Knauer, S.J., "La détermination du bien et du mal moral par le principe du double effect," *Nouvelle revue théologique* 87 (1965) 356–76.

2. Richard A. McCormick, S.J., *Notes on Moral Theology: 1965 Through 1980* (Washington, D.C.: University Press of America, Inc., 1981) 8–13.

3. This is how Germain Grisez once described the import of Knauer's article. See Grisez's *Abortion: The Myths, the Realities, and the Arguments* (New York: Corpus Books, 1970) 331.

4. McCormick, *Notes: 1965–1980* 10.

5. Peter Knauer, S.J., "Überlegungen zur moraltheologischen Prinzipienlehre der Enzyklika 'Humanae vitae,'" *Theologie und Philosophie* 45 (1970) 60–74; and idem, "The Hermeneutic Function of the Principle of Double Effect," *Natural Law Forum* 12 (1967) 132–62. The latter article was reprinted in Charles E. Curran and Richard A. McCormick, S.J., eds., *Moral Theology No. 1: Moral Norms and Catholic Tradition* (New York: Paulist Press, 1979) 1–39.

6. McCormick, *Notes: 1965–1980* 311–22.

7. Idem, *Ambiguity in Moral Choice* (Milwaukee: Marquette University, 1973).

8. In a recent article McCormick lists the following names as the chief propo-

nents of proportionalism: J. Fuchs, S.J., B. Schüller, S.J., F. Böckle, L. Janssens, B. Häring, F. Scholz, F. Furger, W. Kerber, S.J., C.E. Curran, L. Cahill, P. Keane, J. Selling, E. Vacek, S.J., D. Hollenbach, S.J., M. de Wachter, M. Farley, J. Walter, R. Ginters, H. Weber, K. Demmer, G. Hallett, S.J., B. Hoose, and, of course, himself. Idem, "Moral Theology 1940–1989: An Overview," *Theological Studies* 50 (March 1989) 10.

9. McCormick lists the following names as the chief opponents of proportionalism: G. Grisez, J. Finnis, J. Boyle, W.E. May, and the late J. Connery, S.J. Ibid.

10. Idem, *How Brave a New World?: Dilemmas in Bioethics* (Washington, D.C.: Georgetown University Press, 1981) 433.

11. For two essays that argue that Aquinas rejected the structural independence of the elements of the human act, see Louis Janssens, "Ontic Evil and Moral Evil," *Moral Theology No. 1* 40–93; and idem, "Saint Thomas Aquinas and the Question of Proportionality," *Louvain Studies* 9 (Spring 1982) 26–46.

12. Bruno Schüller, S.J., "Typen der Begründung sittlicher Normen," *Concilium* 120 (1976) 648–54.

13. Richard A. McCormick, S.J., "Notes on Moral Theology: 1985," *Theological Studies* 47 (March 1986) 86.

14. Bernard Hoose has sharply made this point in his *Proportionalism: The American Debate and Its European Roots* (Washington, D.C.: Georgetown University Press, 1987) 41–67.

15. See McCormick, *Notes: 1965–1980* 710; and Joseph Fuchs, S.J., "The Absoluteness of Moral Terms," *Readings in Moral Theology No. 1* 126.

16. E.g. see Richard A. McCormick, S.J., *Notes on Moral Theology: 1981 Through 1984* (Lanham, MD: University Press of America, Inc., 1984) 64–66; Louis Janssens, "Norms and Priorities in a Love Ethics," *Louvain Studies* 6 (Spring 1977) 231; and Fuchs, "The Absoluteness of Moral Terms" 119–20.

17. Hoose, *Proportionalism* 95.

18. E.g. see John Finnis, "The Consistent Ethic: A Philosophical Critique," in Thomas G. Fuechtmann, ed., *Consistent Ethic of Life* (Kansas City, MO: Sheed & Ward, 1988) 150.

19. McCormick has consistently, and rightfully, denied that proportionalism can be identified with consequentialism or with some utilitarian calculus. E.g. see his *Ambiguity* 97; *Notes: 1965–1980* 717; and "A Commentary on the Commentaries," in Richard A. McCormick, S.J. and Paul Ramsey, eds., *Doing Evil to Achieve Good: Moral Choice in Conflict Situations* (Chicago: Loyola University Press, 1978) 233 and 253.

20. Idem, "Notes: 1985" 86. Emphasis added.

21. Louis Janssens, "Ontic Good and Evil—Premoral Values and Disvalues," *Louvain Studies* 12 (Spring 1987) 81.

22. See McCormick, *Notes: 1965–1980* 710.

23. Bruno Schüller, "The Double Effect in Catholic Thought: A Reevaluation," *Doing Evil* 176–91; and McCormick, ibid. 257–58.

24. E.g. see Thomas J. O'Donnell, S.J., *Medicine and Christian Morality* (New York: Alba House, 1976) 30.

25. McCormick, *Notes: 1965-1980* 701.

26. The best sources for McCormick's position on proportionalism are his: *Ambiguity: Notes: 1965-1980; Notes: 1981-1984;* and *Doing Evil.*

27. I had originally proposed this way of structuring an analysis of the debate in James J. Walter, "Proportionate Reason and Its Three Levels of Inquiry: Structuring the Ongoing Debate," *Louvain Studies* 10 (Spring 1984) 30–40. McCormick and others have not always adequately distinguished these three levels in their writings, and so some of the confusions and misunderstandings that have arisen on both sides of the debate are at least partially attributable to this fact.

28. E.g. see McCormick, *Ambiguity* 76–77; *Doing Evil* 215; and "Notes on Moral Theology: 1984," *Theological Studies* 46 (March 1985) 62.

29. E.g. see idem, *Doing Evil* 232.

30. E.g. H. Noldin, S.J. stated, "Ad obtinendum igitur bonum effectum quandoque licitum est permittere malum, *si adsit ratio excusans proportionate gravis.*" *Summa Theologiae Moralis, Vol. I* (Rome, 1914) 101. Emphasis Noldin's.

31. Brian Johnstone, C.SS.R. has analyzed these ways of describing the term "proportionate reason" in his "The Meaning of Proportionate Reason in Contemporary Moral Theology," *Thomist* 49 (1985) 233–37.

32. This understanding of proportionate reason relies heavily on what Janssens argues is Aquinas' position. See Janssens, *Readings in Moral Theology No. 1* 66–84; and idem, "Saint Thomas and the Question of Proportionality" 31–45. The definition which I have offered probably cannot be entirely extended to how several other proponents of proportionalism have defined this term. For example, it appears that Knauer's understanding of "proportionate" entails a comparison between the long-term consequences of an action and the end sought, not a proper relation between the means and the end. See Peter Knauer, S.J., "Fundamentalethik: Teleologische als deontologische Normenbegründung," *Theologie und Philosophie* 55 (1980) 321–60. Because McCormick has approvingly cited Janssens' definition of "proportionate" as a way of expressing his own position, I take it that this definition is at least one of those which he would give to the term. See McCormick, *Doing Evil* 201 and at 224 where he cites Janssens.

33. For a more extensive discussion of his position on how exceptions are made to a *principle* (not a *norm*) by the subsumption or nonsubsumption of instances under the principle's terms of reference, see Richard A. McCormick, S.J., *The Critical Calling: Reflections on Moral Dilemmas Since Vatican II* (Washington, D.C.: Georgetown University Press, 1989) 147–62.

34. Idem, "Notes: 1985" 87.

35. Ibid. Also, see *Ambiguity,* p. 82, where he notes that there is a difference between "evil-as-effect" and "evil-as-means." This distinction may be an additional reason why he has used different criteria.

36. Knauer, *Moral Theology No. 1* 10–14.

37. Janssens, ibid. 71–2.

38. Knauer, "Fundamentalethik" 331–33.

39. McCormick, *Doing Evil* 224.

40. E.g. see ibid. 208–09.

41. Idem, *Ambiguity* 76–77.

42. Idem, *Doing Evil* 229.

43. E.g. see idem, *Ambiguity* 94.

44. E.g. see idem, *Doing Evil* 254.

45. Ibid. 238.

46. Ibid. 210. Also see idem, *Notes: 1981–1984* 63–64.

47. Sanford S. Levy, "Richard McCormick and Proportionate Reason," *Journal of Religious Ethics* 13 (Fall 1985) 261.

48. McCormick, *Notes: 1965–1980* 812–13.

49. Idem, *Ambiguity* 82–83.

50. Ibid. 87. McCormick borrowed this term from Donald Evans. For Evans' essay, see "Paul Ramsey on Exceptionless Moral Rules," *The American Journal of Jurisprudence* 16 (1971) 184–214.

51. Ibid. 92.

52. Ibid. 94–95.

53. Ibid. 87.

54. For example, Baruch Brody realized that McCormick was not a consequentialist in the way he judged the rightness/wrongness of acts, but he did believe that McCormick was committed to a consequentialist methodology for establishing exceptions to norms. See Baruch Brody, "The Problem of Exceptions in Medical Ethics," *Doing Evil* 54–68.

55. McCormick has stated that he no longer accepts his earlier formulation of the direct/indirect distinction, but now he has adopted Schüller's. See McCormick, ibid. 257.

56. McCormick has frequently cited this school of thought and its proponents as the background to his own position. E.g. see his "Proxy Consent in the Experimentation Situation," in James Johnson and David Smith, eds., *Love and Society: Essays in the Ethics of Paul Ramsey* (Missoula: Scholars Press, 1974) 217; idem, "Does Religious Faith Add to Ethical Perception?" in John C. Haughey, ed., *Personal Values in Public Policy: Conversations on Government Decision-Making* (New York: Paulist Press, 1979) 164; and idem, "Bioethics and Method: Where Do We Start?" *Theology Digest* 29 (Winter 1981) 304–05.

57. Idem, "Bioethics and Method" 305.

58. Idem, "Proxy Consent" 217. Emphasis added.

59. Idem, "Bioethics and Method" 305. Emphasis added.

60. E.g. see idem, *Ambiguity* 82–98.

61. E.g. see idem, *Doing Evil,* 251–53.

62. See John Finnis, *Natural Law and Natural Rights* (Oxford: Clarendon Press, 1980) 92. For a more recent attempt by Finnis to argue against any hierarchy of the basic goods, see John Finnis, Joseph M. Boyle, Jr., and Germain Grisez, *Nuclear Deterrence, Morality and Realism* (Oxford: Clarendon Press, 1987) esp. 275–87.

63. McCormick, *Doing Evil* 253.

64. Though McCormick only assumes the validity of this theory without any argument, there is at least some evidence in the Christian tradition to support its validity. See John Langan, "Augustine on the Unity and the Interconnection of the Virtues," *Harvard Theological Review* 72 (January–April 1979) 81–95.

65. McCormick, *Doing Evil* 237–38.

66. Ibid. 257.

67. Ibid. 265.

68. Idem, *Notes: 1965–1980* 319. The difficulty of knowing that a proportionate reason is present or absent in our acts has been one of the persistent objections to proportionalism in general. E.g. see John Connery, S.J., "Catholic Ethics: Has the Norm for Rule-Making Changed?" *Theological Studies* 42 (June 1981) 248–50.

69. McCormick, *Notes: 1965–1980* 686.

70. Idem, "Notes: 1985" 87–88.

71. E.g. see idem, "Bioethics and Method" 304; and idem, *Doing Evil* 250.

72. Idem, "Bioethics and Method" 305.

73. Idem, *Doing Evil* 250–51.

74. Ibid. 251.

75. Ibid. 250–51.

76. See also idem, *Notes: 1981–1984* 16.

77. Idem, *Doing Evil* 251–52.

78. Idem, *Notes: 1981–1984* 16.

79. Idem, *Doing Evil* 250.

80. Idem, *Notes: 1965–1980* 649.

81. Idem, *Notes: 1981–1984* 62.

82. Idem, "Does Religious Faith Add to Ethical Perception?" 156–57.

83. Idem, "Notes: 1985" 78.

84. Idem, *Notes: 1965–1980* 592.

85. Idem, *Doing Evil* 200.

86. Charles E. Curran, "Utilitarianism and Contemporary Moral Theology: Situating the Debates," *Readings in Moral Theology No. 1* 341–62.

87. McCormick, *Notes: 1965–1980* 650; and idem, *Doing Evil* 245.

88. Idem, *Doing Evil* 231.

89. Ibid. 232.

90. See idem, *The Critical Calling* 148–53.

91. Recently, McCormick has sought to distinguish the substance of a principle from its formulation-application. When he has applied this distinction to the direct taking of innocent life, he has argued that "the presumption against taking life" is the substance of the Catholic principle and "no direct taking of innocent life" is the formulation-application of the principle. Since all formulation-applications have the character of provisionality, flexibility and contingency, he has concluded that the prohibition against the direct killing of the innocent is, like Aquinas' secondary precepts, valid in most cases (*valent ut in pluribus*). Ibid. 150–51 and 221–31. McCormick may very well be correct in making this distinction, but anyone who has accepted Schüller's understanding of "direct" as signifying "approval" *in a moral sense,* and McCormick has, then the direct

killing of anyone cannot be open to provisionality, etc. Whatever it is, e.g. a principle, application, precept, norm, etc., there does not seem to be any possibility of making an exception to the prohibition against direct killing for the reasons I have given. However, if McCormick is only critiquing the Catholic tradition's formulation of this norm in these passages, then his analysis is correct. What I would suggest, though, is that when proportionalists use "direct" in their own positions, they should clearly state that the meaning of the term signifies approval in a moral sense. In other words, I suggest that proportionalists should not use "direct" as a qualifier when its meaning is merely descriptive or unless it can be shown by specific criteria that the agent's disposition toward the premoral evil involved in the means or consequences was one of moral approval.

92. See idem, "Notes: 1985" 87; and Janssens, "Norms and Priorities in a Love Ethics" 230.

93. Philip Keane, S.S. has offered four additional questions that need further study. See his "The Objective Moral Order: Reflections on Recent Research," *Theological Studies* 43 (June 1982) 274–78.

94. Walter, "Proportionate Reason and Its Three Levels of Inquiry" 35–36.

95. Lisa Sowle Cahill, "Teleology, Utilitarianism, and Christian Ethics," *Theological Studies* 42 (December 1981) 618–24.

96. Edward V. Vacek, S.J., "Proportionalism: One View of the Debate," *Theological Studies* 46 (June 1985) 308–09.

97. Ronald H. McKinney, S.J., "The Quest for an Adequate Proportionalist Theory of Value," *Thomist* 53 (January 1989) 56–73.

98. Garth L. Hallett, S.J., *Christian Moral Reasoning: An Analytic Guide* (Notre Dame, IN: University of Notre Dame Press, 1983) 137–43.

99. McCormick himself has said that he is not wedded to the formulation of the hierarchy through the association of basic goods. See his "Notes: 1985" 87.

100. E.g. see idem, *Doing Evil* 252.

101. See Timothy E. O'Connell, *Principles for a Catholic Morality* (New York: The Seabury Press, 1978) 159.

102. Johnstone has made this point in his "The Meaning of Proportionate Reason" 237.

103. Cahill has also noted this in her "Teleology, Utilitarianism, and Christian Ethics" 617.

104. Augustine, *On Christian Doctrine,* trans. J.F. Shaw (Chicago: Great Books, Encyclopaedia Britannica, 1952) chaps. 27–33; and Thomas Aquinas, *Summa Theologiae,* IIa–IIae, q. 26, aa. 1–13.

105. Janssens' attempts at formulating a moral anthropology are noteworthy, especially because of his insistence on the fact that some of the conditions for conflict are grounded in our very nature of being a human person. See his following four articles: "Personalist Morals," *Louvain Studies* 3 (Spring 1970) 5–16; "Artificial Insemination: Ethical Considerations," *Louvain Studies* 8 (Spring 1980) 3–29; "Ontic Good and Evil—Premoral Values and Disvalues" 62–82; and "Time and Space in Morals," in Joseph A. Selling, ed., *Personalist Morals: Essays in Honor of Professor Louis Janssens* (Leuven, Belgium: Leuven University Press, 1988) 9–22.

106. Idem, "Ontic Good and Evil—Premoral Values and Disvalues" 74–75.

107. Ibid. 75.

108. Bernard J.F. Lonergan, S.J., *Method in Theology* (New York: Herder and Herder, 1972) 30–32.

109. Janssens, "Ontic Good and Evil—Premoral Values and Disvalues" 75. Emphasis Janssens'.

110. For a more complete description of my position on affective conversion, see Stephen Happel and James J. Walter, *Conversion and Discipleship: A Christian Foundation for Ethics and Doctrine* (Philadelphia: Fortress Press, 1986) 21 and 39–40.

111. Lonergan, *Method* 31–32.

8

The Teaching Function of the Church in Morality

Charles E. Curran

The Christian community has always seen its belief in Jesus as entailing a way of life and influencing how the individual Christian and the Christian community should live in this world. The distinctive aspect of the Roman Catholic Church involves a hierarchical teaching office in the church. Pope and bishops have a special teaching office in the church which is often said to have as its object both faith and morals. An important question for moral theology as the scientific and thematic reflection on the Christian moral life in the Catholic tradition concerns exactly how the hierarchical teaching office functions in the teaching of morality and its relationship to the consciences of believers and to other roles and functions in the church.

In the last few decades the role of the hierarchical teaching office in moral questions has come to the fore as the most significant moral question that the church has faced. Moral theologians have often had to delve deeply into the related theological discipline of ecclesiology to address this question adequately. Many of the practical implications of ecclesiology have surfaced in the contemporary discussions and disputes which often center on the possibility and legitimacy of dissent from authoritative, noninfallible hierarchical teaching in moral matters.

This perennial question came to the front and the hottest burner in contemporary Catholic life and theology in the reaction within the church to *Humanae Vitae,* the 1968 encyclical of Pope Paul VI which condemned any use of artificial contraception for spouses.[1] Since that time both in theory and in practice the question of dissent has been central in Catholicism. Is dissent from authoritative church teaching on moral matters legitimate? Is there a right to dissent? How frequent can dissent be? What are the limits of dissent? How does the hierarchical teaching office in the church work? How should it work? What is the proper response of Roman Catholic believers to this teaching office?

Richard A. McCormick, a Jesuit priest and now the John A. O'Brien Professor of Christian Ethics at Notre Dame University, not only has lived through this stormy period in the life of the Catholic Church, but he has been one of the most significant voices in interpreting what has been happening and why. Moral theologians by the nature of their vocation deal with the practical day-to-day issues facing the life of the church. The particular talents and gifts of Richard McCormick have only emphasized this scholarly involvement in the practical moral issues facing the Catholic community and the world. For twenty years beginning in 1965 McCormick wrote the "Notes on Moral Theology" for the Jesuit publication *Theological Studies.*[2] These "Notes" reviewed the most important periodical literature in the western world dealing with moral theology and won McCormick worldwide recognition for the perceptiveness of his analysis and criticism. McCormick has not written a systematic treatise on moral theology. In addition to the "Notes" he has often addressed the burning issues of the day in short articles in *America,* the Jesuit weekly. Our author's discussion of the hierarchical teaching office in moral matters has been developed in this same context.

This essay will document the change which took place in McCormick's own positions with regard to the teaching office in the church as he related to the practical and theological issues raised by the official Catholic teaching on artificial contraception in the 1960s. A second section, in the light of McCormick's approach and other contributions, will develop a more systematic understanding of how the teaching-learning process should function in the church in moral matters. A final section will criticize the way in which the hierarchical teaching office has been operating in practice in the life of the church.

McCormick's Own Development

In recent years Professor McCormick has often pointed out two different understandings of the hierarchical magisterium and how a change from one to the other took place in the light of developments within the church, especially Vatican Council II (1962–1965).[3] The older juridical model of church and teaching authority, which was supported by a neoscholastic theology, put heavy emphasis on the authority of the teaching office. These authoritative decrees required submission and obedience on the part of all. Theologians had the primary function of explaining and defending these teachings. In a 1969 more systematic discussion the Jesuit moral theologian pointed out three characteristics of this overly juridical and neoscholastic understanding of the hierarchical teaching office in the church. Such an approach unduly separated the teaching and learning functions with consequent heavy emphasis on the right to teach with little attention to the duty incumbent on the teacher to learn. The total teaching function of the church was one-sidedly identified with the hierarchy and not enough importance was given to the role of all in the teaching office as seen especially in the *sensus fidelium* and the scholarly work of theologians. Such an understanding highlighted and isolated a single aspect of the teaching function—the judgmental.

Theological changes brought about by Vatican Council II produced an understanding of the church as a communion and as the people of God and did away with the pyramid model with the hierarchy as the real church. Likewise the concept of authority was decentralized with a call for dialogue and participation. In an ecumenical environment we must be more willing to be open to learning from other Christians and all human beings. Clergy and laity are now much better educated and informed. The laity have their own areas of competence. As a society we are more conscious that teaching involves an openness to learn through dialogue and entry into the learning and teaching process which is ongoing. As a result of these and other influences a new understanding of teaching has emerged in the church. This renewed approach has three characteristics: the learning process forms an integral part of the teaching process; teaching must be a multidimensional function with the judgmental being only one aspect; the teaching function involves the charism of many people, not just that of the hierarchy.[4] Thus by 1970 McCormick recognized a new understanding of the teaching role of the church in moral matters. This new understanding did not dawn on him as a result of armchair theologizing but was the product of his own scholarly and personal involvements in the tumultuous period of the late 1960s. Richard McCormick himself began teaching moral theology in 1957 with a very juridical notion of the church and of teaching authority in the church. McCormick's development came through his struggles with the question of authoritative church teaching in the late 1960s, especially as seen in the Catholic condemnation of artificial contraception for married couples.

In his writings as late as 1964 the American Jesuit strongly defended the official teaching of the Catholic Church condemning artificial contraception for married couples.[5] In this context dissent from official church teaching was not a burning issue for him. The historical context is necessary for understanding and interpreting what was taking place. No Catholic theologian had publicly questioned the official teaching of the church on artificial contraception before 1963.[6] Dissent was not really talked about as a significant theological issue. In retrospect one is amazed by the rapidity of the changes which took place in Catholic self-understanding. The spirit of Vatican II certainly influenced much of this change, but cultural and societal influences also entered in. Five years after his strong defense of Catholic teaching on contraception McCormick publicly questioned such teaching and upheld the right to dissent. Ironically, some statements made by Pope Paul VI actually contributed to McCormick's own change.

The historical record shows that McCormick has always been a moderate, often presenting his own position as a middle position between two extremes. On both the substantive question of contraception and the ecclesiological question of dissent McCormick clearly had to be convinced before he changed his earlier positions. But with his own honesty and dedication to the truth he had to clearly express his positions once he was convinced of them.

In 1965 Father McCormick maintained that the church can infallibly teach with regard to matters of the natural law, since such teaching is essential to the protection and proposal of Christian morality itself. According to the accepted understanding Catholic teaching could be either infallible or noninfallible. At that time our author also addressed the question of the relationship between authoritative, noninfallible church teaching on the natural law and the arguments proposed for such a teaching. Here again McCormick seeks a middle way between a new rationalism which would not accept a church teaching unless the reasons were clear and convincing and an abdication of reason which would see no connection between the authoritative teaching and the reasons to support it. The magisterium makes sense precisely because arguments are not clear or at least not universally persuasive. We should not always expect to have clear answers and arguments *now*.[7]

McCormick at this time was still not convinced about the arguments for a change in the church teaching on artificial contraception, but the practical aspects of the question surfaced in the light of a June 1964 papal statement. Pope Paul VI admitted that the question of artificial contraception, especially in terms of the pill, was under study by a special commission. At that time the pope could not find sufficient reason for changing the norms reaffirmed by Pope Pius XII. In the meantime Catholics should wish to follow a single law which the church authoritatively proposes. No one for the present should presume to speak in terms divergent from the prevailing norm. The problem for moral theologians concerned the status of this teaching. Was it now in doubt? Could Catholics in accord with the accepted theory of probabilism claim that the teaching was in doubt and be free to disagree with it in good conscience? According to McCormick, the pope has reserved this matter to himself, knows the practical urgency of the decision, is well informed on the literature, and has promised to speak soon and authoritatively. If the pope fails to speak soon on the issue, then one can only conclude that a state of practical doubt exists in the church.[8] Notice the juridical way in which the question is solved. Practical doubt will exist because the pope has not spoken on a matter of great importance which he is studying. The possibility of doubt arises from an omission by the pope and not from the intrinsic arguments or evidence.

A year later McCormick moves away from this juridical approach to the question. He interprets Pope Paul VI as saying that as of 1964 the arguments against the norms proposed by Pius XII are not persuasive. As long as these arguments are not persuasive, the existing norms must be regarded as obligatory. The pope is the ultimate judge as to whether these counter-arguments are persuasive and conclusive. However, the statement of Pope Paul VI cannot mean that only if and when the pope speaks will it become clear that the counter-arguments are sound and persuasive. For the pope to make such a statement the arguments would have to be clear and sound before he speaks! The papal utterance does not make the arguments clear and persuasive. Notice the move within one year from an omission by authority to the intrinsic evidence of the arguments. But despite this change the author of the "Notes" cannot bring himself to say that the arguments against the church's teaching on contraception are now convincing.[9]

Contraception continued to be the number one topic in Catholic moral theology in the next year (1966). The Majority Report of the papal commission arguing for a change in the official teaching was leaked to the press. Father McCormick, writing in 1967, cautiously leaned toward the reasoning of the Majority Report maintaining that not every act of contraceptive intercourse is morally wrong. But again, McCormick as a Catholic theologian had to deal with the practical aspects of the question. What was to be the proper attitude of spouses, priests, and other counselors in practice? Paul VI had brought up the problem again in an address in October 1966. The norm against artificial contraception cannot be considered not binding. The magisterium of the church is not now in a state of doubt but in a moment of study and reflection. McCormick now firmly rejects a legal and juridical understanding of the obligation resulting from the teaching of the hierarchical magisterium. The obligation of the faithful to obey church teaching comes from the teaching or doctrinal statement itself. If there are good and probable intrinsic reasons why the church may change its teaching on contraception, then the foundation for a certain obligation to follow that teaching has ceased to exist. This new papal address has not changed the practical aspects of the question. The teaching of the church is in practical doubt, and in good conscience church members can act against the existing teaching on the basis of a probable opinion to the contrary.[10] It could very well be that the pope was appealing to a legal and juridical obligation to continue to uphold the older teaching, but the author of the "Notes" could not accept such an understanding of the response due to the teaching office in the church.

Our Jesuit theologian later (1968) appealed to another papal address to justify his position. Speaking in 1966 while the birth control commission was studying the question of contraception, Pope Paul VI explained the delay by saying that the magisterium cannot propose moral norms until it is certain of interpreting the will of God. To reach this certitude the church is not dispensed from research and from examining the many questions that are proposed. McCormick draws the obvious conclusion that the teaching is now doubtful.[11]

The Catholic world had known since 1964 that the church was studying the issue of contraception. The majority of the members of the papal commission favored a change in the teaching.[12] However, Pope Paul did not act on that recommendation. Finally on July 29, 1968, the shoe dropped. Pope Paul's encyclical *Humanae Vitae* firmly condemned all contraception for spouses and upheld the older teaching of the church. *Humanae Vitae* touched off an explosion in the life of the church.[13] As a leading Catholic moral theologian, McCormick was very much a part of the ensuing discussion and controversy. However, he did not join in any immediate public dissent from the papal encyclical as did many other theologians in this country and abroad.

To go against the teaching on artificial contraception one could no longer appeal to the words of the pope about doubt in the church's teaching. One has to directly disagree with the papal teaching. McCormick crossed the Rubicon with regard to the legitimacy of dissent in his response to *Humanae Vitae*, but his conclusions were more cautious than his premises. Theologians and others must be docile to church teaching, but such teaching can be wrong. After much analysis the American Jesuit concludes that the intrinsic immorality of every contraceptive act remains a teaching subject to solid and positive doubt. He will not go so far as to say that the teaching is certainly erroneous. If other theologians agree and if bishops and spouses arrive at the same conclusion, it is difficult to see how the teaching would not lose the presumption of certitude enjoyed by such teaching. In practice the dissent of reflective and competent married people should be respected. Absolution in the sacrament of penance should not be refused to those who do not accept the teaching of *Humanae Vitae*. A strong case can be made for saying that individual acts of contraception are not subjectively serious sin.[14] Notice that McCormick is not saying here that contraceptive acts are objectively good acts or can be objectively good acts. The principles he held at that time logically called for more venturesome conclusions. One would have expected him to conclude that there are good and intrinsic reasons why the church's teaching on artificial contraception even in *Humanae Vitae* is doubtful. Consequently, there is no certain obligation for the faithful to follow that teaching. However, one must situate McCormick's response at this time in the light of the swirling controversy that engulfed the life of the Catholic Church in the United States and throughout the world.

The controversy over artificial contraception in the short period between 1964 and 1969 was the context in which McCormick changed and developed his understanding of the hierarchical teaching office in the church and the response due to it. At the meeting of the Catholic Theological Society of America in June 1969 the American Jesuit presented his most systematic and sustained treatment of the teaching role of the magisterium and of theologians.[15]

The Teaching of the Church
in Moral Matters

How should the hierarchical magisterium in the Catholic Church function on moral issues? Richard McCormick's 1969 paper gave the basic skeleton which he has followed since that time for a proper understanding of the role of the hierarchical magisterium. In the last twenty years, our author has addressed this issue in many different contexts. McCormick's latest book *The Critical Calling* discusses the teaching office of the church at length in a number of different chapters which were originally written as essays dealing with particular issues.[16] This section of the essay will develop in a necessarily skeletal but more systematic way an approach to the proper functioning of the church's teaching role in moral matters, which will rely heavily on insights provided by McCormick and others, but which I will present as my own.

The proper understanding of the teaching function of the church in moral matters depends heavily, as Richard McCormick has often pointed out, on one's ecclesiology or theology of the church. The Second Vatican Council brought about a dramatic change in Catholicism's understanding of the church. The model of the church as a pyramid with the hierarchy on top gave way to the model of the church as the people of God or as a *communio* (communion). The newer approaches attempted to overcome the overly juridical understanding which existed in the period before the council and leaned heavily on scriptural and patristic testimonies about the church. Obviously the hierarchical role in the church is not denied but is now contextualized as a service within the people of God. The *Constitution on the Church* discusses the mystery of the church in chapter one, the people of God in chapter two, and the hierarchical role in the church in chapter three.[17]

A second general context for a proper appreciation of the teaching role of the church in moral issues concerns the very concept of teaching itself.[18] Teaching is not primarily a juridical category and should not be understood on the basis of such a model. The purpose of teaching is to convince by appealing to the intellect of another. Teaching attempts to persuade and not to command. Teaching relies heavily on competence and not on authority. The proper response to teaching is not obedience. Obedience is a proper response to the exercise of jurisdiction but not to the teaching function.

The very process of teaching is not a one-way street but always involves a learning process. Every good teacher we have experienced in this world is also a learner. The church is no exception. The teaching office in the church tries to discern the word of God and the truth. The teaching office does not make something true or good but discovers truth and goodness.

A third general perspective reminds us that truth is not something which is possessed totally and once for all. Many, including McCormick, have pointed to the significance of the shift from classicism to historical consciousness in Catholic theology and thought.[19] Classicism thought in terms of the immutable, the eternal, and the unchanging, whereas historical consciousness gives greater importance to the particular, the changing, and the historical. Whereas classicism espoused a deductive methodology, historical consciousness employs a more inductive approach. Human beings are always searching for the truth in the midst of the changing circumstances of time and place. The church is constantly striving for the truth. This search, even with the existence of revelation and the assistance of the Holy Spirit, is a never-ending process which involves refinements, developments, and even changes.

A fourth general context for understanding the moral teaching role in the church recognizes that truths dealing with faith can never be fully possessed, for faith ultimately deals with the mystery of God. Yes, through faith we can arrive at some true knowledge, but our knowledge will always be imperfect, for we see now only in a mirror and not face to face.[20] The Catholic theological tradition has rightly emphasized that the church tries to understand, appropriate, and live the word and work of Jesus in the light of the changing historical realities. Catholicism rejects both the fundamentalistic and the *sola scriptura* approaches. The church today cannot merely repeat the scripture but tries under the Spirit to understand God's word in the changing realities of the different worlds in which we live. Catholicism has traditionally appreciated the need for the development of doctrine. Our faith must be expressed in human concepts and words which are related to different theologies or systematic ways of understanding reality. Different theologies mean that there can be different ways of understanding the same faith reality. In addition all human systems, concepts, and words are necessarily somewhat inadequate in fully expressing the faith reality of our deepest religious convictions. However, this is not to say that we cannot know some truths about God and faith. In this connection one recalls the shift in the understanding of revelation from the neoscholastic emphasis on revelation as propositional truths to the approach of the Second Vatican Council, which describes God as revealing in the acts and deeds of history and especially in the life, death, and resurrection of Jesus.[21]

A fifth general perspective emphasizes that moral truths and moral teaching in the church have quite distinctive characteristics.[22] The Catholic Church has traditionally insisted that its moral teaching on most specific issues is based on the natural law theory. Such an approach stresses the rational character of such teaching. Truths of the natural law are per se intelligible to all human beings. Thus, for example, the Catholic teachings opposed to liberalistic capitalism or totalitarianism or artificial contraception are proposed as positions which should be held by all human beings since they are based on human nature and human reason. This distinctive understanding of moral truths in the Catholic tradition must affect the way in which the church learns, teaches, and proposes its morality. In addition, all recognize the different levels of moral discourse. One can and does speak about attitudes or virtues such as hope or generosity, moral principles such as the obligation to protect innocent human life, moral norms such as the condemnation of divorce and remarriage, and prudential judgments such as the conclusion that the first use of even the smallest nuclear weapon is morally wrong. Different levels of certitude attach to these different aspects of moral teaching.

Within these general perspectives and contexts the teaching function of the church in moral matters can be developed. The first and perhaps most significant characteristic of this teaching function is its pluriform nature. The whole purpose of McCormick's 1969 more systematic essay was to prove that the total teaching function of the church in moral matters cannot be identified with the hierarchical magisterium. The term magisterium suggests a pluridimensional function in the church in which all have varying responsibilities. McCormick spells out three distinguishable components of this magisterium: the prophetic charism understood very broadly to include the many competencies involved, especially those of the laity and of people who have experience about a particular issue, the doctrinal-pastoral charism of the hierarchy, and the scientific charism of the theologian.[23] In subsequent years the author of "Notes on Moral Theology" often comes back to this question. He frequently cites other theologians such as Rahner, Congar, Dulles, Coffy, and others to support the contention that the magisterium cannot be limited just to the hierarchy.[24] Two comments are in order here. First, in his later writings McCormick in characteristic modesty does not give his own position enough importance. The American Jesuit clearly proposed his position in 1969 which was before many of the people he so often quotes in later years. Second, McCormick later recognized that he was not wedded to the terminology of a dual or plural magisteria in the church. All he wanted to do was point out that the total teaching function in the church cannot be reduced to the hierarchical teaching role, and the hierarchical role needs the independent work of theologians and others.[25] The various aspects of the total teaching function of the church will now be discussed in greater detail.

The Hierarchical Teaching Office. In keeping with the pluriform aspect of the teaching function in the church I will use the term hierarchical magisterium to refer to the teaching role of pope and bishops in the church, but I will avoid referring to multiple magisteria in the church. This hierarchical teaching office is connected with the office of bishops in the church. Catholic theology and canon law today distinguish between the infallible and the noninfallible teaching of this magisterium.

Debate exists within the church about the possibility of infallible teaching on specific moral questions. A comparatively few theologians hold that in theory the hierarchical magisterium can teach infallibly on specific moral matters. In particular some hold that the condemnation of artificial contraception belongs to the category of infallible teaching since it has been taught throughout the church by the pope and all the bishops.[26] Most theologians reject the infallible status of the condemnation of artificial contraception. Teaching can be infallible either through the extraordinary teaching office of the pope or ecumenical councils in defining a doctrine or through the ordinary teaching of pope and bishops. All admit there has been no extraordinary definition with regard to contraception. The vast majority of Catholic theologians hold that the condemnation of artificial contraception is not infallible because it does not fulfill the three conditions necessary for such a quality. The matter must be divinely revealed or necessary to explain what is divinely revealed, taught with moral unanimity by the pope and the body of the bishops, and proposed as having to be held definitively by the faithful. The first and third conditions, and maybe even the second, are not met in the case of contraception.[27]

On specific moral questions there cannot be an infallible teaching because of the very nature of such specific moral teachings. McCormick embraces the distinction between the transcendental and the categorical aspects to prove that no categorical aspect could be a saving truth and connected with revelation.[28] Perhaps this distinction does not give enough importance to inner worldly realities and their relationship to salvation. However, specific moral teachings by their very nature are removed from the core of faith, involve much complexity, and are subject to historical development so that one cannot claim to achieve a certitude in these matters that excludes all possibility of error. Note that we are talking about specific moral norms such as divorce, contraception, no first use of even tactical or small nuclear weapons. In this light, moral theologians do not have to deal with the question of infallible teaching which is being discussed today. We are dealing with what contemporary Catholic theology and law call the authoritative, noninfallible teaching. How should the hierarchical magisterium go about its authoritative, noninfallible teaching?

The hierarchical magisterium must always conform itself to the truth and serve the truth. Thus the pope and bishops must be in dialogue and contact with the sources of truth such as scripture, tradition, reason, and experience. In the area of moral teachings great importance must be given to reason because of the recognition that Catholic moral teaching is reasonable and also to experience because the people of God are the ones who live out this moral reality in their daily lives. This dialogue must include other Christian churches and all people of good will. The hierarchical magisterium has an obligation to use all the means available to arrive at the truth in these questions.[29]

The hierarchical teaching office in the church involves both the pope and the bishops. The bishops are true teachers in the church and not just delegates or spokespersons for the pope. Bishops do not really fulfill their teaching office if they merely repeat what the pope has said.[30] Bishops as individuals, as national and regional groups, and as the total college have their own teaching function and role in union with the pope.

This teaching function is connected with the office of pope and bishop, enjoys the special assistance of the Holy Spirit, and constitutes authoritative teaching. No individual in the church can claim to be an authoritative teacher, for this is the role of the pope and the bishops. However, the assistance of the Holy Spirit does not dispense these teachers from the human means of learning and searching out the truth.

Yes, pope and bishops have a teaching office and a special assistance of the Holy Spirit, but these distinctive features of this teaching role do not substitute for the human process of discerning the truth.[31] It is a truism in the Catholic tradition that the divine works in and through the human. McCormick associates the assistance of the Holy Spirit with the two fundamental human processes of evidence gathering and evidence assessing.[32] The Holy Spirit helps in the discernment process, but the Spirit does not overrule or substitute for the normal ways of human discernment.

Every member of the church can appreciate the help which church teaching in general and the hierarchical magisterium in particular can provide. As individuals in our pursuit of truth we are limited by our own finitude. We see only one part of the pie. This limited vision can bring about distortion in our moral analysis and conclusions. In addition all of us must recognize our sinfulness. Our sin at times does blind us and prevents our arriving at moral truth. The church as a community which exists over time and space helps to overcome the limitations which characterize every individual human being who exists in a particular culture, a particular place, and a particular time. In addition, through the gift of the Holy Spirit, the church strives to overcome the reality of sin. Yes, the church itself is also sinful, but through God's grace help exists to resist the power of sin. Thus the church in general and the hierarchical teaching office can help to overcome the innate human limitations of finitude and sinfulness in our search for moral truth. The church is a community of grace and not just a group of individuals.

Theology too needs and profits from the hierarchical magisterium. The theologian by definition studies the word and work of God in a thematic, reflexive, and systematic way. The moral theologian examines the Christian moral life in an analytic and critical manner using all the tools of the human search for the truth as illumined by faith. The faith experience of the church community serves as the source of theological reflection. Theology in its attempt to understand systematically Christian experience knows the inherent difficulties of trying to express this experience in a coherent, adequate, and systematic way. The moral theologian realizes that human reason and human constructs can never perfectly express moral experience. Moral intuitions need to be expressed in appropriate, adequate, and coherent systematic moral discourse. Theologians are constantly looking for better and more adequate understandings. Theology by its very nature is thus dependent upon the experience of the Christian community and the teaching proclaimed by the hierarchical magisterium.

The Christian in the Catholic community as well as the Catholic theologian believes in the teaching office of pope and bishops in the church and the assistance given to that office by the Holy Spirit. In a spirit of faith one graciously accepts and appreciates such a teaching office. However, the assistance of the Holy Spirit does not do away with the human processes of discerning truth in moral matters. Nor is such a teaching function the only way in which the church is involved in the learning and teaching process.

Perhaps the best illustration of how the hierarchical teaching office should function in moral matters comes from the process used by the United States bishops in writing their two pastoral letters on peace and the economy. In both cases much study and dialogue went into the process itself. Experts in scripture, theology, philosophy, and all the pertinent human and social sciences were consulted as well as many who have experience with the particular matters involved. Such wide and broad consultation recognizes the competence and contribution of scholars and of personal experience.

In moral teaching one must distinguish the various levels of moral discourse such as values, attitudes, virtues, principles, norms, and judgments. Logic and Catholic theology as exemplified by Thomas Aquinas have taught that as one descends to the more particular and specific one cannot claim the same degree of certitude as in more general matters.[33] I do not see, for example, how anyone can deny the principle that human life should be respected. This principle is certain, but it is also somewhat formal and vague. The principle that human life should not be killed is somewhat more material and specific so that almost all humans admit some exceptions in this principle. The very specific principle of Catholic moral teaching maintains that one cannot directly take innocent life on one's own authority. Such a principle depends on a number of aspects including the philosophical theory behind the distinction between direct and indirect. Since theologians and philosophers disagree about this theory it is hard to claim that one can have absolute or even moral certitude about the position on direct killing. In my judgment, absolute, specific moral norms involving human behavior described in a concrete way (i.e. this very specific act is always wrong) can never claim a certitude that excludes the possibility of error or exceptions. All have to admit that murder is always wrong, but murder by definition is unjustified killing. I would maintain that lying is always morally wrong because lying by definition is a moral term and not a behavioral term. However, telling a falsehood (a behavioral term) is not always wrong. The malice of lying consists in the violation of my neighbor's right to truth, so that not every falsehood is a lie. Concrete behavioral norms are by definition so specific and involve so many possible circumstances that they cannot claim to have a certitude that excludes the possibility of error or of exception. The perennial danger is to claim more certitude on moral matters than logic and human reason allow. Yes, at times it will be difficult to agree on the level of certitude or probability existing in a particular case, but all should recognize that absolute, specific, concrete behavioral norms cannot claim a certitude that would exclude all exceptions or differences.

Again, the United States bishops' pastoral letters on peace and the economy indicate the general direction that should be taken by the hierarchical magisterium. The bishops distinguish three different levels of their teaching: binding moral principles, statements of recent popes, and practical judgments.[34] On the latter level they recognize that in the midst of such specificity others in the church might disagree with their practical judgments. I agree with the recognition of different levels of specificity and certitude, but three comments about the approach of the U.S. bishops are in order. First, bishops should not merely repeat recent papal teaching just because it is papal teaching, for mere repetition means that the bishops have abdicated their own teaching role. Second, one might not be able to claim moral certitude even on the level of some moral principles. One of the important principles and the linchpin of much of the bishops' letter on peace is the principle of discrimination or noncombatant immunity. However, as a matter of fact there is disagreement within the Catholic Church on this issue as illustrated by the unwillingness of the West German bishops to uphold this principle in their pastoral letter on peace and the nuclear question.[35] Third, the area of legitimate diversity in the church because of the specificity of the positions held can exist on levels other than that of practical judgments. However, at least the approach taken by the American bishops is a step in the right direction.

What is the proper response of all the Catholic faithful to such authoritative, noninfallible teaching proposed by the hierarchical magisterium? By definition such teaching is noninfallible. In other words the teaching is fallible; it might be wrong. Catholic theology has traditionally spoken about a presumption in favor of such teaching. On the basis of what has been said above one can see the fundamental reasons supporting such a presumption, but two important caveats are required. First, the presumption is weakened to the extent that the hierarchical teaching office does not properly carry out its own function in gathering and assessing the evidence. Second, attention must be paid to the different levels of moral discourse and to the fact that the possibility of certitude diminishes to the extent that one becomes more specific.[36]

The *Constitution on the Church* of the Second Vatican Council repeats the terminology in use since the nineteenth century in calling for a religious *obsequium* of intellect and will. The problem concerns the meaning of *obsequium.* Is it obedience? Submission? Respect? McCormick with others maintains that the approach of the conciliar document is too juridical in tone. He understands the proper response of the faithful in terms of a docility to accept the teaching. The Holy Spirit assists the hierarchical teaching office. The faithful and the theologians recognize their own limitations and sinfulness. All affirm at times the difficulty in properly articulating the reasons for the positions we hold. Thus in a docile spirit one hears this teaching and is open to be persuaded by it. However, it can and does happen that such teaching might not be persuasive. Since we are talking about teaching, the proper response cannot be obedience or submission, for these are juridical terms which respond to the exercise of the power of jurisdiction.[37]

The Role of the Faithful. The teaching-learning process in the church involves multiple competencies including the role of the Christian faithful. The ecclesiological shift at the Second Vatican Council reminded us that the church is not just the hierarchy but is the people of God. The entire people of God share in the teaching-learning process in the church. The *Constitution on the Church* emphasizes that all the baptized share in the prophetic or teaching function of Jesus.[38] Catholic theology traditionally has maintained that through baptism all Christians share in the threefold function of Jesus as priest, teacher, and sovereign. The liturgical renewal in Roman Catholicism found its theological grounding in the priestly function of all believers. Just as there exists the priesthood of all believers and a hierarchical priesthood, so, too, there exists the teaching or prophetic function of all Christians and the hierarchical teaching office. The primary teacher in the church remains the Holy Spirit, but all share in the grace, gifts, and charisms of the Holy Spirit. In this context the *sensus fidelium* takes on an important significance. The consensus of the faithful has traditionally been accepted in the church as a criterion of saving truth.

The Second Vatican Council and contemporary theology have recognized an important role for the laity as a most significant part of the people of God. One must recognize the compromise nature of the conciliar documents, but the expanding role of the laity in Catholicism in the last few decades testifies to the changes brought about by the council. By their competence in secular fields and by their personal activity assisted by grace the laity must learn the deepest meaning and value of all creation so that the world is permeated by the spirit of Christ.[39] The *Pastoral Constitution on the Church in the Modern World* recognizes that the church does not always have at hand the answers to particular problems.[40] The laity are urged to take on their own distinctive role and responsibilities.[41] Here too one must remember the changed educational background and formation of the people of God. No longer can the faithful be looked upon as the sheep who must be told what they are to do.

The experience of Christian people constitutes a true *locus* or source of theology. The whole church can and does learn from the experience of Christian people. To discern such experience requires more than a majority vote, but the experience of Christian people is a source of learning and teaching for the whole church. The *Declaration on Religious Freedom* of Vatican II explicitly recognized this role of the experience of the people of God. Recall that the hierarchical teaching office did not accept religious liberty until 1965. The declaration itself recognizes that the demand for religious freedom has been impressing itself more deeply on the consciousness of contemporary human beings. The document takes careful note of these desires in the contemporary human heart and mind and declares them to be greatly in accord with truth and justice.[42] When did the teaching on religious freedom become true? The moment a document was signed in Rome? The document itself admits that the teaching was already true before the document was written.

The function of the faithful in the teaching-learning process of the church has played a central role in the concept of reception. A teaching must be received by the whole church. If a teaching is not truly received, that teaching does not really represent the whole church and should be changed. Again, the criteria for understanding reception are by definition somewhat vague and difficult to apply. In retrospect it is always much easier to recognize when reception did not occur. Reception involves the many different roles of the people of God in general and of theologians and scholars. J. Robert Dionne has recently examined how the teaching of the hierarchical magisterium was modified, changed, and developed on seven specific issues: papal social teaching, collegiality in the church, Catholicism and non-Christian religions, church-state, religious liberty, the church, and membership in the church.[43] Dionne concludes that one of the ways in which doctrine developed and changed from the time of Pius IX in the nineteenth century to the end of Vatican II was through the interplay of two forces: the authentic, noninfallible teaching of the ordinary hierarchical magisterium and the modalities whereby these pronouncements were received by the rest of the church.[44] I do not see how people can deny the changes and modifications that have taken place on these and other issues in the history of the church—e.g. sexual ethics and the place of procreation, interest taking, the rights of the accused, slavery, the teachings of the biblical commission, etc. Such changes not only underscore the role of reception in Catholic self-understanding, but they also point out again that the teaching-learning function in the church is truly an ongoing process which is never fully achieved. In this context, too, one can see the positive reality that dissent can and should play in the life of the church, but that will be discussed shortly.

The Scholarly Teaching Function of Theologians. Theology and theologians have an important role to play in the teaching-learning process of the church. Theology involves a critical, reflexive, thematic, systematic study of Christian faith and life. Moral theology is the branch of Catholic theology which deals with the issues of Christian living in our world. To a certain extent anyone who reflects on Christian faith and life is involved in the work of theology, but academically developed theology uses scientific tools and methods in its attempt to understand better the realities of Christian faith.

The relationship between the role of the hierarchical magisterium and the role of theologians by necessity will always involve some overlapping and some tensions. The hierarchical teaching function is a pastoral role connected with the office of pope and bishops in the church. Only the hierarchical teaching office authoritatively and authentically proposes church teaching. The theologian exercises a scholarly role which ultimately depends on the scholarship of the individual theologian and of the theological community. The role of the theologian is cooperative with, somewhat independent of, and complementary to the hierarchical teaching role.[45] Such an understanding coheres with the recognition that learning and teaching in the Catholic Church involve an ongoing process. On the one hand theologians must give a proper reception to the teaching of the hierarchical magisterium since the pope and bishops are official teachers in the church. Recall, however, the different levels of hierarchical church teaching and the type of response required by all the faithful. On the other hand, the hierarchical teaching office needs the work of theology. Once one begins to try to explain and teach the faith one is entering into the broad territory of theology. In discussing moral goals, attitudes, virtues, principles, and norms one must use the understandings of moral theology.

In past ecumenical councils theologians have even had official votes. At the Second Vatican Council all recognized the important roles played by theologians. No teaching document of the hierarchical magisterium could be published without using theology. Almost always theologians have been consulted in the writing of such documents. Some have suggested that documents should also be signed by the theologians who have helped to write them.[46]

In this context one can better realize the role that dissent can play in the church. For our limited purposes in discussing moral theology we are dealing only with authoritative, noninfallible church teaching and the role of dissent from such teaching. Dissent rightly can involve all in the church, but our discussion will center on theological dissent. Dissent from such teaching is not only a legitimate possibility at times but also a positive service to the ongoing search for truth within the church.[47]

Such a positive evaluation of dissent stems from the understandings of the hierarchical teaching office and the total teaching-learning function of the church described above. Theologians can be irresponsible in their dissent. Theologians can and will be wrong. Scholars should always use scholarly reserve in proposing their findings and research. However, theological dissent has a positive role to play in the life of the church.

The Catholic faithful can and should recognize both the role and the limits of theological discourse in the church. Theologians are not authoritative teachers who teach officially. Their teaching is based on their scholarship and subject to the criticism of the church and of other theologians. However, they and the whole people of God have a necessary and irreplaceable role to play in the teaching-learning process in the church.

Some have expressed uneasiness over the word dissent.[48] The word does have a somewhat negative ring to it, but I think it accurately describes what is taking place. By using the word one admits very clearly that one differs from authoritative and official hierarchical teaching. The negative aspects of the term also point up the presumption that should be given to authoritative hierarchical teaching. However, the reality of dissent is not primarily something negative. First of all, dissent is only one aspect of the work of the theologian who is constantly striving to understand better and in a more systematic way the word and work of Jesus in the light of our contemporary circumstances. Most of the theologian's work will not involve dissent, but at times theological scholarship will result in dissenting positions. However, dissenting positions, even at times some erroneous ones, must be seen as something positive in the light of the ongoing process by which truth is sought within the church.

The role of the theologian is both critical and public. The theologian serves many different publics both within and outside the church. The whole search for truth in our society today and in the church is public and dialogical. However, the theologian who publicly dissents must act responsibly. This responsibility calls for proper restraint in proposing one's positions and respect for the hierarchical teaching office in the church. All the people of God must recognize the need for such public dissent and should not be scandalized by it.[49]

This section has described the teaching-learning process in the church and three very important components of that process—the hierarchical teaching office, the role of the faithful, and the role of theologians. There will always be a tension in the search for the truth. Sometimes that tension can be unnecessarily exaggerated and exacerbated. If there were no tensions, there would be no real people of God. The pilgrim people of God will always know and experience the tensions of trying to do the truth in love.

CRITICISM OF THE HIERARCHICAL MAGISTERIUM TODAY

In the light of the development of how the hierarchical teaching office and the total teaching-learning function in the church should operate, this section will now criticize the way in which the hierarchical teaching office has been operating in the contemporary church. McCormick has recognized in theory and in practice the need for theology to criticize the way in which the hierarchical magisterium functions but has also insisted on the need for theologians to be self-critical in carrying out their role in the church.[50] Theologians should show respect for the hierarchical teaching office, recognize they are not official teachers in the church, and be conscious of their own limitations. Theologians must be more willing to dialogue with all other theologians in the church, especially with those who hold opposite positions. All of us have succumbed to the danger of dividing theologians into various camps and writing off those who belong to a different camp. Also, theologians with the same general perspective must be more willing to criticize one another and point out deficiencies and problems. Theologians who recognize the positive aspects of dissent must also address the limits of dissent in the church. But this section, in following a schematic approach often used by McCormick, will propose seven corrective criticisms of the exercise of the hierarchical teaching office today.

1. *Admit the different levels of church teaching.* The hierarchical teaching office must admit clearly and publicly the different levels of church teaching. Noninfallible church teaching by its very nature cannot claim an absolute certitude, but can possibly be wrong. The charge of creeping infallibility still rings true today because the provisional character of noninfallible teaching is not recognized. In moral issues acknowledge that the possibility of certitude decreases as specificity increases.

2. *Admit past mistakes in official hierarchical church teaching.* History proves the existence of some errors. An honest recognition of such mistakes will not detract from the role of the hierarchical teaching office but will in fact enhance it. In my judgment this unwillingness to admit mistakes in the past and especially in the present constitutes one of the greatest problems facing the church today. Most agree that Pope Paul

VI's decision not to change the hierarchical teaching on artificial contraception stemmed from his inability to admit that the teaching had been wrong. Could the Holy Spirit allow the church to be wrong on such an important matter? Instead of helping people in their Christian life has the church really been hurting them all these years? People who share my positions must squarely face this question. I think the root of the problem comes from the failure to publicly recognize the provisional nature of this and all noninfallible church teaching.

3. *Bishops must exercise their own independent teaching role in the church.* Bishops are not mere delegates or spokesmen for the pope. Each bishop has a teaching function, and all the bishops together with the pope form the college of bishops with its solicitude for the total church. At the present time bishops really do not exercise any independent teaching role. The role of the bishop and the college of bishops as teachers in the church will not be a reality until a bishop or group of bishops humbly and responsibly but publicly disagrees with a papal teaching. Do you think that any bishops would have publicly disagreed with Pope Paul VI if he had concluded his study of contraception by changing the teaching of the church?

4. *The hierarchical teaching office must consult widely.* In keeping with the understanding of the teaching-learning process as it takes place in the church the hierarchical magisterium must be exercised in a dialogical fashion. Today too often the hierarchical magisterium, especially in moral matters, follows only one theological school, the neoscholastic, and refuses to recognize other legitimate theological positions existing within the church. This narrow approach is bound to skewer the efforts of such a teaching office. Documents which emerge from such a narrow basis will continue to meet with disapproval from many in the church.

5. *The hierarchical teaching office must admit the processive nature of the search for truth in the church.* Such an understanding not only calls for a more consultative, tentative, and dialogical approach to its own role but must also recognize the positive function of dissent in the church. Theologians and faithful will make mistakes, but the expression of dissent at times is necessary for the good of the whole church. Yes, problems will always exist in determining what is the truth in a particular moment. History makes it much easier to discern what was true a hundred years ago. However, dissent has a legitimate and positive role within the church, even though dissent like anything else has been abused and will be abused.

6. *The process of promoting, dialoguing with, and overseeing theologians needs radical revision.* The Congregation for the Doctrine of the Faith has recognized the need to change its own procedures.[51] These

processes must respect the rights of all concerned and incorporate the procedures of due process. Above all theologians must not be judged on the basis of just one orthodox school of theology. Many have recently called for changes in the way in which the Congregation for the Doctrine of the Faith operates.[52] Above all the hierarchical teaching office and the Congregation for the Doctrine of the Faith must adopt a positive and supporting role for the work of theologians. Today most of its efforts seem to be negative and confrontational. Theologians will make mistakes. In the give and take of theological discussion other theologians should enter into the argument and the dialogue. At times the hierarchical church might have to publicly disagree with some theological positions. However, the primary thrust should be the encouragement of the theological enterprise. Richard McCormick has gone further than many others in his criticism of the Congregation for the Doctrine of the Faith as it operates today. The congregation is dominantly western, situated within an authority structure to which it is subordinate and sensitive, and almost exclusively negative in its approach. The congregation should be abolished and its guardian and promotive functions exercised by others.[53] This comment by Father McCormick leads to a final corrective criticism.

7. *Significant structural change in the church and in the teaching function of the hierarchical magisterium is necessary.* McCormick and others have pointed out the basic differences between an overly juridical understanding of the church and of the hierarchical teaching office often associated with a pre-Vatican II approach and a more communitarian or people of God model associated with post-Vatican II thinking. All recognize the danger of oversimplification in such a stark contrast, but the thrust of such an approach is basically correct. For many people the theology and the understanding of the teaching-learning process in the church have changed, but basic church structures have not changed. The new Code of Canon Law, which went into effect in 1983, has really not modified many of the older structures. In many ways today the primary problem facing the theology and practice of the church is the structural problem. A collegial, consultative, dialogical, and differentiating hierarchical teaching office will not emerge until the structures and styles of operating in the church are significantly changed.

This essay has attempted to deal with the teaching role and function in the church. The first part traced Richard McCormick's own development away from the juridical model which stressed the judgmental role of the hierarchical magisterium and tended to identify the hierarchical magisterium with the total teaching function in the church. The second part developed in a systematic but necessarily sketchy way how the teaching role should function in the church. The third section criticized the present way in which the hierarchical teaching office is exercised in the church. In the judgment of Richard McCormick and many others the Catholic Church urgently needs to change the way in which its teaching-learning function is exercised.

Notes

1. Pope Paul VI, *On the Regulation of Birth* (Washington, DC: United States Catholic Conference, 1968).

2. These articles have been collected in two volumes: Richard A. McCormick, *Notes on Moral Theology 1965 through 1980* (Washington, DC: University Press of America, 1981) and *Notes on Moral Theology 1981 through 1984* (Washington, DC: University Press of America, 1984).

3. Richard A. McCormick, "The Teaching Role of the Magisterium and of Theologians," *Proceedings of the Catholic Theological Society of America* 24 (1969) 239–254; Richard A. McCormick, "Conscience, Theologians, and the Magisterium," *New Catholic World* 220 (1977) 268–271; Richard A. McCormick, *The Critical Calling* (Washington, DC: Georgetown University Press, 1989) 25–46.

4. "The Teaching Role," in *Proceedings of CTSA* (1969) 239–254.

5. Richard A. McCormick, "Conjugal Love and Conjugal Morality," *America* 110 (1964) 38–42 and "Family Size, Rhythm, and the Pill," in *The Problem of Population* (Notre Dame, IN: University of Notre Dame Press, 1964) 58–84.

6. Louis Janssens, "Morale conjugale et progestogenes," *Ephemerides Theologicae Lovanienses* 39 (1963) 787–826; Josef Maria Reuss, "Eheliche Hingabe und Zeugung," *Tübinger Theologische Quartalschrift* 143 (1963) 454–476; William van der Marck, "Vructhbaarheidsregeling," *Tijdschrift voor Theologie* 3 (1963) 386–413; Louis K. Dupré, "Toward a Re-examination of the Catholic Position on Birth Control," *Cross Currents* 14 (Winter 1964) 63–85.

7. *Notes 1965–1980* 16–20.

8. Ibid. 50–52.

9. Ibid. 114–116.

10. Ibid. 164–168.

11. Ibid. 211–215.

12. For the story of the struggle over contraception in Roman Catholicism, see Robert Blair Kaiser, *The Politics of Sex and Religion* (Kansas City, MO: Sheed and Ward, 1985).

13. William H. Shannon, *The Lively Debate: Response to Humanae Vitae* (New York: Sheed and Ward, 1970); Joseph A. Selling, "The Reaction to *Humanae Vitae:* A Study in Special and Fundamental Theology" (STD dissertation, Catholic University of Louvain, 1977).

14. *Notes 1965–1980* 225–231.

15. "The Teaching Role," in *Proceedings of CTSA* 24 (1969) 239–254.

16. For the places outside the *Notes* where McCormick treats the teaching function of the church see note 3, including many chapters in *Critical Calling,* and also "A Moral Magisterium in Ecumenical Perspective," *Studies in Christian Ethics* 1 (1988) 20–29. Three important essays, "L'Affaire Curran," "The Search for Truth in the Catholic Context," and "Dissent in Moral Theology and Its Implications: Some Notes on the Literature," are found in Charles E. Curran and Richard A. McCormick, eds., *Readings in Moral Theology No. 6: Dissent in the Church* (New York: Paulist Press, 1988) 408–420, 421–434, 517–539.

17. *Constitution on the Church,* in Walter M. Abbott, ed., *The Documents of Vatican II* (New York: Guild Press, 1966) 14–56.

18. McCormick has insisted on this in almost all his writings on the subject; see especially "The Teaching Role," in *Proceedings of CTSA* 24 (1969) 239–245 and *Critical Calling* chapter 5.

19. *Critical Calling* 42.

20. For the implicit eschatological considerations in McCormick see the essay by Kenneth R. Himes.

21. Avery Dulles, *Models of Revelation* (Garden City, NY: Doubleday Image Books, 1985).

22. "The Search for Truth," *Readings No. 6* 421–434. For a discussion of the meaning of morals in the famous phrase "faith and morals," see John Mahoney, *The Making of Moral Theology: A Study of the Roman Catholic Tradition* (Oxford: Clarendon Press, 1987) 120–135.

23. "The Teaching Role," in *Proceedings CTSA* 24 (1969) 239–247.

24. *Notes 1965–1980* 652–668, 768–785; *Notes 1980–1984* 42–48.

25. *Notes 1965–1980* 783–785.

26. John C. Ford and Germain Grisez "Contraception and Infallibility," *Theological Studies* 39 (1978) 258–312.

27. Joseph Komonchak, "*Humanae Vitae* and Its Reception: Ecclesiological Reflections," *Theological Studies* 39 (1978) 221–257.

28. *Critical Calling* 98–100.

29. "The Search for Truth," in *Readings No. 6* 424–434.

30. "Dissent and Its Implications," in *Readings No. 6* 543.

31. *Critical Calling* 35.

32. *Notes 1965–1980* 262–266.

33. Thomas Aquinas, *Summa Theologiae* (Rome: Marietti, 1952) *Ia IIae* q94 a4; *Critical Calling* 131–162.

34. National Conference of Catholic Bishops, "The Challenge of Peace: God's Gift and Our Response," *Origins* 13 (1983) 2. McCormick cites these levels in *Critical Calling* chapter 5.

35. For an analysis of the position of the West German pastoral letter, see my *Tensions in Moral Theology* (Notre Dame, IN: University of Notre Dame Press, 1988) 140–148.

36. "The Search for Truth," in *Readings No. 6* 425.

37. As one might expect, McCormick deals with the proper response to non-infallible teaching in just about every discussion of magisterium. His later approaches (e.g. *Notes 1980–1984* 191) are dependent upon Francis A. Sullivan,

Magisterium: Teaching Authority in the Catholic Church (New York: Paulist Press, 1983) 157–166.

38. *Constitution on the Church* par. 12, in *Documents of Vatican II* 29–30.

39. Ibid. par. 36, 62–63.

40. *Pastoral Constitution on the Church in the Modern World* par. 32, 232.

41. Ibid. par. 43, 244.

42. *Declaration on Religious Freedom* par. 1, in *Documents of Vatican II* 675–676.

43. J. Robert Dionne, *The Papacy and the Church: A Study of Praxis and Reception in Ecumenical Perspective* (New York: Philosophical Library, 1987) 1–282.

44. Ibid. 353.

45. "In Service to the Gospel: A Consensus Statement of the Joint Committee," in Leo J. O'Donovan, *Cooperation Between Theologians and the Ecclesiastical Magisterium* (Washington, DC: Canon Law Society of America, 1982) 175–189. For the "somewhat independent" role of theologians, see my *Faithful Dissent* (Kansas City, MO: Sheed and Ward, 1986) 52ff.

46. *Notes 1965–1980* 665.

47. McCormick addresses the issue of dissent every time he treats of magisterium. For his latest discussion see *Critical Calling* 25–46.

48. Ladislas Örsy, *The Church: Learning and Teaching* (Wilmington, DE: Michael Glazier, 1987) 90–93.

49. "L'Affaire Curran," *Readings No. 6* 416–420.

50. *Critical Calling* 142–145.

51. *National Catholic Register,* August 12, 1984, 6.

52. Two theologians have recently criticized the Congregation for the Doctrine of the Faith for the way in which they were treated. See Walbert Bühlman, *Dreaming about the Church: Acts of the Apostles of the Twentieth Century* (Kansas City, MO: Sheed and Ward, 1987) and Bernard Häring, "Intervista di Gianni Licheri," *Fede, Storia, Morale* (Roma: Edizioni Borla, 1989).

53. *Critical Calling* 91.

9

The Focus and Its Limitations:
Reflections on Catholic Moral Theology

James M. Gustafson

Although a study of "Notes on Moral Theology" in *Theological Studies* is not sufficient for a non-Roman Catholic to learn moral theology, it comes close to being an essential aspect of one's education. Protestantism can offer nothing comparable to the non-Protestant for many reasons I shall not adduce. Rabbi David Bleich's essays in *Tradition* do provide a somewhat similar resource for the study of Jewish law and ethics.

My education in Catholic moral theology began with interest in the social encyclicals and moved back in time and out in various directions from that point through the years. "Notes" early on became important. McCormick's predecessors, contemporaries, and now successors as authors have all been significant, but the concentration of his research and contributions for so many years has made him my instructor through print. The printed word has been incalculably enriched by oral interaction and personal friendship, particularly during the years we were both residents of the Hyde Park neighborhood of Chicago. But his "Notes" have been preeminently significant.

Indeed, "Notes" might well be a distinctive genre of academic publication and one that is not easily appreciated by persons habituated to other ways of research and writing. "Notes" are literature surveys, of course, and thus aid the reader in keeping abreast of scholarship that his or her own time and attention do not permit. They are not, however, mere annotated bibliography. While the materials are presented with fairness, they are rigorously analyzed, their most crucial features highlighted, their arguments compared with others, and their implications judiciously evaluated. McCormick's capacity for empathy enabled him to disclose often profound underlying concerns that probably motivated very technical arguments—concerns of authors across a spectrum of moral and theological sympathies. The reader must turn to other of McCormick's writings for more comprehensive and systematic accounts of his thinking, but from his "Notes" one is deeply impressed by his extremely careful development of arguments on both substantive and procedural issues. There are evidences of a kind of inductive method; from his assessment of the arguments of others he formulates his own position. Yet, the Catholic tradition is always present critically informing his more constructive moves.

In preparation for this modest and inadequate tribute to a friend I read all of McCormick's "Notes" sequentially for the first (and no doubt last) time. My response is, unfortunately, drawn in large strokes; it is reflections on the twentieth-century legacy of the moral theology tradition as they are evoked by both the literature McCormick attends to and by his own contributions. I say "unfortunately" because many precise qualifications of which I am aware are not developed, and even my main themes are not supported by the many particular citations.

"Notes on Moral Theology" are properly named; they are in focus on the literature already deemed to be moral theology on the basis of either historical or philosophical and theological judgments about what aspects of theological literature are moral. Thus there are boundaries within which attention is given. The boundaries are somewhat porous; attention is given, for example, to liberation theology and its themes from time to time. The boundaries are practically required to make an already vast task manageable as well as justified on intellectual principles. This marginalizes certain interests and concerns which, from another perspective, might be closer to the center of attention. It does not preclude them; for example, as matters of theological anthropology are adduced in more specifically moral literature they are attended to. But the concentration of attention is on both moral issues and methods of adjudication that are deeply conditioned, if not determined, by a disciplinary tradition.

This is not to say that tradition is used as authority in some heteronomous way. What is received and continued methodologically from tradition is rationally justified, not only in terms of the continued use of precise distinctions and careful argument but also in terms of a profound confidence in and respect for certain modes of rational activity. One notes over and over McCormick's comments on lack of precision in writings he assesses, his reconstructive efforts to make more precise and defensible writings whose contributions are marred by lack of clarity, as well as his remark about "vintage Häring," "characterized by obvious Christlike kindness and compassion, pastoral prudence, a shrewd sense of the direction of things, and a generous amount of haziness."[1] The rigor of his development of the principle of double effect forged on the anvil both of classic and contemporary writings, including his development of the principle of proportionate reason, is an example from his constructive work. It is on the basis of his respect for this kind of rational activity that he cogently criticizes not only Catholic but also some Protestant writings, and it is on this basis that his profound admiration of the work of Paul Ramsey has rested even as they engage in disputes.

My impression is that the traditional concentration of moral theology on acts is largely continued, and that those acts and their circumstances which have occupied attention for religious reasons continue to receive dominant attention, e.g. war, sexuality, contraception, abortion, euthanasia and suicide. Thomas Aquinas' "Treatise on Human Acts" seems always to be in the background. The focus on particular acts is necessary because McCormick stays within the tradition that the moral by definition is intentional and voluntary; acts of will are the locus of moral accountability. Circumstances and consequences are important, of course, but intentions and actions are at the center.

McCormick and many of the materials he uses consequently and quite logically are concerned with the avoidance of moral culpability, i.e. of sins. While the intellectual milieu of our time is different from the seventeenth century in which the debates on probabilism flourished, the distinctions regnant in those debates can have heuristic value in interpreting current discussions. McCormick is not a rigorist, and he fairly and judiciously analyzes the arguments of moralists who might be called that. Nor is McCormick a laxist; while acknowledging the honesty of impulses of writers who might be called laxist, he engages in penetrating critiques of their arguments—the evidences they adduce as well as the procedures by which they arrive at their conclusions.

Indeed, one characteristic of his work is to find ways in which some moral culpability can be avoided while supporting outcomes of actions that take into account human values worthy of realization. It is quite clear that a view of human values underlies even his concern to avoid sins, and the espousal of certain values is a basis for modification of some traditional proscriptions of activity, e.g. contraception. But he has a low tolerance for moral ambiguity; he develops rigorous arguments to direct the consciences of persons in circumstances that others more readily accept as muddled in moral ambiguity. A generalization can be hazarded: McCormick's concern to avoid sinful acts while realizing sound human values is in the service of a deeply pastoral purpose. He has empathy and sympathy for the anxiety and suffering of persons, e.g. Roman Catholics who are divorced and remarry, and thinks through ways in which their suffering can be relieved without giving up certain traditional definitions of sinful acts. His writings and those he most approves seek to avoid misplaced guilt while holding persons responsible. In the end, however, they are held morally accountable even though this does not provide a balm for all their pains. But where the tradition and other authors create and sustain a kind of moral suffering that McCormick believes is unwarranted he cautiously but forthrightly comes to another conclusion.

McCormick's long and deep concern to defend the relative independence of the moral theologian from that other teaching authority of the church, the official magisterium, can be interpreted in this context. He and colleagues he supports have a calling to teach what they argue is authentic human and Christian morality. Their work is in this service, and where it cannot be harmonized with institutionally authorized dicta they take their stands on the validity of their arguments. A view of the church that is partly explicit and partly implied backs this degree of independence. McCormick's carefully measured prose on this issue is not given to sweeping rhetorical generalizations; he does not make rousing claims for the Spirit-filled renewed church and for living in an age of historical rather than classical consciousness that are sometimes invoked by others. Nor is he given to searching out some source in the tradition that has been long neglected in order to offer historical justification for this relative independence and the specific conclusions to which it sometimes leads. He knows history and can draw on it, but does not authorize the vocation of the moral theologian by simply historical arguments. He can be interpreted as arguing that moral theology has been at its authentic best, and always should be, in the service of Christian and human morality. While this is an ecclesial vocation, its task is to be faithful to a more profound reality than the historic institutional church—indeed to a reality to which the institution is also obligated.

I have noted that McCormick, continuing the dominant tradition of moral theology largely, but not exclusively, focuses on particular moral acts. It is the voluntariness and intentionality of actions that make persons blameworthy or praiseworthy. A strong but not utterly exclusive theme is that immoral, sinful, acts are to be avoided. No more needs to be said about the important contributions that such a focus has made and continues to make. I shall reflect upon the limitations of the moral theology tradition that follow from this focus. In this I move from particular references to McCormick and "Notes on Moral Theology."

First, the outsider is impressed with how little attention is given to praiseworthy acts; the dominant attention is given to the avoidance of sin. No doubt there are historical reasons for this, some of which can be drawn from the sacrament of penance. But one cannot avoid an impression called to attention by Bernard Häring in many places that an outcome of this is "negative" morality more than "positive" morality. To separate too sharply the doing of various kinds of good from the avoidance of evil is, of course, an error. But one finds few discussions in the moral theology tradition of virtuous actions, of actions that are exemplary instances of realizing various human and other values. I have noted that McCormick's work is basically grounded in values, but the tradition, like Paul Ramsey's work in Protestant moral theology and Alan Donagan's work in moral philosophy, holds strictly to the "Pauline" principle that we are not to do evil that good may come (Rom 3:8).[2] Certainly McCormick's work on the principle of double effect is dedicated to finding ways in which values can be realized without doing evil, but the weight of attention is finally on avoiding moral culpability in the agent.

Why can this focus be interpreted as a limitation? First, the focus on avoiding sinful acts opens the door to an egocentric concern for the agent which can diminish concern for the well-being of other persons, society and even the world of nature. It is susceptible to what can become self-interestedness, not merely in the deplorable form of moral pride but also in the less obnoxious preoccupation with avoiding risks of moral guilt and occasions for remorse. A different Pauline injunction can be cited. "Each of you must regard, not his own interests, but the other man's" (1 Cor 10:24, NEB). One's own interests that ought not be excessively regarded can, I maintain, include a highly moral self-interest. Sins of commission are sometimes avoided at great pain and suffering to other persons, or have the effect of not acting in ways that can be beneficial to other individuals, communities and the world of nature. Physicians who elect to permit a radically defective infant to die intend the death as a good; by doing nothing to hasten the death they avoid moral accountability for a committed act. This is to their moral benefit and not to the benefit of the infant.

Second, in an odd way actions or omissions that have escaped the net of attention as intentional and voluntary can be treated with indifference even though their long-range outcomes are destructive of various values. The life-style of rampant consumerism is an example. The wasting of limited resources, the disposal of nonbiodegradable packaging into land-fills, the devastation of productive soil by erosion due to agricultural practices, the use of disposable income for luxurious meals which might be given to agencies seeking to avoid starvation in other parts of the world—these and similar activities are marginal to the boundaries within which moral theology has traditionally considered moral accountability. As a consequence they receive much less attention in the literature than contraception, homosexuality and similar matters.

A third limitation is that the rational activity by which acts are judged to be sinful or not sinful, moral or immoral, can mask their deeper and mixed underlying motives. The commendable search for clarity and precision in giving reasons for action or forebearance does have the good outcome of generating and sustaining a good conscience; Catholic couples can rationally justify the use of contraceptives within responsible parenthood and avoid feelings of guilt. But in sexual activity as in many other activities the motives—that which moves the act—are often, if not always, not reducible to the reasons which justify it. Rational justification for actions can readily become a rationalization that blurs the deeper and mixed motives that persons have. Human sexuality is not the only arena in which this occurs. I recall, for instance, one of my earliest presentations before the Moral Theology section of the Catholic Theological Society of America in which participation in war was being discussed. My observation was that soldiers are motivated to kill by fear and hatred, and I recalled my own basic training during the Second World War in which "Kill or be killed" was impressed on us not only by verbal abominations but also by training exercises. Moral theologians, reinforced on that occasion by Paul Ramsey, somewhat blithely assured me that the motive was self-defense and that the soldier's moral intention was only to maim and not to kill.

A deeper philosophical issue underlies this limitation, namely what constitutes an adequate interpretation of human agency. To use some traditional distinctions, descriptively what is the relation between the passions, the will and the intellect or rational activity? Does the focus on acts as voluntary and intentional simplify the relations between profoundly biological and psychological wellsprings of action on the one hand and the powers of self-determination (intellect and will) on the other? These issues pertain not only to how actions that are blameworthy are interpreted and judged; they also pertain to praiseworthy actions. The deeper motives for praiseworthy benevolence and beneficence may be as mixed as those for malevolence and evil. In my judgment, traditional action theory that informs much of moral theology isolates such motives as "premoral" virtually by definition and does not take them adequately into account.

The fourth limitation of the focus on acts follows from the third. The locus of the human moral fault, or at least of accountability, is delimited in such a way that the orientation of profound human desires, the loyalties and commitments that direct whole lives (of which particular acts are expressions), are relatively unattended. The qualification of "relatively" is important. In matters of sexuality discussed in the "Notes" some attention is given to the pervasive sexualization of the culture, to the lifestyle of affluent consumerism, and related matters. When loyalties and desires are deeply conditioned by pervasive social and cultural forces it is difficult to locate the decisive and significant actors (intentional and voluntary agents) who foster those that are morally deplorable. Or, they are so many and so widely distributed, and their activity is immersed in institutions that are important for the state of the economy, that the target of critical analysis becomes diffuse. But *ethos,* because of its pervasive and usually unself-conscious shaping of desires and orientations toward values, predisposes agents to act in certain ways. Loyalties to ways of life or to limited communities such as race or class affect valuations expressed in many human choices. While we find discussions of excusing conditions for certain objectively immoral actions, e.g. biological dispositions toward homosexuality, there are not equally precise analyses of ethos and loyalties and how they shape ends, aspirations and character. It falls outside the limits of act analysis.

To interpret the effects of ethos on institutions and individuals requires social analysis. One thinks, for example, of the work of Emile Durkheim as one resource from construing human communities as moral communities and the ways in which the participation of persons in the symbols and rituals of such communities shapes our loves, our orientations toward particular and general values. A more thoroughgoing retrieval of the Augustinian and Thomistic strands of sin as a fundamentally flawed orientation of persons toward ends, toward apparent goods, would turn moral theology more toward those deep conditioning factors that act analysis can too easily judge to be "premoral." And to grasp how such orientations are determined requires more social, psychological and cultural analysis than act analysis normally undertakes. The idea of structural sin does attend to social analysis with reference to matters of economic and political injustices. Should not a parallel analysis be more consciously undertaken with reference to the acts on which moral theology tends to focus? If I can, for purposes of discussion, posit a technological ethos, ought its medical manifestations not be addressed more critically and thoroughly as a source of the powerful motives to make the delay of mortality the end of much of medical practice? Do moral theologians avoid an ambiguous source of many quandaries of modern medical care by focusing too much of their attention on particular choices that are created by technology? Is not a widespread idolatrous desire to overcome human finitude at the root of many particular occasions of voluntary and purposive action in medicine?

It can be argued that an intellectual division of labor locates such matters in another discipline. Such an argument can be countered by interpretations which stress the continuities between what are often separated as the premoral from the moral. This leads to what is, in the minds of some moral theologians, a confusing unclarity. Accountability is diffuse and thus the assessment of blameworthiness difficult to determine. I suggest that the precision of act analysis may lead to an over-simplifying clarity that falsifies dimensions of moral life, and that a more complex understanding of moral life would expand the boundaries of what is properly addressed by moral theology per se.

Yet another way to address what I am describing as a limitation is to call to attention the relationship between sin and sins. Moral theology tends to focus on sins, on particular immoral and sinful acts of individuals. In the Protestant tradition the other extreme has often been the case: the depth of sin resultant from the failure to trust in God. Bad trees bear bad fruits, and the occupation has been with the problem of the roots of the trees. Too frequently the affirmation that good trees bear good fruits has led to excessive assurance that a fundamental conversion will issue in morally praiseworthy deeds. But moral theologians need only to retrieve for more concentrated attention what I noted above, namely the deep strand in the tradition that roots acts in loves: faulty object of love and excessive or defective loves of appropriate objects. It needs, as well, to retrieve more centrally in its literature St. Thomas' "Treatise on Habits" to compensate for the limitation that concentration on acts, and particularly sinful acts, creates.

The attention given to acts in the literature also tends to diminish the evaluations of various relationships. "Tends to" is important to note; justice as a right relationship between persons and institutions, for example, is not overlooked. Perhaps some relationships are classed as part of the circumstances of acts, and thus are deflected from the focus of attention in moral theology. From another perspective, however, the moral qualities of relationships ascend in importance, and it is to indicate how such ascendance would complicate and enlarge moral theological literature that I now move.

There are historical precedents for the concentration on sexual activity in moral theology. These are being examined with some frequency, but to illustrate my contention here I introduce the issue again. A reader of moral theology might too readily get the impression that the ethical quandaries in the relations between male and female are principally those that arise in choices about sexual conduct. One is impressed with how little attention is given to those interactions between persons in families, parents and children as well as between the adult couple, which are a much larger part of family life than is copulation. It is all too easy to get the impression that faithfulness, for example, is important only with reference to temptations to adultery. But faithfulness and unfaithfulness are relationships present in the very fabric of the family as a community and both are expressed in, and affect deeply, countless daily actions. Indeed, a glaring oversight in moral theology is located here. To the outsider this is all the more ironic if the family is a natural community (as well as a covenanted one) that manifests the moral ordering of life ultimately grounded in the divine ordering.

Why is not more attention given in moral theology to right relationships, to a right ordering of interrelationships, between wives and husbands, between parents and children? I shall note examples that are worthy of far more attention than they have received. One can discern a fabric of interdependent obligations between a married couple and between them and children that is essential to the well-being of each member of a family as individuals and to the common well-being of the family. The failure to meet these obligations is not trivial and has both immediate and long-term outcomes that are destructive. Meeting them sustains the well-being of individuals and the common good of the family. Many of them are so ordinary that they are easily overlooked, for example, obligations to share responsibilities for the care of infants, obligations to not unfairly burden others with work (such as keeping rooms neat) that is one's own responsibility, and obligations to take time to communicate with each other on matters of common interest and concern. The quality of relations frames and predisposes conduct, and those qualities deserve attention in their own right.

Respect for persons, which is a relationship between them, gets attention in limit situations in moral theology, e.g. our relations to persons who are dying or born radically defective. But for most persons the locus of relations of respect is present daily in the family (as well as the workplace and countless other loci). What does it mean to respect one's wife or children not only as means but as ends in themselves? What qualities or relations are respectful, and what kinds of relations and actions violate respect? The life-enhancing outcomes of respectful relations as well as the corrosive outcomes of disrespectful relations are worthy of more serious attention in moral theology than they receive.

Trust and fidelity are necessary conditions of human well-being and of the common good of family. Betrayal of trust and faithfulness, as well as expression of it, is a daily event in the interpersonal relations in natural communities. Betrayal in little things, like failure to keep a promise, can unleash resentment which can lead to alienation and even to hatred between persons. No doubt such fractures of right relations lie behind issues that receive attention in moral theology at their "end-states" such as divorce and adultery. The sustenance of those relations enhances human well-being. Or, similarly, justice is a form of right relations, and we have literature about justice in the distribution of health care, in the sphere of economy and in relations between nation states. But why have moral theologians given so little attention to just relations between husbands and wives, parents and children? Injustice in such relations, like betrayal of trust, has corrosive and debilitating effects on individuals and the community as a whole.

St. Thomas' discussion of charity contains distinctions and assumes an order of life that is in part offensive to modern persons, but its fundamental purpose seems to me to be sound. To be sure, it also attends to acts primarily, but the acts of charity are grounded in and backed by a pattern of right relationships. Is there not a larger place in the literature of moral theology for a description and analysis of the morphology of loving and just relationships? One that spells out relationships the qualities of which are respect for persons, faithfulness and loyalty, trust and trustworthiness, and patterns of fairness? If, as it can plausibly be argued, the erosion and rupture of right relations is a causal factor that leads to sinful and immoral actions, should not more attention be given to the moral qualities of patterns of interrelationship and interdependence?

My impression is that a deliberate enlargement of the scope of concern beyond actions would also have implications for how repentance, forgiveness and reconciliation would be construed. Erosion and rupture of relationships, often heedless and unintentional, is an important item for the agenda of moral self-examination. Forgiveness is important for the daily undramatic incidents that generate the conditions of acts more overtly and visibly immoral and sinful. Reconciliation involves rectification and restoration of relationships and of attitudes and outlooks that sustain them. Quite rightly, in my observation, the Catholic tradition has classically never radically divorced the moral dimensions from pastoral care; perhaps greater attention can be given by moral theologians to the moral conditions out of which arise crises and morally wrong acts.

And even wider patterns of interdependent relations, between the human culture of technology and nature physically and biologically understood, are of increasing moral significance in our time. Among the many books that address this are, for example, John Passmore's *Man's Responsibility for Nature,* Hans Jonas' *The Imperative of Responsibility,* and Albert Borgmann's *Technology and the Character of Contemporary Life.* If one were to attempt an assessment of the seriousness of long-range outcomes for humans and for the natural world of which they are a part, I think one would find the rapid development of technology and its impact on nature (humans as well as plants, soil, and weather) to rank high on any list. One is surprised that the Catholic moral theology tradition with its pattern of an ordering of nature, not only descriptively but also morally, has not been exploited more than it has to analyze the human and social problems that arise in this regard, and to propose guidelines for further developments.[3] Again, one wonders whether the concentration of attention on particular acts has limited the vision of writers.

If the above named analysts of the issues are correct, it is the incremental development and extension of technology that makes it difficult to locate the decisive choices that are being made. Indeed, some argue that there is a powerful, but not fully conscious, technological imperative that drives human beings to extend the development and uses of technology without due consideration of the outcomes for human life and the natural world. Like many complex moral issues, attention finally is evoked by crises or pending crises. For example, in ethical literature, both theological and philosophical, the issue of responsibility to coming generations received little attention until recent decades. Theology, and Roman Catholic theology particularly, seems to provide grounds for concern about such a matter as well as a conceptual framework from which to address it.

Perhaps I have overinterpreted the focus of attention on particular acts, and laid more accountability at that doorstep for limitations in the literature than is fully warranted. I forewarned my readers that this essay is drawn in large strokes and requires more qualifications than it has. Perhaps it is too impressionistic. And nothing I have written deters from my indebtedness to Richard McCormick and the literature he has analyzed in "Notes" through the years. I also recognize how much effort and time it took to provide the breadth and depth of coverage of literature that he mastered year after year. A division of labor is essential in an age of specialization. The responsibility for continuing the tradition of "Notes" has now fallen to another generation, and the pattern is becoming clear; different writers attend to different areas of concern. But they have a model of scholarly comprehensiveness and precision to emulate bequeathed to them by the person whose identification with "Notes" will remain as long as moral theology in North America is given attention.

For McCormick's intellectual, academic and ecclesial contributions I remain, and always will, a thankful recipient. For his personal friendship to me and to members of my family, other memories are cherished.

Notes

1. Richard A. McCormick, S.J., *Notes on Moral Theology, 1965–1980* (Washington: University Press of America, 1981) 340.

2. The principle is implied throughout Ramsey's writings on war and medical research and practice. See Donagan, *The Theory of Morality* (Chicago: University of Chicago Press, 1977) 154–155 and elsewhere.

3. For the beginning of such use, see William C. French, "Christianity and the Domination of Nature" (Ph.D. diss., University of Chicago, 1985), especially 510–557.

SEXUAL AND MEDICAL
ETHICS

10

Human Sexuality

Lisa Sowle Cahill

---

1. SEXUAL ETHICS: THE PRESENT SITUATION OF CATHOLIC THOUGHT

Has serious discussion of sexuality and sexual ethics in Roman Catholicism been eclipsed by intraecclesial struggles about defining magisterial authority and fidelity to it in terms of teachings about sex? This possibility has been made forcefully and painfully obvious by Bernard Häring, lamenting the tone of a recent international meeting[1] in commemoration of *Humanae Vitae*. Speaking in turn of attempts to dissociate orthodoxy and fidelity to the papacy from the acceptance of the encyclical on which traditionalists insist, Häring also objects, "People no longer answer the intransigents' hymn of victory with valid arguments, even though that is still possible, but rather with anger, irony and sarcasm."[2]

In an address to the Rome conference attendees, the pope himself dwelt on the authority issue, emphasizing that challenges to the ban on contraception lead to questioning of "other fundamental truths of reason and of faith." He insisted that to reserve agreement "is equal to refusing to give God himself the obedience of our intelligence."[3] The one hundred and sixty-three signatories of the Cologne Declaration objected shortly thereafter that "without considering the differing degrees of certitude and the unequal weight of church statements, the pope has connected the teaching on birth control with fundamental truths of the faith such as the holiness of God and salvation through Jesus Christ."[4] Alluding to Häring's article, the Vatican newspaper published a front-page rebuttal, unsigned but reputedly authored by an influential Vatican source. It warns against creating "[g]reat error and confusion . . . in the minds of the faithful" by means of theological commentary on magisterial pronouncements. It names as "the central question" in the current debate "the position of the magisterium of the church."[5] All but lost in the volley of accusation and defense was Häring's plea for more attention to the relevant arguments, and his rather mild suggestion that a thorough understanding of the moral implications of birth control would need to "seriously consider" which method will "foster the marriage in its broadest sense," and "favor that love and harmony which are so basic to mutual fidelity and so necessary for raising children."[6]

Yet these are questions of immense magnitude for any Roman Catholic moral theology of sexuality: What are the "broadest" meanings and contexts of sexuality and sexual commitments? What are the human and moral relationships among sex, commited love, and parenthood?

The polarization Häring regrets yields little occasion for either faction to nuance its position in dialogue with those of different convictions, or to appreciate the areas of validity in the arguments of opponents. Yet it is often the case that the appropriation of a few of a discussion partner's better insights might enhance one's own position—not just as a bastion to be defended in the fray, but, in the present instance, as a more truthful account of some human realities (sex, marriage, parenthood) now too often approached merely as potential hostages in the ongoing conflict.

Moreover, the battle seems largely confined to the meaning and authority of relatively recent official formulations, barely extending back beyond *Humanae Vitae* (1968). As John T. Noonan[7] and others have made abundantly clear, a longer historical angle on church teaching on contraception and other sexual matters would yield a developmental perspective, as well as a more distanced and comprehensive view of the strands of continuity and change in the evolution of Catholic sexual ethics. Notable among these strands would be the constancy with which the importance of procreation has been affirmed, along with the shift in articulation of that importance from the theory of sex's primary and secondary ends (procreation; mutual help and the allaying of concupiscence) to that of equal ones (love and procreation). Perhaps less noted are the values potentially to be retrieved from obsolete formulations of the "primacy" of procreation. For instance, the notion that procreation is somehow written into the physical structure of the "natural" act of sexual intercourse is one way of attending to the embodied nature of sexuality, and of incorporating embodiedness into moral evaluation. And the argument that human intervention in fertility is illicit because the individual's reproductive capacity is ordained "to the good of the species" at least recognizes that the individual's sexuality and sexual acts have an indispensable social significance. The task that emerges in the post-Vatican II and post-*Humanae Vitae* era is to envision sexuality in its broadest possible historical and anthropological context, even while reflecting in the most profoundly personal way on sexual intimacy, love, and parenthood.

This task is unavoidable if contemporary sexual ethics is to be well-argued and experientially true, and to aim not only to persuade but to inspire.

2. The Contributions of Richard McCormick

To begin with, Richard McCormick saw quite clearly at the time of *Humanae Vitae*'s publication not only that authoritative assertion was no substitute for convincing argument, but that any attempt to make it so would effectively undercut authority itself. Although authoritative pronouncements should enjoy a presumption of correctness, noninfallible teaching is not to be evaluated in total independence from supporting reasons. Otherwise, the very notion of legitimate discussion and even dissent would become meaningless—as would the distinction between infallible and noninfallible. The assertion that a given teaching "is clear and certain simply because the papal magisterium has said so" would have to rest ultimately "on the supposition that the clarity and certainty of a conclusion of natural-law morality are independent of objective evidence." In a remark which, regrettably, remains as pertinent twenty years later, McCormick continues, "In the discussion that has followed *Humanae Vitae,* those who have supported the conclusions of the encyclical have argued in just this way. I believe this is theologically unacceptable."[8] In his judgment, for a theologian either to become a "second magisterium" or to "abandon" his or her "honesty and integrity of thought" would be "disastrous" for the church.[9]

In the years of Vatican II and in those since Paul VI's encyclical, McCormick has sought persistently to rethink the arguments behind the church's teaching, as well as those backing differing proposals about sexual morality. Put briefly, McCormick's project has been to rearticulate the unity of committed love and procreation as meanings of sexual intimacy—a unity upheld by Paul VI—in a way which is personalist rather than act-oriented and biologistic in character. Drawing on the experience of persons in sexual relationships, especially marriage, he has advocated the moral interdependence of love, sexual expression, and parenthood within a permanent commitment. But he has linked the realization of those three values with the ongoing marital relationship rather than with specific sexual acts isolated for moral scrutiny. The practical outcome has been the delineation of a sexual ideal of spousal partnership in creating a community of life which nurtures children, but which does not exclude occasional intervention in the *acts* of sex and conception. Some such interventions—for example, contraception or homologous infertility therapies—might indeed further that partnership. McCormick's recent writings, especially his constructive interpretations of sexuality's meaning, will be examined in more detail below. First, however, it may be instructive to excavate three early essays in which McCormick's writing both exemplifies the state of moral theology before the council, and reveals some of the fresh currents which were already beginning to signal a sea-change.

In 1960, McCormick contributed a well-received pair of articles on teenage sexuality to *The Homiletic and Pastoral Review;* the editor commented upon publication of the second that he was "still receiving requests" for the first.[10] It was taken for granted not only that monogamy is the normative context for sexual expression, but also that this ideal could tolerate no exceptions. McCormick accepts as general principles that to seek or consent to even slight venereal pleasure outside marriage is a serious matter; that any act involving proximate danger of such consent is also serious; and that, without any directly immoral purpose, engagement in acts which may lead to venereal reactions are grave or not in proportion to the adequacy of the reason for so acting. Nonetheless, he warns, the application of these simple principles to the case of the adolescent is "harrowingly difficult."[11] Not only does McCormick appreciate the emotional, developmental, and cultural circumstances of the teenager, he also highlights the inadequacies of a "sin-centered" approach.[12] In the case of adolescent masturbation, the priest-counselor ought to refrain from condemnation or discouragement, instead fostering "a renewal of realistic confidence," and education in "the total meaning of sex as God intended it."[13] "The priest's task is not merely to get others to adopt good conduct exteriorly, but to get them to do it freely and from solid motivation."[14] He should facilitate growth toward sexual maturity, which McCormick defines as *"purposeful control"* of sexuality—not just "chastity" in the form of "static continence." In one of his few portrayals of celibate sexuality, he draws an analogy between marriage and celibacy based on sexual control.

> The purpose is to bring order into the area of sexual instinct, and this in either of two ways: by regulating the instinct according to the ends of married love; or in the case of celibacy, by assuring the spirit total dominance over this instinct.[15]

Only the regulation and integration of sexuality in a mature way "renders the person capable of true love, of self-donation," in a lifetime commitment to another human person or to God.[16]

A few years later, McCormick probed further the meaning of sexuality in marriage in an essay which attempted to ground the church's current teaching on birth control in the nature of the marital relationship as expressed sexually.[17] In his shift in emphasis from the individual's task of integration of the sexual "instinct" to the interpersonal relationship which sexuality enables and expresses, McCormick reflects the influence of "personalist" interpretations of sex and marriage. These had been gaining currency since the 1930s, despite initial Vatican attempts at suppression.[18] The initial thrust of the personalist authors, notably Herbert Doms, was to highlight the "one immediate purpose of the sexual act" as "the representation and realisation by husband and wife of their state of two-in-oneship."[19] Even *Casti Connubii* (1930), reflecting trends at work, and possibly creating what appeared to the personalists to be a supportive environment, had called love "a mutual and intimate harmony" which is "the elemental cause and reason for matrimony."[20] But while Pius XI still regarded procreation as the primary end of marriage and of sexual acts, the personalists saw more radical implications of grounding the meaning of sexuality in love. According to Doms, experience teaches that, in marriage at least, sexual intercourse serves first of all as an expression of love, particularly since women's cyclical fertility keeps conception a relatively infrequent occurrence. In his view, it is the oneness of the couple which should be and usually is the dominant motive in sexual intercourse. Although this argument initially was rejected by the magisterium in favor of the primacy of procreation, the personalist vocabulary and its attempt to ground sexual morality in the experience of the sexual couple (especially spouses) were to have profound reverberations in the Roman Catholic theology and ethics of sexuality. One thinks of the oft-repeated keynote of *Gaudium et Spes,* "the nature of the human person and his acts,"[21] as well as the same document's reference to marriage as an "intimate partnership of life and love," as a "covenant,"[22] and of the refusal of the council fathers to rank the ends of marriage.[23] Even those who, since *Humanae Vitae,* have considered the unity of love and procreation to demand "openness" to procreation in each and every sexual act, have anchored the essential character of procreation in the love relationship of the spouses, rather than in physical reproductive processes merely.[24]

Richard McCormick's writings of the early 1960s demonstrate that near the time of the council, marriage and sexuality had been reenvisioned in interpersonal and intersubjective terms. This shift reflected twentieth century, western perceptions of greater equality between sexual and conjugal partners, the romantic and affective potentials of sexuality, and the importance of sexual and marital fulfillment for the spouses as well as of their familial and social roles. At the same time, thought about sexuality within the parameters of magisterial teaching tried to wed personalist revisions to traditional conclusions about sexual behavior, especially birth control. McCormick himself makes a theological argument about the "vocation to marriage" which is formulated in terms of an analogy between the "two-in-oneness" of spouses, and the "three-in-oneness" of the Trinity. In each case the "relationship is nothing less than a total oblation of persons," one not "self-contained" but "fertile." As the "sexual symbol" of the marital relationship, sexual intercourse is not only "a communion of *persons*," but "an act of total self-giving."[25]

In marital sexuality, he continues, there are two aspects, reproduction and personal love. These "merge" in the act of intercourse.[26] Contraceptive acts are immoral not only or primarily because of the naturally reproductive character of sex, but because they "do not preserve a completeness of donation," and so "fail to express the relationship of total oblation." "Hence, objectively, they are not acts of love."[27] Present readers will not be slow to note that very similar arguments about the character of the marital sexual experience have been put forward more recently by Pope John Paul II.[28] Interestingly and importantly for later development, though, McCormick viewed the procreative aspect of the sexual act not as an essential requirement, but rather as "a *practical criterion* of complete self-giving," a way to "safeguard" self-giving.[29] He allowed that it might not have been so clear that contraception and sterilization impair self-giving, were it not for the guidance of church teaching. And he concludes both that "there is nothing sacrosanct . . . about this or that formulation of natural law,"[30] and that "re-evaluation and reassessment is and always has been the job of theology."[31]

McCormick was later to see that to link the personal partnership of marriage so tightly to the procreative potential of single sex acts was too narrow and too "physicalist" a reading of sexuality's significance as an expression and enhancement of love. However, an even more fundamental objection may be leveled against his repeated insistence that marital love must achieve "totality" of commitment and of symbolization of the divine, a demand unparalleled in any other area of the moral life.[32] In reference to the self-giving represented by the sex act, McCormick uses the words "total," and "complete," or their cognates, twenty-seven times in the course of a four-and-one-half page essay. Surely the cumulative effect of such rhetoric is to hit married couples over the head with an unattainable norm for their conduct—one which, moreover, is hardly left at the level of the ideal, being translated into rules for action of the most concrete and absolute sort. This observation is not meant merely to berate a youthful and perhaps romantic Fr. McCormick, now twenty-five years distant. Suffice it to note that in *Familiaris Consortio* is found the following passage:

> [S]exuality, by means of which man and woman give themselves to one another through the acts which are proper and exclusive to spouses . . . is realized in a truly human way only if it is an integral part of the love by which a man and a woman commit themselves totally to one another until death. The total physical self-giving would be a lie if it were not the sign and fruit of a total personal self-giving, in which the whole person, including the temporal dimension, is present. . . . This totality which is required by conjugal love also corresponds to the demands of responsible fertility.[33]

When the language of personal sexual and marital experience is co-opted in support of traditional teaching on the role of the procreation, a subtle distortion easily occurs. "Experience" is read through the lens of the advocated teaching, and assumes an ideal and abstract character little reflective of the give-and-take of enduring sexual relationships, especially marriage. Once the foundational importance of married love is acknowledged, or even if procreation is conceded not to have a primary importance in that relationship, the absolute exclusion of artificial birth control does not sit so congenially within the always practical and often complex demands of marriage and family life. In the first instance, the demands of love for spouse and family can gain ascendency over the goods of further parenthood; in the second, the demands of "openness" to procreation may conflict with those of responsibilities to spouse or existing children, requiring a practical compromise in which realization of one of the "equal" goods will need to be deferred. The publication of *Humanae Vitae* crystallized many of the ambiguities in the Catholic teaching about sexual relationships, both because it tried to combine a clear rationale for excluding contraception with an appreciation of the value of marriage as a partnership of love, and because it projected the unconvincing result into a practical, ecclesial situation in which the laity were being encouraged to contribute constructively to the renewal of theology and ethics. The mood of "aggiornamento" had fostered hope that, in regard to sexuality, their concerns and experience would be incorporated with an unprecedented profundity and enthusiasm on the part of the magisterium.

In 1968, Richard McCormick retracted his preconciliar agreement that contraception is immoral, and rejected the supposition of *Humanae Vitae* that "every act of coitus has and therefore must retain a *per se* aptitude for procreation." Calling the biological warrants for such a contention "obsolete," McCormick argued that the meaning of every act of coitus cannot be derived from "what happens with relative rarity."[34] A more personalist vocabulary, consistent with *Gaudium et Spes,* should replace biologically oriented language about sex's moral meaning. "Contemporary theological thought insists that the basic criterion for the meaning of human actions is the person, not some isolated aspect of the person."[35] Although biology is certainly relevant to the totality of the person, and although sex indeed has some natural orientation to conception, the *moral* dimensions of this potential must be understood in relation to the meanings of marriage as a whole, including the fertility of the entire relationship. The encyclical had not succeeded in showing (as against the so-called "Majority Report" of the Papal Birth Control Commission) that each and every individual act "deliberately deprived of its procreative power is intrinsically evil."[36]

Expanding a few years later, in the context of sterilization policies in Catholic hospitals, McCormick questions whether "the power to procreate is an element so essential to sexual intimacy that to deprive freely-chosen intimacy of this power is in every instance to assault the ethical or moral good of the person." He observes that if this point had been clearly proved and not merely asserted, the birth control controversy would not have so flourished.[37] Developing the method of analysis which would come to be tagged "proportionalism" by its opponents, McCormick objects that the moral character of an act cannot be identified simply with a physical act; nor has it been so in other spheres of moral reasoning, e.g. property rights and theft, or speech and lying. What counts is "an assessment of an action's relation to the order of persons, to the hierarchy of personal value. . . . The significance (total moral object) [of a sexual act] must be determined as in other instances, by relating the physical act to the order of persons and by seeing it as an intersubjective reality."[38] In other words, there can be proportionate reason for performing even those acts which are in a "premoral" sense "disorders," if those acts are respectful and fulfilling of the integral good of those persons whom they affect.

Of course, to fully appreciate sex as a personal and an intersubjective reality—to have a background against which to illumine the moral status of sexual acts and relationships—would require the "profounder analysis of sexuality in our time, a broad and deep systematic synthesis"[39] for which McCormick has on more than one occasion called, and toward which he has offered some tentative contributions. In a chapter on "Sexuality" in a book on health care, he notes that only when the challenge to rethink sexuality can be carried out in an atmosphere which is "pacific, unthreatened, open," instead of clouded by "panic, fear, and denunciation," can present hints of a new "understanding of sexuality as the radical capacity for interrelatedness (ultimately intimacy) and its actuation as the language of relationship" be followed out.[40] Moreover, the church needs to overcome sexism in its anthropology in general, and in its interpretation of sexuality specifically.[41]

McCormick's own efforts in these directions have occurred for the most part during sallies into the moral complications of particular sexual choices, much as they did two and a half decades ago in his discussions of adolescent sexuality. His most recent collection of revised essays, *The Critical Calling*,[42] provides some offerings which are traditional in their basic contours, but imaginative in expression and explorative in practical content.

As groundwork for a recent foray into today's even more "harrowing" terrain of teenage sexuality and premarital sex, we find reflections on the basic question of the "meaning and purpose of sexual expression." Consistently with the recent tradition, McCormick emphasizes that sexual intimacy is a language which ought to express a special relationship, one formed by the dual aspects of totality and procreation. Two persons take responsibility for the births and education of children within a relationship in which they "are given unreservedly to each other, have taken permanent and public responsibility for each other, have undertaken the risk of shared lives."[43] Monogamous marriage remains the "best chance" human persons have to channel sexuality in a fully human way, that is, into "the friendship of a permanent covenant."[44] This position is traditional in that it upholds monogamous, permanent, heterosexual marriage as the ideal, and grounds the ideal in two morally important dimensions, the unitive and the procreative, proposed as integral to the human realization of sexuality. At the same time, by emphasizing the potential of sexual relationships for "friendship," McCormick has loosed the tie of sexual morality to individual acts and elevated it into the context of mutual respect, commitment, and companionship. He sees this development as having characterized Catholic sexual ethics generally since Pius XII. Its result is that the relationship of the couple becomes a broader criterion with which to evaluate their sexual and reproductive decisions.

For instance, reproductive technologies which further the parental potential of spouses can be accepted, even though, in a few particular acts, they separate the act of conception from that of sex. That a somewhat higher priority is at least tacitly given to the unitive dimension of marital friendship than to the procreative is revealed in McCormick's belief that third party involvement would violate "conjugal exclusivity."[45] In previous writings, he has drawn on the work of the late Paul Ramsey to articulate the non-act-focused unity of parental and spousal love in terms of "spheres" of relationship which should not be separated. "This means that we may not procreate apart from the union of marital love, and that sexual love may not be expressed apart from a context of responsibility for procreation."[46]

One of McCormick's more creative and sensitive explorations of sexual ethics is a chapter on male homosexuality. The real contribution of this discussion is a nuancing of what it means to apply a norm in concrete and perplexing circumstances. Following through on suggestions such as those made by McCormick himself in response to *Humanae Vitae,* some other theologians have justified certain homosexual relationships, even while adhering to an understanding of heterosexuality as normative, by suggesting that anomalous sex acts or relationships are "premoral evils." These may or may not be justified depending on the total complex of factors which encourages or discourages a particular sexual orientation and the life circumstances in which it can be realized. Other thinkers have found this approach excessively negative toward persons with the "minority" sexual orientation, and have chosen to affirm their concrete moral agency by describing basic sexual orientation as "neutral."[47] McCormick (justifiably) finds neither of these alternatives fully satisfying. His point of departure, like those in the first category, is the premise that heterosexuality is somehow normative both for orientation and acts. Yet out of concern for the quality of ministry to gay people in their often painful situations, he does not assert that ideal until point five in a six-point "modest suggestion" about a Christian view of "the gay phenomenon."[48]

> It has been and remains the Church's conviction (based on biblical, anthropological, philosophical evidence, her own experience and reflection) that the sexual expression of interpersonal love offers us the best chance for our growth and humanization —therefore for our maturation as loving persons in Christ's image—if it is structured within the man-woman relationship of covenanted (permanent and exclusive) friendship.[49]

As a prelude to this ideal and as a context for reading it, there are offered four caveats about (1) the power of sin in the world which touches everyone, both through personal characteristics and through "enslaving structures," (2) the liberation which Christ offers all through love, (3) the mission of the body of Christ to change the world through presence to individuals and by remedying oppressive institutions, and (4) the manifold distortions of human sexuality to which the community as kingdom has a healing mission. Although the church in its ministry encourages heterosexual monogamy, McCormick states in a final point that if "an individual is incapable of structuring his sexual intimacy within such a relationship (is irreversibly homosexual), and is not called to celibacy for the Kingdom [subject to his own decision before God], the liberating presence and concern of the community will take a different form. . . ." The church will encourage the cultivation of fidelity and exclusiveness, will offer social and sacramental support, and will combat discrimination against homosexuals.[50] McCormick calls this a "pastoral of approximation" of the ideal, calling to our attention both that the ideal does not cease to claim moral attention even in circumstances of difficulty, and that few if any persons in their sexual lives reach more than an approximation of ideal morality.[51] This analysis goes beyond others' previous efforts, in that it seeks a positive language to articulate the relationship of gay persons within the Christian community, at the same time giving heterosexual marriage an illuminative and guiding role in shaping human sexual expression.

3. TOWARD THE FUTURE

In a recent essay on the state of moral theology in the last half-century, Richard McCormick offers several observations about "significant developments," "where we are now," and "suggestions for the future."[52] Pinpointing as they do many of the major landmarks, as well as some interesting byways, on the map of Roman Catholic ethics in its ecclesial setting, several of McCormick's flags can be turned usefully to the highlighting of his own contributions. All of the items on his agenda for the future have already been significantly furthered in sexual ethics by his own work—among these, four or five preeminently so.

Since the years of Vatican II, he has done much to make this sphere of moral reflection and guidance more "honest," "realistic" "collegial," and "adult." Certainly his twenty-one year protest against pronouncements put forth without adequate analysis has amplified the call for an *honest* reexamination of sexual teaching, one in which, as he puts it, there will be no " 'theology' rigged to justify pretaken authoritative positions." On the side of *realism,* McCormick has warned that wariness is the only appropriate attitude toward any system or author who is so intolerant of ambiguity that he or she insists on having all the answers. Instead, theologians and ethicists must admit readily the limits of all "human concepts and verbal tools." In striving to clarify concepts, improve on systems, and, above all, mediate between the theoretical and the practical, the moral theologian must be informed *collegially* by "the experience and reflection of all those with a true competence." In view of his priestly vocation, the ruminations of McCormick on sex, marriage, and parenthood will have their practical limitations. Yet he has provided for many years a model of the sort of critical openness which permits any ethicist to reflect upon and assess human realities with which he or she has an empathetic and imaginative familiarity rather than a first-hand, experiential one. Along similar lines, since at least his 1960 plea that the counselor encourage the teenager to be more mature and self-motivated, he has with increasing insistency voiced the expectation that *adult* personal responsibility be taken seriously, in sexual conduct no less that in any other sort. "The older paternalism is dead." And, finally, one must not forget that McCormick has done much to make sexual ethics more "scientifically informed," especially in regard to the relevance of the natural cycle of fertility to the morality of interventions to control it, and also in regard to basic questions of psycho-sexual development and orientation, and of the integral role of sexuality in personality.[53]

In other provocative suggestions about the environment of contemporary moral thinking, McCormick fosters movement toward an ethics of sexuality which can guide mutually respectful, personally rewarding, and socially responsible forms of intimacy. Importantly for sexuality, McCormick calls ours an "age of women" and an "age of justice."[54] He notes the already considerable influence of feminist thought on the Catholic theology of marriage and sexuality, facilitated greatly by the multiplying presence of women theologians in the "academy." More fundamental and more drastic implications of this "age of women" become evident when we join the specifically academic enterprise with the more fundamental mandate to inform moral theology generally with the experience of those most involved in the moral realities.

Concerted attention to the experiences, claims, grievances, and exhortations of women on issues of sex and gender has the potential to transform the Roman Catholic understanding of sexuality, marriage, and parenthood. One must grant both that experience-based expressions will be diverse, and that "experiences" as such do not yield moral norms. Moreover, women's and men's experiences are not absolutely separate or incommensurable; in these spheres, they overlap, complement, challenge, and enrich one another. Nonetheless, it is the female dimension in each of these shared spheres which has been historically downplayed and even suppressed by church teaching focusing on the definition of women's (but not men's) fulfillment in terms of sexual and parental roles; and the concentration even in the female-aligned spheres of marriage and reproduction on items such as semen, penetration, and paternity. The solution to such distortions is to disregard neither the importance of parenthood in filling out sexual relationships, nor the physiological components of procreation, as potential moral markers. But how are the physiological and psychological aspects of sexuality, in their importance for both men and women, for both parenthood and interpersonal commitment, to be successfully united? A real "solution" is nowhere yet evident on the horizon. A transformed consciousness of sexuality's moral opportunities and obligations will come slowly to birth only if nurtured by each sex's honest introspection and receptive other-regard, with attention to the social contexts which either distort or support interpersonal bonds, commitments, and projects

A related dimension of the sexual consciousness of tomorrow is indicated by McCormick's invocation of "the age of justice." He notes, for instance, that the emergence of liberation theology has already served to redirect attention from "the individualism of the west, since one form of that individualism is overemphasis on the personal (especially sexual) dimensions of the moral life."[55] An obvious juncture of justice and sexual ethics is concern for the welfare and autonomy of women in sexual relationships and in the many areas of social relationship where gender concerns are prominent. It is just such questions which have been raised poignantly and powerfully by feminist authors.

At the same time, ethical reconsideration of sexuality often takes place in an intellectual and cultural context which still reflects an individualist and liberal bias. Despite the fact that these strands of western, democratic culture have made positive contributions to moral understanding—the dignity and importance of each person, and the centrality of freedom and autonomy in safeguarding the moral life—they also carry along certain limitations of perspective. The emphasis on freedom, personal fulfillment, and autonomous decision-making is a corrective to a pre-modern inclination to interpret sex and its relational potential almost only in terms of their contributions to family, tribe, nation, church, or species. At the same time, the couple cannot be viewed realistically or truly "experientially" if it is dissociated from the wider bonds which sex and parenthood inevitably create.

In one of his early essays, McCormick (denying the legitimacy of contraception) grounds procreation as the "primary end" of marriage and sex in their social and institutional functions.[56] "The couple is seen in a context that transcends them." "Their union constitutes a segment or a cell within the whole human family."[57] Since at least the mid-1960s, the focal point in Catholic interpretations of sexuality has been the personal relationship of the couple, in light of which even the moral quality of procreation has been primarily explained. Indeed, as has been shown, the quest to anchor sexual ethics more convincingly in the love relationship extends back to the "personalism" of the 1930s, although it only gradually became incorporated substantially into "official" teaching. Certainly this relationship is crucial, has been in need of a more experiential reexamination, and is appropriate as a key to moral analysis of sexuality. Yet a too exclusive focus on the "self-gift" or "conjugal love" of spouses precludes adequate understanding of the social conditions of possibility of that relationship (and also tends to confine discussions of sexuality to marriage). Although it is no longer appropriate to call procreation the primary end of sex, nor to see reproduction of the species as the eminent social contribution of the couple, it is nonetheless important to craft a moral vocabulary to express intelligibly sexuality's social side. This includes not only the ways in which couple and family reach out to the community, but also those in which social expectations and patterns help determine what the nature of an interpersonal relation can be. Studies of sexuality and sexual relationships which sort out factors of culture, class, economics, and gender will be indispensable here.

These reflections on the relevance of women's experience and of a justice-oriented perspective on the future shape of sexual ethics have certainly been more suggestive and programmatic than substantive and definitive. I would like to organize some concluding reflections touching on both areas around the possible interrelation of sex, marriage, and parenthood in a view of sexuality which both values women's perspective and tries to set the whole issue in a context broader than the intimacy and "self-gift" of the individual couple. These comments again will hardly exhaust the pertinent issues, but may provoke further reflection and eventual clarification in dialogue with others.

The question posed by the lengthy furor over *Humanae Vitae* is what integral relation procreation can have to commitment sexually expressed, once it is recognized that it is the person who is the ultimate referent of morality and not his or her biology or physical acts as such. The encyclical and its more traditional interpreters try to safeguard the procreative values and responsibilities of sex by giving procreation a foothold in the intimacy of love itself, and, more crucially, by locating that foothold in one place where love and procreation can clearly and tangibly coincide: the act of sexual intercourse. What the encyclical neglects is that marital love and parenthood (beyond "conception") are essentially *relationships,* and neither comes into being nor receives full expression in any one act or symbol. The symbol has no meaning apart from the web of realities whose meaning it helps to focus and communicate. It stands for something larger and must be subordinated to that grounding reality. The larger reality is the totality of a committed sexual relationship, in its dimensions both of loving partnership and of shared parenthood.

Because the encyclical concentrated attention on a particular sort of physical act, critiques of it have counterbalanced by uplifting the personal and downplaying the physical. The parental, as "procreation" or "reproduction," is not infrequently implicated in physicalism. Critiques can yield the impression that only the affective aspects of sexuality really "count" morally, and that the only valid sexual norm is the quality of relationship between sexual partners. Yet such an angle on sexuality is also limited because it virtually eliminates from view those aspects of sexual "experience" to which *Humanae Vitae* clings too desperately. Sexual persons are still embodied persons, even if the whole significance of sexuality is not enclosed by reproductive biology.

Sexuality connects persons with one another in physical, intergenerational, material, and broadly social ways, as well as in the ways of one-to-one intimacy and commitment. Parenthood can fulfill the physical capacities of human sexuality, even while it enhances affective and social partnership. Two persons who extend their creativity, commitment, and hope to children will in doing so rely on, necessarily place trust in, affect permanently, and be morally bound to improve the cultural setting and social institutions into which their family ties them. Shared parenthood brings to fruition the multidimensional human potential of sexuality in a unique and poignant way. It is not a merely incidental or casually dispensable aspect of sex, but one which, other things being equal, should be communally encouraged and personally anticipated as a key meaning dimension of faithful and loving sexual commitment.

The Birth Control Commission's Majority Report, which argued ultimately in favor of artificial means of controlling births, asserted forcefully the complementarity of parental and spousal love. Conjugal love "is not exhausted in the simple mutual giving in which one party seeks only the other," but "according to the condition of each is made truly fruitful in the creation of new life."[58] A "truly 'contraceptive' mentality" is not one which intervenes occasionally to limit births, but one which loses sight of this basic and intimate connection. "A right ordering toward the good of the child within the conjugal and familial community pertains to the essence of human sexuality."[59] Part of the moral meaning of sexual acts is an "ordering" to "responsible, generous and prudent parenthood," just as part derives from "the requirements of mutual love."[60] Responsible parenthood, of course, "does not depend upon the direct fecundity of each and every particular act."[61] But if the severance of procreation from sexuality is moved from the sphere of occasional interventions to the basic definition of sexuality, then a "truly contraceptive" sexual mentality wins.

One wonders whether an insidious disconnection of sex, love, and nurturing children does not underlie many debates over abortion, infertility therapies (especially heterologous ones), and sexual intimacy without long-term personal and social commitment. At the same time, it surely will be admitted that challenges to traditional sexual rules often are occasioned by commendable commitments to dislodge patriarchal definitions of sex, marriage, and family, or to push beyond an act-centered analysis to one that is more just to persons in their total set of personal circumstances and needs. A final and crucial issue, then, remains the specific normative force of the essential and morally important dimensions of sexuality: "love" or affective and social life-partnership, and "procreation" or parenthood shared with one's sexual, affective, and social partner.

Richard McCormick's contributions in the area of sexuality may be even more important as far as this issue is concerned than they are on that of the substantive meaning of sexuality—a meaning about which persons in sexual relationships should have at least as much to say. In responding to the normative import of the values ("life" and "love") affirmed by *Humanae Vitae,* McCormick depicts the moral life as an arena not only of fulfillment, but of struggle. In this light, the encyclical can be seen as "outlining a horizon toward which we must move rather than a casuistry to which we must conform," a horizon whose compelling authority is accepted as long as it remains a beacon even in relentlessly cloudy circumstances. Regarding birth control, he concludes, "as long as the couple resolve to do what they can to bring their marriage (and societal conditions) to the point where the fullness of the sexual act is possible, their practice of contraception would not represent moral failure."[62] Extending the point, we may suggest that sexuality always be seen against the horizon of a committed love which in physical intimacy hopes for the shared task and opportunity to nurture children, and promises to bring both sexual and parental love to fruition in mutual respect and social accountability. Yet this ideal of the human sexual experience is just that, an ideal prophetically stated, not a "casuistry" which can solve every particular problem which the diversity of human circumstances thrusts forward. At the existential level, the overriding norms will surely be the dignity and moral responsibility of each person before God, first; and, second, the love and unity of the couple in the partnership to which they give sexual expression. In circumstances of limit and conflict, their commitment to parenthood will be third. Within that commitment, responsibilities to existing children, and even to the community surrounding the family, will take precedence over potential increase in family size.

As a final note, Roman Catholic sexual ethicists are increasingly sensitive to sexuality's vast experiential range outside the so-called "conjugal couple" as well as within it. This range cannot be comprehended fully using only the three principles dealing with "venereal pleasure" upon which McCormick was able to rely in 1964. His recent essays on homosexuality and teenage sexuality exemplify a collective struggle to think more creatively about the parameters of sexual integrity, and more comprehensively than the monogamous marital context. Experiential and cross-cultural "collegiality" will be crucial to a breakthrough in our understanding of sexuality and moral obligation, an item of the first order on Catholicism's future ethical agenda.

Notes

1. *"Humanae Vitae:* 20 Years After" was convened in Rome in November 1988, under the leadership of Monsignor Carlo Caffarra, and with the sponsorship of the Lateran University, Opus Dei, and the Knights of Columbus.

2. Bernard Häring, "Does God Condemn Contraception? A Question for the Whole Church," *Commonweal* 116 (1989) 70. The essay was published originally in the Italian biweekly, *Il Regno* (Jan. 15, 1989).

3. As cited in a "margin note," *Origins* 18 (1989) 632.

4. *The Cologne Declaration,* released Jan. 25, 1989, *Origins* 18 (1989) 633.

5. "The Moral Norms of 'Humanae Vitae,' " *Origins* 18 (1989) 632. Originally published in *L'Osservatore Romano* (February 10, 1989).

6. "Does God Condemn Contraception?" 71.

7. John T. Noonan, Jr., *Contraception: A History of Its Treatment by the Catholic Theologians and Canonists* (enlarged ed.; Cambridge: Harvard Univ., 1986; original ed., 1965).

8. Richard A. McCormick, S.J., *Notes on Moral Theology: 1965 through 1980* (Washington, D.C.: University Press of America, 1981) 227–28. This source consists of McCormick's contributions to the bibliographical essays on moral theology published in *Theological Studies.* The contribution here cited appeared originally in 1968. Future references to this volume will include the year of original publication in TS in parentheses after the page citation in *Notes.*

9. Ibid. 228.

10. Richard A. McCormick, S.J., "Adolescent Masturbation: A Pastoral Problem," *The Homiletic and Pastoral Review* 60 (1960) 527–40; and "Adolescent Affection: Toward a Sound Sexuality," *HPR* 61 (1960) 245–61.

11. "Adolescent Affection" 247.

12. Ibid. 246.

13. "Adolescent Masturbation" 534.

14. Ibid., 249.

15. "Adolescent Affection" 251.

16. Ibid.

17. Richard A. McCormick, S.J., "Conjugal Love and Conjugal Morality: A reevaluation of the Catholic position in terms of total marital commitment," *America* 110 (1964) 38–42.

18. The most influential personalist authors were Herbert Doms, *The Meaning of Marriage* (New York: Sheed and Ward, 1939); originally *Vom Sinn und Zweck der Ehe* (Breslau: Ostdeutsche Verlagsanstalt, 1935); and Dietrich von Hildebrand, *Marriage* (New York: Longmans, 1942); originally, *Die Ehe* (Munich: Kösel-Pustet, 1929). For treatments of the early personalist debate, see John C. Ford, S.J., and Gerald Kelly, S.J., *Contemporary Moral Theology* 2: *Marriage Questions* (Westminster, Md.: Newman, 1964) 18–35; Theodore Mackin, S.J., *What Is Marriage?* (New York: Paulist, 1984) 225–35. A Vatican condemnation of 1944 is cited in full by Ford and Kelly, 27–28.

19. Doms, *The Meaning of Marriage* 84–85, 94–95.

20. *Pius XI on Christian Marriage: The English Translation* (New York: Barry Vail Corporation, 1931) 12.

21. *Gaudium et Spes (The Pastoral Constitution on the Church in the Modern World)*, in Walter M. Abbot, S.J., ed., *The Documents of Vatican II* (The America Press: New York, America Press, 1966) no. 51.

22. Ibid. no. 48.

23. Ibid. no. 50.

24. See writings of John Paul II on the "theology of the body," which was the theme of his Wednesday afternoon general-audience talks in 1979–81. The series was published in three volumes by the Daughters of St. Paul (Boston): *Original Unity of Man and Woman: Catechesis on the Book of Genesis* (1981); *Blessed Are the Pure of Heart: Catechesis on the Sermon on the Mount and Writings of St. Paul* (1983); *Reflections on Humanae Vitae: Conjugal Morality and Spirituality* (1984). See also Ronald Lawler, O.F.M. Cap., et al., *Catholic Sexual Ethics: A Summary, Explanation & Defense* (Huntington, Ind.: Our Sunday Visitor, 1985).

25. McCormick, "Conjugal Love and Conjugal Morality," *America* 110 (1964) 38.

26. Ibid. 40.

27. Ibid. 39.

28. E.g. John Paul II, *Reflections on "Humanae Vitae."*

29. "Conjugal Love" 40; italics added.

30. Ibid. 41.

31. Ibid. 42.

32. Offering an early interpretation of *Gaudium et Spes,* McCormick uses similar language, even while arguing that the council had left open the contraception issue. He says "that conjugal love is a total personal commitment ordained to parenthood, and that therefore the intimate expressions of this two-in-oneness must 'preserve the full sense of mutual self-giving and human

procreation in the context of human love' " ("The Council on Contraception," *America* 114 [1966] 47–48, at 48). That the struggle for authority in interpreting the council's language had already begun is confirmed by the reply of John C. Ford, "Footnote on Contraception," *America* 114 (1966) 103–07; and by McCormick's reply, ibid., 107.

33. John Paul II, *Familiaris Consortio* (Apostolic Exhortation, "On the Family," December 15, 1981) (Washington D.C.: United States Catholic Conference, 1982) no. 11.

34. *Notes* 218 (1968).

35. Ibid. 219.

36. Ibid. 221.

37. "Sterilization and Theological Method," *Theological Studies* 37 (1976) 474.

38. *Notes* 220 (1968). In an essay on the tenth anniversary of *Humanae Vitae* (*Notes* 774–75 [1979]), McCormick develops the insight that premoral evils such as contraception are still not "neutral." They are to be avoided all other things being equal, but are not wrong absolutely.

39. *Notes* 778 (1979).

40. Richard A. McCormick, *Health and Medicine in the Catholic Tradition: Tradition in Transition* (New York: Crossroad, 1984) 104.

41. Ibid. 101–02. On the issue of feminism, McCormick has commented that the Church is missing an opportunity for leadership, and is shortselling its mission. "If the 'official Church' continues to turtle across the finish line in this way, is she not but a pale image of her radical and innovative Founder?" (Notes 392 [1972].)

42. Richard A. McCormick, S.J., *The Critical Calling: Reflections on Moral Dilemmas Since Vatican II* (Washington, D.C.: Georgetown University Press, 1989).

43. Ibid. 392.

44. Ibid. 393. Three times on the same page McCormick emphasizes that marriage is friendship and covenant.

45. Ibid. 341.

46. *Notes* 406 (1972).

47. McCormick surveys some partakers in the discussion (including John Harvey, Lisa Cahill, and Charles Curran) in *Critical Calling,* 291–93.

48. *Critical Calling* 307–08.

49. Ibid. 308.

50. Ibid.

51. Ibid. 309. McCormick builds his position on a distinction between "specific and individual rectitude." The former refers to those characteristics of moral analysis which are "independent of personal dispositions, attitudes, goals, circumstances." The latter refers to "the personal attitudes, actions, circumstances that qualify our conduct" (302).

52. Richard A. McCormick, S.J., "Moral Theology 1940–1989: An Overview," *Theological Studies* 50 (1989) 3–24.

53. Ibid. 24.

212 / Lisa Sowle Cahill

54. Ibid. 23, 19.

55. Ibid. 15.

56. See also McCormick's quite traditional formulation two years earlier ("Anti-Fertility Pills," *Homiletic and Pastoral Review* 62 (1962) 695):

> Thus whereas the individual organs of the body are immediately ordained to the good of the whole person and so absorbed by the whole that they possess no finality independent of the person, the generative function has a primary finality of its own, the good of the species. Hence the principles governing its suppression must take this teleology into account.

In support, McCormick gives the following bibliographical information: J. Lynch, S.J., *Linacre Quarterly* 20 (1953) 86; D. O'Callaghan, *Moral Principles of Fertility Control* 18; J. Connery, S.J., *Theological Studies* 17 (1956) 559.

It should be noted that McCormick's purpose in this essay was not primarily to give a moral analysis of "the pill," but to provide the solid scientific understanding of its function and possible uses which would be essential to a firm moral grasp. However, he reflects the literature and ethical approach of the day in briefly considering, primarily in relation to "direct intention," uses of contraceptives to correct menstrual disorders, to regularize the cycle to enhance rhythm, to suppress ovulation during pregnancy and so avoid pregnancy, to enhance fertility with an "ovulation rebound," and to delay menstruation (697–700).

57. "Conjugal Love" 38.

58. "The Theological Report of the Papal Commission on Birth Control," June 26, 1966, in Odile M. Liebard, *Official Catholic Teachings: Love and Sexuality* (Wilmington, N.C.: McGrath Publishing Co., 1978) 299.

59. Ibid. 302.

60. Ibid. 303.

61. Ibid.

62. *Notes* 226–27 (1968).

11

Divorce, Remarriage, and Pastoral Practice

Margaret A. Farley

The last twenty-five years have seen significant changes in Roman Catholic belief and practice regarding divorce and second marriages. These changes are sharply visible in the writings of moral theologians, in the activities of marriage tribunals, and in the general perceptions and judgments of growing numbers of persons who consider themselves faithful members of the Roman Catholic community. Sympathy with the changes is not unanimous among theologians, but it is widespread enough to be characterized fairly as a clear majority response.

Major changes so cautiously but relentlessly forged in theological circles are often not reflected in the pronouncements and teachings of church officials, however. They are generally not to be found, for example, in the positions articulated by Pope John Paul II or in documents promulgated by Vatican congregations and commissions or in the 1983 Code of Canon Law. Indeed, the polarization between opinions of many theologians and canonists on the one hand, and traditional positions taken by Vatican officials on the other, now seems extreme. This is true despite the fact that the impetus for change (here as in so many other ethical questions) is traceable at least in part to the Second Vatican Council and to national episcopal conferences as well as individual bishops who have pressed for just the sort of changes that theologians are formulating. The perception of a need for change is fueled by western culture's massive contemporary experience of the breakdown of marital relationships and by the gradual recognition of legitimate differences in cross-cultural interpretations of marriage and family.

DEVELOPMENT AND IMPASSE

Changes in theological opinion and pastoral practice regarding divorce and second marriages lean strongly in the direction of allowing first efforts at marital union (first marriages) to end and second efforts (in new marriages) to be sustained by full participation in the sacramental life of the church. Key changes have to do, therefore, with new understandings of the requirement of permanence in Christian marriage. No one proposes eliminating this requirement, but ways are sought to interpret it which appear more adequate to human and Christian experience and less likely to place unjust and tragic burdens on individual persons and partnerships. The ultimate goal of such changes can be described in terms of nurturing lifelong marriages, but the proximate concern is with the irretrievable loss of (or failure to achieve) union in some marriages and the possibilities for subsequent new marriages in a Christian context.

More specifically, the issue for Roman Catholics has become the meaning and application of the notion of "indissolubility": Insofar as indissolubility characterizes a first marriage, can a second marriage ever be justified (so long as the spouse of the first marriage remains alive)? This question often translates into: May persons in a second marriage ever be allowed to share fully in the life of the church, even to the point of receiving the eucharist? The last quarter century of theological and pastoral responses to these questions may be understood best against the background of the tradition that stretches directly and most identifiably from the twelfth century to the 1983 Code of Canon Law and that continues to be strongly represented in the teachings of Pope John Paul II. As a tradition it has had its own developments, primarily legal but also theological, and it has not been without some pluralism in its interpretation.[1] It found its focus in the mediating decisions of Pope Alexander III, received further articulation at the Council of Trent in opposition to the Protestant reformers, became incorporated into the first Code of Canon Law in 1917, and remains relatively intact in the revised Code of 1983.

The Tradition

According to this tradition (with its evolved specifications), some marriages are absolutely indissoluble, and some are not. Those marriages which may never be dissolved (short of the death of one of the spouses) are marriages between two baptized persons who have validly consented to and sexually consummated their marriage. These are considered sacramental marriages, and the absoluteness of their bond is sealed by sexual intercourse. While the partners in such marriages may be "separated" (according to church law as well as by civil separation or divorce), they may never marry another—precisely because their first marriage is considered in an important sense still to exist. If they do remarry (civilly), the church does not recognize their second marriage; and as long as they continue to live with this new partner (unless they do so not only for serious reasons but with sexual abstinence), church discipline requires that they be excluded from receiving the sacraments. The only way they may be declared free to enter or remain in a second marriage (again, short of the death of their original spouse) is if it can be determined that something was so deficient, so invalidating, in their first "marrying" that in fact no marriage took place. If it can be determined, for example, that there was not full and free mutual consent, or that some invalidating impediment prevented a marriage from being effected, or that the required form for valid marrying was absent, then it may be concluded that the first marriage does not continue to exist because, in fact, it never existed. The "annulment" of such a marriage must be pronounced officially by an ecclesiastical marriage tribunal.

But, also according to this tradition, some marriages do indeed exist whose indissolubility is not absolute (the marriage is vulnerable to being dissolved on some conditions). If a marriage, for example, has never been sexually consummated, it may in certain circumstances be dissolved by papal authority. Or if either or both of the partners were not baptized at the time of their marriage, the marriage can be dissolved for a variety of serious reasons that are determined to constitute a "privilege of faith" for the spouse who did or comes to believe. In these cases, it is possible to justify a second marriage and to admit spouses in second marriages (who either were or later became baptized Catholics) to the full sacramental life of the church. Determination of such cases must also be made officially —sometimes by a marriage tribunal, sometimes by papal authority.

Loosened by Vatican II, a veritable avalanche of literature in moral theology has poured forth since the mid-1960s, struggling with both the logic of this tradition and the logic of contemporary human experience regarding marriage and divorce. Richard McCormick's "Notes on Moral Theology" in the volumes of *Theological Studies* from 1965 to 1989 provide a remarkable view not only of the avalanche of literature but of what can happen to a thinker who tries to be faithful to both of these logics. In these years McCormick directly addressed the problem of divorce and remarriage nine times, and indirectly addressed it several more times (in relation to, for example, questions of moral reasoning or general problems in sexual ethics). The changes in moral theology that characterize this period of thinking about divorce and remarriage are clear in McCormick's chronicles, and the key issues and sub-issues emerge in his analyses. What comes into view, too, is the rather dramatic collision course or stand-off of much of moral theology on the one hand and Vatican leadership on the other in a struggle for the evolution of the tradition.

Theological Development

In 1966 McCormick reported on four articles that discussed the situation of persons divorced (from sacramental, consummated marriages) and remarried. Of these articles, two accepted the present formulation of the church's traditional position, and two attempted to move beyond it.[2] Of the first two, one simply reinforced the view that persons in second marriages must either separate or, if this is not possible, continue to live together but only insofar as they resolve to avoid sexual activity. In no other way can they return to the sacraments of the church. The second article acknowledged that persons who remain sexually active in second marriages cannot be admitted to the sacraments—in particular, the eucharist—but it probed the reasons for this. Because of the "adulterous situation" of a second marriage, the partners' life together is at odds with the faith of the church. Hence, they are in basic conflict with the sign-dimension of the eucharist (insofar as it is a sacrament of the unity of individuals in the church with one another and with God). Nonetheless, persons in second marriages must not be rejected by the church, and they should even be encouraged to participate in the life of the church to the extent that it can be open to them—to come to mass, to avail themselves of devotional practices, etc.

A third article in these 1966 "Notes," however, disputed the necessary exclusion of persons in second marriages from the sacraments, arguing that reception of the eucharist does not require perfect holiness and that, moreover, if it is justified at all for two persons to continue to live together in a marital relationship, their engagement in sexual activity is not necessarily a moral evil. Theirs need not be, in other words, an "adulterous situation." A fourth article goes beyond discussion of pastoral policy to raise theological questions about the nature of Christian sacramental marriage—to ask, therefore, about the status of the first marriage of these divorced persons. If, for example, the concepts of "consent" and of "consummation" are expanded to include elements of process and development, might it be the case that what looked like an absolutely indissoluble marriage was not yet that (and hence, implicitly, persons who had been in such marriages might after all be free to live legitimately as full Christians in their present second marriages)?

While these articles seem hardly revolutionary, their details are important because they signal some of the key issues which will preoccupy moral theologians for the decade to follow: the moral status of the conjugal lives of persons living in stable second marriages; the possibility of their returning to the sacraments; the meaning of both the sacrament of marriage and of the church's other sacraments (especially the eucharist); the minimal and maximal requirements for absolutely indissoluble marriages.

McCormick's own response to the articles and issues in these early "Notes" is also important. In 1966 he saw little reason for any serious change in the traditional formulations to which as a moral theologian he was heir. "There are legitimate questions," he agreed, but "one only hopes that this continuing theological task can be acquitted quietly and unsensationally without offering the cruel comfort born of false hopes."[3] He left open the possibility of a pastoral solution to the problem of reception of the sacraments by those in second marriages whose first marriage was invalid. But when a first marriage was genuinely sacramental (that is validly consented to by two baptized persons) and sexually consummated, its indissolubility cannot be ignored no matter how important the relationship may be in a second marriage. Someone in this situation still belongs to another. To ask whether she or he can nonetheless approach the eucharist may be a legitimate question, but, McCormick concluded, ". . . it is not clear to me how anything but a negative answer to this question is possible."[4] In 1966 McCormick's position probably represented a majority opinion among moral theologians.

In 1971 Richard McCormick returned to the question of divorce and remarriage.[5] It was obvious by then that doctrinal winds were blowing, and they had already turned McCormick himself around in some significant respects. In place by now were at least three important contributions from Vatican II: a description of the nature of marriage as a "community of love"[6]; a history of council interventions such as Melchite Archbishop Elias Zoghbi's proposal to allow acceptance of divorce and remarriage on the model of the eastern churches;[7] conciliar openness to sharing the eucharist with persons not fully in union with the Roman church (as articulated in the *Decree on Ecumenism* and the *Decree on the Eastern Churches*).[8] Also in place were initial groundbreaking biblical and historical studies that served to relativize for many moral theologians what had been previously perceived as absolutes in the tradition regarding divorce and remarriage.[9]

McCormick's primary focus in the 1971 "Notes" was on the issue of admission of persons in second marriages to the eucharist. Treatment of this issue in the literature, of course, necessarily included treatment of the status of both first and second marriages. McCormick identified four positions advanced by writers in the immediately preceding years. The first was the traditional position that Roman Catholics in second marriages are living in a "state of sin" and hence cannot be admitted to full participation in the sacraments (a problem, of course, ameliorated only if the couple agrees to forego sexual relations). A second position suggested that individuals in second marriages might be accepted by the church under a "sign of forgiveness." When a first marriage is both valid and absolutely indissoluble a second marriage begins marked by the sin of the divorce which makes it possible. But this is not an unforgivable sin, and though the second marriage can never have the full sacramental status of the first, it can (through repentance and fidelity) be incorporated into the life of the church. This solution approximates the practice of the eastern churches.

The third position was the one that by 1971 had achieved growing support from many theologians and canonists, including Richard McCormick. It was the "good faith" or internal-forum solution. It provided for reception of the eucharist by individuals in second marriages who believe that their first marriage was not a valid Christian marriage even though this fact cannot be verified on canonically acceptable grounds (even though, that is, they cannot obtain an official "annulment"). It also applied to those individuals in second marriages who, despite the fact that their first marriage might have been valid, are nonetheless convinced in conscience that their second marriage is their only true marriage. McCormick himself saw no difficulty with these applications of an internal-forum solution. However, in order to justify an overall pastoral policy "which refuses to unite canonical marital status with sacramental practice,"[10] he was concerned with what it would mean for situations in which persons' consciences are unclear and conflicted—situations in which persons believe their first marriages to have been genuine Christian marriages and who therefore do not experience complete "good faith" about their second ones. Rather than approach such cases by bringing them under a "sign of forgiveness" (as in position 2), McCormick (and others) offered a way in which they, too, might be included in an internal-forum solution. If traditional categories of "consent" and "consummation" were enlarged to include such factors as capacity for a shared life, maturity for choice and human relationship, spiritual as well as physical consummation, etc., there was a good possibility that many first marriages may not have been genuine Christian sacramental marriages at all. This possibility now seemed strong enough to McCormick to justify a broadened internal-forum approach. He favored this approach because it did not imply approval in principle of second marriages. Nonetheless, as a practical solution to the situation of many persons in stable second marriages he recognized that it moved him beyond where he had been in 1966.

Several years ago in these Notes I stated: 'It is not clear to me how anything but a negative answer to this ... question [of admitting to the eucharist remarried persons whose first marriage was apparently canonically valid] is possible.' Recent literature is a chastening reminder that the matter is certainly more difficult and debatable than that sentence would indicate. Indeed, as will be clear, I would substantially modify that opinion.[11]

There was a fourth position, however, that went farther than McCormick at the time thought justifiable. Proposed as theoretically probable by Bernard Häring,[12] it held that it is possible for marriages—even Christian sacramental consummated marriages—to die (truly to end). If a first marriage has been thoroughly destroyed, it cannot any longer be considered an existing marriage. In such a case a second marriage may be not only acceptable to the Christian community; it may be itself a sacramental marriage in the full sense of the term. McCormick recognized that "probably a fair number of theologians would agree that Häring has accurately sniffed the direction of the winds of doctrinal development or, more accurately, pastoral practice."[13] But for McCormick in 1971, "The notion of the 'dead' marriage, especially if it means the Church's ability to tolerate a second 'living' marriage, needs a great deal more study."[14]

One year later McCormick turned again to these questions, noting that "there has been no letup in the flow of literature during the past year."[15] The issues this year were extensions of the year before. The problem of marital failures was addressed by arguments for the power of the church to dissolve marriages ("let no human put asunder" need not rule out a power of divine origin dissolving marriages) and by proposals to institutionalize the developmental aspects of marriage by distinguishing forms and levels of marriage. That is, the church might recognize an initial form of marriage, constituted by mutual consent and aimed at growing union ("consummation" in a personal, integral sense) and an advanced form of marriage, tested by time, faithful, and finally fully consecrated. Only the latter would be sacramental and absolutely indissoluble.

Consideration of the internal-forum solution continued, with growing emphasis on its usefulness and potential expansion as a pastoral policy. This was the pastoral approach which McCormick himself still seemed to prefer to other forms of institutional accommodation of marital failures. For McCormick this solution provided a way to hold the line against what he feared would be complete separation of the moral from the juridical (if indissolubility were to be seen as purely regulatory); against expanding the use of church power to dissolve marriages (though not against calling the church to accept those who fail in their marriages); and against legitimizing a notion of a marriage's "death." The internal-forum solution, as McCormick saw it in 1972, was still to be directed primarily toward discerning the original invalidity of a first marriage, not its validity and eventual demise.

By 1975 a consensus seemed clear on some issues, particularly the issue of the admission of persons in stable second marriages to the sacraments.[16] Here theological opinion had moved strongly in a positive direction. The reasons varied, but the conclusions were strikingly similar. Key arguments and clarifications had evolved to ease some of the remaining troubling questions. Among the most important of these resolving insights were: (1) Persons otherwise welcomed to participate in the life of the church are not reasonably to be judged as living in a serious "state of sin" (that is, since everyone agreed that persons living in stable second marriages should be encouraged to participate as far as possible in the life of the church, it seemed contradictory to continue to assert that they are nonetheless in a lethal state of sin). (2) Individual consciences are to be respected especially in situations of recognized limitations of juridical structures and processes. (3) Pastoral accommodations can be made without denying a doctrine of indissolubility. (4) Dangers of scandal are now minimized by changes in culture and in religious insight. (5) The eucharist has two finalities—not only as a sign of unity but also as a means of grace (so that it is appropriate for it to be shared by persons not yet in complete unity with the church). Expressions of consensus came in documents from national associations of theologians and canon lawyers and in leading religious publications.[17]

Resolution of the question of admission of persons in stable second marriages to the sacraments led inevitably, however, to the more difficult question of the entrance of divorced persons into a second marriage. In a common struggle with this question some significant disagreements became clear among moral theologians who shared the consensus on the earlier question. Positions turned on analyses of the content and form of the requirement of indissolubility. Conflict also centered on whether church doctrine or only pastoral practice regarding indissolubility should be changed. A good example of these disagreements is visible in the joining of issues between Richard McCormick and Charles Curran.

McCormick and Curran shared the majority opinion on readmission of persons in second marriages to the sacraments. They also shared to some extent the view that first marriages, even if they had been sacramental and consummated, could die—could cease to exist. For by 1975

McCormick's reluctance to accept this construal of the ending of a Christian marriage was largely gone. Influenced by writers like Charles M. Whelan, Joseph MacAvoy, and Charles Curran, McCormick was cautious but moving. He was still saying that "the very concept of a 'dead marriage' is somewhat problematical to the Christian,"[18] yet it was clear that this notion was one of the examples of his own "deepening understanding and consequent modification of opinion over the past seven or eight years."[19]

Though offering proposals "very much in the category of a thought-experiment,"[20] McCormick proceeded to reject the traditional view of indissolubility as based on a bond, a *vinculum,* of ontological or juridical proportions. He suggested, rather, that indissolubility is a "moral ought," an "absolute moral precept" grounded in the union of spouses and their responsibilities to children. It is a "most serious obligation" to permanence in marriage, one that implies a couple's (1) obligation to strengthen and support their union and not allow it to die, and (2) if it does fall apart, their obligation to resuscitate it.[21] When a marriage dies, McCormick thought that it does so through the moral fault of at least one of the partners, through some failure on the part of one or both to keep the obligation to the union. Nonetheless, "a marriage, like a human body, can die without any hope of resuscitation."[22] And once a marriage has been utterly and irretrievably lost, the precept of indissolubility becomes moot. The judgment that an ending so definitive has been reached must be made by the partners themselves; it can only be (but presumably should be) notarized by the legal representatives of the church.

Curran had for some time been convinced that a marriage, however genuine in the first place, might nonetheless cease to exist. He recognized (as did McCormick and others) that this view presupposed an interpretation of marriage as an interpersonal relationship (which is also, but not solely or even primarily, a social institution). Within the relationship of every Christian marriage lies an essential requirement of permanence; marriage is under the obligation of indissolubility. Curran argued, however, that indissolubility was not an absolute rule or precept (as it was for McCormick) but a moral ideal. It exists, as the church had long taught, under the call and the command that it participate in and bear witness to the love of God for human persons and of Jesus for the church. This, however, must be understood in an eschatological perspective: Its call is to a goal, to a fullness it will not achieve in this life. Its obligation is limited by the capabilities of individuals and the possibilities of situations. In Curran's view (unlike McCormick's), not every failure to achieve the goal, or every failure to sustain an effort toward it, can be attributed to the moral fault of one of the spouses; for sometimes human limitation and the "not yet" aspects of grace make it impossible to succeed.[23]

Once a marriage does die, Curran and McCormick differed on how we are to think about the freedom to remarry. For McCormick, there can be no general freedom to marry again. In fact, there remains in place a general prohibition against second marriages. The reasons for the prohibition are twofold: (1) a second marriage "continues and memorializes" the failure of the first because it cuts off all hope of reconciliation, and (2) marriage is a social as well as a personal reality. In other words, it is an interpersonal relationship but also a social institution; what happens to any individual marriage has social consequences for other marriages. Remarriage threatens the stability of other persons' marriages, for it blunts the radical imperative of indissolubility. Yet, according to McCormick, the prohibition against remarriage is not absolute. "Proportionate reasons" in favor of other values may override it. These reasons will be particular to each individual (for they relate to special needs, responsibilities, concrete circumstances), so they (just like the reasons for divorce) must be weighed not by juridical institutions or officers but by the individuals concerned.

Curran, on the other hand, argued that when a first marriage has died, there remains no obligation not to remarry. There is no general prohibition against second marriages. It is not remarriage, but divorce, that is against the requirement of indissolubility. If a divorce was justified, so is remarriage. If the divorce was not justified (if the first marriage failed because of sin), repentance is needed; but the sin is not unforgivable, and its repentance does not include a requirement not to remarry.[24]

The differences in McCormick's and Curran's views on indissolubility and on the freedom to remarry coincided with differences in their positions on doctrinal change. McCormick preferred change only in pastoral practice, not in the doctrine of indissolubility. His construal of the obligation of indissolubility did not, he believed, attack the original doctrine itself. An absolute obligation was still in place. Moreover, he argued that invoking a principle of "proportionate reason" to determine the justification of remarriage would simply be an extension of the traditional category of "privileges of the faith."[25] Finally, he thought that if judgments about the demise of marriages and about proportionate reasons for remarriage are left in the hands of individuals it will not be necessary to "institutionalize" exceptions (either to the precept of indissolubility or to the prohibition against remarriage). Hence, no change in doctrine is needed, and pastoral accommodations can be made for individuals without threatening the overall stability of the institution of marriage.

Curran, on the other hand, argued in 1975 that a change only in pastoral practice would not go far enough in assisting persons who struggle with these issues in their personal lives; nor would it be as faithful to the changing insights in moral theology. A minimalist move to change only pastoral practice might be justified pedagogically and politically, but it can only be a "temporary move which logically must go further."[26] One of the logical pressure points will be recognized by individuals contemplating second marriages: "From a theoretical viewpoint it seems very difficult to say that sometime during the second marriage a couple can be reconciled with the sacraments of the Church, but it is wrong for them to enter the second marriage."[27]

The debate over indissolubility as precept versus indissolubility as ideal has not been resolved in the 1980s, though both points of view continue to be represented. McCormick repeated much of his 1975 formulation in a 1979 article and again in an expansion of that article ten years later (though in his 1989 analysis McCormick's notion of an "absolute" precept of indissolubility modulates more clearly into a "serious" precept).[28] Curran, too, has remained convinced of his view of indissolubility as moral ideal and has added to his argument a consideration of the role of culture.[29] There may be little motivation for others to take sides on this matter, perhaps because Curran's "imperative goal" sometimes looks strong enough to be a *prima facie* precept;[30] and McCormick's obligation not to remarry is clearly *prima facie* (even if indissolubility is "absolute").[31] Similarly, there may be little perceived need to draw further battle lines on the question of change in doctrine or in pastoral practice, perhaps because Curran allowed for a gradual movement from one to the other; and McCormick moved in 1979 to advocate change not only in pastoral practice but in pastoral policy, and in 1989 to propose theological as well as juridical "adjustments."[32]

Critical analysis by canonists in response to the revised Code, major new historical studies, and ongoing biblical research all provided the 1980s with rich resources on the problem of divorce and remarriage.[33] But the avalanche of literature in moral theology slackened considerably. Probably a number of reasons accounted for this. Theologians had resolved in their own minds the questions they had been pressed by contemporary experience to confront. Most of the interesting ideas seemed to be already on the table. The urgency for pastoral solutions to concrete situations of anguish and neglect had lessened, for the consensus regarding changes in pastoral practice (though not in doctrine) emerged not only in theory but in action—in the work of marriage tribunals, the pastoral approaches of the clergy, and new forms of ministry with the divorced and remarried. Annulments of first marriages between baptized

persons, dissolutions of first marriages where at least one partner is un-
baptized, readmission to the sacraments of persons in stable second marriages—all of these were more possible now than they were prior
to 1965.[34]

But the complex story of a quarter of a century of change in theology
and practice regarding divorce and remarriage has another part to its
plot—the responses and initiatives of the official leadership of the church.
Significant movement has taken place here, too, though its present results
look very different from the consensus among most theologians.

Official Response to Development

Much of the history of the institutional church's thinking about
divorce and remarriage is in the interpretation and application (and
sometimes formulation) of law. To some extent the changes in moral
theology have a parallel in juridical practices and decision. Broadening
the base for annulments, expanding the use of the Pauline privilege,
evolving the so-called Petrine privilege—all of these have been twentieth
century innovations in the application of canon law. They have reflected,
but also sometimes anticipated and influenced, moral theology.[35] As in
theology, new ways of addressing the indissolubility of nonsacramental
marriages and the nonvalidity of apparently sacramental marriages posed
less than radical problems for the courts once they had been introduced.
The issue of the indissolubility of truly sacramental, consummated marriages was another matter altogether. Here there is little parallel with the
struggles of moral theology, for the institutional question has at least for
now been closed.

Gaudium et Spes had in 1965 provided a new conciliar description
of marriage as an "intimate partnership" of life and love, "rooted in the
conjugal covenant of irrevocable personal consent," and constituting
essentially "a whole manner and communion of life."[36] This description
raised the standards of personal capability for undertaking a marriage
commitment; from then on considerations of psychological health, emotional maturity, and moral character were pertinent in granting annulments of first marriages. The description might also have allowed consideration of the possible "death" of some marriages (for if marriage is
essentially a whole way of sharing life and love, clearly this may in some
cases cease to exist). But here Vatican officials drew a sharp line.

Overturning the Dutch lower courts' decisions in the Utrecht-Haar-
lem Case, the Congregation of the Signatura asserted in 1975 that "It is
false to say that the council changed the doctrine about marital consent,
as if it had substituted for the traditional notion a certain so-called existential consent, so that when this ceases the matrimonial bond automati-

cally ceases to exist."[37] In this same vein, Paul VI reminded the Roman Rota in 1976 that *Gaudium et Spes* actually spoke of marital consent as effecting a "sacred bond [that] no longer depends on human decisions alone."[38] From this he argued that marriage continues to exist as a "juridical reality" no matter what subjective elements in it may die. As an institutional reality, marriage "in no way depends on love for its existence."[39]

The absolute indissolubility of consummated sacramental marriages was affirmed with traditional force also by the International Theological Commission (appointed by the Congregation for the Doctrine of the Faith) in 1978. It allowed no room whatever for such a marriage to end short of the death of one of the spouses. Every consummated sacramental marriage is indissoluble, the commissioners argued, because it comes into being through the total self-gift of each spouse to the other (a "gift of self which . . . transcends any change of mind"[40]); it is established not only by the will of the spouses but by God's will; it not only images the relationship of Christ to the Church but is incorporated into it in a way that empowers the spouses to fidelity and makes their union utterly indestructible; and it is "a demand of the marital institution itself [so that] even when love has ceased to exist, the marriage has not."[41] Here is a theology of indissolubility whose center is a notion of sacramental union which ultimately founds and incorporates a decision for union and a law of fidelity; the absoluteness of the indissolubility lies not only in a juridical demand but in a mystical foundation of the marital union itself.

Following the 1980 Synod on the Family, Pope John Paul II issued his *Apostolic Exhortation on the Family*. Like the Theological Commission he grounded the absolute indissolubility of consummated sacramental marriage ultimately in its reality as a sacrament. His explication of this reality focused on the "total self-giving" of the spouses to each other and the signification of this through sexual intercourse. The bond between them becomes a sign of and a participation in the saving love of Jesus Christ, which is a nuptial love for the church.[42] Should spouses be unfaithful—should they let their love die—they are nonetheless bound to one another irrevocably, and their infidelity becomes a sign of the infidelity of a people who still belong to God.[43] Absolute indissolubility lies in the very being of a relationship that can be violated but not destroyed. In 1983 the revised Code of Canon Law combined the interpersonal covenantal emphasis of *Gaudium et Spes* (and the theology of John Paul II) with the traditional juridical requirement of indissolubility.[44]

The issue of readmission of divorced persons in stable second marriages to the sacraments has not been as effectively closed by church leadership as the issue of the possible ending of a consummated sacramental marriage. The sympathy of large numbers of bishops for this latter issue has been marked. Numerous pastoral letters have addressed it, and many interventions at both the 1980 and 1985 Synods called for better solutions to the problem. But the responses of John Paul II and of the International Theological Commission were clearly opposed to any changes in pastoral policy in this regard. The Commission wrote simply: "From the incompatibility of the state of the divorced-remarried with the command and mystery of the risen Lord, there follows the impossibility for these Christians of receiving in the eucharist the sign of unity with Christ."[45] Citing reasons of disunity with the church and the dangers of scandal, John Paul II also reiterated: "The church reaffirms its practice, which is based upon sacred scripture, of not admitting to eucharistic communion divorced persons who have remarried . . . [unless] they take on themselves the duty to live in complete continence. . . ."[46] Theologians have taken solace in the fact that even in such positions there is included a concern for divorced and remarried persons and a recognition of their needs for special care. Still, the years of inquiry and interchange in moral theology on this question seem either to have been ignored by church leaders or simply and completely rejected.

A stand-off between moral theologians and church leaders cannot be beneficial for those whose lives are at stake in decisions of marriage and divorce. Hence, the work of moral discernment and communication must proceed. The question of readmission to the sacraments of persons in stable second marriages can perhaps be set aside for a time, since its theoretical and practical problems have largely been settled despite Vatican disagreement. But the question of indissolubility as it relates to the ending of first marriages and the right to remarry must be probed still further.

MARRIAGE AS "COMMITMENT": ANOTHER TRY AT THE IMPASSE?

There are three perspectives from which the absolute indissolubility of sacramental consummated marriages has been and is today understood—juridical, moral, and ontological. When the sacramental dimension of marriage is appealed to as the ultimate ground of indissolubility, it, too, is considered from these three perspectives. The categories here of "juridical," "moral," and "ontological" are not completely discrete, nor is their meaning univocal for everyone who uses them.[47] One way to take account of all three perspectives—avoiding in a sense, but perhaps shedding light on, disagreements among those who use them—is to consider the obligation of indissolubility in terms of marriage as a "commitment." Everyone, no matter where they are on the spectrum of positions regarding indissolubility, presupposes that marriage entails an initial and ongoing covenant (a concept and term now in favor over the traditional "contract") to which the parties come in freedom and in which they are bound because of the obligation they have themselves assumed.[48] Indissolubility as a requirement of Christian marriage is part of the content of the marriage commitment, but it also specifies the way in which one is to be committed (that is, unconditionally or with very few conditions). The moral meaning of the marriage commitment bears examination first, and juridical considerations can be incorporated into it.[49]

Like any other explicit, expressed, interpersonal commitment, marriage involves the giving of one's word in a way that gives to another a claim over one's self. It is a promise which, like any other promise, includes an intention regarding future action and a placing of oneself under a moral claim regarding that action. In the case of marriage, the intended action includes interior actions (of respect, love, trust, etc.) and exterior actions (a way of sharing a life together). Marriage, of course, is a mutual commitment—two persons' words given one to the other, two persons yielding and receiving a claim, two persons establishing by their commitments a new form of relationship intended to move into the future.

There are good reasons why marriage involves commitment as such. Love can desire it; experience can show its need. All commitments in the human community imply a state of affairs in which there is doubt about our future actions; they imply the possibility of failure to do in the future what is intended in the present. Commitments are made (claims given, obligations undertaken, bonds embraced) precisely to assure others and to strengthen ourselves—to give assurance that our word will endure and to strengthen ourselves in keeping our word. This is especially true of profound commitments like marriage, where commitment is a way of safeguarding our desire to do what we deeply want to do not only now but in the future. By committing ourselves we give, as it were, a law to ourselves; we bind ourselves by the claim we give to another. A Christian commitment to marry involves a commitment to more than one person.[50] That is, in a marriage not only is a commitment made by each partner to the other, but both partners also commit themselves to God and to a community of persons (to the church and to society, however that is construed in terms of family, community, and wider society). In each of these directions a word is given, intentions and expectations are clarified, an obligation is undertaken, and a newly qualified relationship is formed.

A marriage commitment is made to persons, but its content includes a commitment to a certain framework of life in relation to persons. While those who marry commit themselves to love one another, they do so (precisely in marrying) by committing themselves to whatever is understood to be the institution, the framework of life, that is marriage—not for its own sake but as the form of their life together.[51] This "framework" can have different levels of specification. There is a kind of generic understanding of "marriage" as a social institution that crosses cultures and religions. But "marriage" will also always have a particular framework in particular societies and religious traditions. Finally, there is a level of framework which is the particular structure of the marriage of two individuals—informed by but not necessarily limited to the institutional frameworks of their own historical context. The commitment to marriage as a framework of life and a way of loving at all of these levels is not necessarily explicit in every marriage, but it is nonetheless there.

In our own culture, and certainly in the Roman Catholic tradition, an intention of permanence in the relationship of marriage is included in marital commitment. Given massive historical changes in social contexts, some of the reasons for incorporating the notion of permanence in the framework of marriage have changed, though many remain the same. The importance of interpersonal reasons has grown, and institutional reasons have receded. Yet there have always been reasons intrinsic to the marital relationship itself and reasons of social utility beyond the relationship. Love itself can want to give its whole future, to bind itself irrevocably to the one loved and to express itself in this way. Some interpreters of the possibilities of human sexuality have also argued that sex is best served by being activated in a context of commitment and of commitment that intends to be permanent.[52] Insofar as marriage is a social institution, permanence can serve the good of children (who need a stable context in which to survive and mature), the general good of society (which depends on the institutions within it for its own stability and growth), and the good of the church (in which marriage can function as a way of Christian life and a sign of God's presence to all).

If an intention of permanence is intrinsic to the meaning of marriage, and if marriage as a commitment is self-obligating, can it ever be justified to end a marriage short of the death of one's spouse? In other words, can the claim that is given to another in the commitment of marriage ever be released? This is the central moral question for both divorce and remarriage. It is the central moral question even when the context is a Christian sacramental and consummated marriage (though there are complexities here that we must still address).

We are used to acknowledging release from a marriage obligation when it can be determined that some basic flaw marked the original marrying—a flaw in the procedure, or a lack of capacity to commit to marital life on the part of either partner, or a situation of unfreedom. Strictly speaking, however, this kind of release from obligation is not a "release" but a recognition that no marriage obligation was ever truly undertaken; the marriage did not exist. The much more difficult question is whether or not a truly valid marriage (and even one that is genuinely sacramental and consummated) may no longer bind.

My own position is that a marriage commitment is subject to release on the same ultimate grounds that any extremely serious, nearly unconditional, permanent commitment may cease to bind.[53] That is, an obligation to sustain a marriage ceases when (1) it truly becomes *impossible* to sustain it; (2) the marriage no longer serves the purposes, or has the *raison d'être*, it was meant to have; (3) another obligation comes into *conflict* with, and takes priority over, the marriage commitment. It is a difficult matter to discern when such conditions actually come to be, but that they do and that they can be identified seems to me to be without doubt. Some brief observations about each of these may help to make this clear.

First, then, when it truly becomes impossible to sustain a marriage relationship, the obligation to do so is released. Impossibility has long been accepted as a general justifying reason for release from the obligation of a promise. The kind of impossibility that is relevant for marriage commitments is not, of course, physical but psychological or moral impossibility. Hence, recognizing it is less like perceiving an incontrovertible fact than like making a judgment or even a decision. Still, examples can be given (of irremediable rupture in a relationship, or utter helplessness in the face of violence, or inability to go on in a relationship that threatens one's very identity as a person); and it seems true that a threshold of real impossibility does exist.

Interestingly, while McCormick and Curran do not construe marital obligation in just the way I have, they both appeal to a kind of impossibility as justification for releasing the requirement of indissolubility. The irretrievable death of a marriage relationship is that point at which, according to McCormick, resuscitation of it is no longer possible; it is at this point that the obligation of indissolubility is discontinued.[54] And Curran argues that precisely where it is impossible "for pilgrim Christians to live up to the fullness of love"—whether because of the limitation of creation, or sin, or the lack of the fullness of grace—there the obligation of indissolubility meets its limit.[55]

The second condition under which a marriage obligation may no longer bind is when it has lost its point, its *raison d'être*, its own intrinsic meaning. It is meant to serve love for spouses, for family, for society, for God. In order to do this it includes a commitment to a "framework" for loving, providing love with a way of living. But if the framework becomes a threat to the very love it is to serve, if it weakens it or contradicts it or blocks it, then the very commitment to love may require that the commitment to marriage as a framework must come to an end. Marriage has multiple meanings and purposes, but all of them may be undermined by the marriage itself (or some of them so gravely as to jeopardize them all). If so, the obligation to the marriage commitment is released.

Closely related to this is the third condition under which a marriage obligation may end—that is, when another obligation conflicts with and takes priority over it. Given the seriousness of the commitment to marriage, there are not many other obligations that can supersede it, for it is made with the kind of unconditionality that is meant to override other claims almost without exception. Still, there are times when other fundamental obligations can take priority—fundamental obligations to God, to children, to society, even to one's spouse (when, for example, commitment to the *well being* of the spouse conflicts with continued commitment to relationship within the framework of marriage). It is also possible for a fundamental obligation to one's own self to justify ending a marriage (not because love of self takes priority over love of another, but because no relationship should be sustained that entails, for example, the complete physical or psychological destruction of a person—including oneself).[56]

When under certain conditions a marriage commitment ceases to bind, are there no obligations (human and Christian) that remain in relation to one's spouse? Clearly there are. Though commitment to a framework for loving (to a relationship as an ongoing marriage) is not completely unconditional or absolute, there are unconditional requirements within it. For example, there is never any justification to stop loving someone altogether—not a marriage partner any more than a stranger or even an enemy. When it is no longer possible or morally good to love someone within the framework of a married love, it is still possible and called for that we love that individual at least with the love that is universally due all persons. It may even be that an obligation continues to a particular love that is faithful to the relationship that once existed. But here we come to the most difficult (for the Roman Catholic tradition) question of all: When the commitment to marriage no longer binds as such, when a true divorce is morally justified,[57] is it also justifiable to remarry? This question will ultimately take us to a consideration of the ontological perspective on divorce and remarriage.

The traditional Roman Catholic position has been and is, as we have seen, that even if an end must come to a marriage in the sense of a separation from shared "bed and board," there remains nonetheless an obligation not to remarry. The reason for this lies ultimately in a conviction that the original marriage in some sense still does exist.[58] Against the position I have just been outlining, the issues might be joined in the following ways: (1) Christian sacramental marriage is unlike other commitments in that it is under the command of God and the decree of Jesus Christ; hence, whatever our reasoning about the release of commitments, the indissolubility of marriage remains an absolute obligation. (2) The "framework" or institution of Christian marriage is regulated by the law of the church. Herein is a special stipulation whereby there will always be a juridical "remainder" of the covenant of marriage—to the effect that even if every other aspect of a marriage has become impossible (or without meaning or in conflict with greater obligations), it is still possible not to marry anyone else. This much of the marriage commitment still holds. (3) A commitment to marriage, when it is consummated as a sacramental reality, changes the partners in their very being. No longer is their union only a matter of moral or juridical bonding, but an ontological or mystical, indestructible, new reality. However it is lived out—with or without an actually shared life and love—it remains, and it makes impossible another commitment to marriage. All of these arguments have in one form or another been sustained in the tradition, but it is the third that currently is key.

One should not, of course, dismiss the first two of these arguments too quickly, though the limitations of this essay prohibit more than a brief response. Roman Catholic biblical scholars have effectively shown in recent years the exegetical difficulties of using New Testament texts as evidence of an absolute requirement of indissolubility. Indeed, if the various "sayings of Jesus" show us anything clearly it is that the Christian community from its beginnings believed it was responsible to modify these "sayings" in their application to different contexts.[59] But even if this were not the case—even if we could find in the biblical traditions a clear command in regard to divorce and remarriage—it is difficult to see how the logic of its application would not require the sort of analysis I have proposed. That is, for example, if something is in fact impossible, it cannot in the concrete be obligating.[60]

On the other hand, should the basis of a prohibition against remarriage be a purely juridical requirement, it can be questioned for its appropriateness to life, and it can also be changed. This is in part why the tradition has not appealed to a purely positive law as the basis for its ban on remarriage after divorce. Similarly, social utility arguments for the positive law are subject to empirical verification and to the challenge that the laws sanction the misuse of individuals for the sake of the common good.

The third argument—that indissolubility finally rests on an ontological union between spouses—is strongly entrenched in the Roman Catholic tradition. It has not gone away by the mere insistence on the part of moral theologians that (a) the bond of marriage is obviously not a reality independent of the relationship of spouses, and (b) insofar as the bond is in the "objective order" it is only a juridical or a moral reality. These theses serve as correctives to some popular misunderstandings and some unusual claims made here and there in the tradition. But they do not finally meet the position of those who, recognizing quite well that there is no ontological bond separate from the relationship of spouses, nonetheless find in this relationship an indestructible binding of being.

The most important spokesperson for an ontological perspective on the permanence of marriage today is John Paul II. The International Theological Commission serves as a careful supporter and explicator of the themes he has so painstakingly developed. The substance of the position, as we have already seen, is this: When two persons marry they yield themselves to one another in a kind of ultimate gift, a gift of self that changes them at the core of their being. By a mutual commitment they become so one with each other that they can no longer be separated. They belong to each other, are joined with each other as "two in one flesh."[61] Indissolubility is a consequence as well as an obligation of their mutual exchange. "For the gift of self, which engages one at the core of the person, transcends any change of mind. It is final."[62]

Both anthropological and sacramental foundations are offered for this view. Human persons are essentially intersubjective and essentially complementary as male and female.[63] Even their bodies have a "nuptial meaning" which incarnates the complementarity of their gendered persons and mirrors the relationship between Christ and the church. When a man and a woman come together in the covenant of marriage they are sealed in the grace of Christ's covenant with the church—imaging it, empowered by it, one with it. So transformed are they that even though their union is in process, or even though they choose at some point to violate their own new reality, they are nonetheless absolutely joined. "There is no separation between them in spirit or flesh."[64] This now is the way of their salvation, since it is thus that their sexual union can be redeemed: In being "converted" to one another, they transcend the selfishness in their bodily love.[65] So important is their sexual union that "the sacramental sign is determined, in a sense, by 'the language of the body,' "[66] though it is the whole of two lives that become one.

Here is a position with great appeal. It takes account of persons (and

not only laws), whole lives (and not only bodies or spirits), the transforming power of grace (and not only a theology of marriage as an image
of the relationship between Christ and the church). Yet the picture it
offers of marriage as a bond in being, settled once and for all by freedom
and grace, is finally misleading and potentially harmful to individuals
and to the church. There are at least three grave problems with the
position which I can only point to here (though they deserve a much
fuller response).

First, while this position depends on a description of Christian marriage as a covenant, it takes no account of the limits of human freedom in
the making and keeping of commitments. Our power of choice, self-determining in profound ways as it is, is not a power that can finish our
future before it comes. Commitment is indeed a way to influence our
future; by it we are changed in the present so that a new relationship can
have both a history and a future. But even with the power of grace, the
bonds that we forge are simply not completely indestructible. And while
it is true that freedom may fail only in the sense that we betray, rather
than fulfill, our promises, nonetheless it is also true that we can thereby
destroy the relationships our promises have made. Moreover, there is
surely what philosophers call "moral luck," and situations beyond our
control that also have the terrible power to undo the projects of our
freedom. A view of marriage that borders on a new mysticism can burden
marriage more than liberate it, crush it even while it aims to inspire.

Second, the theological anthropology assumed into this position is
not benignly separable from its core; and it is an anthropology that has
already harmed persons in its consequences for centuries. The complementarity asserted between women and men, structured on a problematic understanding of the relationship between Christ and the church,
perpetuates a cultural "framework" for marriage that (for all its protests
to the contrary) is essentially a union between unequals. Today this
framework is more likely to contribute to divorce than to the sustaining
of marriage.

Third, the ontological union that this position depicts is itself cause
for question, if not alarm. Drawing on the traditional metaphor of "two
in one flesh," it risks violating the human nature it wants to affirm. The
unqualified emphasis on "total self-giving" yields a view of the fusion of
selves that entails loss of autonomy in person and body. Nothing has
been more dangerous in marriage, especially for women, than ideals of
self-giving that mean loss of identity and self-agency. Efforts to explain
the meaning of this in terms of mutuality of giving only make it more
problematic, since they are joined still to a view of a husband as active
and a wife as passive.[67]

All of this is not to say that there is no ontological union effected in and by marriage. I am not myself inclined to dismiss this possibility—nor even the consequence that some bond remains after the breakdown of a marriage and a justifiable divorce. In fact, when two persons commit themselves to one another in a profound sense, and when they share their lives together for whatever period of time, they *are* somehow changed in their beings. There are many ways in which this change continues—call it a bond or a residue or whatever. What remains after the radical rupture of a marriage may even include a "bodily" bonding (now experienced positively or negatively) as a result of the sexual relationship that once was a part of the marriage. It may also include a spiritual bonding (now experienced positively or negatively) as a result of months or years of a shared history together. If the marriage resulted in children, their lives will be held together for years in the ongoing project of parenting. In any case, the lives of two persons once married to one another are forever qualified by the experience of that marriage. The depth of what remains admits of degrees, but something remains.

The question becomes, then: Does a remaining bond from a first marriage disallow a second marriage? My own opinion is that it does not (or at least in some situations it does not). Whatever ongoing obligation a residual bond entails, it need not include a prohibition of remarriage. Indeed, it may be that only a view of marriage that sees it primarily within an economy of sexuality and purity can sustain an absolute prohibition of remarriage after a justifiable divorce. The formulations of a position heavily dependent on extrapolations from a metaphor like "two in one flesh" are at least likely to provide such an inadequate view.

These considerations remain incomplete. That is as it should be while we continue the task of moving beyond an impasse on the issues. Everyone shares a concern to reduce the misery in people's lives and to nurture the possibilities for well-being and love. How theology and law and social responsibility can converge to do these things is part of our question. We know ways in which we cannot go. We cannot solve the suffering of divorce by restoring patrilinear societies, by returning women to situations of economic dependence, by using law simply to coerce or condemn, by crushing expectations of worthwhile shared lives. In a culture where the earth quakes beneath us with the massive shifts in social institutions, discernment cannot be easy. What is certain is that the wisdom we need must come from a communal effort. That is why a serious impasse must be broken.

Notes

1. For ample evidence of this from a contemporary vantage point see the three-volume historical study of Theodore Mackin, *What Is Marriage?* (New York: Paulist, 1982), *Divorce and Remarriage* (New York: Paulist, 1984), *The Marital Sacrament* (New York: Paulist, 1989); John T. Noonan, *Power to Dissolve: Lawyers and Marriages in the Courts of the Roman Curia* (Cambridge: Harvard Univ., 1972); E. Schillebeeckx, *Marriage: Human Reality and Saving Mystery* (New York: Sheed and Ward, 1965), originally *Het Huwelijk: aardse werkelijkheid en heilsmysterie* (Uitgeverij H. Nelissen, Bilthoven, 1963).

2. See Richard A. McCormick, *Notes on Moral Theology 1965 through 1980* (Washington, D.C., Univ. Press of America, 1981) 82–86.

3. Ibid. 83.

4. Ibid. 86.

5. Ibid. 332–47.

6. See *Gaudium et Spes*, no. 47, in *The Documents of Vatican II*, ed. Walter M. Abbott (New York: America, 1966) 249.

7. *Civiltà cattolica* 4, 116 (1965) 603.

8. See *Unitatis Redintegratio*, nos. 8 and 15, in Abbott 352 and 359; and *Orientalium Ecclesiarum*, no. 26, in Abbott 383–84. These texts assume an understanding of the sacraments as *means* to grace, not only *signs* of grace (in this case, graced unity). Hence, the eucharist can under certain conditions be shared with persons not yet in complete unity with the Roman Catholic Church. By extension, this insight has been thought by many theologians to apply to divorced and remarried Roman Catholics.

9. E.g. Schillebeeckx, n. 1 above; W.J. O'Shea, "Marriage and Divorce: The Biblical Evidence," *Australasian Catholic Record* 167 (1970) 89–109. Of course, some of the most important work was yet to come in the late 1970s and 1980s, e.g. Joseph A. Fitzmyer, "Matthean Divorce Texts," *Theological Studies* 37 (1976) 197–226.

10. McCormick, *Notes on Moral Theology 1965 through 1980* 346.

11. Ibid. 338.

12. Bernard Häring, "Internal Forum Solutions to Insoluble Marriage Cases," *The Jurist* 30 (1970) 21–30. It should be noted that McCormick does not interpret Häring's position in this article as a fourth position (as I do).

13. McCormick, *Notes on Moral Theology 1965 through 1980* 341.

14. Ibid.

15. Ibid. 372–81 at 372.

16. Ibid. 544–61. See also Charles E. Curran, "Divorce: Catholic Theory and Practice in the United States," *American Ecclesiastical Review* 168 (1974) 3–34, 75–96.

17. See e.g. an early committee report from the Canon Law Society of America published in *The Jurist* 30 (1970) 12–13; a document from the professional

organization of French theologians published as "Le probléme pastoral des chrétiens divorcés et remaries," *Vie spirituelle: Supplément* 109 (1974) 125–54; a committee report from the Catholic Theological Society of America published in *America* 127 (1972) 258–60; an editorial in *America* 131 (1974) 362.

18. McCormick, *Notes on Moral Theology 1965 through 1980* 557.

19. Ibid. 556.

20. Ibid.

21. Ibid. 557.

22. Ibid. 558.

23. Charles E. Curran, *Ongoing Revision: Studies in Moral Theology* (Notre Dame: Fides, 1975) 101–05.

24. Ibid. 84.

25. McCormick, *Notes on Moral Theology 1965 through 1980* 559. For a succinct description of current canonical meanings of "Privileges of the Faith" see Ladislas Örsy, *Marriage in Canon Law* (Wilmington: Michael Glazier, 1986) 215–33.

26. Curran, *Ongoing Revision* 105.

27. Ibid. 83–84.

28. McCormick, *Notes on Moral Theology 1965 through 1980* 826–41; *Notes on Moral Theology 1981 through 1984* (Washington, D.C.: Univ. Press of America, 1984) 99–104; "Indissolubility and the Right to the Eucharist: Separate Issues or One?" in *Ministering to the Divorced Catholic* ed. James Young (New York: Paulist, 1979) 65–84; *The Critical Calling: Reflections on Moral Dilemmas Since Vatican II* (Washington, D.C.: Georgetown Univ., 1989) chap. 13. See also Lisa Sowle Cahill, "Notes on Moral Theology: Sexual Ethics, Marriage, and Divorce," *Theological Studies* 47 (1986) 102–17.

29. Charles E. Curran, *Issues in Sexual and Medical Ethics* (Notre Dame: Univ. of Notre Dame, 1978) 3–29.

30. What I mean by this is that Curran's notion of an ideal seems to be only analogous to (not univocal with) ideals of virtue or to something like Reinhold Niebuhr's "impossible possibility." That is, it is not an ideal that is in principle impossible to achieve nor is it (as a final achievement of indissolubility) achievable in degrees; and it does hold a radical imperative. See Curran, *Ongoing Revision* 76.

31. What I mean by this is that McCormick's use of "absolute" here is tempered by his apparent willingness to have it go out of existence when one fails of it. He cites approvingly Schüller's term "presumptive precept" which seems to me more apt than "absolute" for what he wants to convey. See *Notes on Moral Theology 1965 through 1980* 556. It may also be that McCormick's "readjustment" of concepts and use of the term "serious precept" in the 1989 *Critical Calling* represents just such a move. An interpretation of this needs to take account also of McCormick's work on moral rules. See e.g. *Notes* 644.

32. McCormick, "Indissolubility and the Right to the Eucharist" 80; *Critical Calling* 26.

33. Örsy, n. 25 above; Mackin, n. 1 above. See also Jean Gaudemet, *Sociétés et*

Mariage (Strasbourg: CERDIC, 1980); and the important work by Piet F. Fransen on the meaning of Trent, in *Hermeneutics of the Councils and Other Studies* (Leuven: Univ, 1985).

34. As a canon lawyer active currently in a marriage tribunal described it to me: "All of the outrageous cases have now pretty much been taken care of."

35. "The main decisions, especially in modern times, have been made at the Curia. Exercising their freedom to shape a central human institution, the makers of the system have been co-makers with the Lord of institutions." Noonan, *Power to Dissolve* xviii.

36. *Gaudium et Spes* nos. 48 and 50.

37. Quoted in Mackin, *Divorce and Remarriage* 511; see also *What Is Marriage?* 316.

38. *Gaudium et Spes* no. 48.

39. Paul VI, *Acta Apostolicae Sedis* 68 (1976) 204–08; quoted in Mackin, *Divorce and Remarriage* 513; see also *What Is Marriage?* 320–22.

40. International Theological Commission, Commentary on Proposition 4.3, as quoted in Theodore Mackin, "The International Theological Commission and Indissolubility," paper delivered at Univ. of Dayton, 1989, forthcoming in a volume ed. by William P. Roberts (Sheed and Ward, 1990).

41. Ibid.

42. John Paul II, "The Apostolic Exhortation on the Family," *Origins* 11 (1981) esp. nos. 11–13, pp. 441–42.

43. Ibid. no. 12, p. 442. See also John Paul II, "The Family, Marriage and Sexuality," *Origins* 13 (1983) 316–18; "Building Family Life," *Origins* 15 (1985) 172–75; "Homily on Family Life," *Origins* 18 (1988) 29–32.

44. See Canons 1056–57 and 1134, 1983 Code of Canon Law.

45. International Theological Commission, "Christological Theses on the Sacrament of Marriage," *Origins* 8 (1978) 200–04.

46. John Paul II, "The Apostolic Exhortation on the Family," no. 84, p. 465.

47. E.g. Örsy interprets the marital "bond" as a legal relationship which gives rise to and is characterized by moral obligations, in *Marriage in Canon Law* 202–05, 270–72. McCormick argues against a juridical interpretation of the indissolubility requirement in favor of a moral interpretation, but he clearly does not rule out institutional considerations (at least as a safeguard for the social dimension of marriage). John Paul II offers an ontological perspective on marriage, but in the last analysis this is protected by law.

48. See e.g. *Gaudium et Spes* no. 48; 1983 Code of Canon Law, Canon 1055; McCormick, *Critical Calling,* chap. 13 (McCormick's theological "adjustments" are in the direction of viewing marriage as a commitment); John Paul II, "Apostolic Exhortation on the Family," no. 12; Curran, *Ongoing Revision* 106.

49. The general theory of commitment that follows is based on my analysis in *Personal Commitments: Beginning, Keeping, Changing* (San Francisco: Harper, 1986) esp. chaps 2 and 7.

50. What I say here would, I believe, apply to a great extent to so-called "natural" marriages as well as Christian marriages.

51. Even if the persons marrying wish to resist the cultural forms of marriage as an institution, their understanding of marriage will somehow be influenced by these.

52. See my treatment of this in "An Ethic for Same-Sex Relations," in *Challenge to Love,* ed. Robert Nugent (New York: Crossroad, 1983) 103–04. See also Paul Ricoeur, "Wonder, Eroticism, and Enigma," in *Sexuality and Identity* ed. H. Ruitenbeck (New York: Delta, 1970) 13–24; and John Paul II, "Apostolic Exhortation on the Family," no. 11.

53. I do not mean to imply here that there can be no commitments that are absolutely binding (for example, commitments to love God and to love one's neighbor as one's self); but any that are absolutely binding are so because they are not vulnerable to the conditions I outline here. Also, it should be noted—though without opportunity to elaborate—that the unconditionality of the marriage commitment is sufficient to rule out simple release by the agreement of the partners—or, for that matter, by the advent of circumstances other than the ones I identify here.

54. McCormick, *Notes on Moral Theology 1965 through 1980* 558; "Indissolubility and the Right to the Eucharist" 82.

55. Curran, *Ongoing Revision* 105. My way of construing here the justifiable end of a valid marriage can be related to the debate in moral theology about the guilt or innocence of the spouses whose marriage ends. Surely there are instances where the death of a marriage comes through the fault of one or both of the partners (as McCormick insists and Curran allows). When this is the case (though I believe with Curran that it is not always so), it is accurate to say that the fault of the partners brings the marriage to the point of impossibility (the death of "capacity" in McCormick's terms); but once this has happened, then the marriage obligation as such no longer holds. The end of a marriage comes finally in a *decision* by the spouses (it does not, strictly speaking, as a marriage just "die"); and it is this decision that can be morally justified and necessary (however unjustified it may have been to reach the point where this decision must be made).

56. This does not mean we are not called to great and noble loves that are self-sacrificing in a radical sense. But to sacrifice oneself is morally unjustifiable if it means violating one's very nature as a person.

57. By "true divorce" here I mean as distinguished from an annulment or a separation.

58. There are, of course, other arguments in the theological tradition as well —as e.g. McCormick's argument that even though the first marriage does not continue to exist, considerations of social utility ground a *prima facie* duty not to remarry.

59. See Mary Rose D'Angelo, "Remarriage and the Divorce Sayings Attributed to Jesus," forthcoming in a volume ed. by William Roberts (Sheed and Ward, 1990).

60. I am presupposing here the fact that the Roman Catholic tradition, unlike some Christian traditions, has never held that God asks the impossible of human persons.

61. John Paul II, *Original Unity of Man and Woman* (Boston: St. Paul, 1981) 75, 106, 110.

62. International Theological Commission, quoted in Mackin, "The International Theological Commission and Indissolubility."

63. John Paul II, ibid.

64. John Paul II, "The Apostolic Exhortation on the Family" no. 13. John Paul II here quotes Tertullian favorably.

65. John Paul II, *Love and Responsibility* (New York: Farrar, Straus & Giroux, 1981) 215.

66. John Paul II, Audience January 5, 1983, quoted from *Osservatore Romano* in *Moral Theology Today: Certitudes and Doubts* (St. Louis: The Pope John Center, 1984) 277.

67. See John Paul II, *Love and Responsibility* 275.

12

Abortion: Questions of Value and Procedure

Joseph F. Rautenberg

The issue of abortion is a painful and divisive one both within the Roman Catholic Church and in society generally. Fr. Richard McCormick's contributions in this area have been manifold and ongoing. His writings, especially his "Notes on Moral Theology" in *Theological Studies*,[1] have provided a fair, if not necessarily neutral, forum for insights and arguments from many opposing positions. In addition to criticizing and comparing the views of others, Fr. McCormick has developed his own position which includes (1) an insistence on the principle of the inherent value of nascent life, (2) careful discussion of the practical implications of this principle in conflict situations, and (3) sensitive and realistic attention to the broader social and ecclesial areas, including cultural, legal, and pastoral issues. In developing his positions McCormick invariably seeks to stake out the "golden mean," adopting both balanced conclusions and a moderate tone.

To characterize Fr. McCormick's tone as moderate does not mean that either his positions lack substance or his tone conviction. McCormick's work is characterized by an unashamedly theological perspective and the confidence that an individual's identity as a theologian, and even the religious origin of certain positions, need not restrict one to a sectarian arena. Thus, a theologian can and should engage in dialogue (or debate) with the philosopher, politician, scientist, etc., both (a) using common rational and cultural tools and presuppositions and (b) unapologetically offering religious insights. Although, in ethical debate in a pluralistic society, the theological or magisterial origins of positions cannot be used as trump cards, neither can such origins be used to exclude a position *a priori*. Some of McCormick's sharpest words and tone are used with those who would attempt to disenfranchise Catholics from speaking on abortion on sectarian grounds.[2]

In this paper I will focus on three major areas: (1) the status of the embryo (i.e. its identity and value); (2) how conflicts between it and its mother are to be resolved; (3) three problematic cases where the principles and decisions from the first two sections come to bear. The first two sections will deal with kinds of arguments for the rightness or wrongness of abortion. The third section will examine the implementation of morally right judgment in this area.

In the first two sections I will look at (a) the basic position advocated by Richard McCormick, (b) some of the major positions opposed to his views and his response to them, and (c) my own position, and identification of some of the crucial issues for future work. This somewhat dialectical approach is fitting because Professor McCormick has developed and published much of his position on abortion in dialogue with, and response to, others.

The Status of the Embryo: Its Identity and Value

Many commentators see the question of the identity of the embryo —the kind of thing it is—as central to determining its value, and consider the issues of both identity and value crucial for correctly establishing basic moral and legal positions on abortion. McCormick would agree, although he would reject reducing the complex questions of fetal status and value to the question of the proper attribution of the word "person."[3] That term can be too variable in its meaning, sometimes being used for any human being, sometimes being restricted to those possessing an acknowledged right to life, or other rights or characteristics. However, despite some danger of confusion, because of its richness and prevalence, I will continue to use "person" (and "personhood") in accord with the latter meaning to designate one who has a right to life. I will thus distinguish it from the meaning of "human being," which could refer to any differentiable entity of human genotype.

McCormick takes a moderate position on embryonic identity and value. He holds a "developmentalist" (as opposed to "conceptionalist") view on personhood or ensoulment, but opts for the early attribution of full human status at the time of implantation, which establishes individuality (c. 14 days). Prior to this, it seems that the zygote can separate into two or more sections each of which can develop into an infant; or, two or more developing zygotes can fuse into a single embryo. Assuming that individuality is essential to full personhood—full possession of human status and rights—these facts entail a lesser status for the zygote. Further, a number of fertilized ova are lost prior to implantation, and such inherent wastage seem incompatible with the sanctity and dignity of persons (assuming the basic meaningfulness and goodness of things, and/or the goodness and sovereignty of the creator God).[4]

McCormick's doubt as to the full personal status of the conceptus does not mean that, for him, it is of negligible value; nor are its value and rights simply derivative from what it potentially can become. What it is now is worthy of our "respect and awe." It is now, already, a developing human life, and life traditionally deserves the benefit of the doubt.[5]

Three basic types of theories link the ontic status of the embryo to its possession of a right to life or the wrongness of aborting it. These base their judgments of status on (1) "internal" characteristics, (2) relational characteristics, and (3) functional or performance characteristics. McCormick's own position may be classified among the first type. But challenges to his views arise from theorists of all three kinds.

A spectrum of positions identify various *internal characteristics* as key to ontic and moral status. One position, often identified with traditional Roman Catholicism, holds that personhood exists from the moment of conception. The kind of thing an embryo is is established by its natural kind, i.e. its human parentage and genotype. An embryo's ontological status is witnessed by its already ordered development. After conception and the coming to be of a new life with its own internal dynamism and ordering principle, there are no developmental transitions of sufficient magnitude to mark a transition from pre-personal to personal status.[6]

As we have seen, McCormick would certainly grant the humanity of the conceptus prior to establishment of individuality, and would agree to a high status for such a being. However, he would continue to maintain the essential importance of individuality for full personhood and thus would see the time of implantation as a dividing line sufficient to signal a major ontological difference.

This places McCormick in the camp of the "developmentalists," i.e. those who would see personhood as depending on internal characteristics, but ones which the embryo acquires or develops subsequent to conception. However, there is a range of developmentalist opinions, a number of which would disagree with the early date he adopts for hominization. For example, some, building on the traditional definition of a human person as rational animal, identify the time of hominization with brain development and the formation of an identifiable cortical substrate for rationality.[7]

Michael Tooley presents an extreme version of a developmental position, based on the acquisition of desires. He is opposed to theories which do not tie the status of a being directly to characteristics which are both inherent in the individual being and actually possessed by that being. However, he would differ from McCormick's view that the characteristics of humanity and individuality were sufficient for full personal status and the possession of a right to life. For Tooley, the possession of rights to something requires the actual existence of desires for it. Thus, two properties are necessary for a being to have a right to life: first, such a being ". . . possesses the concept of self as a continuing subject of experiences and other mental states, and believes that it is itself such a continuing entity." Second, this enduring self must actually desire its continued existence.

Tooley's argument presents the famous "kitten analogy" by which he attacks the "potentiality principle," i.e. the view that the embryo deserves protection not for what it is or for qualities it has now, but for the sake of what it will become or qualities it has the potential to develop. He postulates a serum which, if injected into kittens, would, after a time, cause them to become rational beings. He assumes that no one would say it was murder to kill an injected kitten before it had developed rationality. If so, consistency would seem to say that neither is it murder to kill a human being which currently lacks such properties, even if it will later develop them.[8]

McCormick does not use potentiality in building his position on embryonic value, but he criticizes Tooley's doubling of the middle term in his *reductio ad absurdum* argument, i.e.: injected kittens are potentially rational (cats); potentially rational (humans) have a right to life; therefore, injected kittens have a right to life. They may indeed. But, unless one begins by accepting Tooley's assumption that sheer rationality is a necessary and sufficient condition for personhood, the argument doesn't follow. One could argue that the potentiality which gives embryos or infants a right to life is e.g. the potential for full humanness, not just potential rationality.

McCormick's view of abortion is based on a being's actual individual humanness, not its potential. He recoils from Tooley's position, for it would justify unrestricted infanticide as well as abortion, and also legitimate both the suicide of those who had lost their desire to live, or the "euthanizing" of such, or of those of any age who had lost or failed to develop their rational capacities.

McCormick's repulsion at a system that could yield such conclusions is shared by many commentators. And such a reaction is not just philosophically irrelevant squeamishness. In a discipline which seeks practical wisdom, emotional abhorrence may have the force of argument. ". . . a simple test of an analysis is the fit of its conclusions with the moral convictions of civilized men."[9]

McCormick's key objection to Tooley is the latter's basing of his theory of rights on the possession of desires. Tooley has mistakenly conceived of basic, inalienable, rights according to the same model as e.g. certain property rights which we can wave if we have no desire for a thing. But these two kinds of rights are very different and are grounded differently. If the assertion of rights is, in fact, a statement about others' moral obligations (as both McCormick and Tooley would seem to agree), then Tooley's assertion of the conditions for having (univocally conceived) rights begs the question of different kinds of rights, and whether we have some moral obligations to beings in the absence of their reflective self-consciousness and desires. Tooley asserts his conclusions in his premises, he doesn't argue for them. This style of discourse may exhibit consistency, but cannot really convince anyone who doesn't already agree.[10]

Against all those developmentalists who would argue for a time later than implantation for the bestowal of personhood, McCormick would hold that, after the major watershed of implantation–individuation, the physical evidence was of an unbroken continuum of development which did not justify any radical differences in ontological status nor, therefore, in moral status.[11]

Some of those who hold that the ontological status of the embryo is morally crucial would see that status as established not by reference to qualities inherent in an individual, but by *relational characteristics.* In this view, the person (as distinguished from the human organism) is essentially relational. Recognition and acceptance by others is thus constitutive of our personhood. Beyond a certain point, recognition of human beings as persons may ordinarily be presumed. But, at least in early pregnancy, the one who really "knows" of the existence of the embryonic other, and hence the one who can bestow a personalizing recognition and acceptance, is the mother.

Relational theorists differ as to whether the mother's acceptance is necessary or not. Bruno Ribes speaks in terms of both parents and society.[12] Daniel and Marjorie Maguire, writing from a more strictly feminist perspective, emphasize the mother's role.[13] In either case this approach involves the possibility that two embryos, equal in all other respects, may be radically different ontologically and morally, if one is accepted by its mother and the other is not.

McCormick sees this reliance upon relational criteria as so arbitrary as to be a "total relativizing of personhood and the morality of abortion." And while the feminist perspective claims to redress prior imbalances, here its arbitrariness and subjectivity is such as to be "effectively discriminatory."[14] The physical dependence of the embryo upon the mother does not entail that its ontic and moral status and value are merely derivative.

Nowhere else are basic identity and rights held to be rightly conditional upon others' acceptance.

The arbitrariness of relational theory is thus shown by its inability to treat equally beings which seem to be equal in themselves despite inequality in their relations. Nor do these theorists give any reasons why, if a relation of a certain kind is necessary for identification as a person, personhood could not be lost if relations deteriorated or ceased. The irreversibility of personhood is simply assumed.

Further, the notion of "relation" employed by this type of theory is peculiarly one-sided. No recognition or acceptance is demanded from the child.[15] "Relation" here lacks the mutuality that is found in the very human relationships which are so important to the adult personality, and which the theory viewed as paradigms of what was necessary for persons to be constituted. The relationists have taken the very real importance *relationships* have to the human personality and used this fact to ground their argument that a very different kind of *relation* is a necessary criterion for at least some bestowals of personhood. But "person" is not the same as "personality." And even if personality would be warped and stunted in the absence of relationships this does not mean that the human being, though wounded, would cease to be a person.

There are those who would accept that the ontological status of the embryo was determinative of what could morally be done to it, and would identify certain *performance* or *functional characteristics* as constitutive of a being's identity and value—as necessary criteria for personhood. In one sense such an approach could yield quite traditional conclusions, if it were accepted that the ordered processes of embryonic development were functions or performances which were sufficient to bestow personhood. More typically, however, theorists identified by this type choose characteristics like the exercise of rationality or autonomy, and thus would deny full personal status and value to a human being pre-natally (and, in some cases, post-natally).

Joseph Fletcher, like some of the developmentalists, considers rationality the essential characteristic of personhood. However, for Fletcher, it is not the possession of the organic substrate of rationality, or a potentiality to become fully rational, that is necessary for personhood, but the actual possession of a functional rational faculty.[16]

H. Tristram Engelhardt, Jr. argues that the functional criterion of rational autonomy determines the ascription of rights. In his system, this is not so much because autonomy is the highest human value, but because the (philosophical) moral realm is the realm of autonomous agents interacting with one another according to certain implicit or explicit contracts. If an organism is unable to exercise rational autonomy it is not a member of the moral realm and consequently, though it may be valued and protected by moral agents, in itself it possesses neither obligations nor rights.[17]

As with Tooley, the conclusions of the functionalists certainly flow from their assumptions. But McCormick would argue that the credibility of their assumptions is undermined by the abhorrent nature of their conclusions. Functionalists like Fletcher or Engelhardt would have no way to establish that actions like infanticide or involuntary euthanasia of mental defectives or the comatose were wrong, or in any way problematic, apart from their violating the claims of, or otherwise harming, others who were rational moral agents. Such conclusions run counter to common moral convictions that something wrong was done to those who were killed. It is arbitrary and dangerous to so divorce the personal and the human and to establish such high qualitative criteria for personhood. Such views are obviously dangerous to many classes of human beings, and the rejection of any inherent obligation to care for the most fragile and vulnerable is corrosive of the moral character of a society.[18]

Although it is a type of objection that can be easily overused, I think that McCormick is correct here in his invocation of the threat of a "slippery slope" to moral disaster, a slope which becomes steeper the higher one sets developmental or functional criteria for personhood. ". . . the best way to state why I share the traditional evaluation is that I can think of no persuasive arguments that limit the sanctity of human life to extrauterine life. In other words, arguments that justify abortion seem to me equally to justify infanticide—and more."[19]

In its practical conclusions Fletcher's functional utilitarianism and Engelhardt's libertarianism resemble Tooley's position, with personhood ascribed according to the possession of rationality or the exercise of autonomy rather than the possession of desires. And there is a problem for funtionalists similar to that found with Tooley or the relationists: if function (or conscious desire, or relationship) is lost, is personhood also? For all these theories, personhood seems to be bestowed not only arbitrarily but unstably.

Ultimately, for McCormick, humanity and basic human rights are givens rather than contingent on certain developmental accomplishments, at least once the stage of individuation is reached. A human being has a certain moral status because of the kind of being he or she inherently is, not because of what others think or do with respect to that being, or what that being is able to think or do on its own. "Accidental" factors which delimit what the situation of the embryo *is:* physical development or location, perceptibility or accessibility to treatment, even its perfection or defect—these do not of themselves show what our behavior and attitude toward it *ought* to be. Similarly, "It is not our sense of experience of loyalty or acceptance that shapes our obligations. It is rather the objective reality of the fetus that ought to found our obligations and nurture our sense of loyalty."[20]

I would agree substantially with Professor McCormick's position on the ontic and moral status of the fetus. However, I wonder if his delay at granting the embryo a full share in basic rights, even if only for two weeks, might exhibit something of that illegitimate separation of the human from the personal that he criticized in Fletcher.

I would opt for the time of conception for treating the embryo as a being possessing fundamental personal rights. There are legitimate problems in choosing this most early date: conception itself is not an instantaneous process; implantation and the establishment of individuality is a significant point. However: (1) The new life engendered by the process of conception is undeniably human. (2) It is differentiable from the originating gametes and from the mother, even prior to the establishment of individuality. Whether it is another or others who are present, we do have an organism with its own human genotype and its own developmental and structural dynamic. (3) The unfolding of this dynamic presents a continuum, from pre-individual to individual, from pre-rational to rational. The continuity of development argues for the identity of the developing being across time. If personal rights are essential, and a being is granted such rights at one time, then it has them always. (4) As McCormick remarked in discussing the status of the pre-implantation embryo in the context of in-vitro fertilization: "Kass has stated that the 'presumption of ignorance ought to err in the direction of not underestimating the basis for respect.' That seems correct, and it is the same as the traditional principle that in factual doubts life deserves the preference."[21]

While the physical evidence for establishing a radical ontic and moral difference around the time of implantation is impressive, it is not conclusive. The fact that some developing embryos may split and recombine doesn't mean all have this potentiality. The individuality of some may shift, but, for most, this will not happen. Therefore in all likelihood an individual is already present, an individual whose development will exhibit great changes at many points, but also a continuity of being. It seems to me that the continuity of development after conception is greater than any *particular* discontinuity.

Rather than arguments against my position based on individuality, I am more impressed by arguments that the percent of "natural" wastage before this stage makes it rationally absurd, or unfitting for a loving God, that such a large percentage of persons never get a chance for any more significant development. Yet the move from the factual to the moral seems particularly problematic here. After all, a high infant mortality rate would not legitimate infanticide.

I would argue that despite all the significant developmental changes, the developing human life from its earliest moments should be considered as fundamentally morally equivalent to that life at any later stage, unless in a particular case it is clear that basic developmental possibilities are already foreseeably foreclosed (e.g. hydatidiform mole).[22]

I think McCormick is correct in his critiques of the various theorists who differ from his position. Developmentalists, relationists, and functionalists all tend to select one aspect or capacity of persons as essential and tie the attribution of rights and value to its presence or absence. Yet the selection process is unproven, even arbitrary. The correlation between the ontic and moral reality of personhood and the particular factor which is supposed to provide the reason for its ascription seems weak and forced—"disproportionate."

A certain developmental criterion could very well be personally important or even sufficient to establish identity as a person (and, thus, value and rights), without being necessary for such establishment. If a particular group of kittens does, in fact, go on to develop a rational capacity, that should change our views of what may be done to that kind of kitten. Rationality may thus serve as a marker for identifying the kind of things that deserve respect without its actual presence and function being a necessary pre-condition for all instances of giving respect or attributing rights.

For later developmentalists, relationists, and functionalists, the reality of the whole is made to depend too much on a particular part. Criteria apt for evaluating a facet of a person may not be applicable to the different kind of measuring which judges the whole. For example, failure to adequately develop or exercise rational autonomy or sociability can rightly lead to judgments of brain defect or psycho-social dysfunction, but it may be as incorrect to use these functional disabilities of certain human facets to deny personhood to the whole as it would be to deny it to someone born without a leg. Similarly, the well-known debates about how one can legitimately move from a fact to a value, or an "is" to an "ought," should make us cautious about having basic moral qualities depend on characteristics of a totally different kind, whether these be psychosocial or material.

While the traditional notion of ensoulment was nonverifiable, it at least pointed to some definite way persons were different from nonpersons. If such language is abandoned, things become less clear. Beyond the notions of a differentiable entity with its own principle of organization and structural dynamic, oriented to its own ends, I do not think any (immediately verifiable or falsifiable) thing, whether an internal characteristic, a relation, or a function, correlates with even the extension, much less the intension, of the word "person." However, whatever else it might mean to call something a "person," the term does, at least, assert that others are obligated to behave in a certain way toward it.

I think that beyond a certain point, attempts to "prove" a particular identification or value are futile, because the fundamental nature of identification and valuing leaves nothing more basic to appeal to. Still, reflection on examples of the admitted personhood of some human beings "at the margins," e.g. the retarded, comatose, or infants, may help one to have a broader vision of what protectable human life looks like. And a sense of the continuum of human life, the fact that it makes sense for me to talk of my conception as when I myself came to be, would argue for more caution in identifying developmentally late or qualitatively high prerequisites for granting basic rights. In arguing for a particular view on fetal identity, value, and rights, we cannot, in the end, eliminate the need for a leap of judgment, reasonable—in that it is principled—but not sufficiently determined. But, here again, I would argue that life should be given the benefit of all these doubts.

It is difficult to judge what future issues are likely to arise in the debate over embryonic status, or even what lines of argument should be pursued. While it is dangerous to predict that things can't change, I can't really foresee what kind of likely new arguments or evidence could make a significant difference at the level of assigning a basic identity or value. I think any movement in this area will more probably come from a deeper reflection on and stronger realization of evidence and arguments already available. To reflect on embryonic photographs and one's identity across time, or to experience the added trauma of fears about pregnancy after the crime of rape—these are more likely to be convincing than any new arguments. However, it is possible that significantly new and different information about what is really going on at certain developmental stages like implantation or cortical formation could affect some developmentalist positions.

CONFLICT SITUATIONS

If the embryo was a "non-person" without moral status or rights, then there would be much less objection to leaving the question of abortion to the mother to decide however she saw fit. If, however, personhood or some significant status is granted to the embryo, moral conflicts can arise. In the abortion situation, the interests and rights of many parties can be involved: fathers, other family members, medical professionals, other social groups and society at large. A fuller treatment would need to take more explicit account of all these factors, but here, for the sake of brevity and simplicity I will consider mainly conflict between the interests or rights of the mother and those of her developing child. A number of different strategies are used in attempts to resolve this conflict.

Some theorists seek a solution by commensurating the values involved. What is meant by "commensurating" varies from theorist to theorist and extended discussion of this topic is beyond the scope of this paper. Here, it must be enough to note that most would recognize and claim to be able to overcome the difficulties involved in commensuration, e.g. the impossibility of simply "weighing" different kinds of values, or reducing them to a common denominator, and the dangers of individual or cultural bias.[23] I would also remark that even those who criticize attempts to establish rightness and wrongness by commensurating must claim to be able to do something of the kind in order to have a workable moral theory. For example, to determine what is just one must somehow weigh benefits and burdens. In any case, Richard McCormick could be placed in the broad group of those who think that moral decision can be carried out by commensurating, by determining what is "proportionately" the best or least evil option.

McCormick's own view of the principles that should guide decision-making on abortion have been consistent. In positions published ten years apart he identifies three basic propositions:

1. Human life as a basic gift and good, the foundation for the enjoyment of all other goods, may be taken only when doing so is the only life-saving and life-serving alternative, or when doing so is, all things considered (not just the numbers), the lesser evil. . . .

2. By "human life" is meant human life from fertilization or at least from the time at or after which it is settled whether there will be one or two distinct human beings (this phrase is Ramsey's). . . .

3. For an act to be life-saving and life-serving, to be the lesser evil (all things considered), there must be at stake human life or its moral equivalent, a good or value comparable to life itself. . . .[24]

Curran argues, and I agree, that this phrase ("other values proportionate to life") must be interpreted in a way consistent with our assessment of the values justifying the taking of extrauterine life.[25]

A willingness to entertain the possibility of a "moral equivalent" to life is "both difficult and dangerous." In trying to decide the conflicts involved in an abortion situation, it is difficult enough to weigh the lives of two people and the possibilities and risks for each. The situation is even more complicated if other values must be considered. Nevertheless McCormick is open to this possibility and thinks such a view is supported by "the casuistry of the tradition." However, one must be cautious and "lean against" tendencies to broaden the range of values which can compete with life.[26]

For Richard McCormick, therefore, the status and value of prenatal life is placed very high. Thus, such life is ordinarily inviolable. However, in two situations of conflict, this inviolability does not exclude acting in a way that has the effect of preventing a child from being born: first, in an established pregnancy, when its continuation threatens the mother's life, or an equivalent value; second, conflicts where, because of uncertain individuality, doubt exists as to whether a person is present; here, the threat to the mother must still be serious, but life-equivalence is not required. One practical consequence of the latter point is McCormick's cautious approval of interceptors to prevent implantation in cases of rape.[27]

Fr. McCormick's proportionalism is rooted within the natural law tradition. This tradition begins from the perspective of individual beings and their actualizations and thus possesses an inherent tendency to maintain the importance of each individual. Utilitarians would also seek to establish moral rightness by a weighing of values, but would look strictly at consequences or outcomes for the general good. Their sense of rights which could constrain harm being done to individuals in the pursuit of the general good would also tend to be weaker than Professor McCormick's. If coupled with a tendency to underestimate the status and value of the embryo, such a position yields a very permissive attitude toward abortion.[28]

Other positions do not just look at the consequences of an action, but focus also on the way the will of the agent bears on any harm done. Traditional Catholic moral theology has considered the distinction between the direct doing of harm and the indirect allowing of it to be important. It is never morally justifiable to directly intend harm. Therefore, it was never considered permissible to do a direct abortion, i.e. any act which sought to expel the embryo, whether this was intended as an end in itself or as a means to a further end.

However, a procedure (not itself simply describable as an abortion), which nonetheless caused the embryo's death, could sometimes be justified, e.g. a hysterectomy done to save the life of a pregnant woman with a cancerous uterus. Here the intention was the saving of life, and the means the medical procedure. The loss of embryonic life was not directly intended as either means or end, but was an unintended side-effect. This situation was not considered to be an exception to the prohibition of abortion. Since the action was not considered an (intrinsically evil) abortion at all, and any harm done was unintended—not willed by the agent as either end or means—such an act could be justified for a proportionate reason. The reasoning behind this justification came to be codified under the name of "the principle of the double effect." A further refinement, proposed by Germain Grisez, would consider that even an act which would ordinarily be describable as an abortion in the physical sense could be described otherwise and considered indirect, and hence not morally wrong, if its killing and saving aspects occurred within the same action.[29]

McCormick would reject two points of the traditional formulation of the principle: first, the notion that certain acts could be established as intrinsically immoral when identified only by their "object," i.e. a narrow description of what was going on, excluding the agent's intention, circumstances, etc.; second, the claim that the directness or indirectness of one's action was itself morally determinative. He would see the difference between directness and indirectness as morally important only to the extent that a corresponding difference was expressed and/or effected in the moral attitude or stance of the agent toward basic values.[30] Therefore, he considers direct abortion as allowable when done to preserve life or an equivalent value.

Some theorists, however, have sought to reconceptualize abortion generally as a passive withholding or withdrawing of support (with embryonic death indirect) rather than as active (direct) killing. If abortion is conceptualized as killing, life or a morally equivalent value may be needed for proportionality. However, in the absence of a claim for a special obligating relationship between mother and child, a lesser reason could justify simply a deciding not to save. For we generally recognize that while only a strictly limited range of reasons can justify killing someone, reasons much less significant can exempt us from being morally (or legally) compelled to offer, e.g. our kidneys, or our blood, even to a family member.[31] In Grisez's and Finnis' terms, while we are morally bound in each and every case not to attack basic goods, we have more freedom with respect to pursuing or not pursuing this or that particular good.

One reason for seeking such a reconceptualization has been to finesse the whole question of fetal status and value and the difficulties of commensurating the maternal and embryonic values involved. These theorists could grant the assumption (made by Curran and McCormick) that the situation of aborting nascent life was to be analyzed according to the same principles and values "justifying the taking of extrauterine life."[32] Yet, they would focus on the autonomy of the mother and the demands of justice to argue that we cannot legitimately ask more of a pregnant woman for support of another than we ask other members of society. McCormick has expressed an openness to considering this reconceptualization, but I do not think he has yet systematically responded to it.[33]

An interesting example of this approach has been offered by Patricia Beattie Jung. She builds on earlier attempts, but distances herself from some of their less credible elements, rejecting both Susan Teft Nicholson's denial of all parental responsibilities in cases of rape, and Judith Jarvis Thomson's analogizing of the embryo with an adult stranger.[34] Jung would propose viewing pregnancy as a "bodily life support" analogous to organ donation. Both actions are "gift relations," supererogatory not obligatory.[35] I think her most interesting and powerful argument for her claim for the mother as ultimate decision-maker in this area is based not simply on the mother's autonomy, but on the very conditions which allow her to be a moral agent at all.

As opposed to dualism, Jung argues that an integrated theory of the person recognizes that an unwanted pregnancy, as invasive of the woman's body, violates her person. Bodily integrity is ". . . a foundation for agency or condition necessary for human action. . . ." As with requiring organ donation, requiring the continuation of a pregnancy would be to objectify the body and violate the person's integrity. It would be a failure to respect persons as persons.[36]

Personal integrity (necessarily including bodily integrity) is, then, not just one value among others. It is the basis for valuing and for all moral decision, the necessary condition for moral agency. It has been traditionally thought that the pursuit or preservation of spiritual or moral values could allow the sacrifice of "material" values, even life itself. If any value could be equal to (or even superior to) life, if any reason could justify not pursuing the development of this particular life, it would seem to be this necessary pre-condition for "playing the moral game." I will return to Jung's arguments later on.

I would substantially agree with McCormick's strategies for the resolution of these conflicts, and his caution about the possible danger in accepting moral equivalents to life in the commensurating judgment. However, I would disagree with him on one issue, and possibly another.

First, I remain troubled by McCormick's willingness to allow interceptors, e.g. in cases of rape. For I think that all the arguments he so coherently presents against later developmental views could also be applied to this situation. As I argued in the previous section, I do not see any clear and convincing reasons why human life, even prior to the "accomplishment" of individuality, should be deprived of the same benefit of the doubt that protects embryos only slightly later in time. Rape is obviously an evil and traumatic thing. But I think only in rare cases would a resulting pregnancy truly threaten life or a morally equivalent value. This level of threat was required to justify later abortion, and I would tend to argue that the status of developing human life, even the zygote of uncertain individuality, requires the presence of such a threat to justify even the use of interceptors.

I am, however, less certain about this conclusion than about the status of the embryo. There is a distinction between a conclusion or decision as to a fact, and the application of that decision in moral judgment. The distinction between an "is" and an "ought" is a familiar one and illustrates that knowledge about facts does not translate in an uncomplicated fashion into knowledge of values or moral obligations. What is less often expressed is that doubts about facts also need not translate simply into an equivalent level of axiological or moral doubt. Roman Catholic casuistry even recognized the use of different methodologies to weigh doubts of law as opposed to doubts of fact.[37]

As we have seen, the moral status of the embryo is highly disputed; nor is this a question of a simple matter of fact, solvable by empirical means. Further, while I do not, finally, accept his conclusions, McCormick's arguments for implantation as a watershed do increase the uncertainty as to the status of the pre-implantation embryo. This uncertainty as to factual matters does, I think, make for greater uncertainty in the practical issue of the use of interceptors. I would still judge that it is most likely correct, and therefore safest, to act as if the conceptus possessed personal status. But, as a pastoral matter, I recognize that the uncertainty involved may legitimate greater leeway for individual decision.

There may possibly be a second point of disagreement. In his 1974 *Notes* McCormick approvingly cited John Finnis' response to Thomson. Finnis' main critique was aimed at Thomson's theory of rights: a theory, separated from a more basic theory of moral obligation, where rights and correlative responsibilities depended upon "grants, concessions, etc."

Thomson denies the existence of any presumptive relationship between mother and embryo, in the absence of the specific acceptance by the mother of such a responsibility.[38] However Finnis (and by implication McCormick) while criticizing such a theory of rights also denied the existence of any special relationship or responsibility. "It is rather a straightforward incident of an ordinary duty everyone owes to his neighbor."[39]

I think this is too hasty and too strong, and that the arguments by Jung do show that more is demanded of the woman in an unwilling pregnancy than "the ordinary duty everyone owes to his neighbor." However, I differ from Jung in that I think a special relationship does exist which is sufficient to ground the greater-than-ordinary duty to another which obliges continuing a pregnancy.

Denials of such a special relationship, based simply on the mother's autonomy, are vulnerable to the critiques of McCormick and others against individualism.[40] Persons are essentially social and, willy-nilly, do have responsibilities to others. If the embryo is of personal status and worth, maternal autonomy can be as constrained in dealing with it as it can in acting in ways which damage born persons. Owning our own property, for example, does not exempt us from being obligated to have our garbage picked up lest we affect the health of those next door. In the abortion situation the "neighbor next door" is the child within the woman's body, but, similarly, the fact that her body is her own does not exempt her from certain duties with respect to that neighbor. Her body, like her property, may not be just her own to the extent that what she does with it impacts other persons.

Jung's more nuanced argument is not so easily rebutted. She also claims to recognize the dangers of an over-individualistic approach,[41] and grants that "Agents are naturally interdependent and bound by the obligations of this interdependence."[42] However, I think she still has a tendency to view motherhood as an alien imposition without the mother's acceptance, and to see the embryo as basically an other. These tendencies seem to me to betray individualistic and dualistic assumptions which can be challenged.

If "natural interdependence" is taken to mean mutual dependence, this would exist, in a univocal sense, only between agents. But the natural interdependence which grounds natural obligations need not be restricted to either a univocal meaning or situations of mutuality. "Because gestation is a primordial, prototypical, and physically concrete form of sociality and interdependence, some obligations to the fetus may exist even when they have not been undertaken deliberately."[43] I agree with Cahill that a nondualistic vision of the human would recognize, in the bodily relation of mother and child, the foundation for a moral relationship.

> The unity of body and spirit in human experience should also be taken into account. . . . The fact that a fetus is ineluctably dependent for its very existence on the body of another, and that this relation of dependence is not *prima facie* pathological or unjust, but physiologically normal and natural for a human being in its earliest stages of existence, should count as one factor in a moral evaluation of pregnancy and abortion. The morality of abortion is not reducible to the issue of "free consent." . . . The body makes peculiar demands, creates peculiar relationships, and grounds peculiar obligations.[44]

The dependence of the embryo does not entail a derivative moral status, dependent on the consent or valuing of another. Rather the embryo's vulnerability and the unique role of the mother in meeting its needs entails a special obligation on her part. The dynamic here is analogous to that process, identified by Pellegrino and Thomasma, where the vulnerability of the patient grounds the doctor's obligation to meet his or her needs. The authors themselves draw the implications for abortion:

> . . . attempts to resolve medical-ethical issues, such as abortion, on the basis of a definition of a person as self-conscious, neglect the roots of both medicine and medical ethics in the *living organism* in need. To argue, based on such a definition, that abortion and euthanasia are good ethical actions is to miss the point of medicine and its ontological condition of possibility.[45]

In my judgment, Jung is still too individualistic and dualistic in her view that constraining a woman from aborting a pregnancy which she is unwilling to bear is fundamentally violative of her personhood-moral agency. In fact, I think a stronger argument could be made that it is abortion which is ordinarily destructive for the mother's moral integrity. If a woman is pregnant, it seems to me that her relationship with her child is already a fact, already part of who she is. She is the mother of this child. An important facet of her identity thus depends on the child. Even if the impregnation was invasive, her pregnancy cannot be seen as simply an invasion. Her child is not an invader but an intrinsic good.[46] Perceptions to the contrary may be deeply and tragically felt, but they are mistaken.

The choice, then, is not over whether to initiate a relationship against a woman's will (that would be a kind of rape). The choice is whether or not she should continue being who she is, partly constituted by a relationship that already is. Conflicts may exist, but they are not just between the woman and the embryo, but between elements or facets of the identity, the interests, and the vision of the woman herself.

Certainly something as unjust and traumatizing as rape calls for both sympathy and aid for its victims. But I do not believe that the crime and tragedy of the way impregnation occurred diminishes the ontic status of the resulting embryo or child; nor does it dissolve the natural obligation for a mother to continue a pregnancy. I agree with McCormick that this obligation is not absolute. Abortion can be done to preserve life or equivalent values. I could also agree that the trauma of rape is such as to make it more possible that life or life-equivalent values may be threatened. But I do not think that the fact that a child was conceived by rape lessens the grounds that are required for aborting it. For I feel that if the woman is already identified as the mother of this child, if she aborts without a justification as serious as life itself, she denies her identity—herself in a fundamental way. And, "what can you offer in exchange for your very self?" (Mt 16:26).

The status and value of the embryo establish it as worthy of the same basic respect and rights granted to born persons. However, I would agree that both Fr. McCormick's position and the position I am arguing for do require much more of a mother on behalf of her unborn child than is ordinarily required of one person for another. Some sort of special relationship seems to be required to justify these additional demands. I think that the unique dependency relation between mother and child, and the necessary effect on the mother's personhood of the sheer intimacy of the physical—and hence personal—relation of pregnancy, point to the existence of such a special moral relationship. I say "point to" because I do not think such a relationship can be proved.

Therefore, while I think there is a special, obligating relationship between mother and child, this is a unique kind of relationship whose existence and quality are, at least to some extent, not derived but "self-evident" in the sense Grisez and Finnis argue that basic values are. The mother-embryo relationship cannot be established as simply a special instance of a more general mechanism which grounds obligating relationships, e.g. agreements, vulnerability, etc.

Such an appeal to self-evidence may seem arbitrary. But, after all, any moral decision may be characterized as arbitrary, if "arbitrary" means unproven. For all moral analysis and judgment begin with assumptions—which are unprovable by definition, and include the risk of leaps which are not (usually) sufficiently and certainly grounded. As analogous to the problem of establishing basic goods, the establishing of basic relationships may lead us back to those fundamental recognitions and valuings where everyone must start and beyond which one cannot argue.

THREE PRACTICAL QUESTIONS

Theoretical questions of the bases of identity and status, of rights and recognitions and conflict resolution, come to bear on people facing agonizing decisions. In his pastoral, social, and legislative views, Fr. McCormick shows the same reasoned moderation that was found in his more theoretical treatments. He seeks to balance both his principled objections to abortion and his sensitivity to the moral uncertainties and personal tragedies that would tend to allow it.[47]

The judgment that the embryo should be accorded fundamental personal status and rights establishes a presumption against abortion, at least except for cases of conflict with life or equivalent values. However, in translating this judgment into practice, in addition to the ordinary difficulties of weighing conflicts of values, I would identify four kinds of factors which affect the confidence and force with which one may seek to impose constraints on abortion, whether these constraints be moral, legal, or ecclesial: (1) uncertainty about fetal status, especially prior to implantation; (2) particular circumstances which affect the commensuration of burdens and benefits, especially with regard to the mother and her unborn child (e.g. pregnancy from rape or a doomed fetus); (3) factors arising from the nature of law, especially the criterion of feasibility; (4) factors arising from the respect due the mother's personal autonomy and moral agency, including her irreplaceable (though not absolute or infallible) role in evaluating the level of burden or benefit for her. The first three categories are already considered in McCormick's theory, and, as we saw above, he would be open to examining the impact of the fourth.

These factors shape McCormick's (and my own) position on three practical issues I wish to consider in conclusion: (1) anti-abortion legislation; (2) rape treatment in Catholic hospitals; (3) obligations to maintain pregnancy when the embryo is known to be doomed.

The battle over legislation concerning abortion seems to be heating up. McCormick recognizes that the above factors, particularly the requirement of feasibility, argue for both restraint in imposing restrictions, and the need to look beyond imposing a solution by brute political or judicial force and attack the range of causes that lead women to seek abortions.[48]

McCormick comes out of the Thomistic tradition on the philosophy of law. In this tradition, law is not composed simply of absolute principles of right and wrong, obedience to which is an end in itself. It is, rather, a *means* to the fulfillment of persons both directly, e.g. by protecting them from harm or mandating the pursuit of certain goods, and, indirectly, through shaping a society where persons may flourish. Therefore, it is not enough for a law to resolutely oppose evil; its "possibility" or feasibility must also be considered. That is, is it an apt means? Will it be generally obeyed? Is it proportionally enforceable? Will it truly protect and advance the good?[49] People will not support laws which they feel are unjust or unreasonably burdensome; and institutions perceived to support such laws will be undermined.

Obviously it is a good thing for unjust or unreasonable laws to be opposed. But, as McCormick points out, the distortions of individualism, consumerism, and functionalism warp modern society and hence corrupt people's perceptions of justice and reasonableness.[50] Therefore, the demand for feasibility is not only a constraint on drafting laws, but also a challenge to reshape society so that humanly authentic moral judgments and laws will find support.

Despite his awareness of the factors that militate against legal constraints on abortion, McCormick opts for a fairly restrictive law. Given the status and value of the embryo, the law should prohibit abortion, except for cases of conflict with life or equivalent values, and adjusting, in certain hard cases such as rape, for the qualitatively different status of the pre-implantation embryo. "In other words, I believe that the social disvalues associated with such a law (a degree of unenforceability, clandestine abortions, less than total control over fertility) are lesser evils than the enormous bloodletting both allowed and, in some real and destructive sense, inescapably encouraged (*teste experientia*), by excessively permissive laws. . . ."[51]

In 1974 McCormick suggested that state legislatures, with their opportunity for broader and more direct participation by all citizens, might be a better site than the courts for deciding the legal and social questions of abortion. In any case, not only the protection of unborn life but the maintenance of the social good demands the dialogue between opposing positions continue. This dialogue, painful and wearying as it sometimes is, is not just an unfortunately necessary means in the absence of the raw power to restrict abortion. It is an irreplaceable part of pursuing the good which is a civilized society.[52]

Finally, I wish to briefly consider two practical questions from the field of medical ethics. Even though I do not accept Jung's arguments as decisively establishing a woman's right to end an unwanted pregnancy, I do recognize their force, and also the validity of her position that some abortions are more validly described as the withdrawal of bodily life support rather than killing. Pregnancy from rape is the clearest and strongest example of an unwanted pregnancy and would thus seem most destructive of a woman's moral personhood. I think that consideration of a woman's autonomy and moral agency, the uncertainty of pre-implantation embryonic status, and the increased plausibility that the trauma of being raped would intensify the threat an unwanted pregnancy (or fear of such pregnancy) would pose to life-equivalent values, make more problematic the Catholic Church's prohibition of the use of interceptors in cases of rape. Even assuming the probable personal status of the embryo from conception, and therefore the objective correctness of the church's position, what should be required of Catholic hospital emergency rooms faced with rape victims?

Attempting to take proper account of both moral knowledge and moral doubt; in dealing with a situation of rape, I would maintain at least the following three points: (1) It is appropriate to communicate the church's teaching (and one's personal belief) that if conception has occurred there is the real possibility (even probability) of the presence of life deserving of respect and protection, but the patient should also be informed of the existence of respectable differing opinions. (2) Respect for this possibility, and fidelity to church teaching, precludes the giving of interceptors in Roman Catholic institutions. (3) While not absolutely determinative, individual autonomy (or parental authority) should always be recognized and supported, even more so in such a painful and uncertain situation. Therefore appropriate information should be provided and requests for referral honored. Furthermore, as regards victims who are Catholic, given the uncertainties arising from the factors discussed above, I do not think the ordinary moral and canonical sanctions applied to abortion should be invoked here.

A second problem, one which I think will become increasingly common as predictive and diagnostic techniques improve, is the case where an embryo is known to be doomed to a short life without the possibility of significant participation in spiritual and relational values (e.g. anencephaly, trisomy 13 or 18). Does the continuation of a pregnancy become more "extraordinary" as the embryo's prospects diminish? If an embryo has "less to lose" does that increase the range of values which could make abortion a proportionately good decision?

I would argue that, while the value and status sufficient to justify a right-to-life are present from conception, what one is obliged to endure to maintain pregnancy shifts when prospects for fulfillment are absent, when a life work is going to be over before it can really begin. This does not mean the embryo is less sacred or valuable, only that harms less severe than a threat to life or its equivalent can sometimes justify the removal of maternal support from a doomed embryo, just as medical treatments can be withdrawn when futile due to terminal illness.

From the Christian perspective, one must be careful not to determine futility simply according to "temporal" criteria. "Temporal" here has the dual meaning of both extending in time and secular or this-worldly. The Christian vision of life as transcending this world can influence value commensuration. An existential vision of the self as not pre-given but as created in the processes of experiencing, deciding, and acting, coupled with a belief in eternal life, might imply that preserving life (even for a short time) would be of eternal benefit, if it meant there was "more of a person" to experience eternity. A teleological system could naturally interpret such "transcendent multiplication" of the value of a life as entailing greater obligation to preserve or pursue it.[53]

Such an expanded perspective does not, of course, solve the problem of conflict between a mother and her child. For it could be argued that harm to the mother's character would also be reflected in her eternity. This envisioning of human life as eternal would not eliminate the need for commensuration, but might very well shape one's appraisal of the values which were in conflict. Further, this line of reasoning presumes that the length of time involved and the abilities of the child to profit from this time are such as to make a significant difference in personal formation. A couple of pain-filled days or weeks probably wouldn't make a difference—a couple of years probably would. But even a couple of years might not make a significant difference to a profoundly re-tarded child.

This essay does not pretend to have definitively solved any of the tangle of problems that make up the abortion question. I hope it is able to make some contribution to that ongoing dialogue spoken of earlier, and also to thereby honor Fr. Richard McCormick who has made significant contributions to this dialogue for many years. At a time when we speak of the frontiers of knowledge and some claim that moral purity calls for the elimination of compromise, he has witnessed to the truth to be found at the center and the moral integrity that comes from living with the tensions of complex issues.

Notes

1. Richard A. McCormick, S.J., *Notes on Moral Theology, 1965 through 1980* (Washington, D.C.: University Press of America, 1981). Originally published

yearly in *Theological Studies.* Citations here will be from the collected *Notes* since I judge that is more generally available.

2. E.g. in 1978 *Notes* McCormick offered a strong critique of the "Call to Concern" published in *Christianity and Crisis* 37 (1977) 222–24. McCormick, *Notes,* 730.

3. McCormick, *Notes,* 786. Richard A. McCormick, S.J., *Notes on Moral Theology, 1981–84* (Washington D.C.: University Press of America, 1984) 185. Richard A. McCormick, S.J., *Health and Medicine in the Catholic Tradition* (New York: The Crossroad Publishing Company, 1984) 131.

4. Gabriel Pastranna, O.P., "Personhood and the Beginning of Human Life," *Thomist* 41 (1977) 247–94. Cf. McCormick, *Notes,* 733–35. Cf. also Karl Rahner, "The Problem of Genetic Manipulation," *Theological Investigations,* vol. 9 (New York: Herder and Herder, 1972) 236.

5. McCormick, *Notes,* 796–97; cf. McCormick, *Health and Medicine,* 131.

6. Germain Grisez, "When Do People Begin?" paper delivered at the 1989 American Catholic Philosophical Association, New Orleans, 1989.

7. Bernard Häring, *Medical Ethics* (Notre Dame: Fides, 1973) 81–84.

8. Michael Tooley, "Abortion and Infanticide," *Philosophy and Public Affairs* 2 (1972) 37–65. Cf. McCormick, *Notes,* 506–07.

9. McCormick, *Notes,* 507.

10. Ibid.

11. McCormick, *Notes,* 498–99. Cf. Charles E. Curran, "Abortion: Law and Morality in Contemporary Catholic Theology," *Jurist* 33 (1973) 162–83. (Cf. also McCormick, *Notes,* 515–16.)

12. Bruno Ribes, "Pour une réforme de la législation française relative à l'avortement," *Etudes,* Jan. 1973, 55–84. Cf. McCormick, *Notes,* 493–94.

13. Marjorie R. Maguire, "Personhood, Covenant and Abortion," *Annual of the Society of Christian Ethics,* 1983, 117–45.

14. McCormick, *Notes 1981–84,* 185.

15. McCormick, *Notes,* 498–99, 515–16.

16. Joseph Fletcher, "Indicators of Humanhood: A Tentative Profile of Man," *Hastings Center Report* 2 (1972) 1–4.

17. H. Tristram Engelhardt, Jr., *The Foundations of Bioethics* (New York: Oxford University Press, 1986) 104–09.

18. McCormick, *Notes,* 445–46. Cf. also McCormick, *Health and Medicine,* 133–34.

19. McCormick, *Health and Medicine,* 132–33.

20. Richard A. McCormick, S.J., "Life-Saving and Life-Taking: A Comment," *Linacre Quarterly* 42 #2 (May 1975), 114.

21. McCormick, *Notes,* 796–97; cf. McCormick, *Health and Medicine,* 131.

22. Grisez, "When Do People Begin?"

23. McCormick, *Notes,* 516.

24. McCormick, *Health and Medicine,* 131–32; cf. McCormick, *Notes,* 515.

25. McCormick, *Notes,* 499.

26. McCormick, *Notes,* 516.

27. McCormick, *Notes,* 734–35.

28. McCormick, *Notes 1981–84,* 183–84. McCormick, *Notes,* 478.

29. Germain Grisez, *Abortion: The Myths, the Realities, and the Arguments* (New York: Corpus Books, 1970) 340–41.

30. Richard A. McCormick, S.J., "A Commentary on the Commentaries," in *Doing Evil to Achieve Good,* eds. Paul Ramsey and Richard McCormick (Chicago: Loyola University Press, 1978) 193–265.

31. Patricia Beattie Jung, "Abortion and Organ Donation: Christian Reflections on Bodily Life Support," in *Abortion and Catholicism: The American Debate,* ed. Patricia Beattie Jung and Thomas Shannon (New York: The Crossroad Publishing Company, 1988) 141–42.

32. McCormick, *Notes,* 499. Cf. Curran, "Abortion."

33. McCormick, *Health and Medicine,* 133.

34. Jung, "Abortion," Nicholson, 141, 165, n. 7; and Thomson, 165–66, n. 8.

35. Jung, "Abortion," 142–44.

36. Jung, "Abortion," 152–53.

37. Carol A. Tauer, "The Tradition of Probabilism and the Moral Status of the Early Embryo," *Theological Studies* 45 (March 1984) 3–33; reprinted in Jung and Shannon, *Abortion,* 54–84.

38. McCormick, *Notes,* 504.

39. McCormick, *Notes,* 505. Cf. John Finnis, "The Rights and Wrongs of Abortion," *Philosophy and Public Affairs* 2 (1973) 117–45.

40. McCormick, Notes, 106, 478–94. Lisa Sowle Cahill, "Abortion, Autonomy, and Community," in *Abortion and Catholicism: The American Debate,* ed. Patricia Beattie Jung and Thomas Shannon (New York: The Crossroad Publishing Company, 1988) 94.

41. Jung, "Abortion," 154, 156, 158–64.

42. Jung, "Abortion," 165, n. 7.

43. Cahill, "Abortion, Autonomy, and Community," 87–88.

44. Cahill, "Abortion, Autonomy, and Community," 89–90.

45. Edmund D. Pellegrino and David C. Thomasma, *A Philosophical Basis of Medical Practice* (New York: Oxford University Press, 1981) 185; cf. 208–14.

46. Lisa Sowle Cahill, "Abortion and Argument by Analogy," Paper presented at the annual meeting of the American Academy of Religion, San Francisco, 1981. Cf. Jung, "Abortion," 146–47.

47. McCormick, *Notes,* 496, 501–02, 517.

48. "A New Catholic Strategy on Abortion," *Month* 234 (1973) 163–71. Cf. McCormick, *Notes,* 490–92, 516–17. McCormick, *Health and Medicine,* 138–39.

49. John Courtney Murray, S.J., *We Hold These Truths* (New York: Sheed and Ward, 1960) 166–67.

50. McCormick, *Notes,* 106, 446, 478, 494. Cf. Fletcher, "Indicators." McCormick, *Health and Medicine,* 133–34.

51. McCormick, *Notes,* 518–19.

52. McCormick, *Notes,* 519–20.

53. Cf. e.g. Marjorie R. Maguire, "Personhood, Covenant and Abortion," 118–19.

13

Issues in Death and Dying
(Including Newborns)

James J. McCartney, O.S.A.

One of the principal bioethical concerns of Richard McCormick over the past decade and a half has been the development and description of ethical principles and procedures relevant to the foregoing or withdrawing of medical treatment. He has especially been interested in medical treatments utilized or refused within the context of terminal conditions, both those of adults and those of children. And although American society has, at the present time, achieved consensus (mostly along the lines McCormick suggests) on many of the vexing issues related to the care and treatment of the terminally ill, there are still many important concerns yet to be resolved.[1] In this chapter I will first of all define some important terms, then list the most important of these issues as I see them. I will then consider and critique McCormick's significant contributions in these areas, and finally attempt to look to the future and consider some issues related to death and dying now on the horizon which will have to be discussed and decided in the years ahead.

1. To Save or Let Die[2]

With the advent of modern medicine, it is now possible to cure diseases that were lethal in the past, to correct anatomical and physiological anomalies that would have proven fatal only a few years ago, to mimic the functions of organs and organ systems, to transplant living and cadaveric organs into new hosts who oftentimes will no longer reject them because of the use of immunosuppressive drugs, and to keep some people alive indefinitely through the use of mechanical respirators and/or artificially delivered nutrition and hydration. Unless we subscribe to the theory that holds "if we have a new technology, then we ought always use it no matter what the consequences" (a type of technological deontology), then these tremendous medical advances do and should raise significant ethical dilemmas when we consider their use as either appropriate or inappropriate in a given clinical situation. What are some of these important ethical issues and dilemmas which have arisen as a consequence of our being able to intervene, both medically and surgically, into persons' lives when they are coming to an end?

Before answering this question, I should first analyze some terms whose meaning, when it is not clear, often clouds and makes much more difficult any attempt at ethical discourse. These include such concepts as "brain death" and its relation to "personal death" or even "death," "medical treatment," "basic care," "terminal illness," "persistent vegetative state," and "euthanasia." Different jurisdictions, ecclesial bodies, philosophers and theologians often stipulate different meanings for these terms, leading to the possibility, for example, that what might be construed as "terminal illness" in one state might not be so construed in another. I will, with the help of McCormick in some instances, provide descriptive and/or stipulative definitions for these terms which I hope will clarify rather than obfuscate current ethical debate.

"Brain death," as currently understood and expressed in the law of many jurisdictions in the United States, simply means that the *individual* in question has died because it has been clinically determined that the whole brain, including the brain stem, has permanently and irrevocably ceased functioning. Brain death is not a halfway house between life and death; it is a phrase which describes a means used to determine whether the individual has died or not so that, if the individual is dead, his or her organs, some of which may still be living and functional, might be put to some beneficent purpose such as transplantation or experimentation. And while some philosophers argue that personal death, i.e. the death of the person, happens when the individual has permanently and irrevocably lost the capacity to think, reason, or choose as a result of brain injury or disease, the law and many philosophical and religious traditions hold that as long as functional integrity of the body is present, there is an individual present who is the subject of personal rights, whether or not he or she has the capacity to think. On this reading, brain death is the determination that the brain, which is the organ and seat of bodily integration and holistic operation, has ceased to function and that therefore the individual is dead, even though some organs and organ systems continue to remain physiologically active (with significant medical assistance) for a period of time. In other words, when brain death is established, what we have is a corpse or cadaver, some of the organs and organ systems of which are still maintained in a living, functional state through the use of medical technology.

The next set of terms for clarification are "medical treatment" as contrasted with "basic care." Clarification of these concepts is important because it is generally accepted that persons have the right to refuse medical treatment under certain circumstances while a humane society will always feel itself obliged to provide basic care. I understand medical treatment to include any therapeutic or palliative intervention that entails a physician's supervision, any physician-prescribed pharmaceutical product assimilated into the patient's body, or any manipulative or surgical invasion of the patient's body by a physician or surgeon. Basic care, on the other hand, includes those hygienic and nutritional measures taken to make patients comfortable and which assist the person in self-healing. Basic care measures include keeping the person clean, assuring proper ventilation and heating/cooling of the person's room, turning to prevent bed sores, providing adequate and well-prepared food and fluids for patients to eat and drink, and assisting patients to eat by mouth when it is difficult for them to do so by themselves. It should be pointed out that care, however well-intended, that proves burdensome to patients over the long run is really poor care because basic care is always seen in reference to a patient's overall comfort and well-being. Following from this analysis, I would consider any artificial administration of food and fluids to be medical treatment and not basic care both because of the bodily invasion required by a nasogastric tube (or any other mode of artificial delivery) and because a physician's supervision is necessary. McCormick generally agrees with this analysis and holds that "feeding by I.V. lines and nasogastric tubes is a medical procedure."[3]

With regard to "terminal illness" or a "terminal condition," McCormick rightly points out that "the notion of 'the dying patient' is ambiguous and sometimes related to the technology available. However, the category is often presented as if it were utterly clear."[4] I could not agree with this analysis more. One only has to consider how terminal illness is defined by the various states who have so-called "right to die" statutes to see the truth of this assertion. Some states put a time frame such as "death likely within a year" within their definition while others hold that a person is terminal "when death is imminent. Some hold that persons are terminal if they have a disease or injury which will bring about death *whether or not* life-prolonging procedures are employed; others hold that persons are dying if they have a disease or injury which will bring about death *unless* life-prolonging procedures are employed.

Although it might be important philosophically and legally to achieve conceptual clarity regarding terminal illness, the decision to refuse medical treatment may be ethically reached on grounds other than the fact that the person is terminally ill and so the determination of "terminal illness" may not be as important as some believe. Nonetheless, in some situations it is helpful, both legally and ethically, to have clinicians reach a consensus, however imperfect conceptually, that a person is at least moribund, i.e. headed toward death. This is especially true when we are trying to decide whether a non-palliative intervention is effective or beneficial on the one hand, or futile or harmful on the other.

"Persistent vegetative state" generally refers to those patients who have suffered some brain trauma which has rendered them unable to perform higher brain functions such as thinking, feeling, suffering, or acting, and whose situation cannot be reversed by current medical technology. Often these patients have been in a coma but are now engaged in sleep-wake cycles. Many times these patients' waking periods are characterized by roving eye movements which sometimes seem to follow moving objects or persons in the room. Occasionally persons in a persistent vegetative state seem to recoil from painful stimuli. Persons in a persistent vegetative state are not brain dead but their prognosis is very poor. Although they can be kept alive, sometimes for many years, by artificial medical interventions, they will never again recover cognitive power or function. They will never return to a sapient state of self-awareness or awareness of others.

The care and treatment of persistent vegetative state patients raises many ethical questions which will be considered in the next section. At this point, however, I wish to point out that even though our understanding of what constitutes a persistent vegetative state is reasonably clear, how to make this diagnosis on a given patient is not easy, at least at the present time. Thus, when stories of permanent coma or persistent vegetative state patients "recovering" reach the newspapers, as sometimes they do, the response ought to be that these persons were misdiagnosed in the first place, not that our ethical and legal standards regarding the treatment and care of patients truly in a persistent vegetative state or permanent coma must necessarily be radically revised.

One final definitional issue with regard to persistent vegetative state patients is whether these persons can be said to be terminally ill. Obviously, the answer to this question can only be given in light of the definition of terminal illness employed; and, as we saw previously, this definition is anything but univocal. Suffice it to say that there are major decisions of appellate courts, such as the Quinlan case in New Jersey and the Bludworth case in Florida, that presume that patients in a persistent vegetative state are terminally ill. However, there are also major appellate court decisions, such as the Cruzan case in Missouri, that presume just the opposite. This lack of consensus in the courts reflects the attitude of ethicists and philosophers in general concerning this issue. McCormick himself has not dealt with this issue in any thematic way in his published work, nor does he need to since the ethical criterion he proposes for continuing or discontinuing treatment in specific cases is not concerned with whether or not a person is terminally ill but whether or not he or she has the potentiality for human relationships. In light of the current dispute over this issue, I believe that McCormick's approach is very wise.

Finally, with regard to conceptual issues surrounding death and dying, the term "euthanasia" should be considered. The Congregation for the Doctrine of the Faith of the Roman Catholic Church defines euthanasia as "an action or omission that by its nature or by intention causes death with the purpose of putting an end to all suffering."[5] This stipulative definition of euthanasia, while useful to the extent that it can be used to state the Congregation's categorical opposition to it (since it is used as a moral term, like murder, rather than a descriptive term, like killing), unfortunately does not reflect the way the term is often used in contemporary society. Many people, for example, would consider the foregoing or removal of burdensome or useless medical interventions as a form of passive euthanasia, but would be willing to justify these decisions in certain circumstances. Catholic ethical teaching would also be able to accept these decisions as justified (as long as there was no intention to directly cause death) but the Congregation (and oftentimes the law in the United States) would not consider these actions as euthanasia but as a legitimate refusal of medical treatment. The term "euthanasia" is often confusing, especially when some are using it in a descriptive sense and some are using it in a stipulative way.

In a recent article,[6] McCormick discusses the problem of euthanasia, shows how unclear the concept has become recently, but ultimately maintains that "the ethical problem at the bottom of the euthanasia discussion is the moral difference between killing and allowing to die.[7] I disagree with McCormick's position here for two reasons. First, as I have previously shown, the "ethical problem" of euthanasia is often at root a conceptual one, the disagreeing parties not using the word in the same way. Second, and more importantly, even if one agrees that there is a moral distinction between active killing and allowing to die (and I do agree with McCormick that there is), there are some acts of "allowing to die" that may be morally objectional (acts of omission with the intention of causing death for beneficent purposes) and would be judged by official Catholic Church teaching and by the law as acts of euthanasia (in the stipulative sense described above). On the other hand, these same acts of omission, if decided upon because continued intervention was perceived as burdensome, useless, or not what the patient would have wished, could be (and often are) construed as the ethically proper thing to do even though it is foreseen that death will follow as a result of this decision. Reducing the ethical problem of euthanasia to the distinction between killing and allowing to die does not, in my opinion, help solve some of the hardest cases being considered today, those which involve the discontinuation of feeding or fluids of patients in a persistent vegetative state. I will consider this issue in section 2 in more detail. I bring it up here only to show that euthanasia is a more complicated topic than even McCormick will admit. With this in mind, I will omit use of the term "euthanasia" in subsequent discussions and analyses since it generally serves only to confuse rather than clarify the issues in death and dying at hand.

Having analyzed some terms which very often cause confusion when death and dying are discussed, I will now turn specifically to those ethically dilemmatic issues which have arisen as a result of our ability to stave off death technologically, in some cases for long periods of time, without any restoration of health or improvement. McCormick himself summarizes these issues as three:

1. "First, how should we conceptualize our duties toward the dying?"

2. "The second area of unclarity is the treatment of the incompetent."

3. "The third area that will remain vexing is the treatment of seriously defective newborns."[8]

In section 2 I will respond to these concerns of McCormick using insights he himself has provided as well as my own critical analyses, conclusions and further questions. Finally, in section 3 I will project to the future and consider what shape these problems and issues will take in the decades ahead.

2. QUESTIONS OF SPECIAL URGENCY[9]

The three issues raised by McCormick and cited at the end of the first section are indeed "questions of special urgency," both because of their impact on people's lives and also because in answering these questions we will in many ways have determined what kind of a global community we will be. I will, then, consider each of these questions in detail in this section.

"How should we conceptualize our duties toward the dying?" In attempting to answer this question, McCormick focuses on treatment decisions and concludes that we must decide whether medical treatments are "obligatory" or "optional" with regard to the dying patient.[10] As important as this issue of medical treatments is, I believe McCormick's first question merits a much more expansive response and indeed McCormick himself in other places has provided this.

In an article written in 1978, McCormick emphasizes that "it is conversation about who we are that is so often bypassed in contemporary discussions about health care. But it is precisely *who we are* that will inform us about the shape of our health care responsibilities.[11] So much do I agree with this assertion that I often define ethics itself as "what we ought to do as civilized persons *in the light of who we say we are.*" Especially with regard to our duties toward the dying is the truth of this statement borne out. Death and dying confront us as no other issue can with our ultimate beliefs and convictions about the existence of God, the value of life, the meaning of suffering, and the significance of solidarity with others who are passing from this world. Thus it is not surprising that Orthodox Jews, whose theological views entail respecting life as a most gracious gift from God as well as emphasizing life in this world rather than hereafter, tend to be very aggressive in keeping people alive to the very last and view most foregoing or removal of medical treatment when biological life can be prolonged as either suicidal or homicidal. To conceptualize our duties toward the dying, we must speak within a given cultural and religious tradition, fully realizing that other cultural and religious perspectives will see the matter quite differently. With this in mind I believe it fair to say that McCormick's analysis of our duties toward the dying reflects the values and vision of a Roman Catholic theologian working within the cultural context of the United States in the latter part of the twentieth century.

Duties Toward the Dying

To get to "duties toward the dying" as McCormick understands them, we must first of all reflect upon the value he places on human life. For McCormick, as for most theologians working within the Catholic tradition, human life is a basic but not absolute good, and "an individual has the primary obligation to preserve this basic good in himself or herself, to preserve his or her own life."[12] Nonetheless, McCormick argues that there are limits to this obligation. According to the Christian perspective, for example, one could never do something immoral to preserve one's life. "There are also limitations when there is no question of sin. Not all means must be used, otherwise we would convert life from a basic value to an absolute and unconditioned one, and in the process subvert some profound Christian convictions about the meaning of life. No one has stated this more clearly than Pius XII."[13] The fact that we are called upon to make these determinations entails for McCormick the need for privacy and self-determination, construed here not simply as autonomy or free choice, but the means by which we can best decide and implement those things which best protect our life, health, and human dignity. McCormick understands the Catholic moral tradition as supportive of self-determination in the acceptance or refusal of treatment because "the *over-all good of the patient will best be served* if treatment is controlled in this way."[14]

This is no "freedom as side-constraint" model as espoused by Engelhardt,[15] but rather a rigorous defense for self-determination as a means for pursuing basic human goods and values. Thus one of our first "duties toward the dying" is to enable them, whenever possible, to make decisions as to what kind of care and treatment they will receive and by whom and in what context this shall be delivered. The goal of this enabling should be to help terminally ill persons live the rest of their lives in a "certain acceptable mix of freedom, painlessness, and ability to function"[16] and then "die with dignity" in accord with their basic beliefs and values.

In a previously cited article, McCormick describes responsibility for health care in explicit theological language. His understanding of God is ultimately relational, God as "being-in-and-for-another." And since human beings are made in the image of God, it is not surprising that we discover ourselves as made for relational life, the ultimate meaning of which is discovered in authentic human love. My greatest gift to others is authentic human love because it is their greatest need and vice versa. McCormick then applies this theological vision to the responsibility for health care generally,[17] but I argue that this is an especially apt theological grounding for care and concern for the terminally ill.

Authentic human love must be the context in which our "duties toward the dying" are carried out. This entails treating the patient as a valuable person right until the end and not shunting him or her aside as something hopeless or useless. It also entails providing care and treatment that is in the patient's best interest, not ours. It may also demand allowing the patient to die a natural death if this is the person's wish even when we believe we could prolong life for a period of time by artificial interventions. It especially means that we provide adequate palliative treatment and care so that the patient is as comfortable as humanly possible, even if this treatment brings with it the unintended but foreseen consequence of respiratory depression and subsequent death. "Authentic human love" means solidarity with the patient, helping the person manage his or her affairs and trying to prepare the person spiritually for death.

It is the living out of the belief for the sake of the dying person (and for ourselves) that "ultimately our eternal happiness depends on love and is love."[18]

Treatment of the Incompetent

I have considered those duties we owe to the dying when they are at least sufficiently rational to make medical decisions and are aware of their surroundings. However, the second issue which McCormick cites, and about which he has written extensively, is "treatment of the incompetent." I am obviously here referring to incompetent patients who are terminally ill or at least "moribund," as the Supreme Court of New Jersey describes them in the Quinlan case,[19] and so I shall still be discussing our duties toward the dying, focusing now, however, upon our duties toward dying persons who are either unconscious or not able to interact with their environment in any affective or relational way.

The first topic I would like to discuss in considering this issue is the use of advance directives for health care. Advance directives are understood as (a) instructions given either orally or in writing by persons while still competent as to how they wish to be treated when incompetent (so-called living wills), or (b) the assignment by competent persons of a health care decision maker, either within a living will or by means of a durable power of attorney statute, who is authorized to make medical decisions on their behalf when they cannot do so for themselves.

McCormick's abiding belief that medical decisions regarding the incompetent are best made by loving family members, in partnership with a physician who knows and respects the patient's values and beliefs, initially led him (and fellow Jesuit John Paris) to oppose legislation officially sanctioning advance directives. McCormick and Paris basically felt there should be no need for legislation to guarantee the natural law right of self-determination. They also felt this kind of legislation would unduly confuse the process of decision making in health care and would possibly exclude the family from participation in decision making. They were also worried about "the possibility that the state, construing the right to refuse treatment as a conferral rather than a natural right—one with inherent moral limitations—could also confer the right to be killed."[20]

The authors, although holding that these objections were still valid, changed their position in 1981 and now support legislation empowering advance directives. They changed their opinion because of the decisions of some state supreme courts which seem to restrict the rights of family and physician to act on a patient's behalf when the patient is incompetent and moribund. I believe that in the intervening years since the article was written, McCormick and Paris have been proven correct. This is most clear in the state of New York whose Court of Appeals (the highest appellate court in the state) has set a most rigorous standard (clear and convincing evidence of the patient's wishes) for the foregoing or discontinuation of life-prolonging procedures for incompetent patients. In the state of New York at the present time, one would be foolhardy not to have enacted some form of advance directive in the light of several recent Court of Appeals decisions, all of which support this most exacting (and in my opinion mistaken) standard of evidence of patients' wishes in cases of incompetence. (Ironically, New York State has only recently begun to work on a statute that would legally empower a health care proxy; there is no statute in New York which legalizes living wills but they obviously have great moral and legal suasion because of the standard of the Court of Appeals.)

I share McCormick's and Paris' ambivalence toward the legalization of advance directives. Ideally, we ought not need statutes (or court involvement for that matter) to protect rights as basic as self-determination and family privacy in matters medical. Indeed, several state appellate courts, most notably Florida's in the Corbett case,[21] have held that there is a common law right of self-determination and a constitutional right of privacy which undergird these statutes and which empower patients or families to make medical decisions which statutes often proscribe (the cessation of artificial feeding in the Corbett case). Nonetheless, statutes legalizing advance directives have been helpful for many reasons. First of all, they have educational value in that they help people to realize that they have the right to make self-determining choices now as to what type of medical treatment they wish in the future or whom they wish to make these choices at that time. Second, a person may not have a loving family situation or a physician who knows and accepts the person's wishes and values. In our highly mobile and fragmented society, this is usually the rule rather than the exception. Finally, whether a legal document or not, it is always helpful to have some written account of patients' wishes at a time when they can no longer express them personally because of incompetence.

On a personal note, I always carry an advance directive in my wallet stating both my wishes should I become incompetent and specific individuals to carry these wishes out, even though I live in one of the ten states (Pennsylvania) which has not yet legalized such documents. Before moving to Pennsylvania, I directed a bioethics institute at a community hospital in Florida where I had the opportunity to draft an advance directive in agreement with Florida statutory and case law, thousands of copies of which were distributed to citizens of that state. I have always found that people are most appreciative to know that not only can they make decisions now that will apply in the future, but that these decisions have the power of law. Thus like McCormick and Paris, I am very supportive of statutes which legalize advance directives, even though I, like them, recognize their problems and limitations.

Another significant topic relevant to the treatment of the incompetent is "quality-of life." When people give instructions limiting medical interventions should they become incompetent and moribund, they are obviously considering the quality, and not just the duration, of their lives. When families, physicians, and health care proxies try to determine what is in incompetent patients' best interests, especially when there is no advance directive, they should not look only at the possible prolongation of life, but at what kind of life will be prolonged and at what cost. McCormick and I are in essential agreement on this issue and I concur wholeheartedly that "much of contemporary health care and very many decisions about treatment are concerned with not just the preservation of life and avoidance of disease, but with a certain quality of life. This is absolutely as it should be. Thus we are concerned not just with keeping a patient alive by surgery or medication, but with a certain level of being alive, a certain acceptable mix of freedom, painlessness, and ability to function."[22]

However, quality of life determinations are not all the same, and there are some quality of life judgments that people who believe in God as the author and giver of life ought not to make, e.g. this is a life not worth living and therefore ought to be terminated. Fear that these kinds of quality of life judgments would become acceptable has led many Catholic and Jewish theologians (and some appellate courts, most notably New York's Court of Appeals) to disallow quality of life determinations on others' behalf altogether. The problem with this approach is that it can lead to a vitalism that tends to prolong biological life at all costs until the person is in the throes of death. I prefer to follow McCormick's approach and say that there are some quality of life judgments about others we must inevitably make, but that these judgments need not inevitably lead us to the determination that there are some lives not worth living and therefore ought to be terminated. I believe this to be the position of Pope Pius XII when he states that "where the proper and independent duty of the family is concerned, they are usually bound only to the use of ordinary means."[23]

McCormick argues that even though decisions to forego or discontinue treatment are often couched in terms of the means used to prolong life, many times it is the quality of the life thus saved that helps render the judgment that the means are extraordinary. "Why? Because, it can be argued, human relationships—which are the very possibility of growth in love of God and neighbor—would be so threatened, strained, or sub-merged that they would no longer function as the heart and meaning of the individual's life as they should."[24]

For McCormick, the most important quality of life judgment that must be made to determine whether or not medical treatments should be continued on behalf of others is whether or not there still exists on the part of these others the potential for human relationships. "If that potential is simply nonexistent or would be utterly submerged and undeveloped in the mere struggle to survive, that life has achieved its potential."[25] He especially applies this guideline to the treatment of seriously defective newborns as we shall subsequently see, but I believe the principle is also applicable to incompetent adults who have expressed no other wishes as to how they wish to be treated when they are moribund. To preserve biological life for its own sake, without any reference to the potential for human relationships, is vitalism pure and simple even though in cases where there is no further potential for human relationships we might not wish to directly terminate life on religious grounds.

Finally, when making treatment decisions about incompetent others, I would argue that it is also appropriate to consider the impact this will have on one's own quality of life. If the medical treatments used to prolong a moribund person's life will create excessive psychological, emotional, financial, or spiritual burdens for the caregiver, he or she is under little obligation to provide them. Although McCormick does not deal with this issue in great detail, he does seem reluctant to allow social factors, "institutional or managerial reasons," to impact on decisions to forego treatment of incompetent patients. Therefore, one wonders whether he would agree with Pope Pius XII's position that "if it appears that the attempt at resuscitation constitutes in reality such a burden for the family that one cannot in all conscience impose it on them, they can lawfully insist that the doctor should discontinue these attempts, and the doctor can lawfully comply."[26]

The third and final topic that must be discussed when considering the issue of treatment of the incompetent is the foregoing or withdrawal of artificial life-prolonging medical treatments, including food and fluids. Starting with the Quinlan case in 1976, courts and state legislatures have wrestled with this issue and have developed consensus on some aspects of the issue but not on others. It is generally agreed, for example, that a patient's previously expressed wishes while competent should be followed, even when, in the instance of a Jehovah's Witness' refusal of blood transfusions on religious grounds, the incompetent person could be restored to consciousness and health by the use of this particular medical treatment (whole blood). It is also generally agreed that when death is at hand, i.e. the person is in the throes of death, all medical treatment including artificially delivered nutrition and hydration may be stopped. There is also consensus that life-prolonging medical procedures may be foregone or discontinued when they are causing pain or discomfort to the patient out of proportion to any benefit to be gained by the prolongation of biological life, or if they are experimental or very expensive technologies such as an artificial heart. And I believe there is also consensus that a respirator or surgical intervention may be foregone (or discontinued in the case of the respirator) when the patient is in a persistent vegetative state and will not be helped to regain consciousness by either of these two procedures. Finally, of course, when a patient is declared brain dead, artificial life-prolonging procedures not only should but in some states must be discontinued (unless the organs are to be used for transplantation or experimentation) in order to prepare the body for burial in accord with public health laws.

However, there is little consensus as to whether persistent vegetative state patients are really terminally ill, and second, if they are not, whether artificial nutrition and hydration can legitimately be discontinued for persons in a persistent vegetative state. McCormick's "own opinion on these issues is that the permanently comatose and *some* noncomatose but elderly incompetent patients may be classified broadly as dying; that feeding by I.V. lines and nasogastric tubes is a medical procedure; that its discontinuance need not involve aiming at the death of such patients; and that the burden-benefit calculus may include, indeed often unavoidably includes, a quality-of-life ingredient, providing we draw the line at the right place."[27]

I agree with McCormick that these patients may be classified as dying because they have a fatal pathology which will inevitably bring about death and which already has left them devoid of any meaningful human relationship. Because of this latter aspect of their illness (their loss of the potential for human relationships), both McCormick and I would agree that any and all medical treatments, including artificially delivered nutrition and hydration, may be discontinued, not necessarily with the intention of bringing about death, but of allowing the fatal pathology (manifested by the absence of the ability to swallow or to ingest food) to run its course to natural death. The quality of life component of the burden-benefit calculus that McCormick refers to is precisely this inability of those in a persistent vegetative state to form or sustain human relationships, one of the spiritual dimensions Pope Pius XII could have intended when he wrote that "life, health, all temporal activities are in fact subordinated to spiritual ends."[28]

Nonetheless, there are many at the present time, especially those involved in "right to life" activities, who argue that the provision of nutrition and hydration, however it is administered, is basic care; that those in a persistent vegetative state are not terminally ill; and that to discontinue administration of feeding and fluids is the moral equivalent of euthanasia by starvation. My argument against this position is that if we can justify the discontinuation of the respirator in the case of Karen Ann Quinlan (and most of those who oppose discontinuation of feeding and fluids agree with the decision in the Quinlan case), then by the same logic and for the sake of consistency, we should also justify the discontinuation of artificially administered nutrition and hydration. In both situations we are dealing with natural substances which we need to survive (oxygen in the case of the respirator, nutrients and fluids in the latter case) that the body, because of a serious pathology, cannot spontaneously take in as it should. In both situations, what is artificial (and a medical treatment) is the artificial delivery of these natural substances to the internal organs which assimilate them (oxygen to the lungs; nutrients and fluids to the stomach, intestine, or blood stream). If the former can be foregone or withdrawn, and most people agree that it can, then why not the latter?

One final observation on this issue! McCormick mentions that the discontinuation of artificially delivered feeding and fluids need not involve aiming at the death of the patients upon whom the decision to discontinue is made. I would phrase this a bit differently and say that the foregoing or discontinuation of artificially delivered nutrition and hydration need not involve intending to kill these patients, but of allowing the fatal pathology present to result in natural death, precisely because their potential for affective, cognitive function (human relationships) has been irrevocably lost. I believe we can wish, and even pray for the death of these patients; what religious persons cannot do is intend to kill these persons either by action or by omission. I do not see in this context how withholding or removing feeding tubes is such an omission but there are those who disagree.

In summing up this section, I can think of no better advice than that articulated by Paris and McCormick in a recent article:

> It is this bedrock teaching of theology on the meaning of life and death—neither of which in the Christian framework ought to be made absolute—and not a misplaced debate on "the casuistry of means" that should guide our judgments on the difficult and sometimes trying decisions cast up by modern medical technology. To do otherwise—or to count mere vegetative existence as a patient-benefit—is to let slip one's grasp on the heart of Cath-

olic tradition on this matter. It is that tradition, developed over centuries of living out the Gospel message on the meaning of life and death—and not some immediate political "pro-life" agenda—that ought to be the source of our advice and guidance to courts.[29]

Treatment of Seriously Defective Newborns

The final "question of urgency" I wish to take up is the issue of the treatment of seriously defective newborns. I have been heavily involved in this issue through my service on the ethics committee of Miami Children's Hospital, and I believe there is no more difficult, nor more frustrating, area in all of bioethics than this one. Decision making is made difficult for many reasons. First of all, newborns do not have any wishes, values, or preferences to express, so decisions in these cases must focus on what is in the best interests of the patient, even though this is not the only criterion for decision making as we shall see. Second, diagnosis and prognosis in the case of newborns is notoriously difficult because of their size, their resilient cells and tissues, their reaction to drugs, and their responsiveness to care. Finally, most people react very emotionally to an infant in distress, and sometimes things that are not in these newborns' best interest are done so that it can be said that at least something was tried.

In an article written in the *Journal of the American Medical Association* over fifteen years ago, McCormick began to wrestle with this problem. Here he maintains that we must develop some objective, quality of life guideline that will ground our moral intuitions as to which infants ought to be saved and which allowed to die. The guideline that he suggests, as we have seen earlier, is the "potential for human relationships associated with the infant's condition."[30] He points out that this guideline is not to be understood as "a detailed rule that preempts decisions; for relational capacity is not subject to mathematical analysis but to human judgment."[31] Thus, "individual decisions will remain the anguishing onus of parents in consultation with physicians."[32]

He accepts the possibility that mistakes will be made using this criterion but suggests that we try to err on the side of life when making these decisions. He also stresses that using the criterion of relational potential "does not imply that 'some lives are valuable, others not' or that 'there is such a thing as a life not worth living.' "[33] Here he stresses that every human being is of incalculable worth and that all individuals are valuable in and of themselves. Nevertheless, he wonders "whether this worldly existence will offer such a valued individual any hope of sharing those values for which physical life is the fundamental condition."[34]

I agree with this criterion as a sufficient, but not necessary condition for discontinuing treatment with newborns. For I argue that there are other factors, irrespective of relational potential, that can serve as criteria for decision making in this context. McCormick touches on these factors in a more recent article[35] but sees them as further specifications of the capacity for human relationships. I disagree, and rather see them as other, but equally important, guidelines for termination of treatment of newborns distinct from relational potential.

First of all, Paris and McCormick argue that "life-saving interventions ought not be omitted for institutional or managerial reasons."[36] Here we part company, for I argue that since we are talking about the promotion of a positive good (the saving of the life of the child), there may be limitations and restrictions based not on the infant's questionable ability to benefit from this treatment, but on the sheer fact that it may cost too much, may involve personnel who are more needed elsewhere, may utilize resources that could more readily save many more lives, may involve the family in genuinely excessive psychological, emotional, or financial burdens they are unable to handle, or may involve the child's becoming a ward of the state with all the psychological trauma that entails. While I agree that we ought to do all that we can to mitigate these factors, when they are irrevocably present I hold that they would provide adequate justification for the foregoing or discontinuance of treatment when they are coupled with a fairly serious pathological anomaly.

McCormick and Paris go on to say that "life-saving interventions may not be omitted simply because the baby is retarded."[37] I am in general agreement here but would amplify their notion of "further complications" which would justify the discontinuance of treatment with the points made in the last paragraph. People should not be asked to do the impossible when it is the case of the promotion of a positive good.

The last two specifications (or additional guidelines as I see them) are ones I totally agree with. They are:

> 3. Life-sustaining intervention may be omitted or withdrawn when there is excessive hardship on the patient, especially when this combines with poor prognosis. . . .

> 4. Life-sustaining interventions may be omitted or withdrawn at a point when it becomes clear that expected life can be had only for a relatively brief time and only with the continued use of artificial feeding. . . .[38]

In ending these considerations not only about defective newborns but about the dying and incompetent generally, I believe it is important to stress something McCormick reflected upon several years ago. He emphasizes "that it is the pride of Judeo-Christian tradition that the weak and defenseless, the powerless and unwanted, those whose grasp on the goods of life is most fragile—that is, those whose potential is real but reduced—are cherished and protected as our neighbor in greatest need. Any application of a general guideline that forgets this is but a racism . . . profoundly at odds with the gospel, and eventually corrosive of the humanity of those who ought to be caring and supporting as long as that care and support has human meaning."[39] I do not believe that a Christian theological stance over these important issues can be articulated any more succinctly and powerfully than this.

3. How Brave a New World?[40]

In looking to the future and considering how the issues surrounding death and dying will develop and change, I will highlight only a few items and suggest ways in which McCormick and I might think about them based on our past and present analyses and conclusions. Since people will always be dying, and will always to some extent be terrified in the face of death, issues surrounding death and dying will always be present, even if some of the issues we are dealing with today are resolved because of fresh insights or, in some cases, new technology.

First of all, I believe that the issue of foregoing or withdrawing the artificial delivery of nutrition and hydration will be with us for some time. However, the debate about this issue may be shifted to focus more on the allocation of scarce medical resources than on the care and treatment due this person because he or she is a human being. My guess is that if allocation issues begin to hold center stage, discontinuation of alimentation and hydration, especially when the cost of care and treatment is expensive over a long period of time, will be much more commonplace than it is today. While many of these discontinuations might be justified, McCormick would surely, and I would probably, believe that the right decision had been reached for the wrong reasons based upon the analysis of this and related issues discussed in the preceding section. Whatever new factors become involved, this issue, I predict, will be a contentious one for decades to come.

The second issue is one which concerns a technology not now possible for humans, but which probably will be available, at least experimentally, in the not too distant future. I am referring here to cryopreservation, the process of slowing the metabolism to a very low level by freezing, storing the body thus frozen for a significant period of time, and then restoring it to a normal state. This process is now used with some success in freezing pre-embryos produced from in-vitro fertilization, and there is in principle no known scientific reason why it would not work with adults when the technology is properly developed. But in what context might cryopreservation be used? Suppose someone at a rather young age had a terminal illness, e.g. AIDS, which is incurable now but for which there might very well be a cure in twenty or thirty years. Someone in this situation might be willing to volunteer for cryopreservation as the only alternative that might help him or her live a normal life (even if twenty or thirty years from now).

I believe that McCormick and I would both approach the issue of cryopreservation in a similar way. First of all, all the ethical principles involved in human experimentation would have to be considered and justified. There would also have to be adequate testing done on lower life forms so that a reasonable prediction of success could be made. Finally, because of the nature of the experiment, volunteers should be restricted to those who might gain some therapeutic benefit if the experiment is a success, e.g. persons with AIDS, terminal cancer, etc. However, if all these caveats are heeded, I would find nothing inherently wrong with volunteering for this type of experiment, and I think that McCormick would also share this view. Of course, when the ethical principle of justice is considered, it would have to be shown why this particular technology should be employed when there are so many other pressing needs. Nonetheless, I hold that cryopreservation experiments could be justified in principle and that they might, in time, benefit far more people than just the terminally ill.

The final issue to be considered in this section is far less esoteric and has to do with voluntary, active euthanasia (VAU), a procedure already practiced with some impunity by physicians in the Netherlands and advocated in the United States by such groups as The Hemlock Society. VAU signifies a patient request to have his or her life terminated by active means and the agreement and carrying out of this by a family member, friend, or health care professional.

McCormick is clearly opposed to VAU but very unclear in his reason for such opposition.[41] He would probably approach the issue by trying to tease out the values and disvalues associated with it and try to show that the disvalues virtually always outweigh the values in any society that wants to think of itself as civilized. My approach to this issue is different and reflects at least two differences in moral methodology between McCormick and myself. First of all, I do not find the traditional natural law argument that suicide is against the natural inclination of self-preservation persuasive when a person is terminally ill (and possibly facing a great deal of suffering). Nonetheless, religious persons (specifically devout Jews and Christians) who believe that God reveals himself as the author of life have generally understood that we are stewards, not masters, of our life. The Catholic tradition has developed this religious insight into the ethical principle that the direct taking of innocent human life is intrinsically immoral. I accept this as a deontological, but as a religiously deontological, principle (I think that McCormick would disagree with me on this on both counts). I further argue that since this principle is religiously grounded, there is no good public policy argument in a pluralistic society for prohibiting assisted suicide or VAU, as long as proper safeguards to prevent abuse are put in place. Devout Jews and Christians ought not to avail themselves of these options since their religious traditions stand opposed to such activity, but nonbelievers might be convinced that assisted suicide and VAU are the only rational (and morally sensible) options should they become terminally ill. Where I would use a proportional calculus is to prohibit health care providers from assisting in suicide or VAU. I believe that many disvalues could be marshaled to support this prohibition, such as the breakdown of trust (already weak), a contradiction of professional responsibilities, the possibility of abuse, an increase of litigation, among others. I do think that McCormick would agree with me here. Thus the issue of VAU is a very interesting one since it manifests more clearly than other issues differences in moral methodology even within the revisionist Catholic tradition.

In closing this chapter, I would like to add a personal note. Richard McCormick not only provided me with much encouragement and support as he guided my course of study at Georgetown and directed my doctoral dissertation, he was also a living model of a Christian humanist, a man for all seasons, a man I am proud to call my friend. May his tribe increase!

Notes

1. For an excellent summary of these issues, both those agreed upon and those still disputed, see Sidney H. Wanzer, M.D. et al., "The Physician's Responsibility Toward Hopelessly Ill Patients," *The New England Journal of Medicine* 320 (1989) 844–49.

2. This is the title of one of McCormick's earliest articles (*Journal of the American Medical Association* 229 [1974] 172–76) dealing with these issues. I believe it an apt title for this section.

3. Richard A. McCormick, S.J., "Caring or Starving? The Case of Claire Conroy," *America* 152 no. 13 (April 6, 1985) 269–73 at 273.

4. Ibid. 272.

5. Congregation for the Doctrine of the Faith, "*Jura et Bona*" ("Euthanasia"), *The Pope Speaks* 26 (1980) 289–96 at 292.

6. Richard A. McCormick, S.J., "*Gaudium et Spes* and the Bioethical Signs of the Times," in Judith A. Dwyer, S.S.J., ed., "*Questions of Special Urgency*": *The Church in the Modern World Two Decades after Vatican II* (Washington: Georgetown Univ. Press, 1986) 79–95.

7. Ibid. 92.

8. Ibid. 87–89.

9. This phrase, the title of an aforementioned book, comes from the Pastoral Constitution *Gaudium et Spes* of the Second Vatican Council.

10. McCormick, "*Gaudium et Spes* and the Biological Signs of the Times," 88.

11. Richard A. McCormick, S.J., "Some Neglected Aspects of Moral Responsibility for Health," *Perspectives in Biology and Medicine* 22 no. 1 (Autumn 1978) 31–43 at 38–39.

12. Richard A. McCormick, S.J., *How Brave a New World? Dilemmas in Bioethics* (Washington: Georgetown U. Press, 1981) 368.

13. Ibid.

14. Ibid. 369.

15. H. Tristram Engelhardt, *The Foundations of Bioethics* (New York: Oxford, 1986).

16. McCormick, "Some Neglected Aspects" 36.

17. Ibid. 39–40.

18. Ibid. 39.

19. *In Re Quinlan,* 70 N.J. 14 at 26 (1976).

20. John J. Paris and Richard A. McCormick, "Living-Will Legislation, Reconsidered," *America* 146, no. 4 (1981) 86–89 at 87.

21. *Corbett v. D'Alessandro,* 487 So 2d. 368 at 370–71 (1984).

22. McCormick, "Some Neglected Aspects" 36.

23. Pope Pius XII, "The Prolongation of Life," *The Pope Speaks* 4 (1958) 393–98 at 397.

24. McCormick, "To Save or Let Die" 175.

25. Ibid.

26. Pope Pius XII, "The Prolongation of Life" 397.

27. McCormick, "Caring or Starving" 273.

28. Pope Pius XII, "The Prolongation of Life" 396.

29. John J. Paris and Richard A. McCormick, "The Catholic Tradition on the Use of Nutrition and Fluids," *America* 156 no. 17 (1987) 356–61 at 361.

30. McCormick, "To Save or Let Die" 175.

31. Ibid.

32. Ibid.

33. Ibid. 176.

34. Ibid.

35. John J. Paris and Richard A. McCormick, "Saving Defective Infants: Options for Life or Death," *America* 148 no. 16 (1983) 313–17.

36. Ibid. 316.

37. Ibid.

38. Ibid.

39. McCormick, "To Save or Let Die" 176.

40. This is the title of one of McCormick's books, previously cited, which is a compendium of many of his previously published articles, some of which are cited in this chapter.

41. See, for example, McCormick "Gaudium et Spes" 91–93, where he discusses euthanasia in the context of the distinction between killing and letting die.

14

Reproductive Interventions: Theology, Ethics, and Public Policy

James F. Childress

Among the many areas of biomedical ethics to which Richard McCormick has made substantial contributions is the interpretation and evaluation of "reproductive interventions" from the standpoints of theology, ethics, and public policy. I will first sketch selected elements of McCormick's framework of moral reasoning, particularly his views about theology, ethics, and public policy that are relevant to his interpretation and evaluation of reproductive interventions. Then I will analyze and assess his views on homologous fertilization, heterologous fertilization, and embryonic life in the context of reproductive interventions. Here as in other areas McCormick's moral reflections are sensitive, clear, rigorous, and insightful.

McCORMICK'S FRAMEWORK: VALUES, CONCRETE MORAL NORMS, AND CONSEQUENCES

A major problem for many married couples is infertility, defined as "the inability of a couple to conceive after 12 months of intercourse without contraception."[1] It is estimated that approximately 2.4 million married couples in the U.S. suffer from infertility; this number would be considerably larger if unmarried couples and singles who want to be parents were included. Hence infertility is clearly "an important personal and societal problem" because of widespread frustration of the desire to have children, especially of one's own, and because the remedies are expensive, time-consuming, intrusive, and frequently unsuccessful.[2]

Several reproductive interventions have been developed to enable infertile couples through technological means to have children of their own (or at least of one spouse's own). McCormick defines "reproductive interventions" as "all procedures that *replace,* in part or totally, the natural (by sexual intercourse) process of conception and of in utero gestation."[3] And he notes that such reproductive interventions touch "on some basic human values: marriage and the family, parenting, genealogy and self-identity, human sexual intimacy and even the sanctity of life itself."[4]

Whatever its ambiguities and deficiencies, McCormick's definition is a good starting point. No term—whether reproductive technology, assisted reproduction, artificial reproduction, artificial procreation, artificial fertilization, noncoital reproduction, etc.—is fully satisfactory, for each term presupposes a certain perspective that is often itself subject to dispute. Such disputes will also be evident in other choices of metaphors in this area (e.g. viewing children as a "gift" or as a "product").

Other questions can be raised about McCormick's use and definition of the phrase "reproductive interventions." First, the phrase "reproductive intervention" may be too broad because it could encompass such interventions into reproduction as contraception and abortion, even though the subject is technologies for procreation.[5]

Second, there may be questions about whether the defining term "replace" is adequate to encompass the distinction, stressed by the Vatican, between dominating nature and assisting nature.[6]

Third, McCormick sometimes arranges "reproductive interventions" according to the degree or extent of replacement of "so-called natural processes"—e.g. artificial insemination (AI), in vitro fertilization (IVF) with embryo transfer (ET) and cloning.[7] It is important to note that the degree or extent of replacement does not necessarily correlate with the major ethical issues, unless nature itself is taken as a moral norm. For example, in many ways artificial insemination by donor (AID) raises more complex ethical and societal problems than IVF.[8] Others would argue that IVF raises ethical problems that are common to many other procedures—e.g. risk-benefit ratio, informed consent, truthfulness, privacy, and confidentiality—but that it does not raise many new fundamental ethical problems except for the disposition of extracorporeal embryos. According to Mary Warnock, "If we look at IVF itself, then, as a remedy for certain kinds of infertility, and apart from any spin-off [such as surrogacy], there seem to be no objections to it, and no ethical questions to be raised."[9] Many of the spin-offs, such as surrogacy, can be used with AI as well as with IVF.

If the fundamental ethical problems of "reproductive interventions" do not correlate with the degree of artificiality, i.e. the extent of replacement of natural processes, unless nature is taken as an ethical norm, it is necessary to explore the norm of nature, including human nature.[10]

McCormick insists that artificiality is not necessarily unnatural, and that it is not necessarily immoral.[11] However, he has characterized such interventions by the degree or extent of their replacement of nature.

McCormick defends a morality based on natural law, if we take natural law to mean moral requirements built into human nature and knowable by nature, i.e. apart from revelation, however much revelation may illumine them. According to McCormick, it is inappropriate to talk about "dwindling defendants of natural law" when in fact there are only "dwindling defendants of a certain type of natural law theology."[12] Joining several other moral theologians, McCormick modifies the traditional "classicist" interpretation of natural law in the direction of a broader, more historical, and more personalistic understanding of human nature.[13] This modified interpretation appears in and supports his dissent from the church's prohibition of artificial contraception, voluntary sterilization, and certain reproductive interventions.

McCormick holds that there is no specific or distinctive Christian ethics because there are no concrete moral demands that are in principle unavailable to human insight and reasoning and that can be known only by revelation.[14] The Christian faith does not provide concrete answers on the level of *essential ethics,* i.e. "those norms that are regarded as applicable to all persons, where one's behavior is but an instance of a general, essential moral norm."[15] Nevertheless, the Christian tradition offers an outlook on and illuminates human values; it provides what Franz Boeckle calls "morally relevant insights."[16] And Christians may discharge in a distinctive manner the moral tasks that apply to all people.

There are objective, nonmoral values to which human beings are inclined because these values define human flourishing. By examining these pre-rational inclinations or tendencies—such as to preserve life and to mate and raise children—it is possible to determine certain values and to use practical reason to develop "middle axioms" or "mediating principles" between these values and concrete choices.[17] For McCormick, the fundamental moral criterion, as formulated by Vatican II, is that of the human "person integrally and adequately considered." This criterion, rather than "the intention of nature inscribed in the organs and their functions," is the point of reference for evaluations of reproductive technologies.[18] The human person is embodied as well as spiritual, social as well as individual, etc. McCormick's interpretation of the human person is richer and deeper than the usual liberal interpretations of the person, and respecting the dignity of persons also differs in the two traditions. However, as I will argue later, McCormick does not pay sufficient attention to the moral significance of respect for personal autonomy, in part because of his suspicion of liberal individualism.[19]

McCormick considers two versions of arguments against technologizing marriage through reproductive interventions on the grounds that it is detrimental to the dignity of human persons. The *hard* version views the technology itself as *inhuman*. The *soft* version views the technology as *potentially dehumanizing*.[20] McCormick accepts the second version as a "prudential caution" that "too much technology introduced into a highly personal context (parenting, family) can mechanize and depersonalize the context." However, regarding the hard version, he notes that such dehumanization is not evident to many.

For both AIH and IVF with ET (embryo transfer) McCormick draws a distinction between different ways human love can express itself in marriage in seeking children; one is through normal sexual intercourse, the other is through the use of reproductive interventions to increase the likelihood of procreation. Reproductive interventions cannot, he contends, be viewed as necessarily unloving; they can be an expression of love and the child can be the expression and embodiment of love.[21] One might even note that many pregnancies result from unloving acts of sexual intercourse within marriage. Hence it is important not to compare the best examples of marital intercourse with the worst cases of reproductive intervention.

Still technological replacement is a problem for McCormick. On the spectrum of possibilities, his position falls between the pro-technologists, such as Joseph Fletcher, who view artificial reproduction as more human than natural reproduction, and the hard critics of reproductive technology who view it as intrinsically inhuman. Nevertheless, he does not view reproductive interventions as "neutral" technologies to be evaluated merely according to their ends and consequences. According to McCormick, "the artificial road to pregnancy is a disvalue and one that needs justification."[22] McCormick's statement is, I believe, problematic. There is a sense in which all medical procedures are a disvalue—for example, having to use a kidney machine or having to take medication. That is, they are the sorts of things one would not choose if one did not have some problem for which such procedures were needed. However, it is infertility, not the reproductive intervention, that frustrates the fulfillment of the natural ends of marriage or (in McCormick's language) the realization of some of the values of human flourishing.[23] And it would seem that corrective or compensatory measures would be legitimate. However, it does not follow that the corrective or compensatory measures are themselves disvalues. It would not make sense to view kidney dialysis as a disvalue simply because it does not cure kidney disease and is desirable only as a means to the end of preserving life.

Questions can be raised about whether infertility should be viewed as a "disease," even though it is a departure from natural functioning, and whether reproductive interventions should be viewed as "therapies," even though they compensate for natural dysfunctions.[24] However, it is important to appreciate the genuine suffering of people who want to have children, many of them having being taught by religious traditions about the value of procreation. It is unfortunate, as Edward Vacek notes, that the Congregation does not factor "suffering" into the moral analysis but only reserves it for a concluding spiritual section on sharing in the Lord's cross: "In other methodologies suffering itself is a disvalue and a reason for seeking alternatives."[25] Because suffering is largely subjective, it is important that the experience of infertile couples be considered. Even when sound criticisms of the desire to have a "child of one's own" are noted, it remains true that many infertile couples who would be glad to adopt children are unable to do so. Furthermore, in the context of claims that procreation is one of the natural ends or meanings of marriage, it is difficult to hold that the inability of one spouse to participate effectively in procreative activities is not a condition for which medical intervention is appropriate. The hard question is which interventions and under what circumstances.

McCormick worries about *absolutizing* the disvalue of infertility and thereby justifying various reproductive interventions.[26] However, it is difficult to imagine a position that actually absolutizes the disvalue of infertility and thereby justifies every possible means whatsoever to overcome it. In the film *Raising Arizona,* a couple unable to have children of their own kidnap one of a set of quintuplets in order to have a family of their own. However, no one seriously absolutizes the disvalue of infertility in the sense that having a child justifies such means as kidnaping someone else's children or that having a child of one's own justifies stealing sperm, invading another woman's body to obtain ova without her consent, and so forth.

It is useful to conclude this sketch of major elements of McCormick's framework for analyzing and evaluating reproductive interventions by noting the role of consequences in his moral reasoning.[27] Although our concrete moral norms are derived from values, we do not appeal to those values in conflict situations (e.g. the life of the mother versus the life of the fetus) to *override* concrete moral norms. Rather, teleological and consequentialist considerations are used to determine proportionate reason, which specifies the *meaning* of concrete moral norms. Through balancing nonmoral values, we use proportionate reason to determine which concrete actions are to count as murder, injustice, adultery, lying, abortion, and so forth.[28] An action is always morally wrong when it is disproportionate, i.e. when taken as a whole, its nonmoral evil outweighs its nonmoral good.[29] For example, if an act is properly described as a lie, i.e. as a *moral* evil, no intended good can justify it. But not every falsehood is a lie, and which falsehoods count as lies depends on ends and consequences, i.e. on balancing nonmoral values and disvalues. Another example is McCormick's caution about using the term "abortion" in relation to discarded zygotes after efforts at IVF; I will return to this example below.[30]

Consequences also play an important role in McCormick's perspective on the relation of morality and public policy. His perspective is both interesting and important, in part because of the Congregation's call for reform of civil law regarding reproductive interventions and because of his own role in the formation of public policy (e.g. as a member of the Ethics Advisory Board of the Department of Health, Education, and Welfare, and as a consultant to the National Commission for the Protection of Human Subjects of Biomedical and Behavioral Research, as well as to other governmental bodies and private organizations influencing public policy).

Public policy, which may be defined as whatever governments do or do not do,[31] encompasses permission, regulation, prohibition, and the allocation of resources. McCormick contends that morality and public policy are distinct but related. Although morality is indispensable for public policy, it is not sufficient, for policy-makers must also consider a policy's *feasibility*. Thus, in legislation, as in pastoral care, it is necessary to take into account "the good that is possible and feasible in a particular society at a particular time."[32] Often McCormick relates "feasible" to "realistic" and "sound." Although it would be helpful to have a fuller analysis of feasibility from McCormick, one of his major statements is drawn from Paul Micallef, who defines "feasibility" as "that quality whereby a proposed course of action is not merely possible but practicable, adaptable, depending on the circumstances, cultural ways, attitudes, traditions of a people. . . ."[33]

One example of McCormick's appeals to "feasibility" is his argument that "any law or amendment which proscribes intervention from the moment of fertilization is totally unworkable" in part because pregnancy is not diagnosable until several weeks after fertilization.[34] Another example, to be discussed again later, is McCormick's argument that it would not be possible to ban IVF with donor gametes—even though he contends that it is not ethically justifiable—because of a lack of broad consensus and difficulties of compliance and enforcement.[35] These examples suggest some important standards of feasibility: consensus, compliance, and enforcement. "Sometimes morality can be translated into public policy, sometimes not."[36]

Feasibility is not only invoked when it appears that public policy may have to fall below morality. Sometimes, in view of particular circumstances, public policy may have to go beyond or transcend morality.[37] The society may have to prohibit, regulate, or withhold funds from acts or practices that are not immoral in order to prevent evil. To take an example that will be discussed below, it is not immoral, McCormick holds, for a married couple to use IVF with their own gametes, with low risk to the offspring, and with an intention not to abort if the fetus is abnormal. However, he argues against governmental funding of such research for several reasons, including the dangers of fostering practices beyond marriage.[38]

Homologous Fertilization

Now I now want to examine in more detail the implications of McCormick's framework for reproductive interventions. Rather than considering various reproductive interventions in terms of their degree or extent of replacement of natural functions, I will focus on the different human parties affected by these reproductive interventions in light of McCormick's criterion of promotion of the human person. These parties include married couples using their own gametes in reproductive interventions; users, whether married or not, and providers of gametes; and embryos. Having already raised some of the relevant themes, such as natural and artificial, I will briefly consider homologous and heterologous fertilization before concentrating on embryos.

It is appropriate to begin with what McCormick views as the simplest case for either AI or IVF with ET: a married couple unable to have children by natural means. Official Roman Catholic statements construe the procreative (life-giving) and unitive (love-making) dimensions of the conjugal act as joined by nature and God and then draw implications that oppose both artificial contraception and artificial reproduction. Indeed, McCormick suggests that some of the official intransigence regarding artificial reproduction is actually based on opposition to liberalization of contraception.[39] Acceptance of the artificial separation of the procreative and unitive dimensions in pursuit of the procreative value could lead to acceptance of the artificial separation in pursuit of the unitive value.

McCormick's arguments against the official Catholic position are important and, in my judgment, cogent, even when they do not appear to me to go far enough. First, he rejects the official opposition to AIH or to IVF with spousal gametes, which is based on the prohibition of the separation of unitive and procreative functions and the prohibition of masturbation even when it is directed toward procreative values by providing sperm for AIH or IVF.

In developing his position, which he contends is "a solidly probable opinion" because of the theological authority supporting it, McCormick focuses on the *meaning* of inseparability of the unitive and the procreative. He does not challenge the rule that the unitive and the procreative should not be separated, but he challenges the traditional interpretation of that rule. For McCormick, as noted earlier, the interpretation of this rule may well reflect broader teleological and consequentialist considerations, particularly having to do with the human "person integrally and adequately considered," rather than with nature's alleged intention inscribed in sexual organs and their functions. According to his interpretation, the rule does not require that the unitive and the procreative must be held together in *every act,* whether the act is contraception or IVF. Rather, properly interpreted, the rule requires that the *spheres* be held together, "so that there is no procreation apart from marriage, and no full sexual intimacy apart from a context of responsibility for procreation." One of the implications of this movement away from act-analysis to spheres-analysis is that the inseparability rule "must promote the person 'integrally and adequately considered.' When it becomes an obstacle to that promotion, it loses its (generally operative) normative force, for it is subject to, and judged by, the broader criterion."[40]

As I noted earlier in sketching McCormick's framework, he also argues that spousal co-participation in reproductive interventions can also express and embody marital love so that the one conceived is not, as the Congregation suggested, a mere "product of an intervention of medical or biological techniques" or "an object of scientific technology."[41] Furthermore, McCormick rejects the Congregation's view that procreation by IVF and ET should be opposed because it is "procreation deprived of its proper perfection." He notes that the Catholic tradition has accepted many actions that are less than perfect in that they contain positive disvalues that are themselves morally permissible. Indeed, he notes, the Congregation's allowance of medical interventions that are designed "to assist the conjugal act" fall in this category.[42] However, in his movement away from a physicalist toward a more personalist interpretation of natural law McCormick does not stress the distinction between assisting and dominating nature, so central in the Congregation's *Instruction.*

Regarding the possibility of a casuistical interpretation of the Congregation's *Instruction* to permit some reproductive interventions within marriage, McCormick notes with particular disdain the proposal of *modified* GIFT (gamete intrafallopian transfer). GIFT involves the surgical removal of an egg and its strategic placement beyond the fallopian block to allow in vivo fertilization; modified GIFT involves intercourse with a perforated condom so that some sperm could be collected and then aspirated toward the egg.[43] The use of the perforated condom would seemingly not violate the prohibition on artificial means of contraception. McCormick responds: "Frankly, I find such casuistry debasing and repugnant. If the Congregation wants to insist on a procreation worthy of human beings, it should give no support to such moralistic nit-picking. If it does, it is contributing to a casuistry unworthy of human beings and reducing a healthy morality to an embarrassing moralism. That is the risk inherent in 'precise indications.' "[44]

In short, McCormick concludes that at the level of the individual couple's decision, "there seems to be no argument that shows *with clarity and certainty* that in vitro procedures using their own sperm and ovum are *necessarily and inherently wrong,* if abortion of a possibly deformed child is excluded and the risks are acceptably low." He identifies four necessary conditions for IVF: "(1) the gametes are those of husband and wife; (2) embryo wastage is not significantly higher in the artificial process than it is in vivo; (3) the likelihood of fetal abnormality is no greater than it is in normal procreation; (4) there is no intention to abort if abnormality does occur."[45] The first condition excludes donor gametes; the last three deal with the effect on the offspring. I will now turn to these limits.

HETEROLOGOUS FERTILIZATION

To this point I have considered the justification of AI and IVF within marriage, involving the gametes of the spouses. But major ethical and policy questions surround the use of reproductive interventions by unmarried couples or individuals and by married couples with gametes from third parties. I will concentrate on the latter, making only a few points about the former.

The key distinction for McCormick is between "sexual exclusivity" and "conjugal exclusivity." He does not appear to accept the position that third-party involvement constitutes a form of adultery (though it might lead to adultery through a process of logical justification); it does not involve adultery because it does not involve sexual activity and thus does not violate sexual exclusivity. However, McCormick clearly believes that it infringes on "conjugal exclusivity," and that "having a jointly raised child" does not justify such an infringement. His argument is that "the notion of conjugal exclusivity should include the genetic, gestational and rearing dimensions of parenthood. Separating these dimensions (except through rescue, as in adoption) too easily contains a subtle diminishment of a certain aspect of the human person."[46] However, it is not easy to see how a certain aspect of the human person is thereby diminished.

Even though McCormick accepts and defends a moral rule against the use of third-party gametes, he recognizes that a prohibitive policy would probably not be feasible (though it might be feasible to prohibit commercialized surrogacy). Of critical importance is the form of argument employed, both for the moral position adopted and for the feasibility of public policy. One form of the argument is that "third-party involvement itself violates the marriage covenant, independent of any potential damaging effects or benefits."[47] The marriage covenant involves the exchange of "exclusive, nontransferable, inalienable rights to each other's person and generative acts."[48] McCormick accepts such a view, as articulated by Pius XII and Paul Ramsey, but he holds that it cannot be urged as "a basis for public policy" because it is based on sources of faith.[49]

Another mode of argument for insisting that "marital exclusivity ought to include the genetic, gestational and rearing components" is more secular and can serve as a basis for public policy. This argument holds that relaxation of conjugal exclusivity will produce *harm* to the marriage, to marriage in general, and to the prospective child. An example is that the genetic asymmetry after AIH may have "possibly damaging psychological effects," presumably on the spouses and the offspring.[50]

Another version of this second mode of argument is that "third-party involvement separates procreation from marriage *in principle*."[51] In effect, this version of the argument invokes the metaphors of the thin edge of the wedge and the slippery slope. These metaphors may suggest that the logic of moral justification or social-psychological factors will inevitably lead to bad actions once the first, perhaps legitimate, actions are undertaken.[52]

In a strong dissent to one section of a report of the American Fertility Society Ethics Committee (on which he served as a member), McCormick offered a litany of *possible negative outcomes* of third-party involvement. In addition to severing procreation from the marital union in a fundamental way, third-party involvement brings into the world in a premediated fashion a child "with no bond of origin to one or both marital partners and therefore blurs the child's genealogy and potentially compromises the child's self-identity." Adulteries "might be multiplied": Following the recognition of the moral right to be inseminated by another man's sperm "wives might easily conclude (and it would be difficult to reject their logic) that it is preferable (certainly more convenient and far less expensive) to be inseminated in the natural way." The involvement of third parties would support a "stud-farm mentality . . . with its subtle but unmistakable shift toward eugenics." Finally, "the use of third parties tends to absolutize sterility as a disvalue and childbearing and rearing as a value, thus distorting—and potentially threatening— some basic human values: life, marriage, and the family." McCormick concludes: "Taken cumulatively, such considerations suggest that the use of third parties to overcome sterility is not for the good of persons integrally and adequately considered. It involves risks to basic dimensions of our flourishing. Such risks to basic values outweigh, in a prudential calculus, individual procreative desires or needs. In summary: when calculus involves *individual* benefit, versus *institutional* risk of harm, the latter should take precedence."[53]

This position is largely rule-teleological or rule-consequentialist justification, with a sprinkling of deontological elements, and it is, I believe, fundamentally problematic both as a statement of a moral rule and also as a statement of public policy. McCormick seems to concede that a prohibitive public policy would not be feasible—except perhaps for commercial surrogacy—but his approach focuses on possible (rather than probable) harms and misses the force of the principle of respect for personal autonomy.

It is not sufficient to assert that an individual benefit is in conflict with an institutional risk of harm, and then to conclude from a "prudential calculus" that the latter should take priority. Of critical importance are the magnitude and the probability of both benefit and harm. The *magnitude* of benefit and harm is not settled by noting that the benefit is individual and the harm is institutional, and it is also necessary to consider the *probability* of both the benefit and the harm.

These teleological and consequentialist arguments are very weak because they are pervaded by mere possibilities rather than probabilities. And, as McCormick concedes, the evidence is slim.[54] Consider, for example, the widespread use of AIH; I am not aware of any evidence to support the claim that AIH has led to an increase in adultery because adultery is easier, more convenient, and less costly than the use of medical procedures. It appears that adultery is rarely intended for procreative purposes; it is usually intended for extramarital unitive purposes or sheer pleasure. Furthermore, more evidence is needed about the putative harms to the offspring's self-identity, and the alleged shift to "eugenics" is merely speculative.

McCormick views the use of third parties as absolutizing infertility as a disvalue. But, as I argued above, no one seriously absolutizes infertility as a disvalue that would override all other values in the sense that overcoming sterility would justify any means whatsoever, e.g. kidnaping a woman to be a surrogate. A more important question is whether infertility is enough of a disvalue to the couple that its remedy through reproductive interventions involving third parties should be permitted.

But even this formulation of the question is not morally adequate, because it is necessary to determine seriously whether the probable negative consequences of reproductive interventions to individuals and to institutions are sufficient to outweigh the prima facie principle of respect for personal autonomy (not merely individual benefit) and thus to meet the burden of proof against intervention into autonomous choices. However, by and large, McCormick neglects respect for personal autonomous choices, as a prima facie principle, in determining the stringency and meaning of relevant moral rules and in formulating public policy. Even though McCormick's criterion is the promotion of the person "integrally and adequately considered," personal autonomy is neglected. For example, in reproductive interventions McCormick implies that it would be morally legitimate to override respect for personal autonomy, if it were *feasible* to do so. The lack of feasibility is of course politically relevant, but no moral weight is assigned to the freedom of embodied, social individuals wanting to create a family. The ideal of the family that is allegedly embedded in nature triumphs. The absence of the counterweight of respect for personal autonomy is troubling because the main constraint on governmental intervention appears to be a probable lack of feasibility and constitutionality. Thus, McCormick notes, even though it might be possible to ban commercialized surrogacy, it would not be possible to ban IVF with donor gametes because of problems of compliance and enforcement as well as a lack of broad consensus.[55]

My claim here is not that a case cannot be made for a moral rule and a public policy against the use of donor gametes, but only that such a case needs to include attention to the moral significance of personal autonomous choices, recognizing that they may be compromised by various personal and social conditions and that they may be justifiably overridden to protect other individuals and the society. McCormick has not adequately made that case, perhaps in part because his framework tends to be excessively anti-individualistic.[56] Thus, he fails to acknowledge sufficiently the moral burden of proof that legislators must meet in prohibitive public policies.

Interestingly, the very lack of feasibility of a prohibitive law or policy toward the use of donor (or vendor) gametes in part led McCormick to oppose federal funding for research on IVF with ET (and he would extend this opposition to clinical practice). His argument was not based on the minimal respect owed nascent human life, but rather followed from the "cumulative impact of many arguments." Funding, he suggests, implies "fostering." And he concludes that "if we cannot fund in vitro fertilization between husband and wife without *in our circumstances* funding (and fostering) practices beyond that, we should not do so. I believe this to be the case. *In other circumstances* we could draw a different conclusion."[57]

THE MORAL STATUS OF AND DISPOSITIONAL AUTHORITY OVER THE EMBRYO

Obviously one major party affected by reproductive interventions is the embryo and the child-to-be. I will focus first on the child-to-be before turning to the embryo. Early arguments against IVF focused on the unknown risks of harm to the child-to-be who could not consent to those risks. While some theologians, such as Paul Ramsey, tended to reject the procedure because of the presence of any risks, others required only that the risks be no greater than in normal procreation.[58] Whatever one says ethically about the early experiments, they were conducted and the results indicate that the physical risks are not greater than in natural procreation.[59] Nor is there evidence of serious psychological harms. Hence, there appears to be no reason now to oppose IVF on grounds of risks to the child-to-be. The risks are even less in AI.

Another claim of negative psychosocial effects of reproductive interventions on the child-to-be involves attitudes toward the process of procreation. The Congregation holds that because IVF and ET involve conception "outside the bodies of the couple through actions of third parties whose competence and technical activity determine the success of the procedure," there is a loss of "the dignity and equality that must be common to parents and children"; these are replaced by a relationship of "domination."[60] These concerns are often expressed in the debate about the metaphors that fit with natural and artificial procreation. Our metaphors, often subconsciously, shape the way we think, experience, and act. In each use of metaphor we see something as something else.[61] Critics of reproductive interventions charge that various participants—and the society at large—will come to view offspring as "products" of human technology rather than as "gifts," whether of nature or God. The metaphor of gift will be replaced by the metaphor of product. The Congregation notes that "the child is not an object to which one has a right, nor can he be considered as an object of ownership: rather, a child is a gift, 'the supreme gift' and the most gratuitous gift of marriage, and is a living testimony of the mutual giving of his parents."[62] It argues that generation through IVF and ET is "objectively deprived of its proper perfection: namely, that of being the result and fruit of a conjugal act in which the spouses can become 'cooperators with God for giving life to a new person.' "[63]

As already noted, McCormick argues that marital love can be expressed in the cooperative acts that are involved in reproductive interventions, as well as in natural procreation. This attitude toward reproductive interventions can accommodate the metaphor of gift without succumbing to the metaphor of product. The language of gift and co-responsibility with the creator can be used in expansive or restrictive ways and thus does not provide concrete guidance for decisions about particular acts, however important it is at the foundational level.[64]

Critics of reproductive interventions worry about claims of equality with God in the creation of new life and about claims of inequality with fellow creatures who exist because of reproductive technologies. This inequality may be associated with attitudes of domination and willingness to destroy offspring.[65] However, just as the use of medical technologies does not necessarily reduce the sense of God as the sustainer of life, so the use of reproductive interventions does not necessarily reduce the sense of God as the giver of life. And just as the use of medical technologies to sustain life does not necessarily result in inequality between family members and physicians, on the one hand, and the patient, on the other, so the use of reproductive technologies does not necessarily entail attitudes of inequality and domination toward offspring. The Congregation concludes that every child who comes into the world, by whatever process, "must in any case be accepted as a living gift of the divine goodness and must be brought up with love."[66] However, this imperative could not be met if the artificial procedures necessarily entailed a change in attitudes toward offspring. Replacement of some natural processes by technologies does not necessarily entail replacement of some fundamental metaphors, attitudes, and beliefs.

Suspicion is warranted when critics only identify possible harms to offspring in artificial procedures, without noticing possible harms to offspring of natural sexual relations. One interesting question is what would be the appropriate *moral* response if IVF and ET developed to the point where they actually increased the chances of successful conception for all married couples and greatly reduced the risks of spontaneous abortions and loss of life.[67] It is useful to consider whether under those circumstances a case could be made for a moral obligation to use such means.

In contrast to official Roman Catholic teaching that the embryo is a human being from the moment of conception, McCormick has raised some questions that open the door at least partly to different actions and policies in reproductive interventions. There are three major views regarding the embryo: (1) the embryo has full humanity from the moment of conception and thus merits full protection, (2) the embryo is potential human life and deserves some protection, and (3) the embryo is mere (human) tissue, comparable to an appendix. Stressing that this debate cannot be resolved by science because it is fundamentally evaluative, McCormick believes "that there are significant phenomena in the preimplantation period that suggest a different evaluation of human life at this stage. Therefore, I do not believe that nascent life at this stage makes the same demands for protection that it does later."[68] These significant phenomena include the possibility of (identical) twinning and the possibility of recombination. As Mary Warnock notes, prior to about fourteen days, "the embryo hasn't yet decided how many people it is going to be."[69] Others also stress that the primitive streak that becomes the spinal cord is not yet formed and that there is a heavy natural loss of embryonic life. In view of such significant phenomena, McCormick holds that the absolute protection of the human embryo can only be viewed as "a kind of safeside rule against abuse." He does not reject such rules and concedes that they "are just as valid and persuasive as the dangers that they envisage are unavoidable." However, "if clear lines can be drawn that block this slide toward abuse, the safe-side rule is less persuasive."[70]

The rule of the absolute protection of the human embryo is not justifiable on grounds of the personhood of the embryo. Not only is the evaluation of the early embryo as a person controversial, but also, as McCormick notes, it is unnecessary, for many who deny that the zygote is a person still hold that the zygote "deserves our respect and awe."[71] The language of "preembryo" used by some commentators for the first fourteen days after fertilization is defensible as long as it does not serve to deny any moral significance to the "preembryo."[72]

One important question concerns the appropriate language, actions, and policies toward spare embryos that will be discarded rather than implanted. McCormick recommends caution about the use of the term "abortion" in regard to discarded zygotes. His reasons relate in part to his general views about concrete moral norms such as the prohibition of abortion. Many naturally fertilized ova never implant and are thus lost. Hence, couples engaging in normal sexual relations tactily accept such a loss as a risk and even the price of seeking to have a child (and, one might add, of engaging in sexual intercourse without preventing conception). "If it is by no means clear that couples engaging in normal sexual relations are 'causing abortions' because foreseeably many fertilized ova do not implant, it is not clear that the discards from artificial procedures must be called 'abortions,' especially if the ratio of occurrence is roughly similar."[73] One response to McCormick's position might be that it is inappropriate to reproduce by artifice what happens in nature, i.e. to replicate nature's life-taking, but his rejoinder notes that the proper analogy focuses on achieving artificially what occurs naturally, i.e. of duplicating nature's achievements even with unavoidable disvalues such as the loss of zygotes.[74] Although McCormick concedes the tentativeness of his "probes into a difficult area," his point might be extended because it is questionable whether the term "abortion" can be easily applied to the treatment of zygotes in vitro. The term may be better restricted to the termination of a pregnancy and the biological relationship between the pregnant woman and the fetus she is carrying.

Disputes about the selective termination of the lives of some fetuses in order to save others in multi-fetal pregnancies also raise questions about appropriate language as well as about ethically defensible actions. Such pregnancies may result from infertility treatments as well as from the placement of several fertilized eggs in order to increase the chances of successful pregnancies and to reduce the chances of having to repeat the procedure, and there are ethical responsibilities to try to prevent such multi-fetal pregnancies in which it is highly probable that all will be lost unless some are selectively terminated. Selectively terminating the lives of some fetuses to save others is not a termination of pregnancy because the pregnancy continues (unless the procedure accidentally causes the loss of all fetuses), and the term "abortion" may not be appropriate because it is often construed to mean the deliberate termination of pregnancy. However, the phrase "selective reduction of pregnancy" masks the loss of morally significant embryonic life. Whatever language is used, a pregnant woman in such cases has to consider the probability that all of her fetuses will die unless she chooses to terminate the lives of some; that the procedure has a risk of terminating all; and that there are uncertainties about how many can safely remain.[75]

In contrast to traditional Catholic moral theology, McCormick holds that the selective termination of the lives of some fetuses can be ethically justified in some extreme cases of multi-fetal pregnancies.[76] According to the Congregation, "on occasion, some of the implanted embryos are sacrificed for various eugenic, economic or psychological reasons."[77] And of course such sacrifices are rejected as immoral. However, as McCormick recognizes, it is not possible to reduce genuine conflicts of fetal life with fetal life to these three rubrics.

In addition to questions about how many embryos should be implanted, several other ethical and policy issues arise regarding dispositional authority over extracorporeal embryos. One is experimentation on fertilized ova. McCormick accepts a presumption against experimentation on embryos, based on respect for nascent life; however, this presumption can be rebutted under some circumstances. For example, some research was necessary prior to embryo transfer technology, but this research is not "incompatible with respect" in view of "our strong doubts about zygote status."[78]

The Ethics Advisory Board on which McCormick served reported that IVF with embryo transfer—and certain research necessary to it—is "ethically acceptable" or acceptable from an ethical standpoint. McCormick concurred with this recommendation and introduced the phrase "ethically defensible but still legitimately controverted," which has since been sharply criticized.[79] Evaluative interpretations of nascent human life can be (and are) legitimately controverted, with substantial arguments being offered for and against positions. In a pluralistic society, where there are competing views about the early embryo, it may be necessary—even a matter of "public wisdom"—to resort to procedures in the absence of "shared convictions about substantive outcomes."[80] The procedure McCormick recommends is an authoritative national body. Such a procedure is necessary to rebut the policy presumption against experimentation on embryos.

Where research alone—not embryo transfer—is the object of IVF, public policy should not support such research through the provision of government funds, because "respect for germinating life calls for at least this." Whatever important knowledge about genetic disease and fertility might result from research on fertilized ova, such research cannot be done "without stripping nascent life of the minimal respect we owe it."[81] Thus distinguishing research aimed at embryo transfer from research on the fertilized ova for other purposes, McCormick held that the prohibition of the latter could conceivably pass the feasibility test.[82] Although McCormick did not recommend prohibition of the former, he argued, as noted above, against government funding for research on IVF with ET, based not on the minimal respect owed nascent human life, but rather on the "cumulative impact of many arguments."

Fundamental tensions emerge about the metaphors used to articulate who has what kind of dispositional authority over extracorporeal embryos. Even if the language should not personalize or depersonalize, most metaphors and concepts will tend to do one or the other.[83] On the one hand, for many, property notions are inappropriately applied to extracorporeal embryos. The Warnock Commission recommended legislation to ensure that "there is no right of ownership in a human embryo."[84] Arguments against commercialization focus on the intrinsic value of the embryo (the kind of respect and awe stressed by McCormick) or on the implications of such commerce for our attitudes toward children and others. This latter argument stresses the importance of symbolizing respect for human life. Nevertheless, it may be possible to hold that there are "quasi-property" rights, at least to the extent that individuals can donate embryos but not sell them and to the extent that harm to embryos can be compensable.

However, more personal language is more defensible even if the early embryo is not a person in the strict sense. For example, an Australian report proposes a guardianship model, holding that once a genetically new human life emerges, then guardianship becomes the appropriate moral model. Ordinarily, the report notes, guardianship is exercised by the intended social parents, or, if there are none, then by the gamete donors, or finally as a last resort by some third party. Guardianship should be directed by the welfare and best interests of the ward, and it would be inconsistent, for example, with destructive nontherapeutic experimentation.[85]

These models (and others) have different implications for dispositional authority. One major issue of dispositional authority is the mode of transfer: donation (express or presumed); abandonment; sale; or expropriation.[86] Some arguments already have been suggested for ruling out sales, and additional arguments would include the danger of commodification. Societal expropriation is difficult to justify, but the society may assume dispositional authority over embryos if the primary decision-makers violate their responsibilities. Abandonment is morally indefensible, but if it occurs the state may have to step in. Donation or—if the model is more personalistic—putting the embryo up for adoption may be justified, at least within limits. In view of McCormick's opposition to donation of gametes and wombs, it is likely that he would be opposed to the transfer of embryos in this way too. However, if the alternative is destruction, then transfer by donation may be defensible. Nevertheless, there may be defensible legal and ethical limits on rights to transfer an embryo, whether the embryo is viewed as property-like or person-like. For example, the society may attempt to restrict placement, perhaps by requiring screening of recipients.

Among other possible limits on dispositional authority, the limit on the right to destroy the embryo has already been noted. It is important to note that abortion rights, where recognized in law, do not necessarily cover the destruction of extracorporeal embryos. The right to have an abortion encompasses the right to terminate a pregnancy but may not include the right to have an extracorporeal embryo dead. For example, in Louisiana the extracorporeal embryo is protected as a "judicial person" and thus may not be destroyed, but the irony is that if the same embryo is placed in a woman, she may then abort and destroy that embryo.[87]

Finally, there are important questions about limits on cyropreservation of fertilized ova. Over sixty children have been born in Australia and Europe following cryopreservation.[88] Evidence suggests that fifty percent of frozen embryos are capable of further development after thawing, and these rates can be expected to improve.[89] Cryopreservation may reduce the number of procedures that a woman must undergo. Ethically, how should we think about frozen embryos? John Robertson contends that cryopreservation "poses few unique ethical and social issues," but simply facilitates extensions of IVF.[90] By contrast, the Ethics Committee of the American College of Obstetricians and Gynecologists insists that "embryo freezing raises almost unprecedented metaphysical, ethical, and legal problems."[91] Problems include time limits on storage and use after the deaths of the gamete providers or intended social parents.

Two current cases in courts in the U.S. illustrate the kinds of issues that must be resolved. First, who has dispositional authority over frozen embryos when a couple gets a divorce. In Tennessee a couple seeking a divorce is contesting the disposition of seven frozen embryos, following IVF using her eggs and his sperm. The wife seeks custody of the embryos, arguing that they should be viewed as living and thus subject to family law determining custody as well as to constitutional law relating to the woman's right to choose whether to bring a pregnancy to term. She wants first to have two children from the embryos in storage before thinking about donating the remainder. By contrast, the husband insists that property law should apply and that the embryos should be treated as the joint property of the marriage. He argues that he should retain the absolute right to decide whether or not he will become a parent and he is not willing for his ex-wife to bear his child.[92]

The second case involves a suit by a couple against the Jones Institute for Reproductive Medicine in Norfolk, Va., for immediate release of their frozen embryo (and for $200,000 for emotional damages). In 1986, while living on the east coast, the couple began IVF with the Jones Institute; several fertilized eggs were implanted unsuccessfully, while one fertilized egg was frozen for future implantation. Now living in California, the couple contends that the Jones Institute is holding their frozen embryo "hostage" in refusing to release it for shipment to California for implantation. Their lawyer says that the Jones Institute's action is "like saying a day-care center can't release a child at the end of the day to the parents." At the time of the suit the embryo had been frozen almost two years, and the suit contended that twenty-eight months is the longest period an embryo has been frozen before a successful implant. The Jones Institute responds that the initial contract did not offer the option of transferring the frozen embryo, and that granting the request would set a precedent for the forced release of other fertilized eggs that could then be implanted by physicians who are not qualified to perform the procedure. The Jones Institute said that it regards the "fertilized egg as a small piece of humanity. It's human, not animal." However, the Jones Institute would "thaw" the embryo, causing its destruction, if the couple so indicated.[93]

In its opposition to cryopreservation the Congregation contends that freezing embryos is an "offense against the respect due to human beings by exposing them to grave risks of death or harm to their physical integrity and depriving them, at least temporarily, of maternal shelter and gestation, thus placing them in a situation in which further offenses and manipulation are possible."[94] It is not clear that McCormick's approach to IVF and ET requires such opposition to cryopreservation, but it is also not clear what actions and public policies regarding cryopreservation follow from those principles.[95] If IVF and ET are undertaken in the simple case he accepts, then cryopreservation could be justified as a mode of possible rescue, and donation of frozen embryos could be justified as analogous to putting a child up for adoption in extreme circumstances.

CONCLUSION

A final inconclusive note is in order. I have a deep appreciation of Richard McCormick's important and profound contributions to the debates in moral theology, ethics, and public policy about reproductive interventions—as well as to so many other areas. While underlining many points of agreement, I have identified what I believe are some conceptual and normative problems along the way. My main reservation is more general. McCormick's criterion of respect for or promotion of the human "person integrally and adequately considered" is clearly much richer than the liberal criterion of respect for the person, especially when the latter is reduced to respect for autonomous choices, with little attention to embodiment and sociality; nevertheless, McCormick's own criterion tends to be truncated, at least in the area of reproductive interventions, because respect for personal autonomous choices plays a minor role at most. To be sure, in the assessment of public policies, McCormick comes to some "liberal" conclusions about permission and regulation. However, his reasons usually have to do with *feasibility,* and they rarely, if ever, build on a presumption, even a rebuttable one, in favor of respecting personal autonomous choices regarding reproductive interventions.

Notes

1. U.S. Congress, Office of Technology Assessment, *Infertility: Medical and Social Choices,* OTA-BA-358 (Washington, DC: U.S. Government Printing Office, May 1988) 3.

2. Ibid.

3. McCormick, *How Brave a New World? Dilemmas in Bioethics* (Garden City, N.Y.: Doubleday & Co., 1981) 307. Hereafter *HBNW.* The Congregation for the Doctrine of the Faith defines "artificial fertilization" or "artificial reproduction" as "the different technical procedures directed toward obtaining a human conception in a manner other than the sexual union of man and woman." *Instruction on Respect for Human Life in its Origins and on the Dignity of Procreation: Replies to Certain Questions of the Day* (February 22, 1987), Part II. Hereafter *Instruction.* It is reprinted in Thomas A. Shannon and Lisa Sowle Cahill, *Religion and Artificial Reproduction: An Inquiry into the Vatican "Instruction on Respect for Human Life"* (New York: Crossroad, 1988) 140–77.

4. McCormick, "Therapy or Tampering? The Ethics of Reproductive Technology," *America* (December 7, 1985) 397.

5. McCormick recognizes this and stipulates a narrower interpretation. See *HBNW* 307.

6. *Instruction* Intro., 1.

7. *HBNW* 307.

8. Sherman Elias and George J. Annas, "Social Policy Considerations in Noncoital Reproduction," *Journal of the American Medical Association* 255 (January 3, 1986) 62–68.

9. Mary Warnock, "The Artificial Family," in *Moral Dilemmas in Modern Medicine,* ed. Michael Lockwood (Oxford: Oxford University Press, 1985) 141. A report from the Office of Technology Assessment concludes that most religious traditions in the U.S. "support IVF as long as only spousal gametes (ova and sperm) are used and as long as no embryos are wasted, though support lessens to some degree when there is early embryo wastage and to a much greater degree when donor gametes are used." *Infertility* 214.

10. Shannon and Cahill, *Religion and Artificial Reproduction* passim.

11. McCormick, "Therapy or Tampering?" 399.

12. McCormick, *Notes on Moral Theology, 1965 through 1980* (Washington, DC: University Press of America, 1981) 120–21, fn. 13.

13. *HBNW* x.

14. McCormick, *Notes on Moral Theology, 1965 through 1980* 804, 707, passim.

15. McCormick, "Theology and Bioethics," *Hastings Center Report* 19 (March/April 1989) 6.

16. Ibid. 10; McCormick, *Notes on Moral Theology, 1965 through 1980* 637–38; *HBNW* 9.

17. *HBNW* chap. 1.

18. McCormick, "Therapy or Tampering?" 400.

19. See James F. Childress, "Two By McCormick," *Hastings Center Report* 12 (June 1982) 40–42.

20. *HBNW* 327.

21. Ibid. 328.

22. Ibid.

23. See Edward C. Vacek, "Vatican Instruction on Reproductive Technology," *Theological Studies* 49 (March 1988) 116.

24. McCormick, *HBNW* 325, and "Therapy or Tampering?" 396.

25. Vacek, "Vatican Instruction on Reproductive Technology" 117.

26. McCormick, "Therapy or Tampering?" 402.

27. I will not consider McCormick's views on "double effect." But see Paul Ramsey and Richard McCormick, eds., *Doing Evil to Achieve Good* (Chicago: Loyola University Press, 1978) 70–71.

28. McCormick, *Notes on Moral Theology, 1965 through 1980* 810.

29. Ibid. 710. For an analysis and assessment of "proportionalism" see Bernard Hoose, *Proportionalism: The American Debate and Its European Roots* (Washington, DC: Georgetown University Press, 1985).

30. *HBNW* 330.

31. Thomas Dye, *Understanding Public Policy,* 2nd ed. (Englewood Cliffs, NJ: Prentice-Hall, 1975) 1.

32. *HBNW* 171.

33. Ibid., 72–73, 190.

34. McCormick, *Notes on Moral Theology, 1965 through 1980* 735, fn. 108.

35. McCormick, "The Vatican Document on Bioethics," *America* 156 (March 28, 1987) 247–48; "Therapy or Tampering?" 402.

36. McCormick, "Therapy or Tampering?" 398.

37. *HBNW* 73.

38. Ibid. 332–33.

39. See "Therapy or Tampering?" 399.

40. Ibid. 399–400. For four of McCormick's objections to the inseparability rule, as articulated in *Instruction,* see "Document Is Unpersuasive," *Health Progress* (July-August 1987) 53–55.

41. *Instruction* Part II. B. 4. b.

42. McCormick, "The Vatican Document on Bioethics."

43. See the discussion in and following Donald T. DeMarco, "Catholic Moral Teaching and TOT/GIFT," in The Pope John Center, *Reproductive Technologies, Marriage and the Church* (Braintree, Mass.: The Pope John XXIII Medical-Moral Research and Education Center, 1988) 122–39, with a response by Donald G. McCarthy.

44. McCormick, "The Vatican Document on Bioethics" 248.

45. *HBNW* 332.

46. "Therapy or Tampering?" 401–02.

47. Ibid. 402.

48. "Dissent on the Use of Third Parties," in The Ethics Committee of the American Fertility Society, "Ethical Considerations of the New Reproductive Technologies," *Fertility and Sterility* 46 (September 1986), Supplement 1, 82S. See also McCormick, "Ethics of Reproductive Technology: AFS Recommendations, Dissent," *Health Progress* (March 1987) 33–37.

49. "Therapy or Tampering?" 402. See Paul Ramsey, *Fabricated Man* (New Haven: Yale University Press, 1970).

50. "Therapy or Tampering?" 402.

51. Ibid.

52. See Tom L. Beauchamp and James F. Childress, *Principles of Biomedical Ethics* 3rd ed. (New York: Oxford University Press, 1989), chap. 4.

53. "Dissent on the Use of Third Parties" and McCormick, "Ethics of Reproductive Technology."

54. "Therapy or Tampering?" 402.

55. McCormick, "The Vatican Document on Bioethics," and "Therapy or Tampering?" 398, 402.

56. See again Childress, "Two By McCormick."

57. *HBNW* 333.

58. Ibid. 331.

59. See "Reassuring Study on In Vitro Babies: Group of 83 Conceived in Lab Shows No Increased Risk of Abnormalities," *The New York Times,* August 11, 1989, p. 17.

60. *Instruction* Part II, B. 5.

61. See George Lakoff and Mark Johnson, *Metaphors We Live By* (Chicago: University of Chicago Press, 1980).

62. *Instruction* Part II, B. 8.

63. Ibid. Part II, B. 5.

64. Vacek, "Vatican Instruction on Reproductive Technology" 130.

65. For criticisms of "making" see Oliver O'Donovan, *Begotten or Made?* (Oxford: Clarendon Press, 1984) 85–86, and, building on the Congregation's *Instruction,* William E. May, "Catholic Moral Teaching on In Vitro Fertilization," in *Reproductive Technologies, Marriage and the Church* 107–21. See also J. M. Finnis, "IVF and the Catholic Tradition," *The Month* (February 1984) 55–58.

66. *Instruction* Part II, B. 5.

67. See Vacek, "Vatican Instruction on Reproductive Technology" 122.

68. McCormick, "Therapy or Tampering?" 403.

69. Quoted in Michael Lockwood, "The Warnock Report: A Philosophical Appraisal," in *Moral Dilemmas in Modern Medicine,* ed. Michael Lockwood, 160.

70. McCormick, "Therapy or Tampering?" 402.

71. *HBNW* 328.

72. See The Ethics Committee of the American Fertility Society, "Ethical Considerations of the New Reproductive Technologies" vii.

73. *HBNW* 330.

74. Ibid.

75. See, for example, Mark I. Evans, et al., "Selective First-Trimester Termination in Octuplet and Quadruplet Pregnancies: Clinical and Ethical Issues," *Obstetrics and Gynecology* 71 (March 1988) 289–96; Richard L. Berkowitz, "Selective Reduction of Multifetal Pregnancies in the First Trimester," *New England Journal of Medicine* 318 (April 21, 1988) 1043–1046; and John C. Hobbins, "Selective Reduction—A Perinatal Necessity?" *New England Journal of Medicine* 318 (April 21, 1988) 1062–63.

76. Gina Kolata, "Multiple Fetuses Raise New Issues Tied to Abortion," *New York Times,* January 25, 1988, A1.

77. *Instruction* Part II.

78. *HBNW* 329, 333.

79. See Margaret O'Brien Steinfels, "In Vitro Fertilization: 'Ethically Acceptable' Research," *Hastings Center Report* 9 (June 1979) 5–8, and McCormick's response, "The EAB and In Vitro Fertilization," *Hastings Center Report* 9 (December 1979) 4, along with Steinfels' reply. See also Ethics Advisory Board, U.S. Department of Health, Education, and Welfare, *Report and Conclusions: HEW Support of Research Involving Human In Vitro Fertilization and Embryo Transfer* (Washington, DC: U.S. Government Printing Office, 1979) and *Federal Register* 44 (June 18, 1970) 35033–58.

80. "Therapy or Tampering?" 403.

81. *HBNW* 332.

82. "Therapy or Tampering?" 398.

83. See Andrea Bonnicksen, *In Vitro Fertilization: Building Policy from Laboratories to Legislatures* (New York: Columbia University Press, 1989), esp. 40–45.

84. Department of Health and Social Security, *Report of the Committee of Inquiry into Human Fertilisation and Embryology* (Chairman: Dame Mary Warnock) (London: Her Majesty's Stationery Office, July 1984) 10:11.

85. See the discussion of this legislation in Office of Technology Assessment, *Infertility* 252–53.

86. For an analysis of these categories as used in organ and tissue transfer, see James F. Childress, "Ethical Criteria for Procuring and Distributing Organs for Transplantation," *Journal of Health Politics, Policy and Law* 14 (Spring 1989) 87–113.

87. Senate Select Committee, Human Embryo Experimentation Bill of 1985, *Human Embryo Experimentation in Australia* (September 1986).

88. Office of Technology Assessment, *Infertility* 298.

89. American College of Obstetricians and Gynecologists (ACOG) Committee on Ethics, "Ethical Issues in Human In Vitro Fertilization and Embryo Placement" (Washington, DC: ACOG, July 1986).

90. John A. Robertson, "Ethical and Legal Issues in Cryopreservation of Human Embryos," *Fertility and Sterility* 47 (March 1987) 371–81.

91. ACOG, "Ethical Issues in Human In Vitro Fertilization and Embryo Placement."

92. Ronald Smothers, "Embryos in a Divorce Case: Joint Property or Offspring?" *New York Times,* April 22, 1989, p. 1.

93. "Couple Sues In-Vitro Clinic," *Charlottesville Daily Progress,* May 11, 1989, B4.

94. *Instruction* I, 6.

95. McCormick, "Therapy or Tampering?" 403.

SOCIAL AND POLITICAL ETHICS

15

The Basis of Human Rights

Jack Mahoney, S.J.

In the late eighteenth century the strange spectacle could be observed of heartfelt agreement between a pope and an English free-thinking philosopher. They were both implacably opposed to any idea of human rights. As Pope Pius VI exclaimed in a papal brief to Louis XVI of France, human rights was a monstrous idea. And Bentham, in his diatribe on the same French Declaration of the Rights of Man, expostulated that it was terrorist language and dangerous nonsense.

The complete reversal which has taken place only in more recent times in the church's attitude to human rights is not the scope of this study. Suffice it to say that today in world society there is no greater champion of human rights than Pope John Paul II. As he wrote in his latest encyclical, *On the Social Concern of the Church* (1987, no. 25), one of the positive features of the contemporary social scene is "the full awareness among large numbers of men and women of their own dignity and of that of every human being. This awareness is expressed, for example, in the more lively concern that human rights should be respected, and in the more vigorous rejection of their violation."

In this, and also in praising in principle the *Universal Declaration of Human Rights* promulgated in 1948 by the United Nations Organization, the pope was following closely the major human rights program adopted by his predecessor, John XXIII, in his encyclical *Pacem in Terris* (1963). He too noted as a characteristic of the modern age a progressive improvement in the economic and social condition of working men, first in claiming their rights in the economic and social spheres, and then in claiming their political rights as well (no. 40). John, however, also began his encyclical by providing a classical statement of human rights (no. 9). "Any well-regulated and profitable human association requires the acceptance of one fundamental principle: that every human being possesses the characteristics of a person; that is, a nature endowed with intelligence and freedom of will. As such he has rights and duties, which together stem simultaneously from that nature. For that reason such rights and duties are universal and inviolable, and cannot be alienated in any way."

It is worth noting that the pope here made no reference to God in his exposition of human rights, presumably because, this being the first papal encyclical in history to be addressed, *inter alia,* "to all men of good will," he wished to engage the sympathy also of nonbelievers. It is true that in the following paragraph he added, "When, furthermore, we consider man's personal dignity from the standpoint of divine revelation, inevitably our estimate of it is incomparably increased . . ." (no. 10). Nevertheless, the fact that he thought an exposition of human rights could be propounded without reference to God not only raises the recurring contemporary question of the so-called "specificity" of Christian ethics. It also stimulates the question whether a doctrine of human rights can be reasonably sustained without some formal underpinning in a divine act of creation. The aim of this study is to explore in various key stages of the development of human rights doctrine whether an answer can be forthcoming to this latter question.

Magna Carta

One of the most powerful early landmarks and later touchstones of human rights was the Great Charter of liberties wrested by the barons of England from their king in the meadow of Runnymede in June 1215, to the grave displeasure of Pope Innocent III, who excommunicated the barons and annulled *Magna Carta.* The protracted negotiations were the culmination of a system of government which was based on royal patronage and exploitation and exercised with royal arbitrariness. And this was not untypical of the close association in thirteenth century Europe in general between the urgent royal need of military resources and the concession of liberties in return for the means to satisfy that need. At the same time, as Holt observed, in a wider perspective *Magna Carta* "emerged from the increasing maturity of European political thought and practice, from the concept of rule according to law, from the demand for the preservation of the rights of subjects within a feudal and ecclesiastical hierarchy and from routine patterns of government which went with more disciplined and sophisticated forms of administration."[1]

Our concern is not with the detailed content of the Great Charter ("great" to distinguish it from the smaller charter of the forests) on such matters as property, taxation, standard weights and measures and due process of law, but with its basis of argumentation, and with two features in particular, the basic nature of what was being conceded by the king and the theoretical, as distinct from the immediately pragmatic, grounds for such concessions.

> Know that, in the sight of God and for the salvation of our soul and those of all our predecessors and descendants, to the glory of God and the honour of Holy Church, and the betterment of our kingdom, with the counsel of our reverend fathers Stephen Archbishop of Canterbury, Primate of all England and Cardinal of the Holy Roman Church . . . and of the noblemen . . . and others of our faithful subjects:

> 1. We have in the first place granted to God (*concessisse Deo*) and have confirmed by this present charter for ourselves and our heirs in perpetuity that the English Church be free, and have its rights untouched and its liberties unharmed. . . . We have also granted (*Concessimus*) to all the free men of our kingdom, for ourselves and our heirs in perpetuity, for them and their heirs to have and to hold from us and our heirs, all the following liberties. . . .[2]

> 63. Wherefore we will and firmly enjoin that the English Church be free and that men in our kingdom have and hold all the aforesaid liberties, rights, and grants (*libertates, jura, et concessiones*), well and in peace, freely and quietly, fully and entirely, for themselves and their heirs from us and our heirs, in all matters and places, as has been said.[3]

The pattern of the Charter is a series of acts of royal self-limitation whereby the king's initiative and power are stated not to apply in certain areas of action and behavior in favor of the individuals or parties concerned. There is, however, no mention of the basis of such concession of liberties, rights and grants, other than tradition, whether historical or imagined. The appeal to the force of tradition, whether of custom or of previous legislation, was, however, not a very secure base, and was in fact part of the controversy between John and his barons. As Holt observes, royal government was "securely grounded in the traditional rights compounded in the Anglo-Norman monarchy of [William] the Conqueror"; and John's policy in the years following *Magna Carta* was "to confront the Charter with the traditional rights of the Crown."[4]

"Even if God Did Not Exist"

If *Magna Carta* was "a political document produced in a crisis,"[5] the major endeavor of the Dutch Calvinist lawyer, Hugo Grotius (d. 1645), was to attempt to remove, or at least control, such all too frequent crises throughout the Christian Europe of the seventeenth century. His most important legacy was as a contributor to developing the doctrine of the just war in terms of the ethical restraints which governed not just declaring war but also waging war. However, in the Introduction to his detailed study of the *Law of War and Peace,* he took the occasion to speak of law and legal rights in general, and of natural law and natural rights in particular. As such he constitutes an important contributor to the development of natural rights theory, and one to whom we can address our question as to the justification which underlies these theories.

"Throughout the Christian world I have seen a licence in making war, both in resorting to war and in the conduct of war, which would shame barbarians."[6] As a result, Grotius sought to establish rules for war to which all human beings would subscribe, not from Christian revelation, but from the power of human reason as it considered the nature of law and of rights. In doing so, he was at pains to distinguish their various meanings, particularly in clarifying the different applications of the ambiguous Latin term *jus.*

As he observed, the word can mean what is just.[7] It can also be equated with "law" in its broadest sense, "a rule of moral actions obliging one to what is correct," as Aristotle noted, distinguishing between natural law and legal, or positive, law.[8] In addition, however, *jus* can also mean by derivation something relating to the person. "In this sense, *jus* is a moral quality pertaining to a person to possess or do something justly." Such a right in the strict sense he identified as a claim (*facultas*) which includes power, either over oneself (i.e. liberty) or over others (authority); or a claim which includes ownership, either full (i.e. property) or less full (the use of things).[9]

In exploring the nature of rights Grotius singled out for attack the view that there was no such thing as natural right (*jus naturale*), but that people had simply sanctioned rights as a matter of utility, and that these accordingly varied according to customs and had often changed. Against the basis of this view, that all animals, including the human, are impelled by nature to seek their own advantage, Grotius drew upon the long tradition stemming from Aristotle that every human is kin and friend to every other (*Ethics* VIII, 1). Among the human characteristics, then, is a desire for society—not, however, a mere sharing of existence, but a society which is peaceful and rationally structured with one's fellows.[10] This conservation of society which is in accord with human intelligence is the origin of *jus,* or natural law, covering such behavior as respect for what belongs to others, keeping promises, repairing damages and punishing for transgressions.[11]

Thus far, Grotius was building upon and developing the scholastic tradition. Where he was to make a bold break with that tradition, however, arising from his convictions that Christian morality had failed in practice, particularly in its practice of warfare, but that human reason could provide certainty, was in his asserting that the law of human nature has force even if there were no divine underpinning of human nature. "What we have spoken about would have some weight even if we were to grant what cannot be granted without the utmost wickedness, that God does not exist or that he takes no interest in human affairs" (*Et haec quidem quae iam diximus, locum aliquem haberent, etiamsi daremus, quod sine summo scelere dari nequit, non esse Deum, aut non curari ab eo negotia humana*).[12] The effect of this confident, indeed, overconfident, statement of the autonomy of natural law was to sever it from its roots in creation and, in the term of Köhler, to "detheologie" natural law. "The detheologisation of natural law in a line from Grotius to Pufendorf and Thomasius is at once the foundation of the tolerant state as well as its becoming an absolute concept as the *primum principium* of political and social life."[13] As the non-existence of God became increasingly more than a speculative possibility in society, the difficulties of Grotius' confident claims for human nature and human reason would become increasingly evident.

THE ENGLISH BILL OF RIGHTS 1689

A further milestone in the English development of human rights is to be found in the passing by Parliament of "An Act declaring the Rights and Liberties of the Subject and Settling the Succession of the Crown" in the immediate aftermath of "the Glorious Revolution" of 1688.[14] The Act opens by relating how Parliament had recently presented to William and Mary, then Prince and Princess of Orange, a Declaration that "the late King James the Second . . . did endeavour to subvert and extirpate the Protestant religion and the laws and liberties of this kingdom" in various specified ways, and how Parliament had offered for approval a list of such rights and liberties, together with the throne, to the Dutch royal couple.

After this long preamble, Parliament now addressed itself to the business in hand, which was not just to ratify all the foregoing by act of

Parliament, praying "that it may be declared and enacted that all and singular the rights and liberties asserted and claimed in the said declaration are the true, ancient and indubitable rights and liberties of the people of this kingdom." Nor did Parliament sit just to swear its own and posterity's allegiance to the new monarchs. There were more portentous matters to hand. "Whereas it hath been found by experience that it is inconsistent with the safety and welfare of this Protestant kingdom to be governed by a popish prince, or by any king or queen marrying a papist, the said Lords Spiritual and Temporal and Commons do further pray that it may be enacted, that all and every person and persons that is, are or shall be reconciled to or shall hold communion with the see or Church of Rome, or shall profess the popish religion, or shall marry a papist, shall be excluded and be for ever incapable to inherit, possess or enjoy the crown and government of this realm. . . . All which their Majesties are contented and pleased shall be declared, enacted and established by authority of this present Parliament, and shall stand, remain and be the law of this realm for ever."

Parliament realized that it had been a massive blunder on the part of its predecessors to restore the monarchy without laying down any conditions on its exercise, and this oversight had been further confounded by the growing climate of the absolutist theory of kingship by divine right which was cultivated and exercised by the restored Stuart monarchs. Time, however, was not on the side of Parliament and, as one commentator observes, "a statement of grievances and appropriate remedies was hastily drawn up, embodied in a Declaration of Rights, presented, along with the crown, to the new sovereigns and formally accepted by them. . . . The imposition of conditions or restrictions on the monarch was accepted as a normal thing, though those embodied in the Declaration of Rights were as mild and conservative, and in some cases as vague, as could well have been devised."[15]

Browning's comment on the actual Bill of Rights seems a fair one. The suppliant tone of the document and its substance in terms of rights, laws and liberties do not differ much from the tone and contents of the gracious concessions made in 1215 by King John to his barons, although, as Cranston observes, "The Bill of Rights was not a Bill of 'the Rights of Man,' but of the Rights of Parliament."[16] Nor is the basis of such rights in tradition and history significantly different. In fact, the major development in terms of human rights made by the 1689 Act of the English Parliament was not so much in its first part, that "declaring the rights and liberties of the subject," but in its second part, in "settling the succession of the Crown." The originality of the 1689 act lay in its countering the current of absolutism running strongly in the rest of Europe by dislodging the hereditary right of succession in favor of the will of the nation expressed through Parliament, and in the process adopting in practice the contract theory of government. It is in this respect, then, rather than in the individual rights claimed for Parliament, that one can perhaps see, as Browning observes, the influence of the ideas developed and eloquently expressed by the contemporary English philosopher, John Locke (d. 1704), to whom we may now turn.

JOHN LOCKE

In 1690 Locke published anonymously his *Two Treatises of Government,* with the express aim, as the Preface explains, of legitimating the accession to the throne of England of "our present King William; to make good his title, in the consent of the people . . . and to justify to the world the people of England, whose love of their just and natural rights, with their resolution to preserve them, saved the nation when it was on the very brink of slavery and ruin."[17] In point of fact, as scholars now agree, Locke had written his book on political philosophy some years previously, in the latter years of the Stuart monarchy, but the "Glorious Revolution" provided the occasion to exemplify his theories, while his theory in turn served to bolster the political transition which had recently occurred.

The Two Treatises, then, is not a rushed reaction to events, but the measured statement of views molded over the years through contact with such ancient and modern classics as Aristotle and Grotius, and matured in the political controversy of the last years of the House of Stuart. Central to Locke's political philosophy is the traditional distinction between the "state of nature" and human "society." For him, unlike Thomas Hobbes before him, the state of nature is not a state of war, "however some men have confounded them." "Men living together according to reason, without a common superior on earth, with authority to judge between them, is properly the state of nature."[18] In this state of nature there is a corresponding law, for though men are born free and equal, their state is not one of license. "The state of nature has a law of nature to govern it, which obliges every one: and reason, which is that law, teaches all mankind, who will but consult it, that being all equal and independent, no one ought to harm another in his life, health, liberty, or possessions."[19]

When they enter by agreement into society, men will then proceed by common consent to sanction laws, but these laws do not supersede the law of nature. "The obligations of the law of nature cease not in society but only in many cases are drawn closer, and have by human laws known penalties annexed to them, to enforce their observation. Thus the law of nature stands as an external rule to all men, legislators as well as others. The rules that they make for other men's actions must, as well as their own and other men's actions, be conformable to the law of nature, i.e., to the will of God, of which that is a declaration."[20]

"The objective existence of a body of natural law," then, Laslett comments, "is an essential presupposition of [Locke's] political theory. . . . Natural law, in his system in *Two Treatises,* was at one and the same time a command of God, a rule of reason, and a law in the very nature of things as they are, by which they work and we work too."[21] And this for posterity was to create something of a difficulty. For "it is of importance to see in Locke, [who was] the recognised point of departure for liberalism, the liberal dilemma already present, the dilemma of maintaining a political faith without subscribing to a total, holistic view of the world."[22] For Locke, of course, this was no dilemma. His own Aristotelian predilection for human sociability and reasonableness is evident in his respect for "reason which God hath given to be the rule betwixt man and man, and the common bond whereby human kind is united into one fellowship and society."[23] It was this, combined with his belief in God (and his rejection of original sin[24]), which lay at the root of his rejection of Hobbes' view of the state of nature as brutish and anarchical. As he wrote in a letter on the subject, "the not taking God into this hypothesis has been the great reason of Mr Hobbeses mistake that the laws of nature are not properly laws nor do oblige mankind to their observation when out of a civil state or commonwealth."[25]

In drawing upon the Aristotelian, medieval and scholastic doctrines of natural law, as we have seen, Locke at the same time advanced the subject by applying it to contemporary circumstances and adding to the idea that natural law imposes certain morally right actions the potent consideration that it also confers certain moral rights.[26] The result was, as Melden observes, that these new features of the Lockean doctrine, which made him the notable exponent of the natural rights movement that developed in the seventeenth century, "were important to men of practical affairs who put them to use in the political upheavals that took place not only in England but also in America and France."[27]

NATURAL AND SACRED RIGHTS

The influence of Locke is clear in the next stage of human rights development to be considered, the creation of the United States of

America. The North American colonies, more egalitarian than Europe and lacking hereditary class structures while expanding rapidly in numbers and resources, found increasingly irksome government by a well-nigh absolutist parliament in England. With no ancient historical claims or precedents to which to appeal, they took their stand, in the 1776 Declaration of Independence, on "the revolutionary principle of the natural rights of man" in "the most eloquent revolutionary manifesto in western history."[28] Thomas Jefferson's measured cadences draw heavily on the doctrine of Locke that all human creatures are born in a state of nature with certain God-given natural rights which they bring with them by their free consent into the making and monitoring of society and its laws for their shared human advancement.

> When in the Course of human events, it becomes necessary for one people to dissolve the political bands which have connected them with another, and to assume among the Powers of the earth, the separate and equal station to which the Laws of Nature and of Nature's God entitle them, a decent respect to the opinions of mankind requires that they should declare the causes which impel them to the separation.

> We hold these truths to be self-evident, that all men are created equal, that they are endowed their Creator with certain unalienable Rights, that among these are Life, Liberty and the pursuit of Happiness. That to secure these rights, Governments are instituted among Men, deriving their just powers from the consent of the governed. . . .[29]

In the words of Thomas Paine (d. 1809), the English expatriate whose *Common Sense* had so helped inspire the American colonists to rise against the English monarchy, participation by France in the American War of Independence had greatly influenced the march of events under Louis XVI and provided "the school of Freedom" for French officers and soldiers in alliance with the aspirations of the former colonies.[30] In the manifesto of the French Revolution, the 1789 Declaration of the Rights of Man and of the Citizen, it is not difficult to see both the political influence of successful American claims to human rights and the similar basing of those "sacred rights" upon "nature and nature's God."

> The representatives of the people of France, formed into a National Assembly, considering that ignorance, neglect, or con-

tempt of human rights are the sole causes of public misfortunes and corruptions of Government, have resolved to set forth, in a solemn declaration, these natural, imprescriptible, and inalienable rights: that this declaration being constantly present to the minds of the members of the body social, they may be ever kept attentive to their rights and their duties. . . .

For these reasons, the National Assembly doth recognize and declare, in the presence of the Supreme Being, and with the hope of his blessing and favour, the following sacred rights of men and of citizens:

I. Men are born, and always continue, free, and equal in respect of their rights. Civil distinctions, therefore, can be founded only on public utility.

II. The end of all political associations is the preservation of the natural and imprescriptible rights of man; and these rights are liberty, property, security, and resistance of oppression.

III. The nation is essentially the source of all sovereignty; nor can any individual, or any body of men, be entitled to any authority which is not expressly derived from it.[31]

In these first three articles, identifying the rights of man, are contained the principles which are subsequently spelt out or applied in the remaining fourteen as the rights of citizens in society, in such a way as to exemplify the Lockean analysis of society, summed up in Paine's assertion in his *Rights of Man* that "All the great laws of society are laws of nature."[32] But if this commentary on the French *Declaration,* was "the finest example of political pamphleteering in the Age of Revolution,"[33] it is arguably true that the work of which it was a devastating critique was the finest rhetorical case for political conservatism constructed in that or succeeding centuries.

BURKE'S ATTACK AND PAINE'S RIPOSTE

Edmund Burke (d. 1797) had been not unsympathetic to the plight of the transatlantic American colonies in their bid for some measure of independence, but when revolution came considerably nearer home, just across the Channel, and seemed likely to spread its contagion not only in an England rumbling with social and political discontent but also to his native restless Ireland, Burke was not slow, though at first almost alone, to sound the alarm to the political and propertied classes in England. His *Reflections on the Revolution in France* showed what have been described as "unusual gifts of political foresight" of what terrors still lay in wait for France, though partly as a result of the warring reaction of France's neighbors, including England.[34] And the burden of his attack on recent events in France, and the possibility of their being replicated in England, was to reject political and social revolution in favor of development and gradualism, such as had been achieved in England by the Glorious Revolution of 1688, in spite of the fact that some agitators in England were basing their case for revolution on that same event.

In the circumstances it was less than candid of Burke to describe the transfer of the throne of England on that occasion and the provision made for the Protestant succession as "a small and a temporary deviation from the strict order of a regular hereditary succession."[35] It was, however, part of Burke's argument to establish the liberties of England on tradition and inheritance rather than on any more philosophical basis. "You will observe, that from Magna Carta to the Declaration of Rights, it has been the uniform policy of our constitutions to claim and assert our liberties, as an *entailed inheritance* derived to us from our forefathers, and to be transmitted to our posterity; as an estate specially belonging to the people of this kingdom without any reference whatsoever to any other more general or prior right."[36]

So much so that, although Burke delivers a forthright attack on the doctrine of natural rights, he nevertheless appeals to nature in so doing —but to nature as he understands it; that is, to inherited social structures and the instinctive reliance on the past. "The body of the people must not find the principles of natural subordination by art rooted out of their minds. They must respect that property of which they cannot partake. They must labour to obtain what by labour can be obtained; and when they find, as they commonly do, the success disproportioned to the endeavour, they must be taught their consolation in the final proportions of eternal justice."[37] Again, "The levellers therefore only change and pervert the natural order of things; they load the edifice of society, by setting up in the air what the solidity of the structure requires to be on the ground. . . . The occupation of a hair-dresser, or of a working tallow-chandler, cannot be a matter of honour to any person—to say nothing of a number of other more servile employments. . . . [T]he state suffers oppression, if such as they, either individually or collectively, are permitted to rule. In this you think you are combating prejudice, but you are at war with nature."[38]

It was entirely in keeping with such patrician sentiments uttered from the hierarchical summit of English society that Burke should lament that with the French Revolution "the age of chivalry is gone.—That of sophisters, oeconomists, and calculators, has succeeded; and the glory of Europe is extinguished for ever. Never, never more, shall we behold that generous loyalty to rank and sex, that proud submission, that dignified obedience, that subordination of the heart, which kept alive, even in servitude itself, the spirit of an exalted freedom."[39]

Of a less flamboyant but more savage rhetoric, Thomas Paine's riposte to Burke in his *Rights of Man* made such short shrift of Burke's claims for heredity and tradition, in royal government as well as in political society, as to secure for Paine an indictment for seditious libel. But he rose to the same heights of eloquence when he charged Burke, "Not one glance of compassion, not one commiserating reflection, that I can find throughout his book, has he bestowed on those who lingered out the most wretched of lives, a life without hope, in the most miserable of prisons. . . . His hero or his heroine must be a tragedy-victim expiring in show, and not the real prisoner of misery, sliding into death in the silence of a dungeon."[40]

More philosophically, Paine turns the tables on Burke in his assertion that "It is by distortedly exalting some men, that others are distortedly debased, till the whole is out of nature."[41] What is more, to argue from historical precedent, as Burke mainly does, is to stop short of going the whole way, "till we come to the divine origin of the rights of man at the creation. . . . [E]very child born into the world must be considered as deriving its existence from God. The world is as new to him as it was to the first man that existed, and his natural right in it is of the same kind."[42] But "it is not among the least of the evils of the present existing governments in all parts of Europe, that man, considered as man, is thrown back to a vast distance from his Maker, and the artificial chasm filled up by a succession of barriers, or sort of turnpike gates, through which he has to pass."[43] Society and its structures have a purpose, to be sure; but "Man did not enter into society to become *worse* than he was before, nor to have fewer rights than he had before, but to have those rights better secured." Natural rights belong to man "in right of his existence," whereas civil rights belong to man "in right of his being a member of society. Every civil right has for its foundation, some natural right preexisting in the individual, but to the enjoyment of which his individual power is not, in all cases, sufficiently competent."[44]

THE HEIGHT OF NONSENSE

What purported to be a more rational English onslaught on the whole idea of human rights was mounted by a contemporary of Burke and Paine, Jeremy Bentham (d. 1832), who was so seized by the all-sufficiency of his (or rather Helvetius') principle of utility as the solution to every ethical question that he contemptuously dismissed any other view which did not fit into his categories.[45] The ponderous sarcasm, or what Hart terms the "panic-stricken rhetoric,"[46] of Bentham's analysis of the French Declaration of Rights charges it with being "dangerous nonsense" and "terrorist language" in its "perpetual abuse of words." In what was to become the most famous aphorism on the subject, "*Natural rights* is simple nonsense: natural and imprescriptible rights, rhetorical nonsense —nonsense upon stilts," or the height of nonsense. "*Right,* the substantive *right* [as opposed to the adjective], is the child of law: from *real* laws come *real* rights; but from *imaginary* laws, from laws of nature, fancied and invented by poets, rhetoricians, and dealers in moral and intellectual poisons, come *imaginary* rights, a bastard brood of monsters. . . ."[47] As he was to repeat in a later work, "To me a right and a legal right are the same thing, for I know no other. Right and law are correlative terms: as much so as son and father. Right is with me the child of law: from different operations of the law result different sorts of rights. A natural right is a son that never had a father."[48]

What, however, of the claim that natural rights and natural law may derive from a divine source of creation, as Locke and Paine had maintained, and the American and French Declarations had claimed? Bentham's only reply is to acknowledge that "from a divine law comes a divine right just as intelligibly as from a political human law comes a political human right." In this way from a supposed divine law some have derived the divine right of kings. But "as the existence of the law for the purpose is always denied and can never be proved, it is as perfectly useless"; it has no utility. And in any case natural rights are most often claimed, he added gratuitously, by "those by whom the existence of a divine law and of a divine lawgiver are equally denied."[49] In sum, for Bentham, "The recognition of the nothingness of the laws of nature and the rights of man that have been grounded on them is a branch of knowledge of as much importance to an Englishman, though a negative one, as the most perfect acquaintance that can be formed with the existing laws of England."[50]

INTERNATIONAL DEVELOPMENTS

Bentham's forceful and persuasive advocacy of Utilitarianism came, of course, to dominate the scene of most subsequent English philosophical and political study to the present, and also set the stage for much of the modern debate on the subject of human rights, both in clarifying ideas and terminology, and in exploring the basis, if there is one, of human rights. Just, however, when it might be thought that the subject was outmoded, if not philosophically exploded, it reemerged on the world scene in the closing stages of the Second World War and in the trial and conviction of leading members of the German Nazi Reich by the International Military Tribunal at Nuremberg. According to the Charter adopted as law by the Tribunal, "The following acts, or any of them, are crimes coming within the jurisdiction of the Tribunal for which there shall be individual responsibility. . . . (c) Crimes against humanity; namely, murder, extermination, enslavement, deportation, and other inhuman acts committed against any civilian population. . . ."[51]

In his study of the Nuremberg trials, Woetzel comments that "The IMT had the endorsement of the international community, which also affirmed that the acts listed as crimes against humanity were violations of international law."[52] He cites earlier historical reference to the occurrence of the phrases "interest of humanity" and the "laws of humanity" in the Fourth Hague Convention of 1907.[53] And he concludes that "most of these acts constituted heinous crimes judged by any standard of justice."[54]

The aftermath of the Second World War saw, of course, the formation of the United Nations Organization in 1945, as a result of which the subject of human rights took on an international political dimension. This found expression in the 1948 Universal Declaration of Human Rights, and has subsequently developed in the western world, both in the European Convention of Human Rights, with its Human Rights Commission and its Court of Human Rights, and in the Inter-American Commission on Human Rights within the Organization of American States.[55] The Preamble to the Universal Declaration of 1948 indicates the basis for what follows.

> Whereas recognition of the inherent dignity and of the equal and inalienable rights of all members of the human family is the foundation of freedom, justice and peace in the world,

> Whereas disregard and contempt for human rights have resulted in barbarous acts which have outraged the conscience of mankind, and the advent of a world in which human beings

shall enjoy freedom of speech and belief and freedom from fear
and want has been proclaimed as the highest aspiration of the
common people. . . .[56]

Whatever may be said of the individual "human rights" then listed,
many of which are clearly heavily dependent on cultural, social and
political circumstances, it seems accurate to say, with Little, that in the
Preamble there is "what may be called the assumption of a prior and
independent moral belief in some common and permanent human characteristics that enjoin certain universally specifiable ways of treating
human beings and that prohibit others."[57]

In more recent years the advocacy of human rights on the international scene has made it part of the political agenda of several major
nations, including the Carter administration in the United States and
culminating to date in the proposal of President Gorbachev of the USSR
for a major international conference on the subject in Moscow in 1991.

MODERN STUDIES ON RIGHTS

The purpose of this essay has been partly the interest of surveying the
historical development of human rights to the recent present, and mainly
to explore what justification is proposed for recognizing and proclaiming
them. In this concluding section we may now briefly survey recent
writing on the subject and offer some reflections.

Probably the major division between attempts to justify human
rights is that between those who would see the concept as at root a
theological one and those who would aim to find ultimate justification in
a closed philosophical or socio-political system of thought. The teaching
of recent popes on the subject, for example, has continued to maintain
substantially the classical Christian view, which is to be found also as
more than rhetoric in the statements of Grotius, Locke, and Paine, as
well as in the American and French Declarations of Human Rights, and
which is in principle separable from any form of a contract theory of
society. This broadly theological approach contains difficulties of detail
and specification, but its logic appears impressive. It is true that basing
the idea of human rights on that of natural law in its equally classical
exposition raises difficulties arising from the understanding and concept
of nature, but with the recent shift of emphasis in Catholic thinking from
human "nature" to human "person" several at least of those difficulties
appear to have been surmounted.[58]

For its part, philosophical analysis has, of course, contributed much to clarifying human rights concepts and language. The now accepted distinction is a valuable one between a "(mere) liberty" or what Hart calls a "liberty-right," according to which I can claim a "right" to do something in the sense that I am not obliged to refrain from doing it, and a "claim-right" which gives me a claim on others, either negatively not to prevent me, or positively to assist me. Equally, the exploration of rights in terms of the correlative duties which they may or may not entail for others constitutes a useful reality check in the whole field.

Moreover, the use of rights language has received impressive vindication in some recent literature. It is true that it can be considered grossly inflated in what it claims, or unduly individualistic in its scope, or peculiarly western in its history and rhetoric.[59] The argument is also proposed that the moral claims entailed in the language of rights can just as validly be established or expressed in other moral terms without recourse to talking about rights. On the other hand, inflated and unwarranted claims can be made on the basis of any principle of morality, and reference to *prima facie,* or "overrideable" rights, on the analogy with Ross' analysis of *prima facie* duties, can be of help in moderating rights talk. As to the terminology itself, the suggestion of Macdonald is impressive, that statements made about human, or natural, rights are not so much statements of fact (as Bentham stolidly supposed in easily proving that these were not verified) as "records of decisions" (or perhaps better as records of moral determination).[60] Such an understanding makes good sense of the ringing declaration of Rousseau, that man is born free, and everywhere he is in chains.

In addition, the particular recourse to rights language within moral discourse in general serves to highlight what Nickel has identified as their "high priority, definiteness, and bindingness." "This character would be lost if we were to deconstruct rights into mere goals or ideals."[61] It is also, of course, part of the popularity of the writings of Dworkin on the subject of rights that he introduced the striking phrase of "rights as trumps" into the literature by "arguing for the right to moral independence as a trump over utilitarian justifications."[62] Indeed, Mackie makes the point that Mill himself appeared to feel the need for some distinguishing feature in the final chapter of his *Utilitarianism* when he recognized "a real difference in kind" between "the extraordinarily important and impressive kind of utility which is concerned" with rights and "any of the more common cases of utility."[63]

At the same time, recent philosophical analysis of rights claims and language appears limited in several respects. For one thing, by approaching the subject so regularly from the standpoint of duty it appears not only to be unduly influenced since Bentham by the paradigm of legal rights, which find their main expression in identifying the duties of others, but also to have difficulty in focusing on what precisely it is in the "claimant" which generates such duties. Legal rights are conferred, but human rights are recognized. Harrison, for instance, clearly has a refreshingly realistic point when he writes, "The central point is that if you really want to see what you have got when you are told that you have a right, see what duties are laid on other people."[64] Yet presumably the basic point is not just identifying what duties are laid on others, but precisely why any such duties should be laid on other people in my regard. Starting from duty may clarify, but only starting from right or, more fundamentally, the right-bearer can justify.

At a deeper level, disagreement or skepticism on what such justification might be has the effect of making all the analysis of the language and concepts free-floating with little anchorage in reality, or so at least a theist might conclude. Not untypical is the impressive construction by Mackie of a fundamental right of all persons progressively to choose how they shall live, on which he subsequently comments, "I am not claiming that it is objectively valid, or that its validity can be found out by reason: I am merely adopting it and recommending it for general adoption as a moral principle."[65]

What appears to be in practice the simple contractual "adopting" of human rights by interested parties is possibly most evident in the growing phenomenon of modern statements on the subject. Commenting on the International Legal Code on Human Rights, for instance, Sieghart observes that "it was precisely to overcome this [philosophical] uncertainty that the international legal community established its agreed legal code —much as scientists and engineers have established internationally agreed standards of measurement such as the metre and the gram, in order to short-circuit further disputes about miles, leagues, ells, pounds, ounces, and grains."[66]

Others, it is true, do attempt to establish by reasoning the objective validity of one or more basic human rights; but it is at least questionable how successful they are. Jeremy Waldron in his *Theories of Rights* responds to a "preoccupation with foundations" by usefully classifying various attempts to provide justification for rights.[67] He notes the refinement of the approach by way of duties in the recognition that the reason for imposing duties on others is to be found in the protection or advancement of some interest on the part of the right-bearer.[68] And he details various attempts to justify human rights in society on utilitarian grounds, to conclude rightly that "We must not let the *formal* sophistication of modern utilitarianism blind us to the fact that, at the level of content, utilitarians remain perfectly happy about (indeed are necessarily and profoundly committed to) the possibility of trading off the interests in life or liberty of a small number of people against a greater sum of the lesser interests of others."[69]

Indeed, we might add, following an observation of Dworkin, that one of the main functions of rights and rights language is precisely to be anti-utilitarian. "We need rights, as a distinct element in political theory, only when some decision that injures some people nevertheless finds prima-facie support in the claim that it will make the community as a whole better off on some plausible account of where the community's general welfare lies. . . . We want to say that the decision is wrong, in spite of its apparent merit, because it does not take the damage it causes to some into account in the right way and therefore does not treat these people as equals entitled to the same concern as others."[70]

By contrast, nonutilitarian theories, according to Waldron, either tend to be little more than assertions based on intuition or claimed first principles, or in some few cases they attempt to derive rights from the very conditions or preconditions of rational moral discourse between human beings. Thus it may be significant that, when we propose trading away someone's interests, we feel obliged to produce reasons which he or she can in principle accept. "But this requirement seems to imply that we must leave intact at least those interests that are central to each person's capacity to recognize and understand moral reason and moral argument (again, his freedom of thought and expression and maybe certain basic interests in material well-being)."[71]

From such and other considerations on the modern philosophy of rights one might conclude that their future appears to be either highly problematic or distinctly obscure. Alasdair MacIntyre, of course, would tend to view this as a significant instance of his general thesis of the bankruptcy of modern moral philosophy: "every attempt to give good reasons for believing that there *are* such rights has failed." As for the attempt on the part of some moderns to appeal to intuition in default of an argument as a basis for the existence of human rights, MacIntyre sardonically rejoins that "one of the things that we ought to have learned from the history of moral philosophy is that the introduction of the word 'intuition' by a moral philosopher is always a signal that something has gone badly wrong with an argument."[72]

One may not, however, need to go all the way with MacIntyre in his strictures on modern rights thinking, or for that matter in his general thesis. Some of the analytical and nonutilitarian endeavors to give human rights some measure of clarity as well as existence appear to be steps in the right direction.[73] And if Christianity in general, and the Catholic Church in particular, is persuaded on the basis of its beliefs that every human person is endowed by God with certain prerogatives, presumably it would do better to encourage rather than to dash the hopes of such philosophers to give a rational account of those prerogatives.

It may be, indeed, that the steady and increasing human persuasion that people are not to be explained away without remainder in the pursuit of the general welfare of any society is saying something which is both real and important. Sumner writes, for instance, of "our pre-theoretical intuitions about rights."[74] In a similar way one could maintain that much of what is today said or written to the detriment of human rights is significantly "counter-intuitive" in a sense of "intuition" which is far removed from the intellectual activity derided by MacIntyre. It may even be that such human persuasion, far from being Benthamite nonsense, has paradoxically some affinity with what Edmund Burke described as human "prejudice" or unreflected or "untaught feelings." "You see, Sir, that in this enlightened age I am bold enough to confess, that we are generally men of untaught feelings; that instead of casting away all our old prejudices, we cherish them to a very considerable degree. . . . Many of our men of speculation, instead of exploding general prejudices, employ their sagacity to discover the latent wisdom which prevails in them."[75]

Notes

1. J. C. Holt, *Magna Carta,* Cambridge 1969, 105. For the Latin text of the Charter, cf 316–36.

2. Holt, 316.

3. Holt, 336.

4. Holt, 25, 247.

5. Holt, 6.

6. Hugo Grotius, *De Jure Belli et Pacis,* ed W. Whewell, 3 vols, Cambridge, 1853, *Proleg.* 28; vol. 1, lix.

7. Bk 1, chap 1, 3, 1.

8. Bk 1, chap 1, 9.

9. Bk 1, chap 1, 4–8.

10. Prol 5–6; xl–xli.

11. Prol 8; xliv.

12. Prol 11; xlvi.

13. In H. Jedin & J. Dolan, eds., *Handbook of Church History,* London, 1969, vol. vi, 346.

14. *English Historical Documents VIII, 1660–1714,* ed. A. Browning, London 1953, 122–28.

15. Ibid, 20.

16. M. Cranston, *John Locke,* Oxford, 1985, 325, n 3.

17. John Locke, *Two Treatises of Government,* ed P. Laslett, Cambridge, 1963, 171.

18. Book 2, chap 3, 19; 321.

19. Book 2, chap 2, 6; 311.

20. Book 2, chap 10, 35; 403.

21. Laslett, 95.

22. Laslett, 103.

23. Book 2, chap 15; 172.

24. In *The Reasonableness of Christianity,* 1695; cf Cranston, 389.

25. Laslett, 93–94.

26. See H.L.A. Hart, "Are There Any Natural Rights?" in A.I. Melden, *Human Rights,* Belmont, Cal, 1970; and Melden, 2.

27. Melden, 2.

28. N. Hampson, *The Enlightenment,* London, 1984, 179.

29. The text in Melden, 138–39.

30. Thomas Paine, *Rights of Man,* London, 1984, Part 1, 94.

31. Full text in Paine, Part 1, 110–112; and Melden, 140–42.

32. Paine, Part 2, chap 1.

33. E. Foner in his Introduction to Paine, 17.

34. Edmund Burke, *Reflections on the Revolution in France,* ed. Conor Cruise O'Brien, London, 1968, Intro 21, 71–72.

35. Burke, 101.

36. Burke, 119.

37. Burke, 372.

38. Burke, 138.

39. Burke, 170.

40. Paine, Part 1, 51.

41. Paine, 59.

42. Paine, 66.

43. Paine, 67.

44. Paine, 68.

45. Jeremy Bentham's *Anarchical Fallacies* is conveniently to be found in excerpt in J. Waldron, ed., *Nonsense Upon Stilts,* London, 1987, 46–69, to which the following page numbers refer.

46. H.L.A. Hart, *Essays on Bentham,* Oxford, 1982, 78.

47. Waldron, *Nonsense,* 69.

48. Bentham, *Supply Without Burthen or Escheat Vice Taxation;* cf. Waldron, *Nonsense,* 73.

49. Waldron, *Nonsense,* 73, note.

50. Waldron, *Nonsense,* 69.

51. R.K. Woetzel, *The Nuremberg Trials in International Law,* London, 1962, 274.

52. Woetzel, 180.

53. Woetzel, 181–82, n. 14.

54. Woetzel, 189.

55. See James W. Nickel, *Making Sense of Human Rights,* University of California, 1987.

56. Nickel, 181. The Text of the Declaration is at 181–86.

57. David Little, "Human Rights," in J.F. Childress and J. Macquarrie, *A New Dictionary of Christian Ethics,* London, 1986, 279.

58. Cf. John Mahoney, *The Making of Moral Theology,* Oxford, 1987, 113–14.

59. Cf. Roger Scruton, "The Ideology of Human Rights," in idem, *The Politics of Culture,* Manchester, 1981, 205–09.

60. Margaret Macdonald, "Natural Rights," in Melden, 54–55.

61. Nickel, 18.

62. R. Dworkin, "Rights as Trumps," in Waldron, *Theories,* 165.

63. J.L. Mackie, "Can There Be a Right-Based Moral Theory?" in Waldron, *Theories,* 176.

64. R. Harrison, *Bentham,* London, 1983, 94.

65. Mackie, in Waldron, *Theories,* 178.

66. Paul Sieghart, *The Lawful Rights of Mankind,* Oxford, 1986, x.

67. Waldron, *Theories,* 2–3.

68. Waldron, *Theories,* 11.

69. Waldron, *Theories,* 18–19.

70. Dworkin, *Rights as Trumps,* in Waldron, *Theories,* 166.

71. Waldron, *Theories,* 19–20.

72. Alasdair MacIntyre, *After Virtue,* London 1981, 67.

73. Cf. Waldron, *Theories,* 20.

74. L.W. Sumner, *The Moral Foundation of Rights,* Oxford, 1987, 96.

75. Burke, *Reflections,* 182–83.

16

The Church, Morality, and Public Policy

Leslie Griffin

Ethics is the keynote of recent United States political discourse, with the morality of individual politicians explored in microscopic detail. While many commentators laud the public's rising interest in moral conduct from their representatives, other analysts worry that "there is a danger that some will suffer because the ethicists go too far."[1] The latter concern is that a preoccupation with the personal morality of politicians may inhibit attentive wrestling with broader questions of public policy and public well-being.

The relationship of personal ethics to political office is a complex one, fully worthy of serious scholarly as well as popular debate. We usually think of personal morality as private, but in fact it often has public repercussions. For example, personal financial arrangements with a friend or family member may at some point influence the politician's recorded vote. In addition, personal morality in political ethics also extends to the assessment of the politician's individual choices about public policy, yet this subject is frequently excluded from the current debate. We need reminders that ethical reflection on politics, and ethical analysis of the morality of politicians, is inadequate if it fails to assess the criteria by which politicians make legislative choices about public policy.

Unfortunately, political scientists, philosophers and politicians have long disagreed not only over the standards appropriate to the individual politician's vote, but even about whether or not politicians can be moral. Even when he or she restricts the range of discussion to one religious tradition such as Christianity, the ethicist quickly discovers that the tradition offers different—indeed conflicting—interpretations of the morality of the individual politician. A central concern is that political practice connects Christians to certain deeds which appear morally questionable (e.g. concealing the truth or lying, deceiving the public, employing force, executing criminals, declaring war, etc.). Because of this, portions of the Christian tradition recommend that Christians remain separate from politics, lest their loyalty to Jesus Christ be corrupted by the immoral demands of political power. Other Christians recognize that responsible moral agents "dirty their hands" in politics, and urge them to perform immoral actions for the common good. Traditional Roman Catholic interpretations of political morality have tended to justify political office-holding (at least for those not of clerical or religious status) and to assert the possibility of good and right moral choices in the political arena. Yet even in recent Catholic writings, especially on specific topics such as abortion, there is disagreement about where one draws the line to limit the politician's acts.

Given such divisions of opinion among Christians, ecumenical approaches to political morality become difficult to conceptualize, let alone to identify or enact. If one searches for some compromise position, some middle ground among the different Christian options, one runs the risk of devaluing the prophetic voices of Christianity, or of being too optimistic about the existence of a political ethics. Thus compromise cannot be identified as the best or sole political option available to Christians.

Nonetheless, there are reasons to value an ethic of compromise for the individual politician. In this essay, I will argue that a review of Roman Catholic theological ethics and of American political experience provides grounding for a positive assessment of compromises as morally good choices available to politicians. Yet such an overview will also remind us that there are limits to compromise. Since Roman Catholic thought has been more sympathetic to the morality of compromise than other elements of the Christian tradition, I will focus on contemporary Catholic contributions to a theory of compromise for the individual politician. Here the theological ethics of Richard McCormick will provide the foundation for a contemporary theological ethics of compromise.

MODERN CATHOLIC SOCIAL TEACHING

An obvious starting point for those interested in Catholic interpretations of the role of the individual politician in public policy is modern Catholic social teaching. While there are many features of that century-long tradition which merit our attention, three features of it are pertinent here. First, in *Pacem in Terris,* John XXIII describes the interconnected morality of the public and private spheres: "the individual representatives of political communities cannot put aside their personal dignity while they are acting in the name and interest of their countries; and that they cannot therefore violate the very law of their being, which is the moral law."[2] In Catholic social thought, the division of a politician's personal morality from his or her public morality is nonsensical, for in both realms she or he is subject to the moral demands of the natural law. The tradition is emphatic that there are ethical standards for politicians and appears suspicious of claims that the political arena suspends or overrides traditional moral judgments.

Second, in Catholic social teaching (in contrast e.g. to Catholic sexual ethical thought) the hierarchical magisterium has formulated a general framework of norms and principles for social life, while at the same time respecting political, economic, historical and cultural differences among peoples of every nation. The church has been careful not to offer solutions of "universal validity"[3] which disregard individual differences. Nor has it wished to usurp areas of lay competence (the technical aspects of economics, political science, etc.); instead, the laity are encouraged to apply the church's teaching to their specific circumstances. These features result in a style of social ethics which is inductive, able to learn from concrete experiences in circumscribed settings.

That style at times translates into substantive changes in Catholic social thought. For example, it was John Courtney Murray's experience of constitutional separation of church and state in the United States which led him to reexamine the magisterial formulations condemning such separation of Leo XIII and Pius XII. Murray's work culminated in the new identification of a right to religious freedom in *Dignitatis Humanae* at the Second Vatican Council. In a more recent instance of this process, some commentators now claim the economic experience of U.S. capitalism as the source of the newly-minted "right to economic initiative" lauded in John Paul II's *Sollicitudo Rei Socialis.*[4]

A third theme of Catholic social teaching is that democracy emerges after the Second World War.[5] People learn from the war, Pius XII argues, that they want to control their own destinies. Paul VI pursues this theme in *Octogesima Adveniens,* and identifies two aspirations as central to persons in the modern world: the aspirations to equality and participation. Themes of democracy and participation reinforce the inductive methodology of the tradition noted above.

There is good reason to argue, then, that in Catholic social ethics there is a strong mandate for the careful perusal of the political experience of people in different nations. The inductive style and the centrality of participation ground such a warrant. In addition, however, Catholic social thought reminds its readers that ethical conduct is possible and obligatory for politicians, and challenges those who would reject moral requirements in the political arena.

With such warrants in place, Catholic social teaching can be seen to mandate some attention to contemporary American political life as a source for its political ethics. It is to an overview of that experience that I now turn.

POLITICAL EXPERIENCE IN THE UNITED STATES

While there are many features of American political life that could be noted here, in this section I will highlight three features which pose sharp challenges to political ethics. Such an overview can contribute to some initial identification of norms to guide the conduct of the politician.

1. *There is reason to question a separate morality for politicians.* Polls suggest that many Americans are critical of their leaders for failing to uphold certain moral standards. Sexual and financial conduct receives close scrutiny, and often the winning or holding of political office depends on passing ethical review. Codes of ethics multiply as citizens and legislators try to insure some type of accountability.

Many Americans are skeptical of this new interest in ethics, and argue that it prevents good government. Yet behind the popular dissatisfaction with politicians is an important ethical argument. That insight is well expressed in Sissela Bok's moral philosophical analysis of *Lying.*[6] Bok argues that in order to understand the ethics of lying, it is essential to view the lie from the *perspective of the deceived* as well as from the *perspective of the liar.* Bok's point is that we tend to discover few reasons to oppose our own lies, which are told to forward our own purposes. Yet we can envision many reasons to limit the lies told to us by others.

Because the perspective of the deceived gives one a broader insight into the ethics of lying, Bok advocates a test of publicity for lies. She argues that a "moral principle must be capable of public statement and defense,"[7] and recommends that one consult "the collective perspective of reasonable persons seen as potentially deceived."[8] To meet the publicity test, potential liars must subject their own decisions not only to conscience and to the judgment of their peers, but also to the wide public, to "persons of all allegiances,"[9] especially to those who will be critical of the decision. Bok is thus suspicious of lies, and identifies a general presumption against them. Yet she does not exclude all lies. Lies are sometimes justified, but must be committed to a process of judgment and review.

Bok devotes a chapter of her book to "Lies for the Public Good." In politics, the usual excuses for lying are magnified by appeals to public interest. Now one can pretend to lie for the public good, or for altruism, or as a sacrifice for the nation. Such "noble lies" have a long history, but

Bok vigorously warns against them. Here again she urges the test of publicity. In politics, publicity means that the practices of the government must be subject to broad public discussion. This is especially true if some deceptive practices are going to be practiced by the government. Bok concludes: "only those deceptive practices which can be openly debated and consented to in advance are *justifiable* in a democracy."[10]

Democracy is also a key theme in Dennis Thompson's analysis of political ethics. In his book *Political Ethics and Public Choice* he points to the "mutual dependency of democracy and ethics."[11] Thompson shows how democracy changes the classical interpretation of the morality of the individual politician, and vitiates a dirty hands approach to political ethics. No longer can we think of rulers as princes and kings who perform immoral actions in secrecy. Instead, democracy changes this perception of the political leader: "Because democratic officials are supposed to act with the consent of citizens . . . they are not uniquely guilty in the way that the problem in its traditional form presumes."[12] The result is that the politician cannot be judged alone, by a separate standard: ". . . as long as officials are assumed to act with the democratic approval of citizens, officials cannot be burdened with any greater responsibility than citizens."[13]

Thompson thus changes the focus from the *dirty hands* of one politician to the *many hands* responsible in a democracy. He shows that the politician must maintain accountability to the general public, but also that citizens must share responsibility. Bok cautions against a separate political ethic to cover lying. Her reminder of the perspective of the deceived gives form to the intuitions of those who sense that politicians should not live by a separate ethical standard. From the experience of suspicion of the morality of politicians comes a cautionary norm. Politicians must put themselves in the perspective of the voter and subject their decisions to the test of publicity and to democratic participation.

2. *Democratic politics in the United States is characterized by pluralism in values, beliefs and attitudes.* Political life in any setting brings with it "tragic choices"[14] because of scarcity of resources. When all needs cannot be met because of scarcity of goods, societies employ different criteria to guide decision-making, and to make hard choices among competing goods. Democracy brings with it diversity of opinion about such choices, and pluralism complicates the decision-making process still further. The test of publicity requires that all voices be heard. Yet it is difficult to base political agreements on diversity of opinion and value.

The bitter struggle over abortion in the United States is a constant reminder of American pluralism. Fundamental perspectives on the human person undergird the arguments of opposing camps. Similar disagreements mark our discussions of social justice and human rights. The ethical question becomes: Is it responsible to support one moral position, and yet accept and respect another's commitment to very different values? The political question becomes: Can laws and lawmakers represent their constituencies while still recognizing pluralism and remaining faithful to their own moral judgments?

3. *Experience suggests that compromise is a constructive response to pluralism. Yet, the existence of compromise contributes to persons' moral skepticism about politics and politicians.* Often politicians split the difference, or agree on a middle ground, even if personally committed to other positions. In his detailed study of the decision-making processes of the United States Senate, Barry Seltser concludes:

> Our examination has basically supported the traditional claim that compromise is the heart and soul of American politics. The nature of political action requires it; the institutions of American politics cannot function without it; the complexity of the legislative process mandates it; and the nature of political language is built upon it.[15]

Dennis Thompson's shift from a traditional theory of dirty hands to democratic dirty hands is accompanied by a recognition that public officials are frequently involved in "making marginal choices" with "mixed moral results" leading to "only incremental change." He concludes: "Officials *compromise* more than they *agonize*."[16]

Even though compromise pervades the American political system, its ethical status is uncertain. There are grounds for moral skepticism about compromise, since legislators appear to relinquish some commitment to fundamental principles or beliefs when they compromise. On the other hand, moral praise for compromise emerges when it is viewed as a way of respecting pluralism and diversity, or when it resolves and pacifies serious disruptions of social and political life. The perplexing issue becomes whether or not there are criteria or norms by which one can distinguish good compromises from bad.

Guido Calabresi's treatment of *Roe v. Wade* in *Ideals, Beliefs, Attitudes and the Law*[17] illustrates the dilemma of compromise. In a chapter entitled "When Ideals Clash," he explores the diverse values supported by opposing sides in the abortion controversy. Calabresi argues that when two groups identify conflicting values (here the right to life and the right to equality), then compromise solutions are required which show respect for both sides of the discussion. It is dangerous for laws to dismiss one side of the debate, and to reject an opponent's moral premises.[18] When values conflict:

> We must admit that what needs to be done is something that we
> wish not to do, but cannot avoid doing. We must regret deeply,
> that given the existing, irremediable conflict between two fun-
> damental sets of values, we must inevitably give more weight to
> one than the other, much as we hate to weaken either. Only in
> this way are we *all,* to some extent, shouldering the responsibil-
> ity. When, instead, we deny that anything of value is being
> sacrificed and say that the losing belief is one to which our polity
> gives no weight, we are adding significantly to the loss of the
> losers.[19]

Calabresi concedes that these solutions are not usually admired by
staunch defenders of principle, by the "pure holders of a metaphysic and
belief."[20] Yet, they offer a special advantage in a pluralistic society in
which "most believers of one metaphysic feel strong tugs toward other
sets of beliefs. . . . The recognition of the different values in conflict, then,
mirrors our own internal conflict. Like the society, *we want to have it
both ways.*"[21] For Calabresi, then, compromise must incorporate two sets
of values.

Yet abortion shows that such compromises cannot always be
reached. Numerous middle ground solutions to the abortion dilemma
have been proposed. Moreover, polls suggest that a majority of Americans have espoused some middle ground position which both opposes
abortion and supports a woman's right to choose (an illustration of Calabresi's point? or an immoral compromise?). Yet the discussion remains
polarized, with no end and no agreement in sight, and with refusal to
compromise a source of ongoing division. Some understanding of when
it is appropriate and inappropriate to seek some middle ground is needed.

Seltser reports that senators describe their own refusals to compromise as matters of *principle,* which cannot be compromised (and use such
language most frequently about abortion). Seltser rejects such an interpretation of principles, and warns against employing principles too
readily in politics. He argues that appeals to principle as absolute norms
which prohibit any compromise are mistaken. For principles are often
unclear, or intolerant, or imprecise, offer "poor guides to action"[22] or
come into conflict with other principles. Seltser prefers an approach to
political ethics which sets appropriate limits to compromise. He identifies
four criteria by which the politician can judge compromises:

> I. The representative must represent a range of interests. Such
> interests should be paramount in justifying compromises, and

the *broader* interests have a prima facie claim to recognition over the narrower ones.

II. Concern for consequences to others must be the primary factor in political compromises.

III. Compromises should be progressive, opening up the possibility for future compromises and agreement, and for the resolution of underlying problems.

IV. In cases where moral or political principles are violated by compromise, the compromise is illegitimate.[23]

As examples of criterion four, Seltser lists fundamental constitutional provisions (e.g. federalism) or substantive principles (opposition to genocide) or due process of law, which must never be overridden.

The criteria remain general enough that they may be difficult to apply. Yet for Seltser, such difficulty is the price Americans pay for diversity. Drawing lines to limit human conduct is difficult, as is coming to agreement amidst pluralism. Such is the work necessary to democratic government.

The last criterion of Seltser, of course, poses certain difficulties, since one of the unresolved questions is at what point one must say no to compromise. Seltser himself acknowledges the problem: we continue to respect the integrity of some persons who will not compromise. "Perhaps we are afraid that our political life . . . will not provide us with such opportunities for heroism; as a result, we all too eagerly are potential dupes for such claims. Because we possess no objective standard to identify when integrity is truly at stake, our gullibility may let us settle for too little, while our skepticism may make us demand too much."[24] A positive moral assessment of compromise—one which incorporated limits to compromise—might help to increase our understanding of the integrity of the politician, might enable us to see heroism in the compromises undertaken by the legislator.

Compromises contribute to persons' suspicions about the moral integrity of politicians. Yet in a democracy failure to compromise may dismiss moral beliefs represented in a pluralistic society. One response to this situation is to be clear about when compromise is appropriate and inappropriate. From this overview, certain tentative guidelines for the politician's morality have arisen. First, politics must be practiced from the perspective of the citizen as well as the politician. Second, departures from standard morality require justification and explanation and must be submitted to public debate. Third, the compromises of politicians can be viewed as morally good actions. In particular, they are means of respecting diverse moral commitments in a pluralistic society. However, it is important to set moral limits to compromise. Among these limits are that such actions should serve the common good, serve unity rather than division, and lead toward resolution in the future.

American political experience, then, is one source of insight into some initial norms for the politician. For further guidance, I turn now to theological interpretations of the morality of compromise.

THEOLOGICAL PERSPECTIVES ON COMPROMISE

Compromise and Moral Dilemmas

One argument which offers some theological support to a positive assessment of the morality of compromise is Edward Santurri's work on moral dilemmas, *Perplexity in the Moral Life*. The book's basic question is whether to interpret moral dilemmas as questions of limited knowledge or as genuine dilemmas. In a genuine dilemma, all choices available to the agent are morally wrong. "A moral dilemma is a situation in which it actually is the case (rather than merely seems to be the case) that a moral transgression is unavoidable. Thus, to acknowledge the existence of a genuine moral dilemma would be to rule out *in principle* the possibility of finding an unequivocal moral solution to the problem."[25] On the other hand, moral dilemmas may not exist, and may be due instead to our lack of adequate knowledge to resolve the problem. Santurri's study has obvious implications for the political problem of dirty hands, because some elements of the Christian tradition interpret political choices—especially compromise choices—as examples of real dilemmas and not of the limits to our knowledge.

Santurri's careful and complex book assesses the philosophical and theological responses to this problem and explores Christian presuppositions about the moral epistemology vs. moral dilemma debate. The author suggests that an assessment both of Thomistic natural law theory and of theological voluntarism renders the moral dilemmas thesis problematic. In the former tradition, God's ability and power in creation would be undermined by belief in moral dilemmas; in the latter tradition, "accepting the existence of dilemmas would mean attributing incoherence to the divine will, thereby admitting God's practical irrationality."[26] Santurri's conclusion is that in the Christian tradition, the "burden of proof" rests with the perplexity rather than the knowledge theory.

In his conclusion, Santurri is careful to assess the moral status of the agent's choices in conflict situations. He resists interpretations of such choices as "tragic," preferring the language of moral "regret." He insists that

> ... acknowledging the appropriateness of moral regret in conflict situations does not require acknowledging further that the agent has violated some binding moral obligation. Of course, when moral regret is appropriate, this fact always attests to the sacrifice of some moral value. *But the loss of a moral value or a moral good does not imply the doing of a moral wrong. To assume otherwise is to confuse the categories of the moral good and the moral right.*[27]

Santurri gives the example of "deceiving a corrupt legislator" to bring about just social legislation, as an example of a morally right choice in which there may be moral loss, but not tragedy.

Santurri concedes (in an argument reminiscent of Seltser) that such a theory necessitates difficult decision-making, "increased ethical reflection" on the part of the believer. Santurri's strong conclusion is an important one for theories of compromise. "Most important, if my assessments are correct, then the Christian believer, at any rate, will need to assume that a moral truth is always available for the resolutions of moral conflicts, no matter how intractable those conflicts may appear to be."[28]

Some theological warrant, then, is given for a theory of compromise which recognizes *moral loss* and *moral regret* as part of political life, but which refuses to view compromise as requiring a *moral wrong*. Therefore, positive moral assessments can attach to an ethic of compromise. Theological support is provided as well for a commitment of Christians to sustained ethical reflection and to the ongoing quest for resolution of conflicts of value.

Catholic Contributions to the Morality of Compromise

Theologians and ethicists can also find in the Thomistic natural law tradition described by Santurri some history of making judgments about the morality of compromise. Certain characteristics of Roman Catholic ethics allow it to accept compromise in specific cases. Its natural law foundation insists that politics must be governed by ethical criteria and that Catholics are never under moral obligation to perform morally evil acts. In the past, Catholic casuistry helped to specify the demands of the natural law, and developed criteria and principles by which one could decide whether or not to compromise.

A number of contemporary Catholic writers share this basic perspective, which accepts political life as a locus of moral activity. They support theories which allow some compromise, and yet differ about how to place limits on it. A theory of compromise is at the heart of the general ethical theory of Catholic moral theologian Charles Curran, who states: "From one viewpoint, the act is good because it is the best that one can do. However, from the other aspect the act is wrong and shows the presence of sin in the given situation."[29] Curran thus maintains the Catholic concern for good actions. Yet Curran's reminder that "In the face of the sinful situation man must do the best he can"[30] is also reminiscent of dirty hands categories of thought, in which the situation may place some limitation on the moral choice available to the politician. The full implications of Curran's theory of compromise for political ethics are not made explicit, since it is applied primarily to questions of sexual ethics. Yet its emphasis on sin leaves uncertain the morality of the politician's choices and the status of the politician's dirty hands.

The philosopher Germain Grisez establishes certain limits which politicians must never transgress.[31] Specific basic norms are inviolable, and certain compromises (especially in areas such as abortion and nuclear deterrence) are not permitted. However, on other issues, compromise is morally acceptable to Grisez. Thus Grisez offers an ethical theory which allows compromise but which contains some built-in limits.

At the heart of Grisez's theory is his assertion that agents must not act directly against basic goods. Here he opposes the proportionalist reasoning represented by Curran and by Richard McCormick. Because the taking of an innocent human life acts against a basic good, direct abortion is always prohibited. So too are systems of nuclear deterrence, for they target innocent civilians.

On the subject of abortion, Grisez opposes those who believe that public officials can in good conscience choose to fund abortion. He states: "Support of public abortion funding is not simply a case of law and public policy. It is a personal moral act whose object is direct abortion."[32] A limit to compromise emerges. Catholic thought (and basic moral principles) do not allow public officials to support abortion in public policy. Grisez rejects the Cuomo approach (of private opposition but public support) to this question as a confusion of morality's demands. He rejects as well the employment of the traditional Catholic principle of cooperation for this case.

In Catholic moral theology, cooperation meant "concurrence with another person in an act that is morally wrong."[33] The tradition distinguished between formal and material cooperation. Formal cooperation with evil was never permitted, but material cooperation was allowed when one had a proportionate reason for so acting. Decisions about whether an action is permitted, once it is defined as material rather than formal cooperation, depend upon the discernment of what "proportionate reason" means. The discussion of material cooperation establishes criteria which help one to decide if the cooperation is permitted.

Grisez's conclusion in the abortion case is: "since it is wrong to want abortions done, it is wrong to want them done by means of public funding."[34] Those who promote abortion are *not* "cooperators" but "prime moral agents,"[35] and therefore morally culpable. In a footnote on the principle of cooperation, Grisez rejects the use of the principle for such political cases. In the tradition, he argues, the principle applied to employees under the command of superiors, and not to individuals who possess power in government.

In a book written with John Finnis and Joseph Boyle, Grisez pursues an analysis of legislators and nuclear deterrence. In chapter thirteen, the authors assess the responsibilities of individual lawmakers who themselves reject deterrence as immoral. The negative norms are clear: "Everyone's fundamental responsibility is not to choose or do anything which itself adopts, participates in, or supports that public act or any of the subordinate acts with which it is constituted and sustained. For the public act includes an unacceptable proposal: to kill innocents in city swaps and/or final retaliation."[36] The member of Congress must not vote for proposals to support or fund the deterrent. Yet, the member could vote for an omnibus bill, which includes some provisions for the deterrent, if he or she cannot remove these provisions and if "the bill's other provisions legitimately promote some aspect(s) of the common good."[37] In that case the deterrent provisions are viewed as a side-effect. Nor are politicians under obligation to oppose the deterrent at first opportunity. Moreover, Grisez et al. add that such members could vote for a "deterrence-stabilizing weapon" in order to prevent the weakening of the deterrent. "In doing so, they would not be choosing the deterrent but presupposing its existence, which they regard as immoral."[38] Citizens, for their part, can vote for candidates who support deterrence, especially when other candidates back other immoral policies. Voters are not morally connected with all the positions of a candidate.

There is moral advice as well for those who do not view the deterrent as evil. These persons are wrong. Yet "counselling the lesser evil" to them (which is in fact "dissuading from the greater evil") is allowed, even encouraged.[39] In this case, they should be urged to support a strong and effective system of deterrence, rather than a weak one. Supporting nuclear deterrence is wrong. But if one is committed to nuclear deterrence, it is better to support an effective rather than an ineffective system.

In both cases, the negative prohibitions on conduct are easier to define than the positive obligations. Yet individual persons do possess positive obligations to promote human life and well-being, which depend on the circumstances of their lives.

The difference between the treatment of abortion funding and nuclear deterrence funding is not treated explicitly by Grisez. There are features of his ethical theory (such as directness, proximity, etc.) which might help one to judge what the difference is. Yet the question remains: What distinguishes compromise on abortion from other compromises, especially from compromises on nuclear deterrence? Is one permitted to "counsel the lesser evil" to advocates of abortion? Is there a compromise position on abortion which respects Catholic principles but also heeds the voices raised in support of the morality of the pro-choice position? A Catholic theory of compromise which could deal more consistently with the question of abortion would be better able to meet our initial criteria of openness to the perspective of the other and respect for pluralism.

The theological ethics of Richard McCormick possesses a number of characteristics which equip it to deal more ably with questions of compromise. These traits also provide further insight into the morality of the individual politician.

One important component of McCormick's political ethics is his theory of law as it relates to public policy and morality. McCormick roots this concept in the writings of Thomas Aquinas and John Courtney Murray, and concludes from them that law is not required to address all issues of personal morality. Instead, laws must be enforceable, and all matters of private morality are not enforceable. Americans learned from the failure of prohibition that all moral issues cannot be legislated. "Morality can translate into public policy only if it survives the test of feasibility."[40]

The feasibility test is used by McCormick to address specific questions of public policy. In the sphere of reproductive technology, McCormick criticizes the morality of third-party participation, opposing AID and donor IVF. Yet he acknowledges that in the United States a law against such practices would not be feasible. On the other hand, there is good reason to believe that laws against surrogate motherhood are feasible. In the matter of abortion, McCormick argues that "an absolutely prohibitive law on abortion is not enforceable."[41] An absolutely prohibitive law defines human life as commencing at the moment of conception and outlaws all abortions, including the life of the mother, rape and incest cases. Clearly, McCormick argues, laws prohibiting abortion from the moment of conception are not feasible, since they could not be enforced.

McCormick notes that Mario Cuomo appropriately used the language of feasibility in his speech at Notre Dame: "One may disagree with Cuomo's political assessment of feasibility in our times. One cannot, however, disagree with his criterion."[42]

At the same time, law is not without moral concerns. "Law, or public policy, has an inherently moral character due to its rootage in existential human ends (goods). The welfare of the community cannot be unrelated to what is judged to be promotive or destructive to the individual."[43] Laws must serve moral ends. Yet they cannot legislate all aspects of morality.

A second component of McCormick's ethical theory is his distinction between principles and the application of principles. McCormick warns that the statement of principles is in itself difficult; it is easy to confuse applications of principles with principles. This is due to "the close relationship of the two and the very malleability of the concepts."[44] The danger occurs when "The changeable is taken to be unchangeable, the contingent to be abiding, the formulation to be the substance."[45] When this occurs, applications of principles become mistaken for principles, and they appear to be beyond challenge to many members of the church.

McCormick argues that such confusion is present in the formulation "no direct killing of the innocent," which we have already identified as a cornerstone of Grisez's writings about abortion and nuclear deterrence. Some supporters of the consistent ethic of life identify "no direct killing of the innocent" as the ethic's fundamental principle, which undergirds the prohibition against abortion, or against killing of noncombatants in warfare. However, McCormick asserts that "no direct killing of the innocent" is not a principle: "I suggest that the presumption against taking human life is the substance or principle and 'no direct taking of innocent human life' is a kind of formulation-application."[46] Those who center the consistent ethic of life on "no direct killing of the innocent," then, may be misstating the principle. On the subject of abortion, McCormick identifies the basic principle as "human life, as a basic human good, may be taken only when such taking is, all things considered, the only life-saving and life-serving option available."[47] Moral agents, concedes McCormick, will disagree over certain applications of this principle.

A third component of McCormick's theological ethics is an element that we have seen present in the American political experience—pluralism.[48] McCormick (like Seltser) values diversity and respects pluralism, not only in society, but also in the church. Vatican II was a major contributor to pluralism in the church. It fostered an ecumenical spirit in which

Catholics began to appreciate the worth of Christian commitments other than their own. But Vatican II fostered pluralism within Catholicism as well. For it disbanded the teaching/learning dichotomy of the Vatican I church, as the church moved to value the insights and contributions of lay Catholics to the church.

McCormick identifies pluralism as especially important to the field of moral theology. Many in the magisterium fear pluralism in moral matters, and advocate a system of moral reasoning which places certain absolute limits on human conduct. In particular, as we have seen, McCormick opposes the rigid formulation of principles by the Catholic magisterium, and defends the ability of Catholics to apply principles. In Catholicism, then, McCormick finds room for acceptance of pluralism about concrete moral norms, moral methodology, as well as the status of magisterial teaching. Here McCormick differs from Grisez, who views certain magisterial formulations as unchanging. By respecting pluralism in the moral life, McCormick encourages the role of the individual decision-maker and the discernment of the individual believer.

Fourth, undergirding McCormick's treatment of political ethics is his use of a "proportionalist" approach to moral norms. As in the principles/application of principles discussion, much of the debate over proportionalism has focused on the meaning of direct and indirect intention. McCormick treats this question at length in his 1973 lecture *Ambiguity in Moral Choice*. His use of the word "ambiguity" is appropriate for our discussion of compromise, for it captures the sense of moral ambivalence that we have about the limited nature of our accomplishments.

In a later commentary on *Ambiguity in Moral Choice,* McCormick acknowledges the finitude and sinfulness which characterize human choice. For human persons, "The good they achieve is often at the expense of the good left undone or the evil caused."[49] Then McCormick poses the question quite sharply:

> Theological compromise with evil has always been an uneasy, fragile thing; for Christians know deep in their hearts and down their pulses that their Lord and Master did not hesitate to demand of them that they swim upstream, that their world view, profoundly stamped by the proleptic presence of the eschatological kingdom, be countercultural, that they suffer at times in dumb, uncomprehending silence and trust. It is a risky venture, therefore, for a Christian to deliberate about the evil he may rightfully do as he attempts to shape his life in love of Christ and the neighbor God's Christ redeemed. But that is precisely what

that discussion is all about. How do we come to terms with unavoidable evil?[50]

In his development of a proportionalist method in moral theology, McCormick rejects a physicalist reading of direct and indirect. As Richard Sparks notes, "Proportionalists suggest that no act viewed in itself —killing a human being, telling a falsehood, having an orgasm, cutting one's fallopian tube or vas deferens—yields an absolute moral conclusion."[51] Instead, as McCormick explains in this brief summary of proportionalism in *The Critical Calling:*

> . . . causing certain disvalues (ontic, nonmoral, premoral evils) in our conduct does not ipso facto make the action morally wrong. The action becomes morally wrong when, all things considered, there is no proportionate reason justifying it.[52]

In *Ambiguity in Moral Choice,* McCormick explains what he means by "proportionate reason." "Proportionate reason means three things: (a) a value at least equal to that sacrificed is at stake; (b) there is no less harmful way of protecting the value here and now; (c) the manner of its protection here and now will not undermine it in the long run."[53]

For proportionalists, then, attention turns to the moral agent, whose intention is crucial. For the politician, there are not certain acts that are by definition ruled out in advance. Such an approach emphasizes the judgment of the individual and is part of moral pluralism in the church. It also, however, makes it more difficult to discern when to draw the line against compromise.

The approach is not unlike that taken by Bok. Lying is not always wrong, nor is it morally neutral. There is a presumption against it. Lying requires explanation, defense—proportionate reason. For the proportionalists, so too with other acts of human beings.

A fifth component of McCormick's thought, which provides specific guidance for our topic, is his use of the principle of cooperation. McCormick applies the principle to Agnes Mary Mansour's connection to the Medicaid funding of abortion. McCormick argues (contra Grisez) that not all funding of abortion is by definition formal cooperation. Instead, participation in funding abortions need not involve formal cooperation, if the agent has proportionate or "sufficiently grave" cause for his or her cooperation. It is interesting to note that in the Mansour case, McCormick believes proportionate reason was not present because of the "disproportion of disvalues to values."[54] Yet, proportionate reason must enter into the assessment of the morality of action by the individual, and so funding cannot be ruled out in advance.

So far, then, methodological concerns (proportionalism, principles/ application of principles direct and indirect and cooperation) combine with McCormick's theory of law and his vision of pluralism to provide an ethic for the politician which allows some cooperation with evil, some compromise under limited circumstances. Such actions can be viewed as morally good if they are undertaken with proportionate reason. Yet one further element in McCormick's writings strengthens and refines his theory of compromise. This is his insistence on civil conversation about moral issues. Such discussion mandates *respect for the convictions of the other* as well as *witness to one's own point of view.*

Both of these components are evident in McCormick's writings on abortion. In a 1978 essay in *America* which proposes rules for the abortion debate, McCormick advocates that persons from different perspectives identify areas of agreement between them, admit to weaknesses in their own positions, and represent the other side fairly.[55] In a more recent essay which seeks to develop a middle ground on abortion, McCormick reminds readers "to examine perspectives foreign to their own."[56] Moreover, he advises those engaged in the abortion discussion that "*Whenever a discussion becomes heated, it should cease* ... shouting sessions on abortion only alienate and divide the shouters."[57] Proper perspective is kept, then, through respect for the opponent and the opponent's position.

In the same essay, McCormick states that "*Witness is the most effective leaven and the most persuasive educator concerning abortion.*"[58] In a letter to Mario Cuomo, McCormick commends the governor's use of feasibility as a criterion in legislative decision-making. Yet McCormick also argues that one must work for change. "Hence I have always felt that there is a middle ground between private conviction vs. public passivity: persuasion."[59] Positive obligations, then, accompany the morality of compromise. One must respect the opinion of the other. Yet continued commitment to one's own principles is part of one's obligation. McCormick urges both groups in the discussion to "emphasize what they are for rather than what they are against, and [do] so in action ... putting one's money where one's mouth is can be done at least as effectively (and far more so, I believe) through means other than picketing."[60] What one learns from McCormick, then, is that an ethic of compromise calls for attention to the other's moral perspective as well as to conviction and commitment in pursuing one's own. An illustration of such an approach can be found in McCormick's own participation on public policy boards (such as the Ethical Advisory Board and the American Fertility Society) while representing a minority viewpoint.[61]

It is interesting to note that in these two essays on abortion, both of which offer middle ground positions on abortion, McCormick is reluctant to use the language of compromise. In his 1978 essay, he states: "I do not believe these guidelines call for compromise or abandonment of anyone's moral conviction."[62] In the 1989 essay, McCormick notes that any search for middle ground always runs the danger of an inappropriate lessening of moral commitments. Indeed here he uses the word "compromise" pejoratively, and asserts: "diverting attention to the middle ground is not an invitation to compromise. To attempt to discover what we might agree on is not to forfeit our disagreements."[63]

Yet, as we have seen, the morality of the politician—and thus the resolution of serious issues of public policy—may be served by a more positive assessment of compromise in the life of the politician. While rejecting the terminology of compromise, therefore, McCormick's theological ethics seems to offer a positive ethical assessment of some compromises by politicians. His discussion of dialogue and mutual understanding, his commitment to the resolution of moral dilemmas, and his recognition of the perspective of the other complement those criteria which emerge from American political experience. He adds to our analysis a reminder that persons can remain supportive of their fundamental convictions even in the midst of compromise.

CONCLUSIONS: THE CHURCH, PUBLIC POLICY AND THE MORALITY OF THE POLITICIAN

A theory of compromise in political ethics offers advantages to those who distrust the morality of politicians and yet desire moral action from their representatives. In American experience, pluralism brings the question of compromise into focus, as values conflict in a democracy. In Catholic thought, theological and ethical arguments combine to propose a picture of politicians capable of making moral judgments according to the natural law. In both traditions, reason and reflection can aid the individual to discern whether or not a specific compromise accords with moral standards.

What emerges as central to the analysis of the morality of the politician in both American and Catholic thought is the judgment of the individual legislator. That individual is called to the difficult task of respect for the moral commitments of others. He or she must envision the perspective of the served, work for broad social interests and for the common good. At the same time, he or she must maintain some fidelity to self and to his or her fundamental beliefs. That individual must learn to draw lines and to distinguish good from bad compromises.

The Catholic magisterium has much to teach such a legislator, about moral norms, natural law reasoning, and principles such as cooperation. Yet a focus on the individual politician's moral choices about public policy also instructs the church. In an ethic of compromise, the church is reminded of its own pluralism, and of the tentativeness of its formulation of principles. The church is reminded to listen to the moral arguments of those with whom it disagrees, and to continue the quest for resolution of conflicts of values. An ethic of compromise for individual politicians does not automatically translate into a justification of compromise by the institutional church. Yet it does suggest to all church members that it is praiseworthy to heed the perspective of the other and to let "persons of all allegiances" voice their moral insights.

Notes

1. Richard E. Cohen, "Misjudging the Ethical Boundaries," *National Journal,* May 20, 1989, 1253.

2. In Joseph Gremillion, *The Gospel of Peace and Justice* (Maryknoll: Orbis, 1976) 219, no. 81.

3. Paul VI, *Octogesima Adveniens,* in Gremillion, *The Gospel* 487, no. 4.

4. For such commentaries on *Sollicitudo,* see Kenneth A. Myers, ed., *Aspiring to Freedom: Commentaries on John Paul II's Encyclical 'The Social Concerns of the Church'* (Grand Rapids: Eerdmans, 1988).

5. For a recent treatment of democracy in Catholic social teaching, see Paul Sigmund, "The Catholic Tradition and Modern Democracy," in Leslie Griffin, ed., *Religion and Politics in the American Milieu,* 3–21.

6. Sissela Bok, *Lying: Moral Choice in Public and Private Life* (New York: Vintage, 1978).

7. Ibid. 97.

8. Ibid. 98.

9. Ibid. 103.

10. Ibid. 191.

11. Dennis Thompson, *Political Ethics and Public Choice* (Cambridge: Harvard, 1987) 3.

12. Ibid. 11.

13. Ibid. 22.

14. I take this expression from Guido Calabresi and Philip Bobbitt, *Tragic Choices* (New York: Norton, 1978).

15. *The Principles and Practice of Political Compromise: A Case Study of the United States Senate* (New York: Edwin Mellen, 1984) 234.

16. Thompson, *Political Ethics* 7, my emphasis.

17. Guido Calabresi, *Ideals, Beliefs, Attitudes and the Law* (Syracuse: Syracuse University, 1985).

18. Calabresi argues that this occurred in *Roe v. Wade.*

19. Ibid. 98.

20. Ibid.

21. Ibid., my emphasis.

22. Seltser, *Principles* 233.

23. Ibid. 236, 238, 241, 245.

24. Ibid. 281–82.

25. Edward Santurri, *Perplexity in the Moral Life: Philosophical and Theological Considerations* (Charlottesville: University Press of Virginia, 1987) 2.

26. Ibid. 5.

27. Ibid. 206.

28. Ibid. 211.

29. Curran, *A New Look At Christian Morality* (Notre Dame: Fides, 1968) 172.

30. Ibid. 171.

31. For a complete statement of Grisez's work, see *The Way of the Lord Jesus, Volume One: Christian Moral Principles* (Chicago: Franciscan Herald, 1985).

32. Germain Grisez, "A Critique of Two Theological Papers," *Homiletic and Pastoral Review* 84 (1984) 10.

33. Edwin Healy, *Medical Ethics* (Chicago: Loyola, 1956) 101.

34. Grisez, "Critique" 13.

35. Germain Grisez, "Public Funding of Abortion: A Reply to Richard A. McCormick," *Homiletic and Pastoral Review* 85 (1985) 45.

36. John Finnis, Joseph M. Boyle Jr. and Germain Grisez, *Nuclear Deterrence, Morality and Realism* (Oxford: Clarendon, 1987) 343.

37. Ibid. 345.

38. Ibid. 346.

39. Ibid. 358.

40. McCormick, "Therapy or Tampering? The Ethics of Reproductive Technology," *America* 153 (7 December 1985) 397.

41. McCormick, "Abortion: The Unexplored Middle Ground," *Second Opinion* 10 (1989) 46.

42. McCormick, *The Critical Calling: Reflections on Moral Dilemmas Since Vatican II* (Washington, D.C.: Georgetown University, 1989) 200.

43. McCormick, "Abortion: A Changing Morality and Policy?" in Thomas Shannon, ed., *Bioethics* (Ramsey, NJ: Paulist, 1981) 26.

44. McCormick, "Catholic Moral Theology: Is Pluralism Pathogenic?" in *Critical Calling* 150.

45. Ibid. 149.

46. Ibid. 150.

47. Ibid. 152.

48. McCormick, *Critical Calling,* chaps. 7–8; McCormick, *Health and Medicine in the Catholic Tradition* (New York: Crossroad, 1984), chapter 3.

49. In Richard McCormick and Paul Ramsey, *Doing Evil To Achieve Good* (Chicago: Loyola, 1978) 194–95.

50. Ibid. 195.

51. Richard C. Sparks, "The Storm Over Proportionalism: Choosing the Lesser Evil," *Church* 5 (1989) 12; see also Bernard Hoose, *Proportionalism: The American Debate and Its European Roots* (Washington, D.C.: Georgetown University, 1987).

52. McCormick, *Critical Calling* 134.

53. McCormick, *Doing Evil* 45.

54. McCormick, "Medicaid and Abortion," *Theological Studies* 45 (1984) 717, n. 5. See "The Physician and Teenage Sexuality," in *Critical Calling* 398 for discussion of counselling the lesser evil.

55. McCormick, "Rules for Abortion Debate," *America* 146 (1978) 26.

56. McCormick, "Abortion: The Unexplored," 46.

57. Ibid. 49.

58. Ibid. 47.

59. McCormick, *Critical Calling* 201.

60. McCormick, "Abortion: The Unexplored" 47.

61. McCormick, *Critical Calling,* chapter 11.

62. McCormick, "Rules" 26.

63. McCormick, "Abortion: The Unexplored" 42.

17

Catholic Teaching on War and Peace: The Decade 1979–1989

J. Bryan Hehir

Catholic moralists are indebted to Richard McCormick for many reasons, preeminently for the way in which he has blended knowledge, wisdom and judgment in helping us all absorb, integrate and apply the post-Vatican II developments in moral theology. Proportionally speaking, McCormick has written less on war and peace than on a series of other topics. But the attention he gave to the issues of war and peace in the 1980s was a solid sign that these topics had resurfaced in the wider Catholic community.

Unlike some other conciliar themes, the teaching on war and peace found in *Gaudium et Spes* did not draw immediate attention in the United States. While it did contribute to the debate about conscientious objection during the Vietnam War, and also informed the emergence of a Catholic pacifist community in the 1970s, the principal theological attention to war and peace surfaced in the last decade.

This chapter will examine the decade 1979–1989 as a case study in Catholic thinking on war and peace, particularly on the nuclear question. Using the method of *Gaudium et Spes,* the chapter will first sketch the signs of the times in political-strategic developments, then turn to the moral response found in papal teaching, the pastoral letters and theological analysis. Finally, I will sketch themes which point to the emerging agenda of the 1990s for ethics and strategy.

I. THE SIGNS OF THE TIMES

The Vatican Council, through *Gaudium et Spes,* instructed the whole church—and moralists particularly—to read the signs of the times and interpret them in the light of the gospel.[1] Reading the signs which marked the nuclear debate in the 1980s was not a simple matter. Intellectually and politically the decade stands out in the history of the nuclear age as a time of notable complexity and change.[2] The council taught the church to see its relationship to the world in reciprocal terms; the conviction of *Gaudium et Spes* was that the church should learn from the world and that it had something to teach the world.

The change and complexity of the nuclear debate offered the church an opportunity to enter the public discussion at a moment open to insights and ideas which were neither political nor strategic. In turn the church's commentary helped to shape the public argument. Here I will comment on three signs of the times which created this open moment.

A. Doctrine and Dissent

Although this heading sounds like an introduction to a chapter on *Humanae Vitae,* it in fact has equal relevance to the political-strategic argument about nuclear weapons in the 1980s. The strategic theory which has shaped the U.S. debate about nuclear weapons, nuclear strategy and arms control has the character of a doctrine. There are canonical concepts, rules of argument, recognized authorities and an established orthodoxy.[3] This conceptual framework to guide nuclear policy developed in the 1950s, became established in the official policy of the U.S. government in the 1960s, and has served as the baseline for analysis and debate since then. Terms like "assured destruction," "first and second strike," "crisis stability," and "window of vulnerability" constitute a shared vocabulary even if the participants disagree on conclusions.

A principal sign of the times in the decade of the 1980s was the way the established doctrine came under review and criticism from diverse places. In many ways the orthodoxy weathered the storm and maintains its viability. But in both political and strategic terms the 1980s were a time of deep and dramatic shifts.

Politically, the decade opened as "a new cold war" and it closed with the orthodox opinion holding that the cold war is over. In the area of arms control President Reagan moved from disparaging the idea to signing the first arms reduction treaty in the history of the nuclear relationship. Although Mr. Reagan's conversion on many points provided a fascinating pilgrimage in the 1980s, the longer term impact was surely the appearance of Mikhail Gorbachev's "new thinking" in the Soviet Union.

While these broader changes were taking place, the specifics of the nuclear argument were also in flux. The dissent from the doctrine which had governed both strategy and arms control policy moved to the left and the right of the received opinions. In 1982 four patriarchs of U.S. strategic policy—McGeorge Bundy, George Kennan, Robert McNamara and

Gerard Smith—proposed movement toward a "no first use" policy for the NATO alliance;[4] while the idea had been proposed previously the combined authority and standing of these authors gave this dissent from the doctrine a new edge. Kennan and McNamara pressed the standard consensus in other ways, the former calling for fifty percent reductions in the strategic arsenals (just when the Reagan strategic modernization program was being pressed forward) and the latter arguing that nuclear weapons had no military utility.[5]

These proposals moved left of the doctrine; the premier dissent from the right was President Reagan's proposal of March 1983 for a defensive shield as a method of reversing the nuclear relationship of the superpowers. While the proposal was and continues to be a subject of enormous technical controversy, the point here is simply that it challenged the basic premises of deterrence even as that policy remained the foundation of U.S. security planning.

Indeed the debate about deterrence was the best example of the changing pattern of the nuclear argument in the 1980s. For thirty years deterrence had been the organizing concept of strategic discourse. The discussion had always been about what kind of deterrence, how much was needed to deter, or how to explain the meaning of deterrence to the general public. In the 1980s, the idea of deterrence came under review from the left and the right of the intellectual and political spectrum. In the mainline strategic literature articles appeared with the title "Deterrence Is the Problem"; book length studies appeared asking whether we could "go beyond deterrence."[6] This kind of questioning at the political-strategic level provided both an opening for moral assessment of deterrence, and was itself impacted by the moral arguments being pursued about nuclear strategy and arms control. The substantive issues of doctrine were under reexamination in this decade and the scope of the review was a second sign of the times.

B. The Public Debate

One of the differences of the nuclear debate in the 1980s was not only what was being discussed, but who was speaking. The constituency for the nuclear strategy and arms control argument traditionally had been a small, intensely involved corps of people in the government, in a few public policy institutes and in a select group of universities. The subject they were addressing was of universal concern, but the participants were an aristocracy of planners, intellectuals and policymakers.

The 1980s saw the democratization of the nuclear debate. New participants emerged from the general public. The primary shift of participation was generated by the freeze movement; the importance of the freeze was less its specific proposal and more its method of drawing a broad spectrum of the public into the nuclear argument. Other groups like the Physicians for Social Responsibility introduced a previously unengaged but immensely influential profession into the nuclear arena. They were followed by groups of lawyers, corporate executives, and union leaders.

The effect of the democratization of the debate was not only to enlarge the nuclear argument, but to center certain questions which often remained marginal in the standard strategic literature. Prominent among the "new" questions was the moral problem posed by the nuclear age. When ordinary citizens, unschooled in the arcane logic of the nuclear relationship, were introduced to the nuclear question, the moral issues (i.e. the human significance and human consequence of living under the nuclear threat) were a prominent topic of interest. Because religious organizations had both a broad popular constituency and a capacity to engage the moral questions systematically, they fitted into the new public debate in a unique way.[7]

C. The New Dialogue

The new dialogue of the 1980s was a product of the first two signs of the times. The combination of pluralist views in the professional strategic community and wider public participation in the political arena created the opportunities for dialogue and joint exploration among specialized groups that previously had little contact or common purpose.

One example was the dialogue of religion and science which found new impetus because of the nuclear question. The role of the scientific community in the discovery and development of nuclear weapons, the explicit moral examination which had gone on among scientists about the results of their work and the renewed public interest in the moral meaning of the nuclear age opened scientists to the moral-religious assessment of the nuclear question found in *The Challenge of Peace* and other religious documents of the 1980s.

A second example of the new dialogue was the body of literature, produced on an interdisciplinary basis, examining the relationship of strategic doctrine and ethical analysis. Strategists such as Albert Wohlstetter, Herman Kahn and Joseph Nye and political analysts such as Stanley Hoffmann, Robert Tucker and Bruce Russett addressed the moral dimensions of the nuclear question in detailed fashion. Moralists such as John Langan, Francis Winters, Kenneth Himes and David Hollenbach were read in the political and strategic community. George Weigel's and Michael Novak's dissent from *The Challenge of Peace* became a staple in the political and moral literature.

Neither the religion and science nor the strategy and ethics arguments need to be examined here. The point is simply to highlight that in the period 1979–1989 change in the way people thought about nuclear weapons, changes in who talked about them and changes in the relationship among key actors created a dynamic setting for moral analysis.

II. THE MORAL RESPONSE: THEOLOGY AND NUCLEAR ETHICS

The moral response to the nuclear question in the last decade included papal teaching, episcopal statements and theological reflection. My purpose is not exegesis of these texts but a synthesis of major themes in the Catholic literature.[8]

A. John Paul II: Continuity and Change

The period analyzed in this chapter coincides with the first decade of the papacy of John Paul II. During this time the pope has spoken frequently to the nuclear question using encyclicals, special messages to the United Nations and addresses to the diplomatic corps at the Vatican.[9] While these statements show clear ties to both his predecessors and to the teaching of *Gaudium et Spes,* on this question as on other aspects of the social teaching John Paul II has imprinted his own distinctive style. To some degree the character of his teaching is due to the visibility and urgency the nuclear question assumed in the 1980s, but it is also due to the pope's willingness to enter the nuclear debate with greater specificity than his predecessors. In evaluating John Paul II's position, one can distinguish a basic teaching on the use of force, its application to nuclear weapons, a position on deterrence and a commitment to disarmament.

While this chapter is focused on nuclear policy, it is useful to begin with John Paul II's treatment of the moral character of the use of force. His position is both traditional, and yet a reshaping of the tradition. The traditional position within Roman Catholicism was accurately summarized by John Courtney Murray:

> The church does not look immediately to the abolition of war. Her doctrine still seeks to fulfill its triple function: to condemn war as evil, to limit the evil it entails, and to humanize its conduct as far as possible.[10]

In contrast to this description, John Paul II has emphasized much more the abolition of the use of force than he has the humanization of its use. In a series of statements spanning his pontificate, the pope has declared himself to be an advocate of nonviolence. Two texts exemplify the consistency of this position over a decade. At Drogheda, Ireland, at the very beginning of his ministry, the pope stated his case in personal, emotional terms:

> I join my voice today to the voice of Paul VI and my other predecessors, to the voices of your religious leaders, to the voices of all men and women of reason, and I proclaim, with the conviction of my faith in Christ and with an awareness of my mission, that violence is evil, that violence is unacceptable as a solution to problems, that violence is unworthy of man. Violence is a lie, for it goes against the truth of our faith, the truth of our humanity. Violence destroys what it claims to defend: the dignity, the life, the freedom of human beings.[11]

A decade later in Southern Africa the pope returned to his view of violence and the political process: "Above all . . . you must renounce every form of violence and hatred. Violence only begets further violence. . . . The increase of violence in the world can never be halted by responding with more of the same."[12]

Both statements were made in areas of recurring violence, and in cases where participants have made the argument that only violence can change an unjust situation. The pope has not engaged specific arguments; he simply reaffirms his conviction that nonviolence is the rational and evangelical imperative. He has repeated this position—no recourse to violence even in the face of injustice in the social order—throughout Latin America. While the three situations are not identical by any means, the point here is to highlight the frequency and firmness of the papal position.

The character of these statements raises the question whether this pope has in fact abandoned the principle which allows some use of force to oppose other forms of violence and injustice. The answer is negative, the pertinent text being the 1982 World Day of Peace Message. The context of the statement was important; throughout the NATO alliance large public protests were being mounted in a peace offensive; the U.S. pastoral letter was being drafted and debated; within the ecclesial discussion, papal teaching, in particular the texts from *Pacem in Terris,* were being cited to make a strong case against the use of force. The pope responded by taking the Catholic perspective back to its Augustinian roots: "For Christians know that in this world a totally and permanently peaceful human society is unfortunately a utopia, and that ideologies that hold up that prospect as easily attainable are based on hopes that cannot be realized, whatever the reason behind them."[13]

This assessment of the human condition, reflecting Augustine's view that war is both the result of sin and a remedy for a sinful world, led John Paul to his conclusion:

That is why Christians have no hesitation in recalling that, in the name of an elementary requirement of justice, peoples have a right and even a duty to protect their existence and freedom by proportionate means against an unjust aggressor.[14]

This text, based on Vatican II's *Gaudium et Spes,* reasserts the traditional teaching summarized by Murray above. *Gaudium et Spes* provided narrow but solid legitimation for some use of force. John Paul II, in aligning himself with this position, does not attempt to relate it systematically to his repeated endorsement of a nonviolent posture. The sheer number of papal interventions on a topic—particularly in this papacy— makes it difficult to sustain precise connections among addresses and texts designed for very different audiences. But commentators need to examine the corpus of interventions in terms of coherence and consistency.

One method of interpreting the teaching of John Paul II thus far in his papacy is to highlight the context of his various interventions. In Ireland, Southern Africa and Latin America he is addressing situations of internal conflict in societies. Particularly in Latin America and Southern Africa of the 1970s and 1980s, the pope encountered ecclesial communities where many were convinced that they were facing long-standing conditions of tyranny and injustice which could only be overcome by some use of force. Paul VI had addressed this question in *Progressio Populorum,* had seemed to provide some legitimation of use of force as an *ultima ratio,* and then had drawn back from this position in his address to the Medellín Conference of 1968.

John Paul II's commentary on civil conflict distinguishes between the "just cause" argument and the "just means" question. Since the pope has criticized often and in depth the conditions prevailing in both Latin America and Southern Africa, he is not disputing the just cause argument that prevailing conditions are intolerable for human dignity and ought to be changed. Nevertheless, John Paul II has categorically opposed resort to force as a means of social change. His judgment is not based on an unprincipled pacifist position, but on a conviction that the harm done by violence will be disproportionate to the good achieved, and that it will be the poor and defenseless who suffer the most in these conflicts.[15]

The 1982 World Day of Peace Message speaks to a different context, relations among states. Here the pope envisions situations of aggression where all other means have failed and a state must defend itself against an unjustified attack by another state. John Paul II does not address the question in any detail; he seems satisfied to state the principle that "a duty" to resist aggression exists, and then to let the traditional moral calculus of discrimination and proportionality guide the moral assessment of each case. But one of the cases is the possible use of nuclear weapons: here the pope again enters the debate about moral limits on force.

Following his predecessors from Pius XII to Paul VI, John Paul II does not ask and answer the question whether a nuclear weapon could ever be used.[16] Rather he continually stresses the disproportionate nature of nuclear war. At Hiroshima in 1981: "In the past it was possible to destroy a village, a town, even a country. Now it is the whole planet that has come under threat."[17] Without formulating a detailed judgment, the pope by repeated assertion leaves the impression that nuclear war does not fit the logic of limited use of force.

But this means that John Paul must face the dilemma of deterrence, the policies by which states forestall the use of nuclear weapons by threatening nuclear retaliation. The pope's position on deterrence is well known but much debated. The basic judgment was expressed at the United Nations in 1982: "In current conditions 'deterrence' based on balance, certainly not as an end in itself but as a step on the way toward a progressive disarmament, may still be judged morally acceptable."[18] The debate arises from questions about the pope's intent in this text.

Does this general legitimation of deterrence refer to the specific policies of deterrence pursued by states today? Some commentators question whether the text is meant to justify existing force structures and declaratory policies. Cardinal Casaroli acknowledged in an address in 1983 that the traditional moral principles—presumably the just-war criteria—would be needed to apply the pope's statement to "the actual ways of exercising this deterrence."[19]

Another question about the pope's judgment on deterrence is how his limited legitimation of deterrence corresponds to his clearly overriding moral imperative for the nuclear age: disarmament. In his 1988 address to the diplomatic corps, the pope made his position clear; speaking of nuclear weapons, he said, "In this matter one must move toward total disarmament."[20]

The pope is a nuclear abolitionist. But his radical goal is joined with gradualist means. He does not move from the imperative of total nuclear disarmament as an objective to a position advocating immediate disengagement from the nuclear relationship as his advice to states and citizens. This position has been held in the Catholic debate from Walter Stein and Gordon Zahn in the 1960s to John Finnis, Germain Grisez and Joseph Boyle in the 1980s. The Finnis, Grisez, Boyle book contends that the gradualist position of the pope does not mean an endorsement of existing deterrence strategies. At most, they argue, the pope "affirms no more than that the Catholic Church has not yet clarified and reached firm conclusions on the relevant issues."[21] Furthermore, their argument holds that *if* the pope attended to the "facts about the threats and intentions"[22] embodied in existing deterrence policy, or *if* the traditional principles (including discrimination) were used to apply the papal statement to existing deterrent policies, then a judgment of condemnation would be assured.

Thus far in the debate, the Holy See's position is not that clear-cut. Neither of the propositions advanced by Finnis, Grisez and Boyle seems to me to be persuasive. It is difficult to believe that the pope has spoken frequently on the nuclear question but does not understand the basic facts of the problem. Nor does it seem plausible that Cardinal Casaroli, having both set forth the 1982 papal statement on deterrence and called attention to the traditional principles to be used in applying the text,[23] would then draw back from the conclusion that deterrence should be condemned—if that were the conclusion the Holy See had reached. It may well be the case that the Catholic Church has not reached firm conclusions on all aspects of the deterrence question. But the statements of the 1980s from the Holy See grant a limited legitimacy to the deterrence relationship; it is hardly a ringing endorsement, but it is more than the neutrality on the question which Finnis et al. contend is the Holy See's position.

The limited legitimacy is narrowly drawn. John Paul II is hardly an advocate of deterrence as an adequate policy—morally or strategically. Deterrence "cannot be a reliable basis for security and peace"; it is legitimated as a "transitional" method of regulating the superpower relationship, looking toward a more stable foundation in the future.[24] Those who find in deterrence an answer to the nuclear question cannot claim the pope as an ally. He is even an uncertain ally for most arms control theorists. The pope sees arms control as a means of achieving nuclear disarmament; most advocates of arms control describe it as a method of stabilizing the nuclear relationship, not ending it.

At the close of his first decade in the papacy John Paul II's teaching on war and peace is dynamic and still developing. He has pressed the case for nonviolence as a method of social change; he has categorically ruled out resort to force in situations of internal or domestic conflict; he has acknowledged the right of states to use force as a last resort; he has effectively placed nuclear war beyond the bounds of "limited conflict"; and he has provided a narrow measure of support for deterrence, while demanding that nuclear disarmament be pursued as a realistic and necessary objective.

There are tensions in his teaching which are easy to identify but difficult to resolve. Does he hold to a limited legitimation of "just-war" teaching for states but no legitimacy for "just-revolution" for non-state actors? Will he continue to reduce the legitimacy of a state's right to use force? Has he confronted the problems which arms control advocates find in advocating nuclear disarmament in a world where both states and private groups can produce these weapons?

John Paul II has a developed position on war and peace, but not a finished position. He has already addressed the nuclear question more frequently than any of his predecessors. Both the character of his teaching and the changing nature of the nuclear relationship will require further papal responses to complement the major effort the pope has already undertaken.

B. The Pastoral Letters

Since the beginning of the nuclear age, the dominant voice in the church on issues of war and peace has been the papacy. From Pius XII through John Paul II, papal teaching—along with *Gaudium et Spes*—set the framework and defined the themes of the Catholic inquiry. Theologians analyzed the magisterial texts and in some instances applied them to specific issues, but the dynamic moved from the center of the church outward.

The 1980s are notable, from this perspective, for the appearance of a series of pastoral letters produced by episcopal conferences as different as East Germany, Japan, Holland and Poland. The most discussed letters were those of France, West Germany and the United States, all issued in 1983. These three letters had an ecclesiological, moral, and political significance which made them a central part of the story of the decade.

Ecclesiologically, the pastoral letters were a product of conciliar and post-conciliar initiatives which came to fruition in the 1980s. In the first instance, the fact of episcopal conferences was a product of Vatican II; while forerunners existed (notably the National Catholic Welfare Conference in the United States) the post-conciliar entities had a theological and juridical standing in the church which inevitably gave them a broader capacity for engagement in the public arena.

The episcopal conferences were invited into the public arena by the post-conciliar initiative of Pope Paul VI. In his 1971 apostolic letter, *Octogesima Adveniens,* the pope defined a social role for "the local church" which was not confined to the bishops but surely did not exclude them:

> In the face of such widely varying situations it is difficult for us to utter a unified message and to put forward a solution which has universal validity. Such is not our ambition, nor is it our mission. It is up to Christian communities to analyze with objectivity the situation which is proper to their own country, to shed on it the light of the Gospel's unalterable words and to draw principles of reflection, norms of judgment and directives for action from the social teaching of the church.[25]

This text was an invitation to the local churches to become active agents of social teaching, to be sources of insight, the author of ideas which could move from the edge of the church to the center. The invitation was accepted: the Brazilian hierarchy's human rights ministry in the 1960s and 1970s, the emergence of the theology of liberation throughout Latin America in the same period, and the development of the pastoral letters of the 1980s all testified to the potential of the local churches to be teachers in the social ministry.

Paul VI's invitation highlighted what an economist would call "the comparative advantage" of the local church, what it was best prepared by structure and experience to offer the wider church. The teaching of the papal magisterium must be cast at a general level; its strength lies in its ability to project a vision, to protect principles and values of abiding moral significance and to call the community of the faithful to forms of service and witness in the social arena.

The generality of the teaching points to its utility and its limits. Precisely as a universal message it stresses the catholicity of the church and it defines values and principles to be held by all. But the generality of the teaching leaves it open to either remaining isolated from the places and points of decision in society, or being manipulated by multiple parties claiming legitimation for opposing positions. The comparative advantage of the local church is its capacity to engage the specifics of a social question. Specificity here means the ability to enter the concrete complexity of a problem, and to engage the public discussion by which social policies are shaped and influenced.

Comparing the papal teaching with *The Challenge of Peace* illustrates the potential of the local church. There is a trajectory in the papal teaching from Pius XII to John Paul II which increasingly calls into question the moral legitimacy of using nuclear weapons. The moral argument is made in terms of the principle of proportionality. In sharp contrast to the secular debate, however, there is little specific discussion in the papal literature about whether nuclear use could conceivably be limited. The papal texts stay at a very abstract level.

The Challenge of Peace provides a counterpoint to the papal style. It discusses three kinds of nuclear use and makes a different judgment on each of them. The pastoral letter establishes a sliding scale of moral judgments, ruling out counter-population use absolutely, opposing first-use on the basis of a prudential judgment, and acknowledging a very narrow moral permissibility for second strike, counter-force, retaliation.[26]

It would be surprising to find such specificity in a papal text, but at some level of the church this kind of detailed moral evaluation must take place if we are to address the policy process.

Precisely because the ecclesiological position of the local church allows it entrance into the policy discussion in different countries, the moral analysis of the pastoral letters assumes a different character than papal or conciliar teaching. The assessment of deterrence in both the U.S. and the French letters is quite different from that of *Gaudium et Spes* or John Paul II.

Gaudium et Spes opened the evaluation of deterrence in Catholic teaching, but it did so with little analysis of the elements of deterrence strategy and with an almost neutral evaluation: "Many regard this state of affairs as the most effective way by which peace of a sort can be maintained among nations at the present time."[27] Moral reservations can be deduced from the conciliar text, but there is not a moral judgment made in it. This was in sharp contrast to the severe moral strictures leveled against the arms race by which deterrence is sustained.

The French episcopal letter did not provide an extensive review of deterrence literature, but it did sharply portray the rationale of the French deterrent ("deterrence of the strong by the weak"). It also defined the nature of French policy: "Because of the lack of a diversified means of deterrence, our deterrence still rests on an anti-city strategy, itself condemned, without appeal, by the Council. . . ."[28]

The French pastoral was concise in its definition of deterrence, but cryptic about the various debates which have surrounded the evolution of deterrence policy. Perhaps because the origin and locus of these debates have been primarily in the United States, the U.S. letter surveys the central concepts which have shaped deterrence policy over the last four decades. In a thirty page section, the U.S. pastoral reviews: the concept and development of deterrence policy, moral principles and policy choices, and the relationship of nuclear and conventional defenses.[29]

These broad topics, which have generated thousands of pages of analysis in the United States and Europe, were hardly probed in depth. But even the synthetic treatment of the nuclear argument offered in *The Challenge of Peace* was much more detailed than either *Gaudium et Spes* or Pope John Paul at the United Nations. This is not said as a criticism of papal or conciliar statements. It is questionable whether such a technical argument, drawn principally from one region of the world, is appropriate for a universal teaching document. But respect for the empirical complexity—indeed the uniqueness—of the deterrence problem requires that the church's moral analysis somewhere enter the details of the policy debate.

The character of the moral analysis differs among the three pastorals: the U.S. letter is the most detailed, the German letter is the most general in its treatment of deterrence, and the French pastoral stands between them. But all three letters illustrate how the local church is drawn more directly into the arena of policy choices in order to provide guidance for the actual decisions people face as officials or citizens.

The specificity of the moral evaluation in the pastorals generated another characteristic: a pluralist response to the nuclear question. The pastoral letters provide a case study of episcopal pluralism, a too little studied example in a time when pluralism among theologians is so minutely scrutinized. Pluralism among the French, German and U.S. episcopates included differences in ethical method and divergence on specific conclusions.

The methodological split was European vs. American. Charles Curran has noted the consequentialist character of the West German letter in its assessment of deterrence,[30] and Finnis et al. see the French letter as a consequentialist tract.[31] In both cases the problems posed for the principle of discrimination by nuclear strategy and the issue of intentionality in assessing deterrence were not central in the French or German assessments. The U.S. letter uses the principle of discrimination prominently in its analysis of targeting doctrine, and it affirmed—without discussion—the prohibition against intending to kill the innocent. Neither of these efforts satisfied the Finnis-Grisez-Boyle team,[32] but they did limit the role of consequentialist judgments in the U.S. letter. It counted consequences but in a subordinate position to the discrimination and intentionality criteria.

Regarding specific conclusions, the clearest example of European-American differences was the "no first use" section of the U.S. letter. The U.S. bishops, seeking to reduce the likelihood of any use of nuclear weapons, declared: "We do not perceive any situation in which the deliberate initiation of nuclear warfare, on however restricted a scale, can be morally justified."[33]

Neither of the European episcopates took this position, and it was clear from the debates surrounding the pastoral letters that the European view—ecclesial and political—was not inclined toward increased reliance on conventional defense. The "no first use" debate within the church reflected the geographical and strategic perspectives which exist in the NATO debates. On economic grounds and in light of historical experience European governments and analysts were not disposed to return to conventional forces as a first line of defense.

A difference of emphasis rather than moral differences marked the way in which the U.S. and French letters described the *jus ad bellum* dimension of the nuclear problem. The French letter starkly stated the threats facing Europe: "War and Blackmail."[34] The danger from the east, in its ideological and military dimensions, was the overriding reality of the French letter. The U.S. pastoral recognized the U.S.-Soviet competition in its various dimensions ("divided by philosophy, ideology, and competing ambitions"),[35] but focused its principal moral concerns on the qualitatively new *means* by which the classical inter-state competition was now waged.

The French emphasis on the nature of the threat overshadowed its commentary on deterrence strategy, while the U.S. emphasis on an ethic of means was criticized by William O'Brien, and others for failing to give sufficient weight to the values at stake in the U.S.-Soviet competition.[36]

The political significance of the pastoral letters was the manner in which they became part of the wider public argument in the western alliance.[37] As noted above, the ecclesiastical differences on nuclear vs. conventional deterrence or on "no first use" mirrored some of the arguments in the secular community. This is not testimony to a lack of creativity in the ecclesial debate but a sign of the way history and geography continue to have relevance for ethics as well as strategy. Some of the West German authors who opposed Bundy et al. on first use also took public issue with the U.S. pastoral letter. The U.S. letter, even in its successive drafts, became part of the internal European debate. In 1982, between October and December, 10,000 copies of the second draft were sold in West Germany. Similarly, the appearance of the West German and French pastoral letters provided U.S. critics of *The Challenge of Peace* with an alternative Catholic perspective.

Within the United States, the pastoral letter quickly became part of the strategic debate. Stephen Rosenfeld of *The Washington Post* characterized the challenge which the letter posed for citizens, strategists and political leaders:

The Catholic bishops are doing a brave yet questionable thing. They are forcing a public debate on perhaps the most perplexing moral question of them all, the morality of the doctrine of nuclear deterrence. . . . Their logic and passion have taken them to the very foundation of American security policy.[38]

While neither the German nor the French documents were enthusiastic endorsements of deterrence, the general impression created was that the European episcopates supported the prevailing policy while the U.S. bishops posed a political and moral counterpoint to U.S. policy of the early 1980s.

At the end of the decade the three letters stand as a case study of church-state engagement on a major public issue. The engagement varied according to political culture, with the U.S. church-state exchange being the most public, the most detailed, and the most intense. But all three of the letters can be examined not only in terms of their specific conclusions on nuclear weapons, but also in terms of their catalytic role in pressing public analysis beyond purely technical issues.

C. Theologians: Reviewing and Revising the Tradition

The amount of theological writing generated in the last decade on war and peace has been enormous.[39] If one takes the nuclear age from its inception, it is still true to say that papal writing on war and peace has been the driving force in the tradition. For much of the nuclear age, episcopal conferences did not exist, and few individual bishops had either the capacity or the inclination to address the topic of war and peace. Theological writing could claim key contributions: John Ford's uniquely famous article on obliteration bombing; John Courtney Murray's definitive interpretation of Pius XII's impact on the just-war tradition; the original contributions of Gordon Zahn, James Douglass and Thomas Merton to a Catholic theology of nonviolence.[40] But the structure and substance of the tradition was most clearly found in the papal writing from Pius XII through John Paul II.

The 1980s manifested a pattern whereby papal and particularly episcopal documents called forth theological analysis. Properly, the theological writing is broader in scope, more detailed in analysis and more pluralist in character than either the papal or episcopal texts. To examine the theological writing provides not only a review of the 1980s but a sense of direction about the future.

The interpretation offered here is by necessity selective, based on two principles. First, only Catholic writings will be reviewed. Second, the objective is not to provide a taxonomy of the debate, but to select those issues which emerged in the 1980s and will continue to be examined in the 1990s. Three issues will exemplify the range of theological debate in the 1980s: (1) a question of ethical theory; (2) a case of applied morality; (3) an issue of ecclesial teaching style.

    1. *Ethical Theory—Pacifism and Just War Doctrine.* The trajectory of Catholic teaching on war and peace from 1939–1979 (Pius XII to John Paul II) exhibits two themes. First, a process of tightening the limits on justifiable uses of force: Murray showed how Pius XII reduced the scope of *ius ad bellum;* John XXIII and Paul VI strengthened the presumption against resort to force; and John Paul II's strictures against the use of force in situations of civil conflict further limited the range of appeals to just-war criteria. Second, the reemergence of a Catholic position which opposes the just-war argument and espouses a nonviolent option. Both of these developments were particularly striking within the institution which has been the repository of the just-war tradition.

    The Challenge of Peace reflected and sharpened both of these larger developments in Catholic theology. The move to incorporate both the just-war and nonviolent positions in the same document sharpened the focus of theological discussion about their role and relationship in Catholic teaching. But the decision to include both themes in the pastoral letter meant that the bishops had to provide some explanation of the relationship themselves. They made three assertions: (1) that the two distinct ethical positions did share some objective common ground; (2) that the dialogue of the two positions should serve to discipline each position; (3) the difference between the two positions was not only their substantive conclusion on the use of force, but also their function in moral discourse. The nonviolent position is treated in the pastoral letter as a personal position, while the just-war position is regarded as both a personal and social ethic (for individuals and states).[41]

    The response within the Catholic community to the way *The Challenge of Peace* framed the two traditions ran from an indictment that it amounted to a confusion of tongues to an endorsement of the pastoral as a development in Catholic theology.

    The first criticism arose during the drafting of the pastoral letter as part of the convocation held in Rome to review the second draft of the U.S. pastoral.[42] The official summary of the meeting argued that the presentation of the just-war and nonviolence positions gave the latter a status it never held in the Catholic tradition, that it was a mistake to portray two seemingly equal moral traditions, and that a clear distinction had to be made between the public role of the just-war ethic and the personal option provided by the nonviolent position. The Vatican critique recognized the significance of the move being made in the pastoral letter; it was not necessarily to equate the two positions, but it did give a new status to the nonviolent position simply by bringing it into full view in the section on normative theory in the pastoral. Not surprisingly, all of the Holy See's recommendations influenced the subsequent versions of the pastoral letter.

The wider theological debate continued. James Finn argued that the joining of the two positions within a common moral vision not only risked theoretical confusion but gave undue influence to a nonviolent perspective in a policy document presumably based on just-war criteria.[43] Both Charles Curran and David Hollenbach supported the pastoral letter's framing of the ethical debate, terming it an advance beyond *Gaudium et Spes* and an opening to further development in Catholic thinking. Hollenbach saw the move as a product of both the challenge posed to a "limited war ethic" by nuclear weapons, and a recognition of the influence of the nonviolent perspective in the post-conciliar period.[44] Curran argued that models for relating the two distinct but complementary orientations could be found in other areas of Catholic life (e.g. the relationship of religious and lay vocations within the context of a universal call to discipleship).[45]

Even in the more attenuated framing of the positions in the final version of the letter, the theoretical question has been sharpened and commentary on it continues. The way forward in this discussion in the 1990s will require more attention to the structure of the debate. James Finn is willing to acknowledge that the two positions share "an overall moral vision," but he sees nothing beyond that. Richard Miller, on the other hand, is convinced that James Childress' position—reflected in the pastoral—that the two traditions share a common presumption of nonmaleficence is too narrow a description of the shared vision.[46] *The Challenge of Peace* simply acknowledged complementarity, but never specified its structure. To do so will require being clear on what is shared, equally clear on where the sharing stops, and creative about the possibilities of some joint action based on well defined common objectives.

Contra James Finn, more is shared than a common moral vision. The important point made at the level of moral vision, however, is that both the just war and nonviolent positions stand against what Michael Walzer has called "the realist" position, that war is the realm of necessity which places it outside the world of moral choice.[47] Since this argument —or some version of it—is regularly made in times of war or in debates about national security, it is no small benefit to have a "common moral vision" which provides a counterpoint.

Beyond moral vision, however, lies shared moral principles. Childress and Ralph Potter have both made the point that the moral tradition which legitimizes war as the *ultima ratio* must begin at the point where the nonviolent tradition stands, with a presumption against taking life.[48] This shared perspective has its limits, but as Childress notes, it leaves traces of its influence throughout the articulation of the just-war position.[49] Finally, beyond vision and principle, as Miller has observed,[50] the two distinct moral arguments find common ground in the task which the pastoral letter calls "Shaping a Peaceful World." Here the two perspectives can agree that restraint of force involves not only shaping moral limits but also creating political conditions which provide an alternative to achieving social goals through the use of force.

With James Finn, I believe it crucial for the future structure of the pacifism-just-war discussion to be clear about the differences of the two traditions. A clear identifiable line must be drawn at the point where the just-war presumption against force yields to exceptions articulated in just-cause categories. Unless this line can be drawn conceptually and practically, the just-war ethic loses its meaning. To maintain its moral identity the ethic must be able to *legitimate* force as well as to *limit* it.

Even as the task of shaping the peace is commonly encouraged between the two perspectives, it is necessary in a world of sin and of states to instruct personal conscience and inform public policy with the criteria needed to make a *moral* decision to use force. To dispense with the discussion of why the presumption of nonviolence has its limits is to forget the lessons of moral principle and historical experience which first brought the Christian tradition to the conclusion that both human nature and the nature of politics require—this side of the eschaton—the threat of sanction to secure the realm of morality and law.

2. *Applied Morality—The Case of Deterrence.* In the years 1959–1979 the moral debate on deterrence had produced three basic positions: defending deterrence (e.g. Paul Ramsey); denial of deterrence (e.g. Walter Stein) and deterrence devoid of use (e.g. Michael Walzer).[51] The renewed and expanded moral debate of the last decade has produced new substance but has not altered the structure of the argument in terms of these basic positions. Each of them has a successor in the 1980s.

In a corpus of writings William O'Brien has reasserted Ramsey's argument that nuclear weapons and nuclear strategy can, in principle, be accommodated within the tradition of just war norms.[52] Like Ramsey, O'Brien has been willing to set forth a detailed argument about weapons, tactics and limits which would be needed to keep nuclear use justifiable, and to make it possible to deploy a morally acceptable deterrent. On two counts O'Brien differs from Ramsey. He treats the principle of discrimination as a prescription which in certain cases can be overridden; Ramsey treats the principle as an exceptionless norm. O'Brien accepts new limits on strategy in the 1980s through his support of a "no first use" position.[53]

The 1980s version of the Stein position is found in *Nuclear Deterrence, Morality and Realism*[54] by John Finnis, Joseph Boyle and Germain Grisez. Writing in defense of "common morality" and specifically within the just-war tradition, this team of single-minded moralists indict deterrence from its inception to its implementation because it is inextricably tied, they tell us, to an intention to kill the innocent. As one of the authors put it, "The conclusion seems inescapable: the nuclear deterrent is not acceptable to Christian consciences and cannot in the foreseeable future be transformed into an acceptable form of deterrence."[55] This double judgment leaves the authors no counsel for governments or citizens who accept their position other than to dissociate themselves from a policy that is murderous in its intent.

The functional equivalent of Walzer in the 1980s is the position of Francis X. Winters.[56] Functionally equivalent, but not argued in similar fashion, Winters holds that the deterrent posture should be sustained, but that "militarily meaningful use" of nuclear weapons is today recognized as morally wrong and militarily counterproductive. He believes this shared recognition of moral and strategic perspectives will sustain deterrence and provide the time needed to restructure deterrence on a conventional basis which meets moral criteria.

If the structure of the moral debate has remained constant (new names in old positions), what has the extensive analysis and argument of the 1980s produced? Are we simply where we were in the mid-1970s with new footnotes?

Such a judgment does not do justice to the inquiry of the last decade. While there is a certain structural continuity between the early and later stages of the deterrence debate, there has also occurred in the last ten years a sea-change in the empirical and ethical reflection on deterrence. The effect of this shift of themes and tone in the understanding of deterrence cuts across and influences all three of the basic positions on the morality of deterrence, as it also affects the political-strategic debate.

The sea-change was sensed and summarized by one of the most sophisticated and discriminating analysts of the nuclear age, Lawrence Freedman of King's College (London). In a review of three books analyzing the ethics of deterrence, Freedman makes an observation about the state of the nuclear debate in the 1980s:

Thus all these authors accept that *something* must be done about deterrence. This is itself a noteworthy change from the

1950s and 1960s, when deterrence commanded greater political and military support and was promoted with confidence and vigor. In the strategic studies community, as well as in the political and theological establishments, a degree of disillusionment with deterrence is apparent, illustrated by the growing interest in conventional defense and the increasing discomfort within NATO about the reliance on threats to use nuclear weapons first.[57]

The effect of this disillusionment with deterrence shapes the context in which the three moral positions on deterrence are read and received. The Finnis-Boyle-Grisez position has today within the Catholic community a broader constituency than the similar position held by Stein thirty years ago. The constituency is visible in both theological writing and activist groups like Pax Christi, USA. It is still a minority position, as the authors acknowledge, but it is closer to the center of the Catholic debate than a John Courtney Murray would have thought likely.

Those closer to the Murray position, like William O'Brien, must answer questions today from the normative and empirical debates about the possibility of controlling nuclear use which are sharper than those Ramsey and Murray faced in the 1960s. The moral position about controlled use was always a difficult position to hold even where the empirical debate showed fewer doubts about deterrence than it does today. There are variations on the Ramsey-O'Brien position found in the writings of John Langan which broaden the scope of its constituency even as they reduce the legitimation for using nuclear weapons.[58]

In similar fashion one could take the Walzer-Winters conclusions and find connections with David Hollenbach's conclusions, although the case would be argued in a very different fashion.

Somewhere along the spectrum of O'Brien-Langan-Hollenbach-Winters, I believe one finds the majority view on deterrence at the end of the 1980s. In spite of the universal respect for his writing there are few who are prepared to make Murray's proposition ("since limited nuclear war may be a necessity, it must be made a possibility")[59] a leading theme in their analysis. O'Brien does, but I locate the majority opinion between O'Brien and Winters, not with O'Brien. Doubts about usable nuclear forces inevitably create doubts about deterrence. But those holding doubts are still in a quite different position than Finnis et al.

How do the doubters express their moral evaluation of deterrence? The disillusionment about deterrence—morally and strategically—was the soil which produced "conditional acceptance of deterrence," the position of *The Challenge of Peace*.[60] The position has all the untidiness of the phenomenon it seeks to evaluate. Just as nuclear deterrence does not fit nicely in the classical matrix of politics and strategy, so the "conditional acceptance" leaves both moralists and plain citizens less than satisfied with its conclusions.

Conditional acceptance does not contain the certitudes of the Finnis-Boyle-Grisez condemnation of deterrence. The doubters about deterrence are less prepared to reduce the total moral analysis to the prism of conditional intentions. Without disputing the pedigree of the moral reasoning, and while recognizing the internal logic of the argument, one can still remain unpersuaded by the conclusion. It is not clear that intentionality captures the full range of moral judgment needed to assess the reality of deterrence.

The doubters are not prepared to condemn, but neither are they prepared simply to comply with deterrence doctrine. Conditional acceptance carries some of the same moral judgment as John Paul II's comments on the strategy of deterrence: "It is only on the condition of remaining fundamentally transitional and oriented towards the search for another type of international relationship that this strategy can be considered."[61] Unlike O'Brien or Albert Wohlstetter the doubters of the conditional acceptance position are not persuaded that we can rectify the deterrence problem by refining targeting doctrine and reducing the yield of warheads. Acknowledging the utility of these steps, the position of conditional acceptance seeks a more fundamental transformation of the deterrence relationship.

Such a transformation does not require immediate withdrawal from the deterrence posture, but a gradual movement away from the pattern of the last forty years, a long-term decline in reliance on nuclear weapons (as Joseph Nye has advocated), (for some) a change in NATO doctrine about first use, pursuit of a significant number of arms control steps, and an attempt to reshape political relations, so that the role of nuclear weapons in world politics is substantially marginalized.

How do those holding conditional acceptance as a position apply and utilize their conditions in the policy debate. The 1988 statement of the U.S. bishops, *A Report on the Challenge of Peace and Policy Developments 1983–1988,* sought to illustrate how the conditions can be used in an ongoing assessment of policy, particularly—at that moment—the SDI debate. The report defined two kinds of conditions arising from *The Challenge of Peace:* conditions about the "direction" of deterrence policy and conditions about the "character" of weapons proposed for modernizing the deterrent forces.[62]

These conditions and the criteria which flow from them are resources to use in pursuit of the long-term transformation which conditional acceptance seeks to achieve. David Hollenbach, a consistently creative participant in the nuclear debate of the last decade, argues for a style of moral analysis which complements the use of these conditions:

> The real question for moral judgment is whether a concrete strategic option will actually make the world more secure from nuclear disaster or less so. There is no such thing as deterrence in the abstract. Rather there are only specific defense postures involving diverse weapons systems, targeting doctrines, procurement programs, and strategic master concepts. It is these that must be subjected to ethical scrutiny, not some abstract notion of deterrence or intention.[63]

Following the logic of conditional acceptance will require testing the elements and direction of deterrence policy in the style of casuistry advocated by Hollenbach. Some of this testing was done in the 1980s but, as we will see shortly, there are new questions emerging in the 1990s.

3. *An Ecclesial Issue—Specificity of Episcopal Teaching.* A third theological issue, rooted in the debate of the 1980s, but sure to continue, is the style of magisterial teaching in the social arena. While the question has significance for papal and conciliar teaching, it arose and has been debated principally in relationship to the style of the two pastoral letters on peace and the economy. Both of the pastoral letters joined an explanation of the principles of Catholic teaching to a range of policy recommendations, applying principles to the specifics of the public policy debate. While most critics of the style of specificity were also critical of the substance of the positions the bishops adopted, Avery Dulles tried to distinguish the two issues.

Focusing on the question of the style of teaching, he argued that an episcopal conference, "should devote itself primarily to teaching,"[64] leaving applications of the principles to the laity. Dulles returned to the same question at the end of the 1980s in his book *The Reshaping of Catholicism.* While not ruling out specific policy positions for the bishops, Dulles clearly sided with those who see high risks for the episcopal conference, when it moves beyond teaching general principles in the social arena. Dulles' basic concern is that engaging bishops in the debate about contingent policy choices threatens their religious authority and can threaten the transcendence of the church and its teaching ministry.[65]

In other places, I have argued that there are ecclesiological, moral and social grounds supporting the style of specific moral teaching reflected in the pastoral letters.[66] Dulles takes these arguments into consideration, seems to agree with the first two, but doubts the social utility of engaging the bishops in "contentious issues" which inevitably entangle them "in the ambiguities of mundane politics."[67] While it is clear that Dulles has doubts or objections to *where* the bishops come down on issues, he keeps his argument on the point of *how* they should teach.

I continue to believe that the Catholic ecclesial and moral style of argument, reflected in the social, sexual and medical ethics tradition of the church, legitimates, indeed calls for, a process of teaching principles and illustrating their application in specific areas. Both the willingness of the pope to engage very specific questions on his trips and in his allocutions and the 1986 Vatican statement on new technologies of birth, *Donum Vitae*,[68] testify to a Catholic style of using both principles and their application.

Moreover, in making his case against specificity, Avery Dulles draws conclusions which seem to me not conclusive. First, he sees duplication between the bishops' efforts in the specifics of the policy debate and other "foundations, public interest groups and educational institutions" which deal with these questions from a "very similar perspective."[69] While there clearly is convergence and similarity between conclusions of the pastoral letters and other secular institutions, I would argue that there is little or no explicit use of the Catholic moral tradition by other groups in the public debate. By entering the debate, putting the tradition vigorously in public view, and assessing issues from a religious-moral perspective, the bishops do more—for the church and society—than simply support the conclusions of others. Convergence on conclusions does not exhaust what they contribute to the public argument.

Second, Dulles fears that sustained, visible engagement by the bishops in "secular affairs" can give the impression that the "truly important in their eyes is not the faith or holiness that leads to everlasting life but rather the structuring of human society to make the world more habitable."[70] Against this fear stands the possibility that the engagement of the bishops will testify to the truth that both faith and holiness *require* engagement in the task of structuring a society which protects human dignity and promotes human rights. Dulles' understandable concern to protect the transcendence of the gospel and the church's ministry risks, at times, his underestimating the challenge posed for the church by Vatican II's assertion that: "They are mistaken who, knowing that we have here no abiding city but seek one which is to come, think that they may therefore shirk their earthly responsibilities."[71] Dulles does not intend or want to encourage shirking these responsibilities, but he may not attend sufficiently to what needs to be done by bishops and others to catalyze the concern for "earthly responsibilities" which the council calls for.

Rather than report this debate among others, I have engaged it directly, but the argument involves many commentators and is larger than the style of one episcopal conference. Dulles and I share more in principle than we disagree upon in application, but the debate on applications will continue.

III. Beyond the 1980s: Politics, Strategy and Ethics

This essay opened with an assessment of signs of the times which produced the rich debate on war and peace of the 1980s. At the threshold of the 1990s, one can at least catalogue the major political-strategic trends which seem most likely to set the agenda for the next decade, and then list the kinds of issues this catalogue is likely to evoke in the ecclesial-moral literature.

A. Politics and Strategy
The 1990s will be marked by the primacy of the political questions, the return of conventional arms issues, and the necessity to address systemic issues. A word on each of these:

1. *The Primacy of the Political.* The nuclear age has been built on the premise of unyielding hostility of the superpowers, and the quest to find a limited strip of common interest through which the nuclear competition could be contained under conditions of "stability" in spite of the political rivalry. The 1990s open the possibility—far from a certainty—that the political character of the superpower relationship can be changed. This far more ambitious goal than arms control will not dispense with either deterrence or arms control but it opens a new agenda of political and moral questions.

2. *The Return of the Conventional Questions.* The nuclear question has dominated politics, strategy and arms control. But the possibilities of political change in the superpower relationship and the proposals by both the United States and the Soviet Union for substantial change in the NATO-Warsaw Pact relationship brings the questions of conventional arms, conventional deterrence, and the relationship of these to the nuclear question onto center stage. The need for a conceptual framework to relate strategic and conventional arms control negotiations, and for a political vision broad enough to guide the restructuring of the European question, is recognized on all sides. But the conceptual-political work has just begun.

3. *The Rise of the Systemic Issues.* The nuclear question has always had cosmic implications, but it has been a superpower possession. The

1990s will raise the systemic side of the question—proliferation of nuclear weapons—with a new edge. The Nonproliferation Treaty must be renewed by all signatories in 1995. This event will force the nuclear powers to address the wider concerns of non-nuclear states about the shape of the international system in areas beyond the nuclear question. To be too brief about this point, proliferation issues join the east-west debate to the north-south questions. The centrality of the superpowers will continue in the 1990s, but the systemic issues will have to be addressed. The strategic debate will need to attend to justice as well as peace issues.

B. Ecclesial-Ethical Response

The results of the debates of the 1980s and the changing signs of the times of the 1990s point to the following framework of analysis.

1. *Foundations and Fundamentals.* Three different challenges posed in the debate of the 1980s will continue in the next decade. All three challenges can be described in relation to *The Challenge of Peace.* First, the Catholic pacifist argument will continue. The pastoral letter was regarded as useful but not sufficiently profound or prophetic. The case will continue to be made by Gordon Zahn et al. that the logic of the Christian tradition and the character of contemporary warfare both require—finally—a Catholic pacifist position for the church.[72] In contrast, George Weigel and Michael Novak both found in *The Challenge of Peace* a failure to respect the tradition of moderate Catholic realism.[73] The Weigel challenge is that the tradition is adequate for the times, but has been subverted and/or subordinated to the political plans of the Catholic left. Those accused regard their work as development of the tradition, not its corruption. The debate will not be finished in the 1990s. A third challenge—Finnis-Boyle-Grisez's work—may be described in terms of the title of their book, *Nuclear Deterrence, Morality and Realism.* In brief, they find a version of realism so dominant in parts of the ecclesial debate that it has sacrificed the principles of morality which the church must uphold. The realist concerns of some have brought them, wittingly or unwittingly, to sacrifice common morality on the altar of consequentialism. This debate, too, will continue.

2. *Political Ethics.* The primacy of the political opens possibilities for those who have written in the ethics of strategy and arms control. While the latter issues remain, the changing focus of the U.S.-Soviet relationship invites and requires a larger set of reflections on the basic elements of the international system: the superpower relationship, the recasting of the European question, the role of the east-west competition

in regional conflicts. The task here is what Stanley Hoffmann has called an ethic of world order.[74] The writings of the 1990s need to be expanded to meet this test.

3. *Strategic and Conventional Questions.* The critics and the defenders of deterrence will both be challenged in moral terms by the new mix of nuclear and conventional negotiations. It is not difficult to be disillusioned with deterrence in political or moral terms. But replacing deterrence has always been more difficult than criticizing it. The record of conventional deterrence in the European theater has not been such to inspire confidence. But the possibilities of the 1990s will include the recasting of deterrence, the review of the conventional balance in Europe and the restructuring of the European question as it has existed for four decades. The ethical choices involved have yet to be clearly defined in the literature.

4. *Systemic Challenges:* The agenda for linking changing superpower political and strategic relations to the wider array of systemic questions has been best outlined by John Paul II in *Sollicitudo Rei Socialis.*[75] His challenge to join the East-West and north-south issues in systematic fashion has not yet been addressed adequately in either the empirical or the normative literature. It is both a devilishly difficult and urgently necessary task for church and state in the 1990s.

The decade 1979–1989 produced major results and much debate on war and peace in the Catholic Church. The coming decade will require both sorting out our differences of the 1980s and facing authentically new questions required to keep and build the peace.

Notes

1. Vatican II, *Gaudium et Spes,* (1965) #4, 11.

2. For major themes and events which have shaped the nuclear debate in the past decade cf: McG. Bundy, *Danger and Survival: Choices about the Bomb in the First Fifty Years* (N.Y.: Random House, 1988) 543ff; J. Nye, The Contribution of Strategic Studies: Future Challenges, *Adelphi Papers* #235 (London: IISS, 1989) 20–34; S. Talbott, *Endgame: The Inside Story of SALT II* (N.Y.: Harper and Row, 1979); *The Master of the Game: Paul Nitze and the Nuclear Peace* (N.Y.: Knopf, 1988); R. Tucker, The Nuclear Debate, *Foreign Affairs,* 63 (1984) 1–32.

3. Cf. Bundy, cited; L. Freedman, *The Evolution of Nuclear Strategy* (N.Y.: St. Martin's Press, 1981); M. Mandelbaum, *The Nuclear Question: The United States and Nuclear Weapons 1946–1976* (Cambridge: Cambridge University Press, 1979).

4. McG. Bundy, G. Kennan, R.S. McNamara and G. Smith, "Nuclear Weapons and the Atlantic Alliance," *Foreign Affairs,* 60 (1982) 753–68.

5. R.S. McNamara, "The Military Role of Nuclear Weapons," *Foreign Affairs* 62 (1983) 59–80.

6. Cf. M. McGwire, "Deterrence: The Problem—Not the Solution," *SAIS Review* 5 (1985) 105–24; for a defense of deterrence, L. Weiseltier, *Nuclear War, Nuclear Peace* (N.Y.: Holt, Rinehart & Winston, 1983); J. Nye, G. Allison and A. Carnesale, eds., *Fateful Visions: Avoiding Nuclear Catastrophe* (Cambridge: Ballinger Publishing Co., 1988) esp. 1–11.

7. B. Van Voorst, "The Churches and Nuclear Deterrence," *Foreign Affairs,* 61 (1983) 59–80.

8. The best reviews of the literature are the "Notes" in *Theological Studies:* cf. 45 (1984) 122–38; 46 (1985) 80–101; 47 (1986) 117–33.

9. No complete collection of John Paul II's teaching on nuclear issues is available; for selections cf. *Ways of Peace: Papal Messages for the World Days of Peace 1968–1986* (Vatican City: 1987); *Peace and Disarmament: Documents of the World Council of Churches and the Roman Catholic Church* (Vatican City: 1982).

10. J.C. Murray, *We Hold These Truths: Catholic Reflections on the American Proposition* (N.Y.: Sheed and Ward, 1960) p. 270.

11. John Paul II, "Address in Drogheda, Ireland," *Origins* 9 (1979) 274.

12. John Paul II, "Message to Youth on Nonviolence," *Origins* 18 (1988) 253.

13. John Paul II, "World Day of Peace Message 1982," *Origins* 11 (1982) 477.

14. Ibid.

15. Cf. the 1988 Papal Address to the Diplomatic Corps at the Vatican; in discussing a series of internal conflicts, the pope said: "We must always remember that the civilian populations are the first to suffer from these prolonged crises with all the human tragedy that this entails." *L'Osservatore Romano* (English edition) (Jan. 25, 1988) 6.

16. Cf. Murray's commentary on Pius XII's cautious approach to this question, Murray, cited, 262–63.

17. John Paul II, "Address to Scientists and Scholars," *Origins* 10 (1981) 621.

18. John Paul II, *Message to the Second Special Session of the United Nations on Disarmament* (1982) #8.

19. Cardinal A. Casaroli, "The Vatican's Position on Issues of War and Peace," *Origins* 13 (1983) #12, 439.

20. John Paul II, "1988 Address to the Diplomatic Corps," cited, 7.

21. J. Finnis, J. Boyle, G. Grisez, *Nuclear Deterrence, Morality and Realism* (N.Y.: Oxford University Press, 1987) 98.

22. Ibid.

23. Casaroli, cited, 18. Finnis, et al. note that Casaroli specifically cited the principle of discrimination; presumably this would lead to the judgment the authors affirm about deterrence, if Casaroli were convinced this conclusion was as clear as Finnis et al. assert.

24. John Paul II, "1988 Address to the Diplomatic Corps," cited, 6–7.

25. Paul VI, *Octogesima Adveniens,* #4.

26. The National Conference of Catholic Bishops, *The Challenge of Peace: God's Promise and Our Response* (Washington, D.C.: U.S. Catholic Conference, 1983) #147–61, 46–50 (cited hereafter as CP, with paragraph and page numbers).

27. *Gaudium et Spes,* #81.

28. Joint Pastoral Letter of the French Bishops, *Winning the Peace,* in J.V. Schall, ed., *Out of Justice, Peace and Winning the Peace* (San Francisco: Ignatius Press, 1984) #28, 110.

29. C.P., cited, #162–258, 51–81.

30. C. Curran, The U.S. and West German Bishops on War and Peace, in *Tensions in Moral Theology* (Notre Dame: University of Notre Dame Press, 1988) 138–61, esp. 140–41, 144, 150.

31. Finnis, et al., cited, 199.

32. Ibid. 23–24, 172–174.

33. CP, #150, 47.

34. *Winning the Peace,* cited, 102.

35. C.P., #245, 76.

36. W. O'Brien, "The Challenge of War: A Christian Realist Perspective," in J.A. Dwyer, ed., *The Catholic Bishops and Nuclear War* (Washington, D.C.: Georgetown University Press, 1984) 37–64, esp. 42–49.

37. Cf. Van Voorst, cited; J. Castelli, *The Bishops and the Bomb* (N.Y.: Image Books, 1983).

38. S. Rosenfeld, "The Bishops and the Bomb," *The Washington Post* (Oct. 29, 1982) Op-Ed.

39. Cf. *Theological Studies* "Notes," cited above; for a sampling of other writings cf Dwyer, cited above; W.V. O'Brien and J. Langan, eds., *The Nuclear Dilemma and the Just War Tradition* (Lexington, MA: Lexington Books, 1986); G. Weigel, *Tranquillitas Ordinis: The Present Failure and Future Promise of American Catholic Thought on War and Peace* (N.Y.: Oxford University Press, 1987); A. Kenny, *The Logic of Deterrence* (Chicago: University of Chicago Press, 1985).

40. J. Ford, "The Morality of Obliteration Bombing," *Theological Studies* 5 (1944) 261–309; J.C. Murray, cited, 249–73; J. Douglass, *The Nonviolent Cross* (N.Y.: Macmillan, 1966).

41. C.P., #111–21, 34–37.

42. J. Schotte, "Vatican's Official Report on Meeting to Discuss War and Peace Pastoral," *Origins* 12 (1983) 694.

43. J. Finn, "Pacifism, Just War and the Bishops' Muddle," *This World* 7 (Winter, 1984) 31–42.

44. D. Hollenbach, *Justice, Peace and Human Rights: American Catholic Social Ethics in a Pluralistic Context* (N.Y.: Crossroad Publishing Co., 1988) 154–56.

45. C. Curran, *Critical Concerns in Moral Theology* (Notre Dame: University of Notre Dame Press, 1984) 144–70, esp. 163.

46. Richard Miller, "Christian Pacifism and Just-War Tenets: How Do They Diverge?" *Theological Studies* 47 (1986) 448–72.

47. M. Walzer, *Just and Unjust Wars: A Moral Argument with Historical Illustrations* (N.Y.: Basic Books, 1977) 3–20.

48. J. Childress, "Just War Theories," *Theological Studies* 39 (1978) 427–45; R.B. Potter, "The Moral Logic of War," *McCormick Quarterly* 23 (1970) 203–33.

49. Childress, cited, 427–29.

50. Miller, cited, 469ff.

51. Cf. P. Ramsey, *The Just War: Force and Political Responsibility* (N.Y.: Scribner's, 1968); W. Stein, ed., *Nuclear Weapons and the Christian Conscience* (London: Merlin Publishers, 1961); Walzer, cited.

52. W. O'Brien, "Just War Doctrine in a Nuclear Context," *Theological Studies* 44 (1983) 191–220; "The Failure of Deterrence and the Conduct of War" and "The Future of the Nuclear Debate," in O'Brien and Langan, cited, 153–97, 223–48; "The Challenge of War: A Christian Realist Perspective," in J. Dwyer, *The Catholic Bishops,* cited, 37–64.

53. O'Brien, "Just War Doctrine in a Nuclear Context," cited.

54. Finnis, et al., cited above.

55. J. Finnis, "Nuclear Deterrence, Christian Conscience and the End of Christendom," *New Oxford Review* 55 (July-August 1988) 12.

56. F.X. Winters, "The Bow or the Cloud?" *America* (July 25, 1981) 26–30; "After Tension, Detente," *Theological Studies* 45 (1984) 343–51; "The American Bishops on Deterrence," in J. Dwyer, *The Catholic Bishops,* cited, 23–36; "Bishops and Scholars: The Peace Pastoral Under Siege," *Review of Politics* (Winter 1986) 31–59.

57. L. Freedman, "The Limits of Patience," *New Republic* (April 21, 1986) 27–32.

58. J. Langan, "The American Hierarchy and Nuclear Weapons," *Theological Studies* 43 (1982), 447–67; "Introduction" and "Between Religion and Politics: The Morality of Deterrence," in O'Brien and Langan, *The Nuclear Dilemma,* cited, 3–10, 131–52.

59. J.C. Murray, cited, 271.

60. C.P., #186, 58.

61. John Paul II, *1988 Address to the Diplomatic Corps,* cited, 7.

62. National Conference of Catholic Bishops, *Building Peace and A Report on the Challenge of Peace and Policy Developments* 1983–1988 (Washington, D.C.: U.S. Catholic Conference, 1988) #48–51, 37–39.

63. D. Hollenbach, cited, 147.

64. A. Dulles, "What Is the Doctrinal Authority of a Bishops' Conference?" *Origins* (Jan. 24, 1985) 532.

65. A. Dulles, *The Reshaping of Catholicism: Current Challenges in the Theology of the Church* (N.Y.: Harper and Row, 1987) 155, 182, 183.

66. J.B. Hehir, "From Church-State to Church-World: The Ecclesiological Implications," *Proceedings of the Catholic Theological Society* 42 (1987); "Principles and Politics," *Commonweal,* 114 (1987) 169–70.

67. Dulles, *The Reshaping,* cited, 176.

68. Congregation for the Doctrine of the Faith, *Donum Vitae* (1987).

69. Dulles, *The Reshaping,* cited, 176.

70. Ibid.

71. *Gaudium et Spes,* #43.

72. G. Zahn, "The Church's 'New Attitude Toward War,' " in J. Dwyer, ed., *Questions of Special Urgency* (Washington, D.C.: Georgetown University Press) 203–20; "American Catholics and Peace: A Progress Report," *New Oxford Review* (June 1987) 12–17.

73. G. Weigel, cited above; M. Novak, *Moral Clarity in the Nuclear Age* (Nashville: Thomas Nelson, 1983).

74. S. Hoffmann, cf. *The Political Ethics of International Relations* (N.Y.: Carnegie Council on Ethics and International Affairs, 1988); *Duties Beyond Borders: On the Limits and Possibilities of Ethical International Politics* (N.Y.: Syracuse University Press, 1981) 189ff.

75. John Paul II, *Sollicitudo Rei Socialis* (1987), #22, 23.

Bibliography of
Richard A. McCormick, S.J.

1952

"Ghosts in the Wings," *America* 86 (January 5, 1952) 377–379.

"Standards and the Stagirite," *America* 87 (May 3, 1952) 135–137.

1957

The Removal of a Fetus Probably Dead to Save the Life of the Mother (Rome: Pontifica Universitas Gregoriana, 1957).

1959

Callan, Charles J., and McHugh, John A. Revised and enlarged by Farrell, Edward P., *Moral Theology, The Priest* 15 (April, 1959) 342–344. (Book review.)

"The Primacy of Charity," *Perspectives* (August/September, 1959) 18–27.

1960

"Adolescent Masturbation: A Pastoral Problem," *Homiletic and Pastoral Review* 60 (March, 1960) 527–540.

Gilleman, Gerard, *The Primacy of Charity in Moral Theology,* trans. by Ryan, William F. and Vachon, André, *The Priest* 16 (July, 1960) 346–347. (Book review.)

Buckley, Michael J., *Morality and the Homosexual, Homiletic and Pastoral Review* 60 (August, 1960) 1032–1034. (Book review.)

"Adolescent Affection: Toward a Sound Sexuality," *Homiletic and Pastoral Review* 61 (December, 1960) 244–261. [Reprinted in "Adolescent Love: Toward a Sound Sexuality" (Derby, New York: St. Paul Publications).]

Hagmaier, George, *Counselling the Catholic, Review for Religious* 19 (1960) 391. (Book review.)

1961

Gibbons, William J., ed., *Population, Resources and the Future, The Catholic World* 194 (October, 1961) 56–59. (Book review.)

"Moral Considerations in Autopsy," *Linacre Quarterly* 28 (November, 1961) 161–169. [Reprinted in *Hospital Progress* (April, 1962) 102–108. Also in *Trustee* 15 (July, 1962) 18–21.]

de Lestapsis, Stanislas, *Family Planning and Modern Problems,* trans. Trevett, Reginald F., *America* 106 (December 9, 1961) 370. (Book review.)

1962

"Anti-Fertility Pills," *Homiletic and Pastoral Review* 62 (May, 1962) 692–700.

Chafetz, Morris E., *Alcoholism and Society, America* 107 (June 9, 1962) 386–387. (Book review.)

Osborn, Fairfled, ed., *Our Crowded Planet, America* 107 (November 3, 1962) 1000–1001. (Book review.)

"Is Professional Boxing Immoral?" *Sports Illustrated* 17 (November 5, 1962) 71–72, 74, 76, 78–80, 82. [Condensed reprint in *Catholic Digest* 27 (May, 1963) 108–113.]

1963

"Heterosexual Relationships in Adolescence," *Review for Religious* 22 (January, 1963) 75–92. [Reprinted as "Heterosexual Relationships in Adolescence: The Ideal and the Problem," *Adolescence: Special Cases and Special Problems,* Steimel, Raymond J., ed. (Washington, D.C.: The Catholic University of America Press, 1963) 42–65.]

Kelly, George A., *Birth Control and Catholics, America* 109 (October 19, 1963) 465–466. (Book review.)

1964

"Conjugal Love and Conjugal Morality," *America* 110 (January 11, 1964) 38–42.

Ford, John C. and Kelly, Gerald, *Marriage Questions: Contemporary Moral Theology, Vol. II, America* 110 (January 18, 1964) 112. (Book review.)

Bier, William C., ed., *Personality and Sexual Problems, America* 110 (May 23, 1964) 738. (Book review.)

"Toward a Dialogue," *Commonweal* 80 (June 5, 1964) 313–317.

Gibert, Henri, *Love in Marriage, America* 111 (June 27, 1964) 870. (Book review.)

"Whither the Pill?" *The Catholic World* 199 (July, 1964) 207–214.

Gassert, Robert G., *Psychiatry and Religious Faith, America* 111 (September 19, 1964) 312–313. (Book review.)

"Psychosexual Development in Religious Life," *Review for Religious* 23 (November, 1964) 724–741.

Dupre, Louis, *Contraception and Catholics, America* 111 (November 14, 1964) 628–629. (Book review.)

(No author), *Contraception and Holiness,* Introduction by Archbishop Thomas D. Roberts, *America* 111 (November 14, 1964) 626–628. (Book review.)

"Family Size, Rhythm, and the Pill," *The Problem of Population: Moral and Theological Considerations,* ed. Donald N. Barrett (South Bend: University of Notre Dame Press, 1964) 58–84.

1965

"The Priest and Teen-age Sexuality," *The Homiletic and Pastoral Review* 65 (February, 1965) 379–387. Part II in Vol. 65 (March, 1965) 473–480. [Reprinted in *All Things to All Men,* ed. Joseph F.X. Cevetello (New York: Joseph F. Wagner, Inc., 1965) 362–381.

Lepp, Ignace, *The Authentic Morality, America* 112 (March 27, 1965) 433–434. (Book review.)

Häring, Bernard, *Christian Renewal in a Changing World, America* 112 (March 27, 1965) 433. (Book review.)

"Abortion," *America* 112 (June 19, 1965) 877–881. [Reprinted, condensed form, *Family Digest* 112 (December, 1965) 37–43.

Grisez, Germain G., *Contraception and the Natural Law, The American Ecclesiastical Review* 153 (August, 1965) 119–125. (Book review.)

"Toward a New Sexual Morality?" *The Catholic World* 202 (October, 1965) 10–16.

Monden, Louis, *Sin, Liberty, and Law, America* 113 (November 13, 1965) 602–604. (Book review.)

"Notes in Moral Theology," *Theological Studies* 16 (December, 1965) 596–662.

"Practical and Theoretical Considerations," *The Problem of Population: Vol. III Educational Considerations* (South Bend: The University of Notre Dame Press, 1965) 50–73.

1966
"The Council on Contraception," *America* 114 (January 8, 1966) 47–48.

"The History of a Moral Problem," *America* 114 (January 29, 1966) 174–178.

"Worship in Common," *Catholic Mind* 64 (April, 1966) 20–25.

"General Confession," *Catholic Mind* 64 (May, 1966) 10–12.

Häring, Bernard, *The Time of Salvation, America* 114 (June 18, 1966) 859–860. (Book review.)

"Modern Morals in a Muddle," *America* 115 (July 30, 1966) 116.

"The Polygraph in Business and Industry," *Theological Studies* 27 (September, 1966) 421–433.

"Notes on Moral Theology," *Theological Studies* 17 (December, 1966) 607–654.

"Abortion and Moral Principles," *The Wrong of Abortion* (New York: America Press, 1966) 1–13.

"Conjugal Morality," *Married Love and Children* (New York: America Press, 1966) 24–32.

"Panel Talk on Curriculum: Anti-Semitism and Christian Ethics," *Judaism and the Christian Seminary Curriculum,* ed. J. Bruce Long (Chicago: Loyola University Press, 1966) 94–98.

1967
Häring, Bernard, *Christian Maturity, America* 116 (April 8, 1967) 538. (Book review.)

Oraison, Marc, *The Human Mystery of Sexuality, Homiletic and Pastoral Review* 67 (May, 1967) 707–708.

"Conference Without Consensus," *America* 117 (September 23, 1967) 320–321.

"Aspects of the Moral Question," *America* 117 (December 9, 1967) 716–719. (On abortion.)

"Notes on Moral Theology: January–June, 1967," *Theological Studies* 28 (December, 1967) 749–800.

1968

Oraison, Marc, *The Celibate Condition and Sex, Homiletic and Pastoral Review* 68 (February, 1968) 446–448. (Book review.)

"The New Morality," *America* 118 (June 15, 1968) 769–772.

"Past Church Teaching on Abortion," *CTSA Proceedings* 23 (June 17–20, 1968) 131–151.

"Notes on Moral Theology: January–June, 1968," *Theological Studies* 29 (December, 1968) 679–741.

"Human Significance and Christian Significance," *Norm and Context in Christian Ethics,* Gene H. Outka and Paul Ramsey (New York: Charles Scribner's Sons, 1968) 233–261.

"The Moral Theology of Vatican II," *The Future of Ethics and Moral Theology* (Chicago: Argus Communications, Co., 1968) 7–18.

1969

"The Theology of Revolution," *Catholic Mind* 67 (April, 1969) 23–32.

"When Priests Marry," *America* 120 (April 19, 1969) 471–474.

Callahan, Daniel, ed., *The Catholic Case for Contraception, America* 120 (May 24, 1969) 627–628. (Book review.)

"The Teaching of the Magisterium and Theologians," *CTSA Proceedings* 24 (June 16–19, 1969) 239–254.

"Reflections on Sunday Observance," *The American Ecclesiastical Review* 161 (July, 1969) 55–61.

"Notes on Moral Theology: January–June, 1969," *Theological Studies* 30 (December, 1969) 635–692.

1970

"Christian Morals," *America* 122 (January 10, 1970) 5–6.

"Ethics of Political Protest," *Catholic Mind* 68 (March, 1970) 11–22.

"What We Expect from a Priest—What He Expects from Us," *Emmanuel* 76 (April, 1970) 163–166.

Vaux, Kenneth, *Who Shall Live? America* 122 (April 18, 1970) 424–425. (Book review.)

Curran, Charles E., *Contemporary Problems in Moral Theology, America* 122 (May 16, 1970) 527. (Book review.)

Häring, Bernard, *Road to Relevance, America* 122 (May 16, 1970) 527. (Book review.)

"Loyalty and Dissent: The Magisterium—A New Model," *America* 122 (June 27, 1970) 674–676.

"A Moralist Reports," *America* 123 (July 11, 1970) 22–23.

————, MacRae, George W., and Örsy, Ladislas, "Brussels Hosts the Theologians," *America* 123 (October 3, 1970) 232, 234.

1971

"Notes on Moral Theology: April–September, 1970," *Theological Studies* 32 (March, 1971) 66–122.

Grisez, Germain, *Abortion: The Myths, the Realities, and the Arguments, America* 124 (April 17, 1971) 412–413. (Book review.)

"Presidential Address," *CTSA Proceedings* 26 (June 14–17, 1971) 239–250. [Reprinted as "Leadership and Authority," *Catholic Mind* 70 (March, 1972) 8–16. Also reprinted as "Leadership and Authority," *Dimensions in Religious Education,* ed. John R. McCall (Haverton: CIM Books, 1973) 61–68.]

Häring, Bernard, *Morality Is for Persons, America* 125 (September 11, 1971) 155–158. (Book review.)

"Not What Catholic Hospitals Ordered," *America* 125 (December 11, 1971) 510–513. [Reprinted in *Linacre Quarterly* 39 (February, 1972) 16–20.]

"Vom Umgang mit dem Lebensraum," *Theologie der Gegenwart* 14 #4 (1971) 209–216.

1972

Gustafson, James, *Christian Ethics and the Community, America* 126 (February 26, 1972) 214–215. (Book review.)

"Notes on Moral Theology: April–September, 1971," *Theological Studies* 33 (March, 1972) 68–119.

"Autonomy and Coercion: Moral Values in Medical Practice," *Linacre Quarterly* 39 (May, 1972) 101–105. [Reprinted in *Catholic Mind* 71 (March, 1973) 8–11.]

Curran, Charles E., *Catholic Moral Theology in Dialogue, America* 127 (July 22, 1972) 44–45. (Book review.)

"Genetic Medicine: Notes on the Moral Literature," *Theological Studies* 33 (September, 1972) 531–552. [Reprinted in *New Theology No. 10*, eds. Martin E. Marty and Dean G. Peerman (New York: The Macmillan Company, 1973) 55–84.]

————, and CTSA Study Committee, "The Problem of Second Marriages: An Interim Pastoral Statement by the Study Committee Commissioned by the Board of Directors of CTSA—Report of August 1972," *CTSA Proceedings* 27 (September 1–4, 1972) 234–240. [Reprinted in *America* 127 (October 7, 1972) 258–260.]

"The New Directives and Institutional Medico-Moral Responsibility," *Chicago Studies* 11 (Fall, 1972) 305–314.

"Theologians View the Directives," *Hospital Progress* 53 (December, 1972) 51, 53, 54, 68.

1973

"Theologians View the Directives," *Hospital Progress* 54 (February, 1973) 73–74.

"The Abortion Ruling: Analysis and Prognosis Commentary: Fr. McCormick," *Hospital Progress* 54 (March, 1973) 85, 96.

"Notes on Moral Theology: April–September, 1972," *Theological Studies* 34 (March, 1973) 53–102.

"The Silence Since Humanae Vitae," *America* 129 (July 21, 1973) 30–33. [Reprinted in *Linacre Quarterly* 41 (Fall, 1974) 26–32.]

"What the Silence Means," *America* 129 (October 20, 1973) 287–290.

"The New Medicine and Morality," *Theology Digest* 21 (Winter, 1973) 308–321.

Ambiguity in Moral Choice (Milwaukee: Marquette University Press, 1973).

"Issue Areas for a Medical Ethics Program," *The Teaching of Medical Ethics*, eds. Robert M. Veatch, Willard Gaylin, and Councilman Morgen (New York: Hastings Center Publication, 1973) 103–114.

"The Problem of Motivation," *The Population Crisis and Moral Respon-*

sibility, ed. J. Philip Wogaman (Washington, D.C.: Public Affairs Press, 1973) 320–323.

1974

"Response to Professor Curran—II," *CTSA Proceedings* 29 (June 10–13, 1974) 161–164.

"Notes on Moral Theology: The Abortion Dossier," *Theological Studies* 35 (June, 1974) 312–359.

"To Save or Let Die," *America* 130 (July 13, 1974) 6–10. Simultaneously published in *The Journal of the American Medical Association* 229 (July, 1974) 172–176. [Reprinted in *Life or Death Who Controls?* eds. Nancy C. Ostheimer and John M. Ostheimer (New York: Springer Publishing Company, 1976) 254–265.

"The Teaching Role of the Magisterium—and of the Theologians," *The Catholic Leader* (August 11–August 17, 1974) 7–8.

"Fr. Richard McCormick, S.J., on Pope Paul's Encyclical 'Humanae Vitae' and the Church's Magisterium," *The Catholic Leader* (September 22–September 28, 1974) 10–16.

"To Save or Let Die: State of the Question," *America* 131 (October 5, 1974) 169–173.

"Personal Conscience," *Chicago Studies* 13 (Fall, 1974) 241–252. [Reprinted in *An American Catholic Catechism,* ed. George J. Dyer (New York: The Seabury Press, 1975) 181–193.]

"Proxy Consent in the Experimentation Situation," *Perspectives in Biology and Medicine* 18 (Autumn, 1974) 2–20. [Reprinted in *Love and Society: Essays in the Ethics of Paul Ramsey,* eds. James T. Johnson and David H. Smith (Missoula: Scholars Press, 1974) 209–227.]

"The Concept of Authority: A Catholic View," *Seminar on Authority: The Proceedings of a Dialogue Between Catholics and Baptists Sponsored by the Ecumenical Institute of Wake Forest University and Belmont Abbey College,* ed. J. William Angell (Winston-Salem: The Ecumenical Institute of Wake Forest University, 1974) 9–18.

1975

"H. V. in Perspective," *The Tablet* (London: The Tablet Publishing Co., Ltd., February 8, 1975) 126–128.

"Notes on Moral Theology: April–September, 1974," *Theological Studies* 36 (March, 1975) 77–129.

"Life-Saving and Life-Taking: A Comment," *Linacre Quarterly* 42 (May, 1975) 110–115.

"Fetal Research, Morality, and Public Policy," *The Hastings Center Report* 5 (June, 1975) 26–31.

————, and Walters, Leroy, "Fetal Research and Public Policy," *America* 132 (June 21, 1975) 473–476.

"The Social Responsibility of the Christian," *The Australian Catholic Record* 52 (July, 1975) 253–263. [Digested in *Theology Digest* 24 (Spring, 1976) 11–14.]

"Life/Death Decisions: An Interview with Moral Theologian Fr. Richard McCormick, S.J.," *St. Anthony Messenger* 83 (August, 1975) 33–35.

"A Proposal for 'Quality of Life' Criteria for Sustaining Life," *Hospital Progress* 56 (September, 1975) 76–79.

"Transplantation of Organs: A Commentary on Paul Ramsey," *Theological Studies* 36 (September, 1975) 503–509.

"Indissolubility and the Right to the Eucharist: Separate Issues or One?" *Canon Law Society of America Proceedings of the 37th Annual Convention* (October 6–9, 1975) 26–37.

"Divorce and Remarriage," *Catholic Mind* 73 (November, 1975) 42–57. [Reprinted as "Scheidung und Wiederverheiratung," *Theologie der Gegenwart* 18 #4 (1975) 210–220.]

"The Karen Ann Quinlan Case: Editorial," *Journal of the American Medical Association* 234 (December 8, 1975) 1057.

"Experimentation on the Fetus: Policy Proposals," *Appendix: Research on the Fetus* (Washington, D.C.: U.S. Department of Health, Education, and Welfare Publication, 1975) 5-1–5-11.

"The Insights of the Judeo-Christian Tradition and the Development of an Ethical Code," *Human Rights and Psychological Research: A Debate on Psychology and Ethics,* ed. Eugene Kennedy (New York: Thomas Y. Crowell, 1975) 23–36.

1976

"Sexual Ethics—An Opinion," *National Catholic Reporter* 12 (January 30, 1976) 9.

"Notes on Moral Theology: April–September, 1975," *Theological Studies* 37 (March, 1976) 70–119.

"The Preservation of Life," *Linacre Quarterly* 43 (May, 1976) 94–100.

"Experimental Subjects: Who Should They Be?" *Journal of the American Medical Association* 235 (May 17, 1976) 2197.

"The Social Responsibility of the Christian," *Theology Digest* 24 (Spring, 1976) 11–14.

"When the Neonate Is Defective," *Contemporary Ob/Gyn* 7 (June, 1976) 90, 92, 95–96, 99, 103, 107, 109, 111–112.

"The Moral Right of Privacy," *Hospital Progress* 57 (August, 1976) 38–42.

"Sterilization and Theological Method," *Theological Studies* 37 (September, 1977) 471–477.

"Experimentation in Children: Sharing in Sociality," *Hastings Center Report* 6 (December, 1976) 41–46.

"The Principle of the Double Effect," *Concilium* 120 (December, 1976) 105–120.

"Römische Erklärung zur Sexualethik," *Theologie der Gegenwart* 19 #2 (1976) 72–76.

"Morality of War," *New Catholic Encyclopedia* 14 (1976) 802–807.

"Maker of Heaven and Earth," *Christian Theology: A Case Method Approach,* eds., Robert A. Evans and Thomas E. Parker (New York: Harper & Row, 1976) 88–93.

1977

———, and Hellegers, André E., "Legislation and the Living Will," *America* 136 (March 12, 1977) 210–213.

"Notes on Moral Theology: 1976," *Theological Studies* 38 (March, 1977) 57–114.

" 'Sleeper' on DNA," *National Catholic Reporter* (July 15, 1977) 9.

"Man's Moral Responsibility for Health," *Catholic Hospital* 5 (July–August, 1977) 6–9.

McCormick, Richard A., S.J., et al., "A C & C Symposium: Paying for Abortion: Is the Court Wrong?" *Christianity and Crisis* 37 (September 19, 1977) 202–207.

"Christianity and Morality," *Catholic Mind* 75 (October, 1977) 17–29.

"Sterilisation und Theologische Methode," *Theologie der Gegenwart* 20 (1977) 110–114.

1978

"The Quality of Life, the Sanctity of Life," *Hastings Center Report* 8 (February, 1978) 30–36.

"Notes on Moral Theology: 1977," *Theological Studies* 39 (March, 1978) 76–138.

"Abortion: Rules for Debate," *America* 139 (July 15–22, 1978) 26–30.

"Life in the Test Tube," *The New York Times* (August 8, 1978).

"Unanswered Questions on Test Tube Life," with André Hellegers, *America* 139 (August 12–19, 1978) 74–78.

"Some Neglected Aspects of Responsibility for Health," *Perspectives in Biology and Medicine* 22 (1978) 31–43.

"Moral Norms and Their Meaning," *Lectureship* (Mt. Angel Seminary, 1978) 31–47.

"The Contemporary Moral Magisterium," *Lectureship* (Mt. Angel Seminary, 1978) 48–60.

McCormick, Richard A., S.J., and Ramsey, Paul, eds., *Doing Evil to Achieve Good: Moral Choice in Conflict Situations* (Chicago: Loyola University Press, 1978).

1979

"Abortion: A Changing Morality and Policy," *Hospital Progress* 60 (February, 1979) 36–44.

"Bioethical Issues and the Moral Matrix of U.S. Health Care," *Hospital Progress* 60 (May, 1979) 42–45.

Readings in Moral Theology No. 1: Moral Norms and Catholic Tradition, ed. with Charles E. Curran (Mahwah: Paulist Press, 1979).

"Notes on Moral Theology," *Theological Studies* 40 (1979) 59–112.

1980

"Restatement on Tubal Ligation Confuses Policy with Normative Ethics," *Hospital Progress* 61 (September, 1980) 40.

"The Fox Case," *Journal of the American Medical Association* 244 (November 14, 1980) 2165–2166.

Readings in Moral Theology No. 2: The Distinctiveness of Christian Ethics, ed. with Charles E. Curran (Mahwah: Paulist Press, 1980).

"Sterilization: The Dilemma of Catholic Hospitals," with Corrine Bayley, *America* 143 (1980) 222–225.

Notes on Moral Theology: 1965 through 1980 (Washington, D.C.: University Press of America, 1980).

"The Preservation of Life and Self-determination," *Theological Studies* 41 (1980) 390–396.

"Neural Tube Defects," *Maternal Serum Alpha-Fetoprotein: Issues in the Prenatal Screening and Diagnosis of Neural Tube Defects,* eds. Barbara Gastel, et al. (Washington, D.C.: Government Printing Office, 1980) 128–129.

1981

"No Short Cuts to Making Public Policy on Abortion," *Washington Star* (March 23, 1981).

"Marriage, Morality and Sex-Change Surgery: Four Traditions in Case Ethics," *Hastings Center Report* 11 (August, 1981) 10–11.

"The Fifth Synod of Bishops," *Catholic Mind* 79 (September, 1981) 46–57.

"The Ethics of In Utero Surgery," with William Barclay, et al., *Journal of the American Medical Association* 246 (October 2, 1981) 1550–1555.

"Guidelines for the Treatment of the Mentally Retarded," *Catholic Mind* 79 (November, 1981) 44–51.

"Theology as a Dangerous Discipline," *Georgetown Graduate Review* 1 (1981) 2–3.

How Brave a New World? Dilemmas in Bioethics (Garden City: Double-day, 1981).

Readings in Moral Theology No. 3: Morality and the Magisterium, ed. with Charles E. Curran (Mahwah: Paulist Press, 1981).

"Notes on Moral Theology," *Theological Studies* 42 (1981) 74–121.

"Kernenergie und Kernwaffen," *Theologie der Gegenwart* 24 (1981) 147–156.

"Scheidung und Wiederverheiratung als pastorales Problem," *Theologie der Gegenwart* 24 (1981) 21–32.

"Living-Will Legislation, Reconsidered," *America* 145 (1981) 86–89.

1982

"Infant Doe: Where to Draw the Line," *Washington Post* (July 27, 1982) A 15.

"Les sions intensifs aux nouveau-nés handicapés," *Études* (November, 1982) 493–502.

"Ethical Questions: A Look at the Issues," *Contemporary Ob/Gyn* 20 (November, 1982) 227–232.

"1973–1983: Value Impacts of a Decade," *Hospital Progress* 63 (December, 1982) 38–41.

"Pastoral Guidelines for Facing the Ambiguous Eighties," *The Future of Ministry* (Milwaukee: St. Francis Seminary, 1982) 41–44.

"Neuere Überlegungen zur Unveränderlichkeit sittlicher Normen," *Sittliche Normen,* ed. Walter Kerber, S.J. (Düsseldorf: Patmos, 1982) 46–57.

"Notes on Moral Theology," *Theological Studies* 43 (1982) 69–124.

"Theology and Biomedical Ethics," *Église et theologie* 13 (1982) 311–332.

"Theological Dimensions of Bioethics," *Logos* 3 (1982) 25–46.

Readings in Moral Theology No. 3: The Magisterium and Morality, ed. with Charles E. Curran (Mahwah: Paulist Press, 1982).

1983

"Notes on Moral Theology," *Theological Studies* 44 (1983) 71–122.

"Bioethics in the Public Forum," *Milbank Memorial Fund Quarterly* 61 (1983) 113–126.

"Saving Defective Infants: Options for Life or Death," with John Paris, S.J., *America* 148 (1983) 313–317.

"Nuclear Deterrence and the Problem of Intention: A Review of the Positions," *Catholics and Nuclear War,* ed. Philip Murnion (New York: Crossroad, 1983) 168–182.

1984

Readings in Moral Theology No. 4: The Use of Scripture in Moral Theology, ed. with Charles E. Curran (Mahwah: Paulist Press, 1984).

Health and Medicine in the Catholic Tradition (New York: Crossroad, 1984).

"Notes on Moral Theology," *Theological Studies* 45 (1984) 80–138.

"The Chill Factor: Recent Roman Interventions," *America* 150 (1984) 475–481.

Notes on Moral Theology: 1981 through 1984 (Lanham, Maryland: University Press of America, 1984).

"Medicaid and Abortion," *Theological Studies* 45 (1984) 715–721.

1985

"Was There Any Real Hope for Baby Fae?" *Hastings Center Report* 15 (February, 1985) 12–13.

"Genetic Technology and Our Common Future," *America* 152 (1985) 337–342.

"Caring or Starving? The Case of Claire Conroy," *America* 152 (1985) 269–273.

"Theology and Bioethics: Christian Foundations," *Theology and Bioethics,* ed. Earl Shelp (Dordrecht: Reidel, 1985) 95–114.

"Moral Argument in Christian Ethics," *Journal of Contemporary Health Law and Policy* 1 (1985) 3–23.

"Notes on Moral Theology: Moral Norms—An Update," *Theological Studies* 46 (1985) 50–64.

"Therapy or Tempering? The Ethics of Reproductive Technology," *America* 153 (1985) 396–403.

"Gustafson's God: Who? What? Where? (etc.)," *Journal of Religious Ethics* 13 (1985) 53–70.

"The Past, Present, and Future of Moral Theology," *Proceedings of 1984 Theological Symposium* (Villanova University, 1985).

1986

"The Magisterium," *Authority, Community and Conflict,* ed. Madonna Kolbenschlag (Kansas City: Sheed and Ward, 1986) 34–37.

"*Gaudium et Spes* and the Bioethical Signs of the Times," *Questions of Special Urgency* (Washington: Georgetown University Press, 1986) 79–95.

"Health and Medicine in the Catholic Tradition," *Ephemerides Theologicae Lovanienses* 62 (1986) 207–215.

"Symposium: Bioethical Issues in Organ Transplantation," *Southern Medical Journal* 79 (1986) 1471–1479.

"The Best Interests of the Baby," *Second Opinion* 2 (1986) 18–25.

"Biomedical Advances and the Catholic Perspective," *Contemporary Ethical Issues in the Jewish and Christian Traditions,* ed. Frederick Greenspan (Hoboken: Ktav Publishing House, 1986) 30–52.

"The Search for Truth in the Catholic Context," *America* 155 (1986) 276–281.

"L'Affaire Curran," *America* 154 (1986) 261–267.

Readings in Moral Theology No. 5: Official Catholic Social Teaching, ed. with Charles E. Curran (Mahwah: Paulist Press, 1986).

"Notes on Moral Theology," *Theological Studies* 47 (1986) 69–88.

"Bishops as Teachers and Jesuits as Listeners," *Studies in the Spirituality of Jesuits* 18 (1986) 1–22.

"Finality," "Double Effect," "Magisterium," *Dictionary of Christian Ethics,* eds. James Childress and John Macquarrie (Philadelphia: Westminster, 1986).

1987

"Ethics of Reproductive Technology: AFS Recommendations, Dissent," *Health Progress* 68 (March, 1987) 33–37.

"Document is Unpersuasive," *Health Progress* 68 (July/August, 1987) 53–55.

"Notes on Moral Theology: Dissent in Moral Theology and Its Implications," *Theological Studies* 48 (1987) 87–105.

"Surrogate Motherhood: A Stillborn Idea," *Second Opinion* 5 (1987) 128–132.

"Self-Assessment and Self-Indictment," *Religious Studies Review* 13 (1987) 37–39.

"The Vatican Document on Bioethics," *America* 156 (1987) 24–28.

"The Vatican Document on Bioethics: A Response," *America* 156 (1987) 247–248.

"The Catholic Tradition on the Use of Nutrition and Fluids," with John Paris, S.J., *America* 156 (1987) 356–361.

"Begotten, Not Made," *Notre Dame Magazine* 15 (1987) 22–25.

1988

"Bishops' AIDS Letter 'Splendid' Theology," *National Catholic Reporter* 24 (January 22, 1988) 1, 5–6.

"The Future of Chaplaincy: Bioethical Problems That Shape Ministry," *Charting the Future of Pastoral Care* (Special Publications of National Association of Catholic Chaplains, v. 4, Summer, 1988) 24–39.

"Searching for the Consistent Ethic of Life," *Personalist Morals,* ed. J.A. Selling (Leuven: Leuven University Press, 1988) 135–146.

"A Moral Magisterium in Ecumenical Perspective?" *Studies in Christian Ethics* 1 (1988) 20–29.

"The Importance of Naturalness and Conjugal Gametes," *In Vitro Fertilization and Other Assisted Reproduction* (= Annals of the New York Academy of Sciences, v. 541) (1988) 664–667.

"AIDS: The Shape of the Ethical Challenge," *America* 158 (1988) 147–154.

"The Shape of Moral Evasion in Catholicism," *America* 159 (1988) 183–188.

Readings in Moral Theology No. 6: Dissent in the Church, ed. with Charles E. Curran (Mahwah: Paulist Press, 1988).

"The Cost-Factor in Health Care," *Notre Dame Journal of Law, Ethics and Public Policy* 3 (1988) 161–167.

1989

"Abortion: The Unexplored Middle Ground," *Second Opinion* 10 (March, 1989) 41–50.

"Theology and Bioethics," *Hastings Center Report* 19 (March/April, 1989) 5–10.

The Critical Calling: Moral Dilemmas Since Vatican II (Washington: Georgetown University Press, 1989).

"Moral Theology 1940–1989: An Overview," *Theological Studies* 50 (1989) 3–24.

"Pluralism Within the Church," *Catholic Perspectives on Medical Morals,* eds. Edmund D. Pellegrino, John P. Langan, John Collins Harvey (Dordrecht: Kluwer Academic Publishers, 1989) 147–167.

"Moral Theology in the Year 2000: Reverie or Reality" (Regina: Campion College, 1989. The Nash Lecture, privately printed.)

"Foreword," *Why You Can Disagree and Remain a Faithful Catholic,* by Philip S. Kaufman (Bloomington: Meyer-Stone Books, 1989) xi–xii.

"Sterilization: The Dilemma of Catholic Hospitals," *History and Conscience,* eds. R. Gallagher and Brendan McConvery (Southampton: Camelot Press, 1989) 105–122.